Edited by
JEANNINE BLACKWELL &
SUSANNE ZANTOP

BITTER HEALING: GERMAN WOMEN WRITERS

FROM 1700 TO 1830
An Anthology

University of Nebraska Press

Lincoln & London

The paper in this book meets the minimum requirements of American National Standard
for Information Sciences—Permanence of Paper for Printed Library Materials,
ANSI Z39.48-1984.

Library of Congress Cataloging in Publication Data
Bitter healing: German women writers from 1700 to 1830: an anthology / edited by
Jeannine Blackwell and Susanne Zantop.
p.   cm. – (European women writers series). Includes bibliographical references.
ISBN 0-8032-1207-0 (alk. paper). – ISBN 0-8032-9909-5 (pbk: alk. paper)
1. German literature–18th century–Translations into English.
2. German literature–19th century–Translations into English.
3. German literature–Women authors–Translations into English.
4. English literature–Translations from German.
I. Blackwell, Jeannine.   II. Zantop, Susanne, 1945-.   III. Series.
PT1113.B55   1990
430.9'9287'09033–dc20
89-24953
CIP

Contents

1
Preface

9
Trivial Pursuits?
An Introduction to German Women's Writing
from the Middle Ages to 1830

51
Johanna Eleonore Petersen
The Life of Johanna Eleonore Petersen

79
Luise Adelgunde Gottsched
The Witling
Selected Letters

125
Anna Luisa Karsch
Autobiographical Letter to Professor Sulzer
Anger at War, When It Lasted Too Long
In Praise of Black Cherries

147
Sophie von La Roche
Two Sisters

189
Philippine Gatterer Engelhard
Girl's Lament

201
Benedikte Naubert
The Cloak

279
Caroline Schlegel-Schelling
Selected Letters

297
Henriette Herz
Memoirs of a Jewish Girlhood

333
Dorothea Schlegel
Selected Letters

349
Caroline Auguste Fischer
William the Negro

369
Sophie Mereau
Spring
To a Trellised Tree
Flight to the City

401
Rahel Varnhagen
Selected Letters

417
Karoline von Günderrode
Selected Letters
Once a Dulcet Life Was Mine
The Prime Lament
Apocalyptical Fragment

443
Bettina von Arnim
The Queen's Son
Report on Günderode's Suicide

473
Annette von Droste-Hülshoff
Ledwina

527
Selected Bibliography

535
The Contributors

Preface

Die Heilung ist bitter,
Der Weg ist wohl weit,
Doch greif ich zum Stabe
Und ende mein Leid.

[The cure is bitter,
The journey long,
But I reach for the staff
And heal my wrong.]

(Karoline von Günderrode,
The Pilgrims.)

In recent years, interest in women writers has been increasing dramatically. Commercial publishers and university presses throughout the country have started publishing anthologies or reprints of works by women authors and have established feminist series. Every year witnesses the appearance of new collections of critical essays and scholarly dissertations on writers whose works had been excluded from the canon, buried in libraries or archives, and therefore forgotten by the reading public.

While this effort to recuperate a "lost tradition" has been very productive in English and American studies, we have had little access so far to texts from non-English cultures in English translation. As a consequence, generalizations about women's writing, feminine aesthetics, or female perspectives have often been based on limited evidence and bear the mark of parochialism.

The need for an anthology of women writers in translation is particularly pressing in the field of German literature, where women authors have been more consistently excluded from the canon than in England,

France, or the United States. While some German publishers, such as Georg Olms in Hildesheim, are beginning to reprint novels by eighteenth- and early-nineteenth-century women ("Frühe Frauenliteratur in Deutschland"), new translations into English are rare. With the exception of the bilingual collection of German women's poetry, *The Defiant Muse*, edited by Susan Cocalis, and the forthcoming translation of Dorothea Schlegel's "Life, Thought, and Works" (translated by Edwina Lawler and Ruth Richardson; Lewiston, N.Y.: Edwin Mellen Press), no primary texts by German women authors of this early modern period are available or accessible to today's reader of English. This is indeed a step backward, for in the eighteenth century, English writers widely translated, adapted, and anthologized German plays, novels, and tales and maintained close literary ties with their continental sisters. Sophie von La Roche's *History of Lady Sternheim*, for example, which appeared in Germany in 1771, existed in two different English editions by 1777, and five of Benedikte Naubert's fifty-odd historical novels were translated shortly after their first publication.

With this anthology, we hope to fill a major gap. Although this is an anthology of women writers, we do not pretend to establish a "counter-canon" or to suggest that women's writing developed completely apart from and in completely different ways from men's. Instead of creating another ghetto of *Frauenliteratur,* we want to make hitherto inaccessible texts accessible so that women's and men's literature can be seen in conjunction and women's contribution to literary culture can be more fairly assessed. Although this volume represents only a small selection, we hope it will complement, expand, and possibly revise existing histories of German literature and established notions of "literariness." While traditional German literary histories always assumed that women "inspired" male authors and then "copied" and "trivialized" their lofty innovations, a parallel reading of texts by men and by women may suggest the reverse: at times it was the women authors who created new themes and techniques that men later adopted and claimed as their own. This anthology may thus serve to correct traditional literary histories and create a more interactive model of literary historiography.

In order to situate the texts within the larger context of German social and cultural history, we have prefaced them with a historical introduction to German women in the eighteenth and early nineteenth centuries and also referred to traditions that already existed in the Middle Ages. By summarizing and condensing heterogeneous and widely scattered material, this introduction provides some basic background information for readers little familiar with eighteenth-century Germany and even less familiar with the situation of women writers during that period.

Our decision to arrange the authors in chronological order by date of birth instead of grouping them according to location (Jena, Berlin, etc.), genre (tales, poetry, etc.), literary movement, or date of publication of the individual texts has several reasons. By choosing the chronological sequence, we avoided the suggestion that women's literary culture unfolded organically, in a seamless continuity; we were able to connect the authors' biographies directly with their literary production at various stages; and we avoided generic labeling, leaving it up to our readers to group the texts according to their own needs.

Any historical overview or anthology raises questions about aesthetic criteria for the choice of material, and the implied narrative, the ideological agenda hidden in its organization. What should the guiding principles of selection be—aesthetic, historical, geographic? What is, in fact, "German literature"—written or printed texts produced in the German language, or texts published in "Germany," a country that did not exist as a political unit until the late nineteenth century? What is "literature" for that matter—everything in print, or only those works that critics have declared to be high art? What about oral literature, or literature that was not always meant to leave the manuscript stage, such as letters?

In our selection of material, we tried to be as pragmatic and as open as possible. We were aware that we could not avoid what Lillian S. Robinson has called the "agony" of feminist critics and literary historians, "who are torn between defending the quality of their discoveries and radically redefining literary quality itself." ("Treason Our Text: Feminist Challenges to the Literary Canon," *Tulsa Studies in Women's Literature* 2.1 (Spring 1983): 89.) Thus, while we looked for readability and aesthetic interest, we also wanted to provide a basis for a new aesthetic evaluation. In our choice of appropriate texts we therefore aimed to be as inclusive as possible in terms of the social or religious background and political ideology of the authors and as representative as possible of certain literary trends as they emerged. Insofar as possible, we tried to avoid excerpting the texts, since excerpts do not reflect the authors' aesthetic aspirations. We occasionally had to settle for a shorter prose piece rather than for the perhaps more representative long novel, for Sophie von La Roche's "Two Sisters," for example, instead of her *History of Lady Sternheim*. Or we had to exclude authors altogether, such as the novelist Friederike Helene Unger, because their narratives were too long.

The volume includes writers from various social classes: the Prussian farmer's daughter Anna Luisa Karsch as well as middle-class women (Benedikte Naubert and Sophie Mereau) and aristocrats (Karoline von Günderrode and Annette von Droste-Hülshoff); from various religious backgrounds (the Protestant theologian Petersen, the Jewish *salonnières* Herz and Varnhagen, and the Catholic Droste-Hülschoff); and from different political persuasions (the conservative monarchist Sophie von La Roche and the radical social reformer Bettina von Arnim).

Our choice of texts not only provides a sense of the variety of women who took up the pen, but also attests to the variety of approaches women employed to express their convictions, desires, and dreams.

The anthology opens with the "spiritual autobiography" of the Pietist Johanna Eleonore Petersen, because Pietist confessions and letters became the model for many confessional novels later in the century and for autobiographical writing in general. The gradual secularization and literarization of the genre, which can be observed both in the letters and in other autobiographical texts contained in this volume (Luise Gottsched, Anna Luisa Karsch, Dorothea Schlegel, Rahel Varnhagen), culminates in Droste-Hülshoff's *Ledwina*.

Another literary form that appealed to women's imagination was the fairy tale. Benedikte Naubert, who wrote and collected fairy tales before the Brothers Grimm conceived of their project, is represented by her collage *The Cloak*, Bettina von Arnim, intimately connected with the Grimm circle, contributes a self-conscious, critical response to the fairy-tale tradition.

Although fairy tales often became a vehicle to express utopian longings, "moral tales" became a vehicle for expressing concrete educational goals or advocating moral reform. A typical specimen is Sophie von La Roche's tale *Two Sisters,* whose moral impetus is countered, in a sense, by Sophie

Mereau's frivolous *Flight to the City*. While love and marriage within a white bourgeois setting are celebrated in La Roche's tale and parodied in Mereau's, Caroline Auguste Fischer complicates the conventional marriage plot by adding racial difference to that of class and sex. Like Aphra Behn's *Oroonoko*, Fischer's *William the Negro* thus expands the range of "problems" that can constitute literary plots, calling attention to other forms of oppression.

Interspersed with the prose pieces are poems that exhibit a wide range of lyrical "I"s: from the "natural poet" Anna Luisa Karsch and the popular Philippine Gatterer Engelhard to the lyrical Sophie Mereau and the exuberant Tian, the male persona of Karoline von Günderrode. We have chosen poems that in their personal, even confessional, tone depart from given academic models, because they either exhibit a deep discomfort with marginalization (Engelhard and Mereau), a vehement despair at the limitations of a female writer's existence (Günderrode), or an earthy, sensuous response to the physical environment (Karsch and Mereau).

Although space was precious, we decided to include the German poems with their translations. This will allow readers with some knowledge of German to read original and translation side by side and to appreciate the translator's achievement.

The one-act play by Luise Adelgunde Gottsched, the sole theater piece in our collection, only seems to be an oddity. Until recently historians assumed that women writers in Germany rarely wrote for the stage. Yet although prose and poetry were in fact the most popular "female" genres, Kay Goodman, Susan Cocalis, Ruth Dawson, Susanne Kord, Dagmar von Hoff, and other researchers of eighteenth-century German literature are currently unearthing and investigating a host of plays by women writers— plays that enjoyed considerable popularity and prestige in their own time. Gottsched's attempt to create a public persona for herself and to engage in the literary debate with male peers early in the eighteenth century makes her a kind of dramatic forerunner, which compelled us to include her playful one-acter *The Witling* in our anthology.

Although we tried to select texts that would appeal to the modern reader, our choice was determined above all by historical considerations. "Literary quality" is, after all, a matter of taste, of class, of education, all of which are historically and socially determined. We knew from the start that we would not find a female Goethe, since only few German women writers —mostly from the aristocracy, and mostly in the nineteenth century—aspired to artistic prowess, or even conceived of themselves as *Dichterinnen*, poets. The majority of women wrote for a wide audience, for the market, with the intention of contributing toward the support of their families and of educating other women within the confines of socially prescribed roles. Rather than developing individual characters in unique situations who break with conventions—a model we have come to associate with the rise of modern literature—women writers tended to create exemplary heroines who, faced with complicated constellations and dilemmas, make exemplary moral choices within conventional expectations. Most women authors did not allow themselves the luxury of being particularly radical or experimental, formally or ideologically, but insisted on plain language and straightforward plots. Yet the conventionality of the stories and their message is deceptive. The simplicity of the plot lines and the conciliatory happy endings often veil highly explosive "revolutionary" situations. In order to understand the meaning(s) behind the apparently innocuous stories, we have to develop new techniques of reading that are particularly sensitive to nuances, to existential irony. The "healing" that the texts advocate is preceded by "bitter" experiences, as Karoline von Günderrode's poem tells us. It is therefore of great importance to the contemporary reader to read between the lines, and to unveil the conflicts that the texts carefully cover up.

In our choice of texts, we were therefore guided by the following questions: to what extent does the author contribute to expanding the readers' consciousness of gender? Does she introduce new ways of perception and new ways of representation that undermine or challenge the old, both formally and thematically? In what way can these texts by women help us reinterpret the literature produced by men, a literature with which we have been familiar for generations and which has shaped our literary tastes? And to what extent do they teach us new ways of reading—not only in relation to their context, but in relation to our own?

The anthology is the product of a team effort. In most cases, the translations were made by scholars who had been studying "their" women authors for years and who had always wanted to introduce them to a wider audience. We have therefore kept our editorial interference to a minimum to allow for a multiplicity of approaches and styles. Biographical introductions to the authors and bibliographies will help the reader locate writers in their social and historical context. We have tried to interfere as little as possible in the reading process by imposing our own interpretations and have limited ourselves to a few suggestions. A select bibliography of secondary literature in English may serve as a guide for further reading. For more complete information on German women's social and literary history, we refer to our bibliography in the *Women in German Yearbook* 1989, which includes German titles as well.

Research funds provided by the Committee on Faculty Research at Dartmouth College helped with the financing of this project. We would like to thank the following friends and colleagues: Susan Cocalis (University of Massachusetts), Virginia Swain, Diana Taylor-Manheimer, Laurence Davies, Werner Hoffmeister (all at Dartmouth College), and Michael Jones (Ohio State University), who generously donated their time to read and comment on the manuscript in its various stages; Inge Brown, formerly Senior Secretary in the German Department at Dartmouth College, who helped with the typing of the manuscript; Marianne Hraibi and Patricia A. Carter in Dartmouth's Interlibrary Loan Office, who untiringly fulfilled our requests for more and more materials. And last but not least we want to thank David Ward (Dartmouth), whose keen eye, trained ear, and verbal sensitivity helped us check and edit several of the translations. As we gratefully acknowledge, this volume is truly the product of a "concerted" effort.

Jeannine Blackwell and Susanne Zantop

SUSANNE ZANTOP

Trivial Pursuits?

An Introduction to
German Women's Writing from
the Middle Ages to 1830

I for my part do not advise any woman, unless fate has selected her for it through a combination of many circumstances, to venture into *this* career. First, it would lead our sex as a whole too far from our destiny, and second, it is connected with so many difficulties, which barely *one* woman in a hundred is able to surmount! Considering the difficulty of attaining artistic prowess and the loss of one's peace of mind, this is really the saddest female occupation on earth. To produce art, to be able to write *well* and *usefully*, is such an infinitely demanding task, and the many public attacks, the bitter criticism, the prejudice directed at woman's writings, the jealousy which tries to besmirch them, the personal attacks against woman writers, usually denying them all domestic virtues—taken together, these far outweigh the little bit of glory and satisfied vanity. (Marianne Ehrmann, 1792)

I

Although we know that literature does not exist in a vacuum and that its manifestations do not appear all of a sudden, as if by magic, we often play down the collective nature of the literary enterprise. Fascinated by the "sudden" proliferation of great works of art, we tend to forget that specific preconditions must be met to allow for the

9

emergence of a literary culture: without literacy and a general level of education, books will neither be written nor read; without a certain level of economic affluence, books will not be purchased; without printing facilities and a network of distribution and promotion by booksellers and critics, books will neither be produced nor sold in economically feasible quantities; without laws that protect authorship, and adequate honoraria that compensate the authors, there will be little incentive to choose writing as a profession; without a minimum of public recognition, encouragement, and creative freedom, i.e., some form of economic and emotional sponsorship, the extremely vulnerable act of "going public" will be made almost impossible.

It is important to remember these material and spiritual preconditions for writing when we deal with literary history and particularly with women's literary history. They help us explain why written literature flourished only in monasteries, at courts, universities, and in a few towns during the Middle Ages; in commercial centers, and in the residences of the absolute monarchs during the sixteenth, seventeenth, and eighteenth centuries; and in the growing cities of the nineteenth century. And they help us explain why there were relatively few women authors in the past and why their number eventually increased. Not only did women have to face more material and practical obstacles than men—lack of education, legal and economic dependence, lack of patronage—but they also had to contend with the spiritual and ideological preconceptions that had produced these material obstacles and were in turn reinforced by them: restrictive ideas of what a woman was and what she could and should do, notions of women's unchanging "nature" that stressed their reproductive and receptive faculties over their productive, creative ones and justified keeping them in their "natural" place—the home. Any historical account of women's writing therefore has to take into consideration not only the economic and intellectual constraints women had to overcome in order to pursue a literary career but the notions of gender that predefined women's sense of self and predetermined their range of activities. Furthermore, in addition to considering exterior, manifest forms of tutelage or sponsorship, it is important to analyze—as Mary Poovey has reminded us—how the societal boundaries between "natural" and "unnatural," proper and improper female behavior became internalized, domesticating not only women but women's writing.[1] And we must note how women gradually succeeded in undermining or expanding those very same boundaries. For women writers, finding literary patronage and gaining success as authors depended to no small degree on their ability to accommodate themselves within socially prescribed roles or to hide "excessive" claims in seemingly innocuous literary forms. If we examine the complicated maneuvers, the strategies of adaptation and defiance women writers had to develop in order to gain admittance to a realm dominated by male printers, publishers, critics, and peers, we will be able to understand women's literary activity not as separate from but as intimately connected with men's. Ideally, a history of women's literature (and, analogously, of men's) would have to combine two approaches: it would have to observe the genealogical axis by exploring how women's writings "engendered" other women's writing, i.e., how literary "daughters" inherited from their literary "mothers"; and it would have to focus on the dialogical, even dialectical interaction between women's and men's literature to show how profoundly they influenced and modified each other. We might then realize that women's literary history is neither the straightforward "story of victimization" of a literary "subculture" (Elaine Showalter) nor the "success story" of some defiant individuals, but a history of many small steps, some forward, some backward, and some just circular.[2]

II

Historians of women's writing have repeatedly pointed out that women authors do not fit into the traditional literary categories.[3] More often than not, women worked at the margins of the renowned literary movements, such as "Storm and Stress" or "Romanticism," defined by men and their works. Women chose the genres that were open to them—such as religious confession, fairy tale, letter, novel, or lyric poetry—accommodated these genres to their needs, and made themselves "at home" in them. Thus, whereas women writers cultivated the same genres for centuries, constantly expanding, adapting, and refining them, men eventually felt compelled—possibly under the "anxiety of influence"—to create apparently new, "original" ways of expression. This seeming conventionality of women writers may account for their dismissal by literary historians who, since the eighteenth century, have watched for original geniuses rather than for subtle shifts and changes among so-called fringe groups.

It is for this reason that feminist literary historians have recently advocated using the metaphor "spaces" to circumscribe specific geographical, social, and generic locations that afforded women the opportunity to articulate their artistic needs—and defined the boundaries of their literary activity.[4] As these spaces became less isolated from one another and more open for interaction, women's literary activity increased in quantity, variety, and complexity.

In order to understand the situation in the eighteenth century, which is the focus of this anthology, we have to go back briefly to prior centuries, since the eighteenth century is, of course, heir to much previous literary achievement as well as to earlier problems.

Until about 1600, there were only two "spaces" which gave a few privileged women access to learning and to written literature: the convents and the courts. While France and Italy developed a refined court culture in which women occupied important positions—as inspirers of courtly love poetry, as troubadour poets, or as intellectually active "courtesans"—the economically underdeveloped, politically fragmented Holy Roman Empire with its many small autonomous territories, its illiterate nobility, and its constant feuds hardly provided an environment for women's intellectual or artistic growth.[5] Unlike male poets and bards, women were not supposed to move around freely. From the little information that has survived, it appears that female literary and scientific activity in the German lands was therefore limited to a few, exceptional convents in the ninth to the thirteenth centuries and to a few cities in the fourteenth and fifteenth.

Convents and "beguine houses," independent female communes in which women lived under self-imposed vows of celibacy, provided a place of refuge until they were closed by the Reformation. In the almost complete absence of public schooling, convents had a monopoly on formal education for women. Extensive libraries made some of them centers of learning and intellectual exchange, although, as some historians have pointed out, the subject matter they taught to women was generally limited to reading, writing, music, and needlework and rarely extended to more than a few privileged nuns.[6] Relatively free from external interference and with relative autonomy from the church hierarchy in their internal governance, the convents enabled some women to develop administrative, intellectual, and artistic skills in a congenial environment away from familial responsibilities. It must be stressed, however, that the price of personal freedom was a certain spiritual control by the (male) church hierarchy. Like their male counterparts, women who joined the convents had to take a vow of celibacy. Yet unlike monks, nuns could not become priests, celebrate mass, or administer confession. While their physical energies were channeled in spiritual directions and their sexuality denied, repressed, or sublimated into acceptable, "pure" forms of expression, it was the Pope and his deputies, the bishops or priests, who thus decided on the purity and orthodoxy of their thoughts and writings.[7] They were tolerated as authors "only as long as they denied any self-awareness and presented themselves to the public as humble vessels of the Holy Spirit."[8]

Among the most distinguished German women writers of the Middle Ages are Hrotswitha (Hrotsvith or Roswitha) von Gandersheim (ca. 935–968), Hildegard von Bingen (1098–1179), and Mechthild von Magdeburg (1212–82).[9] All of them were of noble birth. They were privileged to be raised in convents that had already created an environment of learning and artistic pursuit, such as the abbey of Helfta; all received a thorough education in theology and classical literature and were encouraged by their peers to explore their literary talents.

Apart from purely scientific tracts, the writings that emanated from convents and beguine houses fall into two general categories: legends or lives of saints often containing personal visions or prophecies, and hymns and sermons celebrating the mystical union of God and the soul ("unio mystica"). Both forms combine the confessional or private with the exemplary or public, the monologue with the dialogue. These public confessions of the most intimate longings must be understood within the context of Christian mysticism, a spiritual movement that granted even women personal access to, or fusion with, God. The nuns' literary activity could flourish in the protected space of the convent and in the confinement of religious subject matter and form; it was legitimized by its association with the divine. As God's mouthpiece and as His interlocutor, the nuns and beguines were speaking with divine—hence spiritual—authority. The language of mysticism allowed them to express a full range of passion and intimacy without the stigma of immorality.[10] Language—first Latin, then the vernacular—became an increasingly refined and flexible tool to express spiritual and physical desires. The cult of the Virgin Mother Mary provided the nuns with another model of the possible fusion of the sensual and the spiritual. Within these confined spaces considerable literary and intellectual experimentation was thus made possible.

We must not forget, though, that this literature was not just the product of a few exceptionally gifted, inspired individuals, but emanated from small communities of women who, with access to the literary tradition, co-operated artistically and encouraged creativity. As soon as these communities ceased to exist, i.e., when the Reformation dissolved religious orders, the ecstatic, confessional literature of the *Nonnenmystik* came to an abrupt end. It was not revived until the seventeenth century, when it re-emerged in the form of Protestant-Pietist soul-searching and hymns.

Two events may have led to the silencing of women in early modern Europe: Luther's Reformation and the persecution of witches. Although it is not quite clear how and why these events are connected, their impact on women's imagination and social role cannot be denied.

What brought on the persecution and executions of so-called witches in the fourteenth to seventeenth centuries, "that uniquely lethal form of western European misogyny," has not been fully explained to date.[11] A host of factors have been held responsible for the explosion of witchhunts particularly during the Reformation, and particularly in Germany. Although estimates vary, it is assumed that between 100,000 and one million individuals, most of them women, many of them unmarried, old, and/or poor, were burned at the stake after they had "confessed" under torture to the crime of being possessed, literally, by the devil. The confessions proved what had been believed and proclaimed all along: that women's sexuality was insatiable, that they were inherently evil or sinful, that they used devilish magic to lead men astray. Women were made responsible for all ills that befell society: bad harvests, famines, and deaths (the plague, for unknown reasons, killed more men than women). In spectacular mass trials, which became a means to propagate the misogynist message, women were forced to tell the same story, over and over again. Recent studies of trial documents suggest that these tortured confessions, which cast women's experiences and dreams into the rigid forms of deviant male "fantasies of the learned," can be understood as dark travesties or inversions of the love literature created by the mystical nuns.[12] Exemplary lives of saints were thus countered with exemplary life stories of sinners; through fear and guilt, women's imagination was (re-)bound into the dual model of sexless saint ("Mary") or sexually depraved witch ("Eve"), with a dangerously thin borderline between.[13] This dual model was reinforced by popular drawings and woodcuts, which with the advent of printing had become the most influential forms of indoctrination for an illiterate public.[14]

Ever since the beginning of the modern period, that is, from the Reformation onward, this dual model of femininity has obsessed both male writers and women writing about themselves. While men created heroines who were either models of incorruptible angelic purity or demonic, obsessed despots [*Machtweiber*], women were developing strategies of dissimulation, hiding behind "rituals of modesty," suggesting that they were indeed harmless and "virtuous," not prone to any such misdemeanor or overt sexuality.

This spiritual and physical domestication was encouraged by Luther, who considered convents a dangerous place for the female imagination and advocated women's return to the hearth. Although the Reformation supposedly ended the "dark" Middle Ages, the *querelle des femmes*, the debate about women's supposed physical, intellectual, and moral inferiority, continued, indeed with renewed vigor.[15] At first, Luther had advocated general literacy so that every Christian could judge the Bible for himself (or herself) and participate more fully in religious life. Yet he quickly retraced his steps and returned to indoctrination and catechization when he realized that too much reliance on the critical individual could lead to deviance from orthodoxy.[16] Thus it is difficult to assess Luther's impact on women and women's literary pursuits: by advocating literacy even for women and upgrading the vernacular as a literary language, Luther helped expand the reading public and the group of potential writers.[17] By challenging religious orthodoxy and engaging in theological disputes, he opened a space for critical thinking that could serve as a model for women, too.[18] Yet by closing the convents, Luther deprived women of intellectual support groups and centers for undisturbed literary studies. By relinquishing the Virgin Mary symbol in favor of the male Trinity of Father, Son, and Holy Spirit, he devalued a powerful if unattainable model with which women had identified.[19] By advocating higher learning for men and retaining the medieval prohibition of women at universities, he widened the gap between the learned few—mostly men, and mostly aristocrats—and the literate, but still uncultured, many—women and peasants. Finally, by defining the home as their exclusive space and marriage as their exclusive goal, Luther degraded those women who for whatever reason preferred to live independently. Even if he upgraded women's role within the family, as assistant to the husband and teacher of the children, he clearly limited their options and creative freedom.[20] Ultimately, Luther's contribution toward the development of a women's literary culture is, at best, ambiguous.

However, the late sixteenth and the entire seventeenth century witnessed an upsurge in female literary activity, which was probably less the result of the Reformers' attitudes toward women than of improved communication, greater circulation of printed materials, the growth of trade centers, the consolidation of the absolutist states, and the creation of an educated class of state officials. Particularly among the aristocracy, women tended to receive a better education—partly because the German political elite aspired to keep up with the rest of Europe and partly because women were expected to fulfill court duties. Education was also available to a few privileged bourgeois women in the cities, generally the daughters of scholars.[21]

Again, women's creativity emanated from two public "spaces," which at times overlapped: the Protestant communities at the margin of the official church, particularly the Pietists, and a few enlightened—sometimes Pietist-inspired—courts.[22] And again, it found expression in two well-known, well-worked generic spaces: the autobiographical "confession" and the hymn or religious poem, genres which have in common a profound piety and a didactic function as *Erbauungsliteratur* [devotional literature]. As in the Middle Ages, the appeal to religion gave spiritual sanction to women writers, while their claim to have led an exemplary and therefore morally uplifting life legitimized their literary activity as a form of social "service." As models of piety women were allowed to break the "silence" that the church fathers and Luther had considered to be their proper state.[23] Occasionally, they used their moral authority to upbraid members of the ecclesiastical and secular hierarchy and to propagate an ideal of virtue that applied across boundaries of rank and station. Women in the religious sects had relatively more protection and support from persecution for heresy than did the isolated women accused of witchcraft; this public space of the sectarian congregation, as fragile as it was, provided some shelter from state and church, as well as serving as an incipient audience and first critical public for uncloistered women's writing. The informal *Hauskirche* (ca. 1670), a gathering of the faithful in homes, gave women a domesticated and therefore more acceptable arena for their religious literary production.

The informal congregational gatherings in Holland and Germany contrast sharply with the courtly salon culture created by French aristocratic women, although both provided a training ground and audience for women's writing. Although the German courts modeled themselves on the French and the translation of French texts became fashionable, we do not find a salon culture in Germany that is in any way comparable to that in France. Like the bourgeois women active in the Pietist movement, women at German courts were primarily interested in spiritual matters and produced almost exclusively spiritual literature. Thus the duchess Sophia Elisabeth and her daughters at the court of Wolfenbüttel, as well as the two sisters Elisabeth and Anna von Baden-Durlach (1620–92 and 1617–72) at the court of Durlach, wrote religious *Gebrauchsliteratur*, i.e., hymns and moral instructional literature designed to help their fellow Christians lead a virtuous life.[24] The female virtues they propagate in their poems are, as Jean Woods remarked, those that have been associated with ideal femininity ever since: submissiveness, chastity, charity, modesty, silence, and patience.[25] Similarly, Catharina Regina von Greiffenberg (1633–94), the most famous woman poet of the Baroque and member of one of the largest language societies, *Die Deutschgesinnte Genossenschaft,* published religious sonnets, hymns and poems, as well as four volumes of contemplations on the life of Jesus.[26]

Curiously, the many dissenting religious cults that sprang up in the seventeenth century provided more freedom of action than did the courts. All of these religious "fringe" groups included substantial numbers of women, and many were organized nonhierarchically, at least in their initial stages. Their general openness was the direct result of their religious convictions: like the mystics in the Middle Ages, "Quietists," "Labadists," and other enthusiast communities of Pietist inclination advocated the soul's direct access to God, without the intercession of priests or other church officials. Their radical distrust of the establishment made them suspect to officials in church and state alike. In these communities, women came to occupy positions of influence and spiritual leadership, because they were considered particularly able to achieve "fusion" with their divine "bridegroom," Christ. Although they were eventually to be removed from leadership and inspirational roles in most of the conventicles and congregations, women were admitted to the most important of these devotional gatherings, the *collegium pietatis*, five years after its founding in 1670, and often gave testimony of their conversions.

The main contribution of the Pietist movement to literature is the introspective, soul-searching confession.[27] Whereas men's confessions followed either the more rigid, impersonal model of spiritual "breakthrough" (unconscious, sinful existence—despair at damnation—suicidal desires—sudden awareness of God's grace-salvation) or an imitation of radical, erotic medieval mysticism, women's confessions merged realistic descriptions of everyday life with dreams and visions, personal experience of the divine with public conflict, intimate autobiographical detail with learned exegesis of the scripture. A typical example of this mixed genre is Johanna Eleonore Petersen's autobiography. It opens this anthology precisely because it shows the transition between purely religious writing and secular literature; it demonstrates clearly how spiritual authority was converted by women into worldly authority and served as an impetus and a justification for telling their own stories.

Although the "female" types of confessions can in many respects be considered forerunners of the eighteenth-century novel (Christian Fürchtegott Gellert's *The Life of the Swedish Countess of G . . .* , Sophie von La Roche's *The History of Lady Sternheim,* Goethe's *Wilhelm Meister,* Johann Heinrich Jung-Stilling's *Youth*), the contribution of Pietist women writers has not been recognized until recently. Literary histories tended to mention the canoness Susanna von Klettenberg (1732–74), whom Goethe immortalized as "Beautiful Soul" in *Wilhelm Meister's Years of Apprenticeship* (1795/6), or the learned Anna Maria van Schurman (1607–78), whose supposed "recantation" preoccupied readers throughout the eighteenth century.[28] Yet although Klettenberg's and Schurman's lives were appropriated as aesthetic material or served as Enlightenment propaganda against female religious "fanaticism," their literary production—poems, sermons, autobiographical writings—fell into obscurity. The same happened to the radical Anna Ovena Hoyers (1584–1656), writer of spiritual

18

and secular lyrics and a satire against the hierarchical Consistory Church (published in 1650 in Amsterdam), and the argumentative, controversial Johanna Eleonore Petersen.[29]

It was not until the second half of the eighteenth century, when Pietist interiority and a Rousseau-inspired language of passion had also modified, or "feminized," men's writing, that women writers were heard and recognized as a new, distinct voice. Curiously and paradoxically, it was the home, the other female ghetto, that now became a space in which literary activity could develop.

III

Compared to the relative scarcity of German women writers during the 800 years of literary history sketched above—which corresponds to a relative scarcity of male authors and of printed works in general—the second half of the eighteenth century witnessed an explosion of literary activity, something akin to a "revolution" in the book market: from 1773 to 1800, the number of writers in Germany rose from approximately 3,000 to 10,648, while the number of publications per year tripled.[30] Basing his observations on an analysis of the Leipzig Book Fair listings, Albert Ward sums up the situation on the German book market in 1800 as follows: "By the end of the eighteenth century, then, the German book market presents a very different picture from that which we saw in 1740. From a total production of 755 items at Easter 1740, to a total of 2,569 items at Easter 1800, from 28 per cent in Latin to under 4 per cent, from a market dominated by the theologian to a market granting pre-eminence to imaginative literature, and—most spectacular of all—from twenty works of narrative literature announced at Easter 1740 to 300 at Easter 1800. Clearly, the driving moment behind book production was now the reading public's pronounced taste and gargantuan appetite for light entertaining works of fiction."[31]

What is not apparent from these figures is that women writers and particularly women readers held an increasing share in the expanded book market. Whereas Georg Christian Lehms, in his encyclopedia *Teutschlands galante Poetinnen* (Frankfurt, 1715) had listed 111 women authors for all of German history to date, Carl Wilhelm von Schindel (*Die deutschen Schriftstellerinnen des neunzehnten Jahrhunderts*, Leipzig, 1825) mentions 550 women writers for the turn of the century alone. Suddenly, there were not only women authors but women publishers and editors of journals (Sophie von La Roche, Marianne Ehrmann, Therese Huber, Sophie Mereau) and eventually even a woman manager of an influential publishing and printing house (Friederike Helene Unger). In fact, reading and writing became such a rage among women that male critics started to condemn this "mania," which they saw as detracting from more serious occupations in the house. The "feminization of culture" was considered by many a threat to the official division of gender and labor.[32] As one anonymous "husband of a Sappho" complained to the editor of the *Berlinische Monatsschrift* in 1784 about his writer-wife: "Her whole peculiar character is gone: gone are modesty, propriety, all femininity, which have changed to bold self-assertiveness, precociousness and pedantry."[33] He ended his lament with the rhetorical question: "Do you know of any reasonable scholar who would want to have a learned wife?" He advocated that writing, just like "horseback riding and tobacco smoking," be left to men, as before. It was too late, though. The amazons of the pen were not to be stopped.

When we attempt to identify these "new" women writers, readers, and publishers, and the reasons for the emergence of a female literary culture, we face problems similar to those in the earlier period: lack of biographical information, lack of reliable sociological data, and general imprecision.[34] Because most women published anonymously, it is often difficult to determine who wrote what. Biographical information is only abundant for women writers who were associated with famous men. Even then, their letters or diaries were often destroyed if they contained embarrassing details about their famous male counterparts, or they were mutilated when editors considered passages on women's everyday life and concerns trivial. Although their association with important men caused some women writers to survive in literary histories as muses, mothers, lovers, or sisters, it often obfuscated their own literary merit. Their works were judged against the works critics labeled "high art" and were found wanting and hence negligible. Furthermore, the moral double standard was extended to literary activity as well. Men were expected to support their families with their pen, but women were condemned if they did; men were hailed for producing daring new works, but women were scolded if they transgressed the narrow boundaries of propriety—a situation that made them choose anonymity over public censure and "modesty" in subject matter over bold inventiveness. The timidity and reserve expected from women writers also contributed to a sense of obscurity and insignificance. Germany's peculiar political situation, its extreme fragmentation, i.e., the political, legal, economic, and cultural differences between regions and classes, between towns and countryside, made women's contributions even more invisible. And finally, invaluable documents, manuscripts, or editions were destroyed or dispersed during World War II.

Some patterns, however, emerge. In her short study of the social background of women writers in the eighteenth century based on the 223 writers presented by Schindel, Natalie Halperin provides us with the following data: 80 percent of these writers were married, 65.5 percent came from bourgeois backgrounds, 21.5 percent were of the lesser nobility, and about 90 percent had fathers and/or husbands who were bureaucrats or officers.[35] With some caution we may conclude then that women's writing generally emanated from upper middle class homes of civil servants, the new educated class.

How the bourgeois home, in spite of its confining character, could become a springboard for women writers can be explained if we focus on the shifts in conditions and attitudes toward marriage, women's education, and literary production that occurred in the course of the eighteenth century.

The eighteenth-century home was not a haven of freedom or inspiration for women. As marriage and motherhood had become the only economically stable female destiny—especially for Protestant women who had no convents for refuge—the home was the place where women were confined by law, socialization, and necessity; it was the exclusive training ground for domestic virtues and skills, it was women's place of work, pleasure, and frustration. The gradual shift from parent-arranged marriages based on property and social station to the "companionate marriage,"[36] which was supposedly based on love and free choice, brought with it both the promise of emotional fulfillment and increased responsibility for women: the woman, not her parents, had to choose a potential partner; she had to make him love her; she was to blame if the marriage did not work. The resulting emotional burden was considerable, particularly since marriages were virtually indissoluble. By law, women were still subject to their husbands, male relatives, or legal guardians, inside and outside of marriage.

Whereas their subordination had formerly been justified by theological arguments—Eve's inferiority to Adam, her greater moral weakness—Enlightenment thinking now sanctioned it by recourse to "natural law." Rousseau's idea of men's and women's complementary "natures," which was widely accepted in Germany and popularized by educators such as Campe and Basedow, provided the intellectual justification for the gender division inscribed in the legal codes.[37] Both the Frederician Code of 1750, and the Prussian *Allgemeines Landrecht* (civil code) of 1794 viewed women primarily as procreators. As the *Allgemeines Landrecht* categorically states in Article 1: "The principal end of marriage is the procreation and upbringing of children. Hence it follows, judging by the sole light of reason, that the husband is master of his own household, and head of the family. And as the wife enters into it of her own accord, she is in some measure subject to his power." The *Landrecht* went so far as to create guidelines for "marital duty" and to mandate that wives breast-feed their infants. This focus on procreation must be seen in the context of the state's desire to "populate" and "colonize" its territory.[38] Although the new emphasis on child care seemed a necessary measure in view of high infant mortality—between 1779 and 1794, 52.4 percent of all newborns died in their first year—it literally locked women into their role of mother. As Ute Frevert has pointed out, a forty-year-old woman in eighteenth-century Prussia had had an average of ten to twelve pregnancies.[39] Birth control was virtually unknown. This meant that a considerable portion of women's lives was devoted to life-threatening childbirths and time-consuming child rearing. It is not surprising, therefore, that a disproportionately large number of women writers were childless (half of the authors in this anthology!), or that women wrote before they were married and after their children had reached adulthood.

Although the *Landrecht* was more restrictive for women than for men, it provided the possibility of legal divorce in case of persistent adultery, abandonment, childlessness, impotence or incurable mental illness, and threat to life, health, freedom, or honor (paragraphs 670–700). The *Landrecht* also contained some provisions to secure women's control over property they had brought into the marriage or inherited or received as a gift while married. To what extent these new laws were applied in practice has not been studied. The important advance for women, though, was ideo-logical: the law took the decisions affecting women's lives out of the hands of the church and placed them into those of the state, thus opening up ave-nues for complaint and redress. Bad marriages were no longer considered to be God-given but could be discussed and challenged in public. Not sur-prisingly, women writers were among the first to expose marital problems in their fiction and to file for divorce in reality.[40]

The relative liberalization the law provided for a few educated or finan-cially well-off women was accompanied, if not caused, by changes in the political and economic structure of Germany. Until about 1740, the more than 300 electorates, principalities, and free towns that composed the Holy Roman Empire of the German nation were recovering from the dev-astating effects of the Thirty Years' War. One-third to one-half the popula-tion had died in the war; the trade routes had been destroyed, the economy disrupted. It took almost 100 years for the country to reconstruct itself and for the rulers to establish absolute power over their territories, each of which had its own government and religion, its own currency, its own in-ternal autonomy.[41] As most cities declined in the late seventeenth and early eighteenth century because trade routes had shifted—the exceptions were easily accessible, traditional commercial centers like Hamburg, Frankfurt, or Cologne—the absolutist princes' residences became the new centers of cultural and political activity. In order to administer their states and armies, princes resorted more and more to university-trained bourgeois bureaucrats, since they could no longer rely on the nobility, among whom learning and letters did not enjoy much esteem.[42] Members of the bour-geoisie were thus co-opted by the aristocracy; they participated in court life and were in intimate contact with their noble superiors. Because a hus-band's chances of climbing the social ladder were enhanced by a *Renom-mierfrau,* a wife who would shine in public, women of the upper bour-geoisie were not only granted access to the social life at court but also to a more worldly education.[43]

In the cities, particularly in Hamburg and Berlin, we can find an equiv-alent to the literary/social circles at the courts in the salons, semipublic gath-erings in the homes of culturally interested bourgeois in which women in-tellectuals played a prominent role as conversationalists, correspondents, or facilitators.[44] The most important salons in Berlin were kept by two

Jewish women, Henriette Herz and Rahel Varnhagen. In these weekly gatherings, bourgeoisie and nobility, women and men, Jews and Gentiles interacted freely. The salons were thus quasiutopian spaces since they permitted Jewish women, double outsiders, to explore and communicate their own thoughts and feelings, their responses to art, politics, and life in an environment relatively free of the class bias, anti-Semitism, and misogyny so common in the society at large. Although the salons did not directly generate literary works other than extensive correspondences, they provided well-read women with an intellectual forum and a mode of interaction—conversation—which would eventually translate into new literary forms.[45]

Along with the new public roles, wives assumed new private functions. Social historians describing family life in the early eighteenth century insist on the quasiservant role of the German *Hausfrau*.[46] In a predominantly rural economy, women, even of the landholding class, were completely involved in the daily chores of agriculture, husbandry, spinning, and weaving. By the end of the century, however, many bourgeois households, particularly in cities and court residences, had ceased to be self-sufficient. The *Ganzes Haus* [the all-inclusive household], where practically all products for the use of the family were manufactured, was gradually replaced by the nuclear-family home, where many items for consumption were bought.[47] Whereas both husband and wife had cooperated within the *Ganzes Haus*—the wife as a subordinate to the husband—their work spheres now became separated: increasingly, the husband worked "outside" to earn the family's living as a state employee or professional, that is, bureaucrat, minister or teacher, while the woman worked "inside," supervising a more reduced household. As a result of this division of labor, bourgeois women were less involved in the productive aspects of the economy. As their leisure time increased and more emphasis was placed on their role as educators of their children and role models for their daughters, mothers were actually encouraged to spend more time reading and instructing themselves rather than succumb to idle luxury.[48] Yet barred from *Lateinschulen* [Latin schools] and universities and hence from any professional life outside the home, admitted only to elementary schools with their rudimentary instruction in reading, writing, and home economics, women were not prepared to fulfill the role of *gebildete Hausfrau*—the literate, culturally re-

fined, morally impeccable, competent homemaker envisaged by proponents of ideal femininity.[49] In fact, by the second half of the eighteenth
century, women's education in some circles had reached a low, since public
schooling for boys had deprived their sisters of the benefit of participating
in classes taught at home by tutors. As a consequence, a mass of educational handbooks, moral weeklies, calendars, and didactic novels—many
of them written by women—sought to improve women's education without turning women into scholars. Paradoxically, although formal educational facilities did not improve for German women until late in the nineteenth century (despite isolated attempts by educators such as Karoline
Rudolphi or Christian Gotthilf Salzmann to create schools for women)
and although there persisted a considerable hostility toward female book
learning [weibliche Gelehrsamkeit], literacy and literary education thus
became more common among the privileged upper-middle classes. Women
writers, even if they publicly professed their opposition to learning, used
their basic reading skills to acquire and impart a considerable body of
knowledge.[50] The publication of more and more texts in German rather
than Latin supported this form of female autodidacticism. When the interest in religious tracts subsided toward the second half of the eighteenth
century, novels became the vehicle for female education. The invention of
smaller, more legible letters allowed printers to produce books in handy
"pocketbook" formats, the octavo and duodecimo, which could be carried
along on travels or outings and which could be easily hidden from the sight
of parents who disapproved of the novels' supposed "immorality."

A further consequence of the shift from a self-sufficient to an exchange
economy based on cash was that occasionally even upper-class women
were obliged to contribute toward the earnings of the household. Since
professions were not open to them, menial labor was frowned upon, and
the position of governess was denigrated, writing became an occupation
that could be pursued in private, almost secretly, without loss of status,
and which—if the writer succeeded in meeting popular tastes—could become a substantial source of income.[51] Many women thus earned "pin
money" by translating from English or French and eventually turned to
writing their own fiction. For Sophie von La Roche, Benedikte Naubert,
Friederike Helene Unger, Anna Luisa Karsch, and Caroline Auguste
Fischer, writing provided less a means for expressing artistic impulses than

a way to support their families in times of economic distress.

It must be emphasized, though, that this combination of leisure, intellectual encouragement, and literary-linguistic preparation can be found only among a small stratum of women in cities and court towns and rarely among wives or daughters of farmers, artisans, or merchants. The latter tended to be much more integrated into and busy with all facets of production because home and workplace were still located under the same roof. As Halperin's figures show, the number of women writers from trade and artisan backgrounds is comparatively small (approximately 6 percent). Nor is writing common among unmarried women, most of whom faced considerable hardship since they were neither trained nor encouraged to support themselves. Unless they were independently wealthy, like Annette von Droste-Hülshoff, or placed by their families in *Stifte* [Protestant cloisters], like Karoline von Günderrode, they were prone to be exploited as a cheap labor force by their families or by employers. Louise Tilly's description of the lot of unmarried women in Europe aptly characterizes the situation in Germany: "Women's work from 1750 to 1850 . . . did not provide an experience of emancipation. Work was hard and poorly paid and, for the most part, it did not represent a change from traditional occupations. Those women who traveled to cities did find themselves free of some traditional village and family restraints. But, as we shall see, the absence of these restraints was more often burdensome than liberating. Young women with inadequate wages and unstable jobs found themselves caught in a cycle of poverty which increased their vulnerability. Having lost one family, many sought to create another."[52] There were no attractive alternatives to marriage. Marriage was also the only "profession" women were trained for and the home was practically the only place in which they could acquire recognition, protection, and respect. It is not surprising, therefore, that the institution of marriage, its promise and its pitfalls, became the main preoccupation of women writers.

If women's greater public presence, increased leisure time, and higher level of literary education eased their entry into the book market, changes in the book market itself and in the reading habits of the general public helped to pave the way toward women's literary, if not political, emancipation.

In 1719, a book appeared that was an immediate success in all of Western Europe: Daniel Defoe's *Robinson Crusoe*. Within a year, three translations appeared in Germany alone; one of them was reprinted five times in 1720.[53] In 1740 and 1748 respectively, Samuel Richardson published his novels *Pamela, or Virtue Rewarded* and *Clarissa Harlowe,* which again became bestsellers on the Continent. All three novels were of crucial importance for the development of the novel in Germany.[54] Crusoe's "autobiography" provided a model for how a bourgeois traveler could build not only his own physical empire but an imaginary universe out of everyday elements. All Crusoe needed for creation was practical intelligence and a few basic tools—no university education, no patronage, no connections. Whereas Defoe's fictional autobiography made everyday life *literaturfähig,* that is, worthy of being transformed into "literature," Richardson's epistolary novels exposed the intricacies of women's and men's inner lives. Both *Pamela* and *Clarissa* explore the feelings of their female protagonists as they respond to power relationships within the family and between women and their "suitors." Again, literature is created out of experiences that are accessible to all. Exotic settings, bold adventures, and extraordinary lives are thus no longer prerequisites for interesting plots: the minute registration and recreation of emotional responses can provide entertaining and instructive reading. It is not surprising that the novels created by Defoe and Richardson held particular attraction for women, whose range of outer experience was limited.[55] Also, spiritual autobiographies and confessions had already been part of women's literary tradition since the Middle Ages; "public" letters had been a way to exert spiritual authority, while "private" letters had served them as means to communicate emotions. If telling one's life, if writing letters about one's feelings could be literature, women could be writers, too. If Robinson Crusoe's "home economics," his agricultural successes and setbacks, his cooking, hunting, carpentry, and homemaking were of literary interest, so were women's. Utopian settings for these activities could be created not only on faraway islands but also in contemporary society, as Sophie von La Roche's moral tales show. Ironically, these very different novels offered women both a space and the authority for literary projection and self-creation. "Robinsonades" and travelogues thus became favorite vehicles for the literarization of women's familiar experiences, while epistolary novels à la Richardson provided them with an opportunity for the creation of a literary self.

Defoe's and Richardson's novels are only two prominent examples of men's novels that were appropriated by women. Other, equally important texts were Rousseau's epistolary novel *Julie, ou la Nouvelle Heloïse* (1761) and his educational tract *Émile* (1762), with its short but significant discussion of an ideal woman's education ("Sophie"). Again, these works not only signaled a general shift in taste toward bourgeois subject matters and more introspective literary forms, but they also opened up a literary space for projections, identification, and polemics. By imagining themselves as literary heroines, as "Julies" or "Sophies," and fashioning their lives accordingly, women readers, almost imperceptibly, turned into women novelists. This transition from reading via identification to writing is the theme, for example, of one of the most popular women's novels, Friederike Helene Unger's *Julchen Grünthal* (1784; expanded version 1798).

The chaos in the eighteenth-century book market due to the political fragmentation of Germany paradoxically enhanced book consumption and production. Censorship regulations were not unified, so publishers could circumvent the more rigid rules of one state by selling their books in another. Also, censorship became a means of publicity: prohibition of a work in one state served as attraction in another.[56] The lack of a unified copyright law and the official toleration of book piracy in many states forced book prices down. Popular books were reprinted *en masse* and sold in cheap copies by traveling salesmen. This practice, so detrimental to publishers and to "serious" authors, not only affected book prices but also encouraged publishers—ever mindful of the profits—to produce books with immediate popular appeal: family romances, *Schauerromane* [gothic novels], historical novels, or a combination of them all. As an analysis of book production at the end of the eighteenth century shows, popular literature dominated the market, while "Classical German literature did not enjoy a wide circulation and the influence it exercised on contemporaries was very much restricted."[57] This entertaining literature could be read by a relatively uneducated public and produced by relatively uneducated authors whose egos were not invested in the making of "works of art." Women, who published anonymously and who wrote to make money, were ideally suited to become authors of this new popular literature. With the increase in the circulation of novels, publishers' income increased and so did the honoraria they were able to pay their authors: by the late 1700s, it was possible "to earn a comfortable living by serving this master [the reading public] well."[58] As Ward points out, publishers made most of their income from translations, since they only had to pay a small translator's fee but no author's honorarium. Again, this aspect of the book market favored bourgeois women writers working irregular hours at home. It favored them in other respects as well: by writing for the market, often at great speed, by translating and adapting works from other languages, women could refine their style, expand their range of literary experience, and develop a sense of competence.

Journals, moral weeklies, calendars, reading societies, and lending libraries all contributed to educating women and creating a public for the popular literature put on the market in the late 1700s.[59] From the 1720s onward, a wide variety of moral weeklies and educational journals had been produced to "enlighten" the general public. The model for these weeklies were Addison and Steele's *Spectator* and *Tatler*. The latter was imaginatively mistranslated into *Die vernünftigen Tadlerinnen* [The Reasonable Women Critics, 1725–26] by Johann Christoph Gottsched and became the first journal specifically dedicated to instructing a female readership. Although few of these journals sold more than 1,000 copies,[60] they in fact reached a much wider audience because they were handed on from family to family, read in reading circles, and distributed by lending libraries. By 1779, women began to produce their own weeklies, and by 1800, eight journals published by women had appeared on the German book market. The most famous ones were produced by Sophie von La Roche (*Pomona for Germany's Daughters*, 1783–84) and Marianne Ehrmann (*Women's Magazine*, 1787–88, *Amalie's Leisure Hours*, 1790, *The Woman Hermit from the Alps*, 1793–95).[61] Although none of these ventures lasted very long, they acquainted the reading public with women's concerns and, through their "letters to the editor" section, provided a forum for exchange and a literary training ground for future women writers. As Marianne Ehrmann formulated the challenge in her introduction to *Amalie's Leisure Hours:* "Notwithstanding the prejudice against women writers, Amalie dares to dedicate her hours of leisure to education, entertainment and instruction."[62] What Ehrmann is carefully veiling in this sentence is that she was not writing a few trifles in her moments of leisure; writing had become her full-time profession.

IV

What did these women writers write, and how were their works received by the reading public? In his 1825 survey, Schindel lists four "genres" for which women were supposedly ideally suited: lyrical poetry, novels or tales, travelogues, and educational tracts.[63] Although many women writers chose didactic narratives and love poetry over drama or epics, they were by no means limited to these genres, as the example of Luise Gottsched, Friederike Helene Unger, or Benedikte Naubert shows; they also wrote plays, criticism, and historical novels. However, it is true that women writers generally preferred more personal literary forms that were less structured or sanctioned by convention: autobiographies, letters, travelogues, novels, moral or fairy tales, occasional and lyric poetry. This had to do with their specific conditions—their "confinement" to the home, their lack of formal education and hence lack of familiarity with classical conventions—but also with their perception of the specific educational task of the woman writer. Since letters, novels, tales, and lyric poems were less codified, for example, than drama or learned poetry, they provided both generic openness, room for experimentation, and a greater closeness to lived experience. They were thus particularly attractive modes for women who were, for the first time, exploring and (re-)creating women's lives from within. And because of sheer size, novels and collections of stories also brought in more revenue.

While sympathetic critics like Schindel praised women's special sensitivity, their ability to observe and portray human behavior, and their educational skills, which "predestined" them to write "moral" narratives, it was precisely women's preference for the open novel form, their choice of domestic subject matter, and their attention to detail that made them dilettantes in the eyes of those critics for whom art was synonymous with control, organization, and grand, universal ideas. Goethe's dictum, "the true artist stands firmly and securely within himself," did not apply to women who had neither the necessary economic independence nor the emotional autonomy to be so self-sufficient.[64] Clearly, the limited social space assigned to women by society corresponded to the limited literary space they assumed and the limited praise they received as writers. The literary historian Gervinus's cynical assessment of women's literary contribution clearly shows women's double bind: "We men should not tolerate such literary coffee societies . . . women's mind is not nourished by science and life." Women's literature has not produced anything lasting, anything new, he affirms; "it could only imitate beautiful forms and had to take its subject matter from the stock of men's literature; for what would we think of a woman who wanted to gather the rich experiences herself in her own life, experiences that would be necessary for a mediocre writer to become independent ?"[65] In other words, women cannot write anything interesting or original, because they have no interesting experiences. They cannot have interesting experiences, because they are women and by definition "dependent."

Carl Wiegand's critique of women's writing, written about 100 years later, exhibits a similar kind of circular criticism: "In the novel and novella, women could express themselves freely and could demonstrate their special social graces: namely to converse [*plaudern*] on a topic with ease, wit, precise and vivid—detail. Woman rarely manages to create a large artistic composition. Most of the time, she only controls the detail, and her creations are therefore, above all, mosaics."[66] His move from historical observation to generic, essentialist argumentation (women-woman) is typical for critical reception in the nineteenth century. Twentieth-century critics, although they take a less openly essentialist position, display a similar ahistorical perception when they reproach women writers for *not* having transgressed gender and generic boundaries imposed on them by male relatives, a male public—and male judges, sympathetic or not.[67] Wiegand's praise, that women wrote light, entertaining works, *Unterhaltungsliteratur,* that they concentrated on precise observation of their immediate environment, implies, at the same time, their condemnation in a culture that considers only the serious, the profound, the complex, to be great art.[68]

As we look at women's writing in the eighteenth and early nineteenth centuries, we must bear in mind that most women writers were confined to the home by education, tradition, and social coercion—that any public activity, writing included, was considered "unfeminine." In order to justify their activity, women therefore had to establish its usefulness. Women's writing, in most cases, was justified by a twofold purpose: to make money and to instruct other women. Few women claimed that their writing responded to an inner need, or that they were creating art.[69] As we read texts by eighteenth-century women authors, we must therefore suspend our desire to evaluate and dismiss according to what have been male criteria and to concentrate instead on how texts and society interacted: how women understood their reality, how they imagined and constructed alternative models, how they were able to expand not only the confined social space reserved for them—defined by the wife-mother-housewife triangle—but also the generic spaces they had inhabited for centuries.

As we have seen, confessions, stories of guilt and conversions, of private (religious) experiences and visions, had formed the bulk of women's writing from the medieval convents to Pietist communities. The association with God legitimized this literary enterprise and empowered women to challenge the doctrine or attack the church hierarchy. This "authorization" is clearly visible in Johanna Eleonore Petersen's *Life,* where visions not only allow her to develop bold new theories of God's grace but also to "raise her voice in song," like the nightingale. In the eighteenth century, these autobiographical writings became more secular and openly descriptive of actual life circumstances, as they dealt increasingly with women's socialization into family and society. When we compare, for example, Petersen's spiritual autobiography with Henriette Herz's secular memoirs of a century later, we notice the shift from exemplary *imitatio Christi* to individual life story, from reflective moral treatise to empirical descriptions by a specifically and consciously contemporary observer. The theologian Petersen has a religious message; the Jewish *salonnière* Herz wants to evoke the specific milieu in which she was raised, the people she met, the anecdotes that constitute her life and her self. Petersen therefore provides little circumstantial detail, concentrating on her dreams instead, whereas Herz is deeply immersed in and determined by everyday reality, a reality that differs from that of her non-Jewish readers and is therefore both familiar and exotic. Annette von Droste-Hülshoff's novel fragment *Ledwina,* finally, the work of a new generation deeply imbued with Romantic ideas, shows how life is transformed into art, how self-representation becomes fiction, and autobiography, novel. Her sense of the division of the self translates into a fragmented narrative in which every water surface, every mirror, reflects fragments of a disintegrating personality. Autobiographies thus become a means to explore women's socialization, to create a public identity, or to demonstrate how gender roles and familiar constellations preclude the formation of an autonomous, integrated self.

Autobiographical narratives are always present in eighteenth- and nineteenth-century women's writings, whether they are inserted as a realistic life story in fairy tales (for example, "Rose's story" in Benedikte Naubert's *The Cloak*), or as plot device that spurs action in a moral tale (such as the letter of Adelinde's son in La Roche's *Two Sisters*); whether they serve as a self-introduction to explain the author's success, or as an assertion of difference (for example, in Anna Luisa Karsch's poetry).

Closely connected with autobiography is the letter, which suggests a direct link between experience and writing, autobiography and fiction. Letter writing had been a prime occupation of literate women from Hildegard von Bingen onward. In the eighteenth century, writing letters becomes the principal leisure-time activity for the bourgeoisie and an important means to cope with the isolation and confinement of the bourgeois home.[70] Letters to (women) friends are often the only means for women to express anxieties, desires, and frustrations (see the letters by Luise Gottsched, Caroline Schlegel-Schelling, or Karoline von Günderrode). As a literary form of address, letter writing becomes a rhetorical testing ground where elegance of style, sharpness of wit, and acuteness of description are being measured by their impact on the reader. Since many letters are meant to be handed on and read in public, they create both a public voice and an audience. Often a correspondence between an aspiring woman author and other women writers or with an established male patron will precede, supplement, or substitute for her "going public."[71] It is therefore important to examine women's letters as literary texts that not only provide us with clues about women's perceptions of their life world, but also offer a glimpse into women's literary practice, where roles are tried out and cast off, where authorship is considered, renounced, or brought to fruition.[72] Since letters do not have a prescribed format, they constitute an ideal vehicle for expressing and testing experience, personal responses to conflicts in a specific time and place, and random reflections on events or principles. Not surprisingly, the first modern novel by a German woman, Sophie von La Roche's *History of Lady Sternheim* (1771), was also the first entirely epistolary novel created in Germany.[73] It was widely imitated and translated. Its immediate success helped to popularize in Germany a genre that critics had frowned upon: the sentimental novel. Juxtaposing the letters of the virtuous Lady Sternheim with those of the depraved Lord Derby, La Roche presents complex psychological responses to the clash between the moral individual and his/her immoral environment. Although La Roche "borrowed" the epistolary format and the basic conflict—female virtue under male attack which culminates in rape—its resolution provides a rational, pragmatic alternative to both Rousseau's and Richardson's: Even in times of greatest distress, Lady Sternheim does not pine away like Clarissa but takes control of her life by changing her name, moving away, and making herself useful as a teacher of other women. Nor does she die from an unresolved conflict between duty and passion like Julie, but, free from paternal interference, chooses the man with whom she will—in Sarah Scott's unsurpassed formulation—achieve "rational happiness."[74] As Barbara Becker-Cantarino tells us, the *History of Lady Sternheim* was important to eighteenth-century German readers not so much because it represented ideal virtue under attack but because it provided a model of how a woman's life could be transformed into literature—or, we might add, how a woman's life could be created through writing.[75] Furthermore, the novel's emotionally charged, nonsyntactical language, which is clearly indebted to Pietism, profoundly affected the literary discourse of the new generation of "Storm and Stress" authors (among them Goethe and Lenz)—despite the editor's (C. M. Wieland) advice to critical readers to kindly overlook the novel's "deficiencies of style," "the unusual nature of some of the formulations," and "the lack of smooth, well-rounded perfection."[76] As in England and France, women's letters thus infused novels with a new language of feeling, of spontaneity and authenticity, a language that was soon appropriated by male writers such as Goethe (*The Sorrows of Young Werther*) and Jung-Stilling (*Youth*) and canonized by the aesthetic theories of Storm and Stress and Romanticism.

How autobiographical and epistolary elements can be combined to create a new hybrid genre was demonstrated in the nineteenth century by Bettina von Arnim. Three of her works, *Goethe's Correspondence with a Child* (1835), *Günderode* (1840), and *Clemens Brentano's Wreath of Spring* (1844), recreate her relationship with other authors by combining

34

authentic and fictional letters with poetry, diary entries, memoirs, and fiction. In these generic hybrids, Bettina von Arnim applies the Romantic concepts of *Gesamtkunstwerk* [the all-inclusive work of art that contains poetry and prose] and "romanticization of life" to transform life into fiction, historical truth into poetic truth, in order to create a reconciliation that actual life precludes. Particularly in the fictionalized (auto-)biography *Günderode,* von Arnim shows that friendship between women poets can become the smallest unit in an incipient women's literary culture. The interaction between women does not create a confining ghetto but rather a place from which to draw inspiration and strength, a place which ultimately permits them to go out and become involved in society.

The epistolary or confessional "sentimental novel" was further expanded by Benedikte Naubert, who projected it into the distant past. In her historical novels such as *Walter of Montbarry* (1786, translated into English in 1803), *Elisabeth, Erbin von Toggenburg* (1789, translated as *Feudal Tyrants; or: The Counts of Carlsheim and Sargans*), *Alf of Dülmen* (1791, translated into English in 1794), and *Hermann of Unna* (translated in 1794), Benedikte Naubert constructed intricate sentimental plots, often in epistolary and/or confessional form, against the background of real historical events. Her technique of double-layered fictional-historical narrative was later adopted by Walter Scott. Although Scott himself credited Naubert with having provided an inspiration and model for his historical novels, German literary historians still refer to Scott as "the father of the historical novel."[77]

Naubert was not only one of the "mothers" of the historical novel— other such mothers were Mme. de Lafayette in France and the English novelists Sarah Scott and Clara Reeve—she was also one of the first eighteenth-century German collectors and writers of fairy tales, another genre which seemed particularly suited to women's sensibility. As part of the oral tradition, fairy tales had always been intimately connected with women's workplaces—the spinning room, the kitchen, the public well—and with women's experience: the anxieties associated with childbirth and mothering, with ugliness, poverty, illegitimacy, old age. Concentrating on female protagonists rather than on the stereotypical "king's son," Naubert explores the connections between tales and women's lives in her *New German Fairytales* (1789–92). In *The Cloak,* structurally the most complicated of the tales, she literally weaves myths, legends, and elements from the folk tradition into the fabric of a fairy tale, combining the coming-of-age story of a young girl with the autobiography of a lower-class woman. Contrary to generic custom, her "fairy" tale touches on questions of women's work and women's art, women's role in society and women's role in the family. As in the visionary literature of previous centuries, the supernatural and the real are inextricably intertwined. In their search for a self, virtuous Genelas and hardworking Rose learn that spinning and weaving are life-sustaining occupations, for the two women spin the thread that will support them economically as they spin the tale that will allow them to demonstrate their true value and achieve everlasting happiness. The frame, a recreation of King Arthur's court, adds an element of social burlesque and critique: the women at court are neither as cunning as they think, nor as virtuous as they claim; while the knights are neither as strong, nor as gallant, nor as noble as they would like the women to believe. The cloak, a garment meant to cover weaknesses, in fact exposes them. What starts out as a self-righteous competition for virtue ends in the realization that human frailty makes bonding, rather than competition, imperative.

Whereas Naubert's complex ironic tale of female bonding and female creativity focuses on the development of the daughter, Bettina von Arnim's Romantic fairy tale, *The Queen's Son,* written one generation later, explores the plight of the mother. Rejected by the king because of her disfiguring, "monstrous" pregnancy, and distressed by the disappearance of her oldest son, the queen learns to look for support among the wild animals of the forest. In her desperate search for her child, she comes to understand the gulf of distrust and resentment separating humans from animals and to identify with nature, which has been oppressed and exploited by man. The queen's son, who was raised by wild beasts and who becomes king over animals and humans alike, embodies Arnim's utopian longing for a new society that reconciles all opposites. The focus on specific female experiences and the wide utopian thrust of Naubert's and Arnim's fairy tales become apparent if we pair them with the fairy tales collected and reworked by the Grimm brothers, for example, with *Mother Holle, The Three Spinners, The Carnation,* and *The Seven Ravens,* where the female characters are rewarded for selfless domesticity and sacrifice, not for an exploration and assertion of the self.[78]

How women writers expanded generic boundaries by formal as well as by thematic innovations, creating small "utopias" within the confines of patriarchal society, can be shown by comparing three moral tales: Sophie von La Roche's *Two Sisters* (1784), Sophie Mereau's *Flight to the City* (1806), and Caroline Auguste Fischer's *William the Negro* (1817). All three were published in journals and were directed at a large female audience.

Sophie von La Roche's tale narrates the heroic attempt by three women to redeem a monstrous act of parental tyranny: the father's rejection and expulsion of his daughter. In a society that values women's beauty and docility as assets on the marriage market, the ugly, headstrong Adelinde constitutes a liability. She is, therefore, in every sense disinherited. Unable and unwilling to brave the patriarch directly, Adelinde's mother and sister conspire to elevate Adelinde and her family, and reinstitute her socially through education and moral and financial support. The pastoral idyll, the somewhat forced reconciliation at the end of the moral tale, and its sentimental tone have led critics to accuse it of conventionality and sentimentality. Certainly, La Roche does not proclaim a social or political revolution. Her criticism of patriarchal abuse, however, and her presentation of a women-made utopia where "nobility" is a state of mind, not a class affiliation, and where relations between men and women are open and companionate (that is, "British," for Lord Kent embodies the new attitude), make her much more progressive than many of the so-called revolutionaries who, although they attack class divisions, fail to challenge the gender structure.

Sophie Mereau's *Flight to the City* is, in many respects, a parody of a moral tale and of bourgeois morality. Although it ends in marriage and a "happily ever after," the story defies all expectations derived from sentimental novels: in a reversal of the Romantic city-country dichotomy, the young couple elopes from the country to the city; they thrive without proper economic basis and in spite of their bohemian life-style; love survives in spite of the flippant personalities of the two protagonists; they become prosperous in spite of their aversion to a bourgeois existence; and they are accepted into the bosom of the family in spite of their immorality. Neither the parents nor the children correspond to the ideal of bourgeois propriety: the soft-hearted father wastes his money on his craze, the theater; the tough-minded mother spends her time increasing her learning, unconcerned with her disintegrating family; the daughter engages in pre-marital sexual activity without remorse or social punishment. Again, this funny "immoral" tale carries no overtly revolutionary message, but inso-far as human relations and morality are political, Mereau's criticism of the sexual politics of her time constitutes an act of political defiance. Although she reestablishes the old order in the end by way of a bourgeois marriage, this old order is based on none of the old values.

Caroline Auguste Fischer's curious story *William the Negro* has the same basic structure as La Roche's or Mereau's: she resolves the initial marginalization of the female protagonist, the neglected, misunderstood, scorned, "mute" Molly, by reintegrating her into the traditional patri-archal family through marriage. She complicates Molly's sexual marginal-ization, however, by introducing another marginalized character: Wil-liam, the Negro. Both the speechless woman and the fatherless black man are "orphans" and outcasts of society. Their love for each other is as much a transgression of the traditional order as William's revolutionary activity in Haiti. The former transgression, however, is tolerated and the latter even encouraged by the enlightened Sir Robert, a kind of utopian super-father to both Molly and William. And although Molly reverts to the old order by eventually marrying Sir Robert, who is white, wealthy, and Euro-pean, William's son—whom Molly and Robert adopt as their own—em-bodies the new order based on a fusion of opposites. One might even argue that William, who shares so many characteristics with the female protago-nist, is her rebellious, defiant "other": he goes on to lead the revolution which she represses by locking herself away into patriarchal marriage.

All three tales—and most women's narratives of the time—have in common a conciliatory ending: rebelliousness ends in acquiescence, mo-rality and propriety are reestablished; the patriarchal system seems un-challenged. Yet a closer look at the preceding conflicts allows us to dis-cover the incongruities and innovative or critical moments in all of these writings, even those that appear most conservative. In La Roche's story women actively oppose the abuse of power, and they *transform* their im-mediate society into a bucolic idyll. Mereau's tale rewards the single-minded pursuit of pleasure rather than "virtue." And Fischer's Molly achieves happiness in marriage only after all protagonists have learned to make conscious, responsible moral decisions instead of acting by unconscious impulses and prejudices. In each case, the new order "restored" at the end certainly differs from the old order the protagonists started out with. Each story offers alternatives to dominant traditions and invites active identification. In some instances, we can even detect elements of social satire, which signal a growing critical distance to the gender structure and its assumptions about proper femininity.

Although it can be argued that women's contribution in the eighteenth and early nineteenth century has been particularly prominent in the field of prose fiction, women writers were also drawn to another genre that was gradually transformed to provide a space for women's experience: poetry. From the Middle Ages onward, women writers had engaged in writing religious poetry, songs, and poetry to celebrate historical events or activities. After the Reformation, many Protestant women were involved in composing texts to existing melodies and collecting hymns for hymnbooks. In the seventeenth century, this religious poetic activity persisted side by side with occasional poetry, which allowed the writer to invent complicated, witty poetic constructions for secular occasions: the praise of a poet upon the publication of a volume of works; the commemoration of a historic date, the celebration of a particularly important day in the life of a monarch (weddings, battles, births); or the public ridicule of an opponent or an antagonistic group. From its very start, occasional poetry was public, social poetry for immediate consumption.

Although occasional poetry still constituted one of the major incentives for women's poetic activity in the eighteenth century, more personal, lyrical poetic forms gradually appear. In Anna Luisa Karsch's poetry, for example, we already perceive a division between "public" and "private": her "official" panegyrics addressed to Frederick the Great brought her literary fame and financial patronage, but it is her love and nature poetry, in which she expresses joy and grief, that constitutes her literary achievement in the eyes of today's critics. This private, confessional tone is also apparent in Philippine Gatterer Engelhard's highly stylized poem *Girl's Lament* as well as in Sophie Mereau's *Spring* and *To a Trellised Tree*. Increasingly, nature becomes the central metaphor in, and space for, women's poetic experience. "Nature," associated with women and femininity for centuries, is now consciously reclaimed and occupied. For Karsch, the prototypical "natural poet," "nature" is above all a poetic "Nutzraum," a place that provides identity, work, and artistic images; for Karoline von Günderrode, nature, the universe, becomes the Great Womb, which the androgynous poet both enters into and from which s/he draws her creativity; for Annette von Droste-Hülshoff, finally, nature is a magic space, slightly menacing, seductive, and full of literary promise.

All of the writers included in this anthology developed their forms of literary expression in close collaboration with men and women of their time. Even if they worked in isolation, they tried to create a "community" by maintaining an extended correspondence with friends and peers or establishing literary salons and "coffee societies." Yet while male authors—particularly after Storm and Stress theorists such as Herder or the young Goethe had proclaimed the "original genius"—strove to outdo their literary forefathers by coming up with innovative literary forms (whose "originality" was often no more than a postulate), women authors appear to have stayed with the traditional generic spaces they had occupied for centuries. By stretching or crossing generic boundaries, however, and by filling given forms with often painful and unmediated personal experience, they deeply influenced, even redirected, the literature written by men. To say that "women could only imitate beautiful forms and subject matter" invented by men, as Gervinus has, is certainly false. In fact, the attempts by Gervinus and others to relegate women writers to a separate, inferior sphere, to fend them off by establishing fences and then to ridicule their forms of interaction and literary production, had paranoid overtones, even then. By the time Gervinus made his contemptuous remarks, women writers had not only appropriated but transformed "male" literary forms, while male writers had appropriated and transformed "female" forms. To speak of separate spheres and to establish an all-male genealogy was a desperate attempt to turn back the clock. It is precisely the mutual challenge, the productive use of "difference," that created a literary culture, in Germany and elsewhere.

NOTES

1. Mary Poovey, *The Proper Lady and the Woman Writer: Ideology as Style in the Works of Mary Wollstonecraft, Mary Shelley, and Jane Austen* (Chicago: Chicago Univ. Press, 1984), pp. 3 ff. For complete citations of English texts used in this introduction see the bibliography at the end of this volume. German references will be cited in full.

2. A recent collection of articles on German/European literature by women, *Women. Literature. History*, tries to convey this sense of historical disjunction in its title: *Frauen. Literatur. Geschichte. Schreibende Frauen vom Mittelalter bis zur Gegenwart,* edited by Hiltrud Gnüg and Renate Möhrmann (Stuttgart: Metzler, 1985). Because of its specific critical focus and organization, the volume does not provide the sense of continuity or of collective development that is the implicit goal of Barbara Becker-Cantarino's important new study, *Der lange Weg zur Mündigkeit: Frau und Literatur* (1500–1800) (Stuttgart: Metzler, 1987). In this work, the author traces the gradual disenfranchisement of German women and women writers from the Reformation until 1800 by exploring the gradual changes in their traditional (wife and mother, nun, courtesan) and nontraditional (governess, actress) roles. A more synchronic focus is offered by the new anthology of historical-critical articles *Deutsche Literatur von Frauen. Vom Mittelalter bis zur Gegenwart.* 2 vols. (Vol. 1: *Vom Mittelalter bis zum Ende des 18. Jahrhunderts*), edited by Gisela Brinker-Gabler (Munich: Beck, 1988).

3. See Gnüg/Möhrmann, *Frauen. Literatur. Geschichte,* ix, and Gisela Brinker-Gabler, "Die Schriftstellerin in der deutschen Literaturwissenschaft: Aspekte ihrer Rezeption von 1835 bis 1910," *Unterrichtspraxis* 9 (1976): 15–28.

4. See Gisela Brinker-Gabler, "Die Schriftstellerin," pp.20ff., and Gnüg/Möhrmann, *Frauen. Literatur. Geschichte,* p. XIII. Becker-Cantarino (*Der lange Weg*) concentrates on "roles" instead, although "spaces" such as the convents or the courts appear in her analysis as well.

5. For the situation in France and England see the chapter entitled "Klöster und Höfe—Räume literarischer Selbstentfaltung," in Gnüg/Möhrmann, *Frauen. Literatur. Geschichte,* pp.1–34; Carolyn C. Lougee, *Le Paradis des femmes: Women, Salons and Social Stratification in Seventeenth-Century France* (Princeton: Princeton Univ. Press, 1976); and Mary Prior, editor, *Women in English Society* 1500–1800 (London and New York: Methuen, 1985).

6. The assessment of the educational function of convents varies considerably. Joan Ferrante ("The Education of Women in the Middle Ages in Theory, Fact, and Fantasy," in Patricia Labalme, editor, *Beyond their Sex: Learned Women of the European Past* [New York and London: New York Univ. Press, 1980], p.14) claims their extraordinary importance as centers of learning; Sara Lehrman ("The Education of Women in the Middle Ages," in Douglas Radclitt-Umstead, editor, *Roles and Images of Women in the Middle Ages and the Renaissance* (Pittsburgh: Center for Medieval and Renaissance Studies, 1975), pp.133–59) siding with Johannes

Scherr (*Deutsche Kultur- und Sittengeschichte*, Leipzig: Wigand, 1902, p.112) seems to go to the other extreme when she affirms that "the educational system of the Middle Ages—that is, the schools attached to the churches, the monasteries, the bishops' households and the universities—were closed to girls and women. Generally, men thought it was better not to make women too literate" (pp.140ff.). See also Becker-Cantarino, *Der lange Weg*, pp.67–75.

7. Hildegard von Bingen (1098–1179) for example, had to obtain papal approval for "publishing" her first book, *Scivias*.

8. Cocalis, *Defiant Muse*, p. XVI.

9. More information on Hrotswitha is given by Wolfgang Stammler, *Die deutsche Literatur des Mittelalters. Verfasserlexikon*, vol.2, (Berlin and Leipzig: de Gruyter, 1936); Lucas, *Women in the Middle Ages*, pp.143–47; and Sticca, "Sin and Salvation." Some of Hrotswitha's works are available in English translation: Petroff, editor, *Women's Visionary Literature*, pp.114–35. On St. Hildegard of Bingen see: *Symphonia. A Critical Edition of the 'Symphonia armonie celestium revelationum'* and Matthew Fox, editor, *The Illuminations of Hildegard von Bingen*. The latter unfortunately does not provide Hildegard's own texts but a modernized "paraphrase." Cf. also Ferrante, "The Education of Women," 22ff.; Frances and Joseph Gies, *Women in the Middle Ages* (New York: Crowell, 1978), pp.63–96. Excerpts of Hildegard's writings also in Petroff, *Women's Visionary Literature*, 151–58. See Petroff, *Women's Visionary Literature*, pp.212–21 on Mechthild, and pp.222–31 on St. Gertrude the Great, another visionary nun from the abbey of Helfta.

10. Blackwell, "Women's Literary Culture," p.58.

11. E. William Monter, *Witchcraft in France and Switzerland*, p.17. The literature of witch persecution and trials is extensive and controversial, as the recent polemic around Gunnar Heinsohn's and Otto Steiger's theory demonstrates. The most useful historical analyses are by H. C. Erik Midelfort, E. William Monter, Richard Kieckhefer and Richard Horsley in the U.S.; Georg Schormann, Gabriele Becker and Sigrid Bovenschen in Germany. A profoundly disturbing fictionalized account of an individual case based on historical research is provided by Kunze, *Highroad to the Stake*. On the impact of the witches' confessions on confessional literature cf. Jeannine Blackwell, "Die Zunge, der Geistliche und das Weib: Überlegungen zur strukturellen Bedeutung der Hexenbekenntnisse von 1500–1700," in *Der Widerspenstigen Zähmung. Studien zur bezwungenen Weiblichkeit in der Literatur vom Mittelalter bis zur Gegenwart*. Sylvia Wallinger and Monika

Jonas, editors (Innsbruck: Innsbrucker Beiträge zur Kulturwissenschaft, 1986), pp.95–115.

12. See Midelfort, "Witchcraft, Magic, and the Occult," p.197; and Monter, "The Pedestal and the Stake."

13. It is a curious fact that Sprenger, one of the most vehement persecutors of women witches, was also one of the proponents of "Mariolatry," the idolatry of the Virgin Mary, in his function as German organizer of the Confraternities of the Rosary. Cf. Monter, *Ritual, Myth, and Magic*, pp.10ff.

14. In her analysis of witches' depictions in book illustrations and paintings, Jane Davidson not only points to the mutual reinforcement between image and word, but also to the fact that witches were generally depicted as "normal" women of all stations who engage in intercourse with the devil or cook babies. The message of such pamphlets is clear: *any* woman was potentially a witch. ("Great Black Goats and Evil Little Women," p.155).

15. Jean Woods and Maria Fürstenwald (*Schriftstellerinnen, Künstlerinnen und gelehrte Frauen des deutschen Barock. Ein Lexikon* [Stuttgart: Metzler, 1984, p. xiii]) speak of "a seemingly endless wave of Latin publications on the subject of women" as late as 1670, of "ever-new variations on the 'mulier non homo' theme."

16. Strauss, "Lutheranism and Literacy," pp.113ff. See also the survey essay by Irwin, "Society and the Sexes."

17. Strauss claims that literacy spread *in spite of* Luther, since the absolute states needed educated bureaucracy and clergy and supported the institution of Latin Schools and Universities ("Lutheranism and Literacy," p.110).

18. The combative Argula von Grumbach (1492–1563), for example, was inspired by Luther to write a tract denouncing financial exploitation and immorality practiced by the clergy (see Bainton, *Women of the Reformation*, p.103, and Becker-Cantarino, *Der lange Weg*, 103–10.)

19. See Miles, *Image as Insight* and Becker-Cantarino, *Der lange Weg*, p.95.

20. A critical assessment of the new domesticity is given by Dagmar Lorenz, "Vom Kloster zur Küche: Die Frau vor und nach der Reformation Dr. Martin Luthers," in *Die Frau von der Reformation zur Romantik: Die Situation der Frau vor dem Hintergrund der Literatur- und Sozialgeschichte*, edited by B. Becker-Cantarino (Bonn: Bouvier, 1980), pp.14ff.

21. For example, Maria Sibylla Merian or Anna Maria van Schurman.

22. See Jean Woods, "'Die Pflicht befihlet mir/zu schreiben und zu tichten': Drei literarisch tätige Frauen aus dem Hause Baden-Durlach," in Becker-Cantarino, ed-

itor, *Die Frau*, pp.36–57, and Ute Brandes, "Studierstube-Dichterklub-Hofgesellschaft: Kreativität und kultureller Rahmen weiblicher Erzählkunst im Barock," in Brinker-Gabler, editor, *Deutsche Literatur von Frauen I*, 222–47. Pietist women's literature has also received increasing attention: Eda Sagarra, *A Social History*, pp.409ff.; Richard Critchfield, "Prophetin, Führerin, Organisatorin: Zur Rolle der Frau im Pietismus," in Becker-Cantarino, editor, *Die Frau*, 112–37; and Jeannine Blackwell, "Herzensgespräche mit Gott: Bekenntnisse deutscher Pietistinnen im 17. und 18. Jahrhundert," in Brinker-Gabler, editor, *Deutsche Literatur von Frauen I*, 265–89. I have left out a third "space": the *Sprachgesellschaften*, the Baroque language societies, because they tended to overlap with the other two. As Karl F. Otto ("Die Frauen der Sprachgesellschaften," in *Europäische Hofkultur im 16. und 17. Jahrhundert* [Hamburg: Hauswedell, pp.497–503]) has shown, only two language societies accepted women and only one, the *Pegnesische Blumenorden*, had female members who exerted any influence within the society.

23. For example, 1 Corinthians 14:34–35. How rigidly the rule of silence for women was observed in some places is mentioned by Sagarra (*A Social History of Germany*, p.406): until 1700, women in Hamburg churches were even forbidden to *sing*.

24. See Brandes, "Studierstube." Brandes points out that the duchess also wrote a pastoral novel modeled after d'Urfé's *L'Astrée* and a drama about politics and morality. Her daughter Sibylle Ursula, correspondent of Mme. de Scudéry and translator of several of La Calprenède's works, participated in the writing of one of the most important Baroque novels, *Aramena*. See also Becker-Cantarino, *Der lange Weg*, 246–59.

25. Woods, "Die Pflicht," pp.43ff.

26. Cf. Peter M. Daly, "Catharina Regina von Greiffenberg," in *Deutsche Dichter des 17. Jahrhunderts. Ihr Leben und Werk*, edited by Harald Steinhagen and Benno von Wiese (Berlin: Erich Schmidt, 1984), pp.615–39. Incidentally, this handbook treats only two women writers in detail, as opposed to the seventy-five Baroque women poets listed in Goedeke, and the 700 women writers and scholars included in Woods/Fürstenwald.

27. Blackwell ("Herzensgespräche") has shown that the Pietist movement created many more genres. The confession, however, was the genre that influenced later literature most. Blackwell's contention that the Pietist theory of divine inspiration became the basis for the theory of the *Originalgenie* (the idea of the divinely

inspired genius poet) during Storm and Stress is corroborated by Ward's observation: "Whoever could intensify sentiment so as to produce a vision was once called a *Wiedergeborener,* now he is a *Genie.*" (*Book Production, Fiction and the German Reading Public* 1740–1800, p.75).

28. Anna Maria van Schurman (1607–78, also spelled von Schurmann) was an extraordinarily learned woman who spoke fourteen languages, corresponded with monarchs and theologians, and, without having studied formally, was given a permanent chair of theology at the University of Utrecht. At age sixty-two she suddenly joined the "House of the Chosen," a radical ascetic religious group founded by Jean de Labadie in Geneva, and moved with them from town to town, persecuted by authorities. In 1673 she published her autobiography, *Eukleria,* in which she rejects all knowledge that is accumulated for its own sake, not for some spiritual end. Her life was understood by many as proof of women's intellectual potential, but also as a negative example: too much learnedness, it was argued, could lead women astray. See Becker-Cantarino, *Der lange Weg,* pp.113–18.

29. See Becker-Cantarino, "Outsiders," pp.151ff.

30. Ward, *Book Production,* p.87.

31. Ward, *Book Production,* p.58. Comparing the situation in Germany with that in England, Ward notes that "from 1770 to 1800 an average of forty novels appeared annually in England—a total of about 1,200 over three decades, whereas the German reading public were "fed" a similar total during five or six years of the nineties alone" (p.35). Although Ward's numbers have been challenged by Erich Schön, they both agree on the general trend. See Erich Schön, *Der Verlust der Sinnlichkeit oder Die Verwandlungen des Lesers. Mentalitätswandel um* 1800 (Stuttgart: Klett-Cotta, 1987).

32. Rolf Engelsing, *Der Bürger als Leser* (Stuttgart: Metzler, 1974), p.334.

33. "Brief an die Herausgeber von dem Ehmann einer Sappho," *Berlinische Monatsschrift,* F. Gedike and J. E. Biester editors, vol.3 (January 1784): 169; my translation.

34. Becker-Cantarino's recent study, *Der lange Weg zur Mündigkeit,* is the first comprehensive literary-socio-historical survey of German women writers. But as its title indicates, it concentrates on authors who paved the *way to* literary emancipation, rather than on those who benefited from this pioneer work; it presents the *emergence* of a women's literary culture, rather than analyzing the works of its most prominent representatives later in the century. Among the older literary-historical analyses, the most useful ones are still Christine Touaillon, *Der deutsche*

Frauenroman des 18. Jahrhunderts (Vienna and Leipzig: Wilhelm Braumüller, 1919) and Natalie Halperin, *Die deutschen Schriftstellerinnen in der 2. Hälfte des 18. Jahrhunderts* (n. p.: Frankfurt 1919). Whereas the former categorizes authors by analyzing the body of their work, the latter attempts a sociological analysis of women writers. More recent interpretative studies are the monographs by Helga Meise (*Die Unschuld und die Schrift. Deutsche Frauenromane im 18. Jahrhundert* [Marburg and Berlin: Guttandin und Hoppe, 1983]) and Lydia Schieth (*Die Entwicklung des deutschen Frauenromans im ausgehenden 18. Jahrhundert* [Bern and New York: Peter Lang, 1986]), and the articles by Heuser, Schlaffer, Bürger, Dawson, Brandes, Meise, et al. in Brinker-Gabler's anthology *Deutsche Literatur von Frauen*, vols.1 and 2. Social histories of Germany that include detailed information on that turn-of-the-century generation are rare. Eva Walter's attempt to recreate the "weibliche Lebenszusammenhänge," the life world, of eleven women authors from their diaries and letters, provides important insights into the conditions and responses of individual bourgeois women writers but no general data, because of the size of the sample (*Schrieb oft von Mägde Arbeit müde. Weibliche Lebenszusammenhänge* [Düsseldorf: Schwann, 1985]).

35. Natalie Halperin, *Die deutschen Schriftstellerinnen*, p.2.

36. I borrowed the term "companionate marriage" from Lawrence Stone, *The Family, Sex and Marriage in England* 1500–1800 (New York: Harper & Row, 1979 [abridged paperback edition]).

37. For a discussion of complementary gender concepts see the articles by Susan Cocalis ("Der Vormund . . ."), Karin Hausen, Barbara Duden (see n. 47, and Silvia Bovenschen's *Die imaginierte Weiblichkeit*, pp.150–256. The legal situation is discussed by Becker-Cantarino, *Der lange Weg*, pp.46–65.

38. *Allgemeines Landrecht für die preussischen Staaten*, vol.3, 2nd edition (Berlin, 1794). The contemporary English translation is quoted by Bell and Offen, *Women, the Family, and Freedom*, vol. I: 1750–1880, pp.31; 29. On Prussia's family policy cf. also Ute Frevert, "Frauen und Ärzte im späten 18. und frühen 19. Jahrhundert—zur Sozialgeschichte eines Gewaltverhältnisses," in A. Kuhn and J. Rüsen, editors, *Frauen in der Geschichte*, vol.2 (Düsseldorf: Schwann, 1982), pp.177–210.

39. Frevert, "Frauen und Ärzte," p.180.

40. For example, Dorothea Schlegel, Caroline Schlegel-Schelling, Caroline Auguste Fischer, and Sophie Mereau.

41. See Sagarra, *A Social History*, pp.8ff. The German population had decreased

in the Thirty Years' War from 18 million in 1618 to 10–11 million in 1650. It did not reach its prewar level until 1750 (p.10).

42. See Bruford, *Germany in the 18th Century*, pp.64ff.

43. Halperin, *Die deutschen Schriftstellerinnen*, p.29.

44. The literature on salon culture is extensive. The most important study to date is Hertz's *Jewish High Society in Old Regime Berlin*.

45. The theory that conversational salon culture created typically feminine literary forms has been developed by Edith Waldstein, among others (*Bettine von Arnim and the Politics of Romantic Conversation* [Columbia, S.C.: Camden House, 1988]).

46. See Bruford, *Germany in the 18th Century*, pp.225ff.

47. See Gotthardt Frühsorge, "Die Einheit aller Geschäfte. Tradition und Veränderung des 'Hausmutter'-Bildes in der deutschen ökonomischen Literatur des 18. Jahrhunderts," *Wolfenbüttler Studien zur Aufklärung*, vol.3, edited by Günter Schulz (Bremen, Wolfenbüttel, 1976), pp.137–58; Hausen, "Family and Role-Division;" and Barbara Duden, "Das schöne Eigentum. Zur Herausbildung des bürgerlichen Frauenbildes an der Wende vom 18. zum 19. Jahrhundert," *Kursbuch* 47 (March 1977): 125–42.

48. Susan Cocalis ("Der Vormund will Vormund sein: Zur Problematik der weiblichen Unmündigkeit im 18. Jahrhundert," in *Gestaltet und gestaltend. Die Frau in der deutschen Literatur*, edited by Marianne Burkhard [Amsterdam: Rodopi, 1980], pp.33–55) points out that Luther had already emphasized the need for a certain basic home education. On the various approaches to women's education in the late eighteenth century cf. Peter Petschauer, "Eighteenth-Century German Opinions about Education for Women."

49. On women's education see Ullrich Herrmann, "Lesegesellschaften an der Wende des 18. Jahrhunderts," *Archiv für Kulturgeschichte* 57 (1975): 475–84 and Ward, *Book Production*, pp.147ff. Primary education became compulsory in Prussia in 1717, in Saxony in 1772, and in Bavaria in 1802. As Ward points out, though, it was not rigidly enforced. The 1786 census indicates, for example, that only 59 percent of the children regularly attended school in Bohemia. The limits of female learning are also discussed by Jeannine Blackwell ("Weibliche Gelehrsamkeit oder die Grenzen der Toleranz: die Fälle Karsch, Naubert und Gottsched," in *Lessing und die Toleranz. Lessing Yearbook Sonderband*. Edited by Peter Freimark, Franklin Kopitzsch, and Helga Slessarev [Detroit: Wayne State Univ. Press]: 1986, pp.325–39), Rolf Engelsing ("Die Bildung der Frau," in Engelsing, *Der Bürger als*

Leser [Stuttgart: Metzler, 1974], p.322), and Sigrid Bovenschen (*Die imaginierte Weiblichkeit. Exemplarische Untersuchungen zu kulturgeschichtlichen und literarischen Präsentationsformen des Weiblichen* [Frankfurt am Main: Suhrkamp, 1979], pp.63–190).

50. Becker-Cantarino, *Der lange Weg*, 177–84 (on women's autodidacticism).

51. Dawson, "Women Communicating," p.111.

52. Tilly, Scott, and Cohen, "Women's Work and European Fertility Patterns," p.235.

53. See Ward, *Book Production*, pp.18ff; Touaillon, *Der deutsche Frauenroman*, pp.21ff.

54. There was also a submerged German novel tradition, in the form of Baroque pastoral, political, historical, or picaresque novels (Reuter, Grimmelshausen, et al.). The British eighteenth-century novels partially resuscitated this tradition and domesticated or "bourgeoisie-fied" it.

55. Cf. Blackwell, "An Island of Her Own."

56. Ward, *Book Production*, pp.97ff.

57. Ward, *Book Production*, p.129. Ward refers to literature that was placed in the "Classical" category by nineteenth-century critics and reflected nineteenth-century aesthetic preconceptions, rather than responses at the time of publication.

58. Ward, *Book Production*, p.84

59. See Ulrich Herrmann, "Lesegesellschaften an der Wende des 18. Jahrhunderts," *Archiv für Kulturgeschichte* 57 (1975): 475–84.

60. Ward, *Book Production*, p.81

61. For more information on women's moral weeklies, see Dawson, "Women Communicating," and her article entitled "'And this shield is called—self-reliance.'" See also Sabine Schumann, "Das 'lesende Frauenzimmer': Frauenzeitschriften im 18. Jahrhundert," in *Die Frau von der Reformation zur Romantik*, edited by Becker-Cantarino, pp.138–69; Wolfgang Martens, *Die Botschaft der Tugend. Die Aufklärung im Spiegel der deutschen moralischen Wochenschriften* (Stuttgart: Metzler, 1968); and Edith Krull, *Das Wirken der Frau im frühen deutschen Zeitschriftenwesen* (Charlottenburg: R. Lorenz, 1939).

62. Quoted in Dawson, "Women Communicating," p.105.

63. Schindel, *Die deutschen Schriftstellerinnen des 19. Jahrhunderts* (Leipzig: 1825), pp.xxff.

64. As Brinker-Gabler points out, the Goethe-Schiller opposition "Künst-

ler"-"dilettante"-made it clear why women could not aspire to this concept of artistry (see *Works*, Weimar edition, vol. 47, p.318). They lacked all prerequisites for the true artist, which, according to Goethe and Schiller's sketch, is based upon: "Ausübung der Kunst nach Wissenschaft" [exercise of art on the basis of knowledge, or systematically]; "Annahme einer objektiven Kunst" [the concept of an objective art]; "schulgerechte Folge und Steigerung" [continuity and improvement according to literary convention]; "Profession und Beruf" [profession and calling]; "Anschliessung an eine Kunst- und Künstlerwelt. Schule" [association with a world of art and of artists. With a literary school] (*Deutsche Dichterinnen vom 16. Jahrhundert bis zur Gegenwart. Gedichte und Lebensläufe* [Frankfurt: Fischer, 1983], p.19).

65. G. G. Gervinus, *Geschichte der deutschen Dichtung*, v, 4th ed. (Leipzig: 1853), pp.328ff [my translation].

66. Carl Wiegand, *Die Frau in der modernen deutschen Literatur* (Berlin: Schünemann, 1903), p.38.

67. The verdict that eighteenth- and nineteenth-century women's literature is "trivial," "banal," or just "conventional," too much concerned with detail, and overly sentimental was reintroduced by Marianne Thalmann (*Der Trivialroman des 18. Jahrhunderts und der romantische Roman: ein Beitrag zur Entwicklung der Geheimbundmystik* [Berlin: E. Ebering, 1923]) and discussed and/or adopted by Marion Beaujean (*Der Trivialroman in der 2. Hälfte des 18. Jahrhunderts* [Bonn: Bouvier, 1969]) and others. It has recently come under attack by Helmut Kreuzer ("Trivialliteratur als Forschungsproblem. Zur Kritik des deutschen Trivialromans seit der Aufklärung," *DVjS* 41.2 (1967): 173–91), Rudolf Schenda (*Volk ohne Buch. Studien zur Sozialgeschichte der populären Lesestoffe 1770–1910* [Munich: Deutscher Taschenbuch Verlag, 1977]) and in feminist criticism (for example, Jeannine Blackwell, "Anonym, verschollen, trivial," *Women in German Yearbook*. Edited by Marianne Burkhard and Edith Waldstein [Lanham, London, New York: Univ. Press of America, 1985], pp.39–60).

68. See Schenda, *Volk ohne Buch*, p.23.

69. See Eva Walter, *Schrieb oft*, p.50.

70. See, for example, Reinhard M. Nickisch, "Die Frau als Briefschreiberin im Zeitalter der deutschen Aufklärung," *Wolfenbüttler Studien zur Aufklärung* 3 (1976): 25–69; and Barbara Becker-Cantarino, "Leben als Text. Briefe als Ausdrucks- und Verständigungsmittel in der Briefkultur und Literatur des 18. Jahrhun-

derts," in Gnüg and Möhrmann, editors. *Frauen. Literatur. Geschichte*, pp.83–103.

71. For example, the correspondence between Sophie von La Roche and Christoph Martin Wieland, Anna Luisa Karsch, and Johann Wilhelm Ludwig Gleim. See also Ruth Perry's analysis of British women's correspondences in the seventeenth century ("Radical Doubt and the Liberation of Women," *Eighteenth-Century Studies*, 18. 4 (Summer 1985): pp.472–93, especially pp.476 and 482.

72. For example, Cornelia Goethe's "diary in letters," letters in which she conceives of her life in terms of literature.

73. As Helga Meise has recently shown, Maria Anna Sagar's *Die verwechselten Töchter* (1771) competes with La Roche's for the title "first important German woman's novel."

74. Sarah Scott, *Millenium Hall* (1762), published by Penguin 1986.

75. Becker-Cantarino, "Leben als Text," p.102. The idea that writing is a substitute for unlived life was expressed by Sophie von La Roche herself who, barred from the education of her daughters because of court duties, claimed that she wrote her novel to educate "ein papiernes Mädchen" [which means both a "girl on paper" and a paper girl]. See Becker-Cantarino, *Der lange Weg*, pp.296–301.

76. Sophie von La Roche, *Geschichte des Fräuleins von Sternheim*, edited by Barbara Becker-Cantarino (Stuttgart: Reclam, 1983), p.14 [my translation], and Becker-Cantarino, *Der lange Weg*, pp.286–88.

77. H. A. and E. Frenzel, *Daten deutscher Dichtung* 2, 13th ed. (Munich: Deutscher Taschenbuch Verlag, 1976), p.355. See also Nikolaus Dorsch, 'Sich rettend aus der kalten Würklichkeit.' *Die Briefe Benedikte Nauberts. Edition-Kritik-Kommentar* (Frankfurt am Main, Bern, and New York: Peter Lang, 1986), p.227.

78. See Boettigheimer, "Tale Spinners."

Introduction, bibliography, and translation by
CORNELIA NIEKUS MOORE

Johanna Eleonore Petersen

(1644–1724)

Johanna Eleonore Petersen (1644–1724)
courtesy of Sächsische Landesbibliothek, Dresden

The following autobiography was written by Johanna Eleonore Petersen, *née* von und zu Merlau (1644–1724), one of the best known and most controversial Pietists in Germany. First published as an attachment to the first edition of *Gespräche des Hertzens mit Gott* [Conversations of the Heart with God, 1689], it was updated for separate publication in 1718, and reprinted in 1719.

As a young woman, Johanna Eleonore became part of the religious reform movement known as Pietism. In her autobiography, she describes her chance meeting with the influential theologian Philipp Jakob Spener (1635–1705) and its far-reaching consequences for her spiritual development. During his years as senior of the Lutheran clergy in Frankfurt, Spener published his *Pia Desideria* (1675), a work that became the foundation of the inner-Lutheran movement of Pietism. Pietism maintained that the Reformation that Luther had begun was to be complemented through a "reformation of life," emphasizing a practical Christianity based on extensive Bible reading. The *Pia Desideria* reflected practices and beliefs held by Spener and his group of followers. One influential member of this *collegium pietatis* was the lawyer Johann Jakob Schütz (1640–90), and it was he who was with Spener when they met Johanna Eleonore. Schütz also participated in the gatherings in the home of the widow Juliana Baur von Eyseneck when Johanna Eleonore was living there and he helped initiate her correspondence with the famous Anna Maria van Schurman (1607–78) whose autobiography *Eukleria* (1673) may have inspired Johanna Eleonore to write her own. Spener also exerted great influence on her future husband: Johann Wilhelm Petersen (1649–1727), a promising but controversial orthodox theologian, who traveled to Frankfurt to meet Spener and came away convinced of the validity of the Pietist way of life. On that first visit to Frankfurt, Petersen also met Johanna Eleonore, whom he presented with a copy of one of his theological treatises. He rather expected to be complimented for his scholarly work, but Fräulein von Merlau refused to flatter him, indeed she called the treatise an encomium to the God Petersen. He was honest enough to admit that she was right, and several years later (1680), when his family urged him to marry, he chose the woman who had refused to flatter him. Although there was a class difference—Johanna Eleonore was from a noble family, Petersen a commoner—the marriage was agreed upon by all concerned. Johanna Eleonore accompanied her husband to Eutin, Lübeck, and Berlin, and on his various journeys, working closely with him as they sought to solve the mysteries of faith, sharing with him the fierce loyalty of friends and the notoriety in the ranks of those who disagreed with their views.

Initially their views were close to those of Spener but gradually became more radical. Far more chiliastic than Spener's "hope for better times," their futuristic aspirations included all of creation. As Johanna Eleonore explains in her autobiography, the dual nature of Christ as both divine and human would enable all humans, even those previously damned, to be eventually saved. She arrived at such convictions through extensive, personalized Bible reading; this reading both instigated and explained personal revelation for those who sought a life of *imitatio Christi*, based on the Scriptures.

In her autobiography, which begins with her childhood during the Thirty Years' War, Johanna Eleonore provides the reader with a highly personal account of her pilgrim's progress, which is supposed to serve as an encouragement for others to follow a similar path and to provide assurances that this can in fact be done. The narrative entices with its anecdotal tales of divine protection, its almost colloquial personal tone, and its heartfelt concern for the salvation of others. In all humility, it warns of temptations and the tricks of the devil. But Johanna Eleonore is human—childhood slights have not been forgotten many years later and the evil tongues of the world disturb her. However, permeating this life story is her faith in God, the testimony of God's glory, and her characteristic consolation of others.

BIBLIOGRAPHY

Petersen's Works

Because her works are rare, the libraries in which they can be found are included here. There is to date no secondary literature in English dedicated specifically to Petersen's oeuvre.

Gespräche des Hertzens mit Gott Auffgesetzet von Johanna Eleonore Petersen, Gebohrne von und zu Merlau. Ploen: Verlegts Siegfried Ripenau, Gedruckt durch Tobias Schmidt, 2 vols., 1689. (Wolfenbüttel: Herzog August Bibliothek; Evanston Garrett Theological Seminary). Vol.3, Frankfurt: Brodthagen, 1690 (Garrett Theological Seminary). Second edition entitled: *Glaubens-Gespräche mit Gott, in drey unterschiedene Theile abgefasset*. Frankfurt: Brodthagen, 1691. (Garrett Theological Seminary; Philadelphia: German Society of Pennsylvania). Third edition, 1715.

Anleitung zu gründlicher Verständniss der Heiligen Offenbahrung Jesu Christi— nach Ordnung einer dazu gehörigen Tabelle. Frankfurt und Leipzig: zu finden bey Johann Daniel Müller, 1696. (Wolfenbüttel: HAB; Göttingen; FdF Nr. 1427a; Washington State Univ., Pullman).

Geistlicher Kampf der berufenen und auserwählten Überwinder. Halle, 1698; with different title: *Die verklärte Offenbarung Christi . . . mit beigefügtem geistlichen Kampf der Erst-Gebohrenen.* [Frankfurt, 1706]. (Göttingen; FdF Nr. 1427; Jantz Nr. 1970). Other edition, Frankfurt 1717.

Das Geheimnis des Erst-Gebornen . . . Frankfurt: Heyl & Liebezeit, 1711. (Göttingen; FdF Nr. 1429; Jantz Nr. 1969).

Einige Send-Schreiben/Betreffende die Nothwendigkeit Verschiedener . . . in Verdacht gezogener Lehren . . . Büdingen, 1714. (Jantz Nr. 1968).

Leben Frauen Johanna Eleonora Petersen . . . auf Kosten guter Freunde, 1718. (Wolfenbüttel: HAB; Chicago: UB; Haverford College). 2nd edition 1719. Reprinted in *Der deutsche Pietismus; Eine Auswahl von Zeugnissen, Urkunden und Bekenntnissen aus dem 17., 18. und 19. Jahrhundert.* Edited with an introduction by W. Mahrholz. Berlin: Furche, 1921, pp.201–45.

The Nature and Necessity of the New Creature in Christ, Stated and Described according to the Heart's Experience and True Practice. Translated by Francis Okely, 2nd edition. London: Lewis, 1772. (Yale; Texas [Austin]; Harvard; Boston Public Library; Haverford College).

Derer Comedien des Herrn Moliere . . . 3 vols. Nürnberg: bey Johann Daniel Tauber, 1694 (FdF Nr. 1812).

The Life of
Johanna Eleonore Petersen

(1689–1718)

Dear Reader, I provide this short account of my life, so that you may know how miraculously the Lord on High has guided me from an early age and provided me with so many opportunities to come closer to Him. I have also been moved to do this, because, like my Savior, I too have been maligned and slandered in many ways.[. . .] In this short treatise I will address these allegations against me. [. . .] If not forewarned, the Christian reader might well think upon reading of these allegations by a deceitful world that they were true, or that they were the primary reason for rejecting this world and its ways. However, I proclaim before God that it was the power of the Lord and His almighty Word that drew me from all transitory pleasures. He saved me from the flagrant sins of the world that bring on the Lord's chastisement. No one on earth can prove a single allegation that has been made against me. Indeed, anyone who has slandered me will have to admit he was only repeating the words of others, words taken at face value. In all humility, however, I can take comfort in the fact that there are people everywhere who have witnessed my life and my actions from youth and have praised the grace of God in me. However, this booklet has a more important mission: to speak of the depravity of the heart. This depravity has to be felt if we are to fully understand what Christ Jesus has done for us and how He has saved us from our sins. Indeed, how can anyone who is unaware of the state of man after the fall of Adam know the Savior. How can anyone believe in the necessity of our dearly bought salvation who has not felt the deprivation in which we live. This realization will dawn on each of us according to the degree to which we partake in Jesus Christ, and to which we need to know ourselves and feel a true humility of the heart which emanates from this knowledge. I thank God that, for a short time, He hid His grace from me so that I could recognize my inability to do good and acknowledge the depraved essence of the human heart. Then I truly came to know that it is His grace which makes us right in thought, word, and deed, and that no sin is so great that we could not fall into it when we avoid His grace. Therefore, when I finally received the gift of God's grace, I did not think too highly of myself, or presume that I was better than others who had fallen into sin. I was only thankful that the grace of God had saved me. I realized that anyone can change his lot for the better, if he realizes the depravity of his own heart. However, hypocrites have too high an opinion of themselves: they believe that they are righteous and good, although they have not washed away their iniquities and instead have inflated themselves in vain in the spirit of the flesh. I say this so that no one will think that I consider myself to be better than others for having been saved from such sins by the grace of God. Rather, from the bottom of my heart I accredit everything to the grace of God and know that the core of depravity lies also within me, that any unpure desire can arise from it, and, if it finds fertile ground, would give birth to sin. Therefore, no one has any reason to be proud, but rather, as Paul says, salvation is to be wrought out with fear and trembling [Phil. 2:12].

The fear of the Lord has kept me, and His goodness and faithfulness have guided me, for which I give Him thanks and praise. I am writing this so that you, dear reader, will also see His manifold wisdom; how in various ways He draws people to Him, some from tender childhood on, others only in their later years. In my case, I experienced the stirrings of His good spirit from an early age, but in my ignorance I often rebelled against this good spirit and thwarted His intentions by paying too much heed to the worldly life of the nobility, until finally I came to my senses, and let His healing Word exert its convincing powers within me.

When I was about four years old, it happened that my dear parents, having lived for a time in Frankfurt because of the ravages of war, returned to the countryside, once again peaceful, bringing their belongings with them.

My dear mother, my two sisters and I lived on an estate called Philippseck near Hettersheim. We were not expecting trouble, but one day the servants came running and reported that a large troop of horsemen were coming, at which news everyone hurriedly gathered their belongings and ran off, leaving my dear mother and her three little children all alone; the oldest was seven years old, I four, and the youngest still an infant. So my dear mother tied the baby to her breast, took the other two by the hand, and, without a maid, set out for Frankfurt more than half a mile away. It was summer, the harvest stood high in the fields and we could hear the noise of soldiers marching on another road about a pistol shot away from us. My dear mother was very much afraid and urged us to pray; but when we came to the outskirts of the city and safety, she knelt down with us and told us to thank God for protecting us. Then my oldest sister, who was three years older than I, said: "Why should we thank God now that they cannot catch us anymore?" Those words struck me deeply. It truly hurt me and I reproached her that she did not want to thank God or that she could think that praying was no longer necessary. I felt an ardent love toward God, whom I thanked with all my heart. Later, when I was told that children come from the midwife, who fetches them from heaven, I sought out a midwife and told her to greet the Lord Jesus Christ kindly for me, and entreated her to tell me whether our Savior indeed loved me, as I had experienced a deep love for Him in my heart. These are the first childhood experiences that I can still remember.

When I was almost six and my dear mother lay again in childbed, I noticed that she was crying. I asked my oldest sister what had made our dear mother cry. She answered that mother had heard that a well-known noblewoman had become a whore. I did not know what that meant, but I thought that it must be something very evil, because it had made mother cry. So I went to a quiet place, knelt down, and prayed tearfully to God to keep me from ever becoming a whore. In His mercy the Lord has answered this simple child's prayer; He has not only kept me from dangerous situations, but also aroused in me an aversion for unchaste words and gestures, and I have never remained in company that was not chaste and honorable. (Nevertheless the slanderous devil has used his tools against me to spread his lies. For instance, it was rumored that my little niece, who lived with me for awhile, was my illegitimate child, although she was really my sister's second child, born in Praunheim, about an hour from Frankfurt, and baptized by Pastor Joh. Harffen, who is still alive at this writing. At the time of her birth, I was forty miles away at court and only returned home nine years after her birth. The girl's father is a von Praunheim and her mother is my younger sister. So the devil should be ashamed for spreading such malicious lies, which are not even worthy of a reply from a child of God. Anyone who loves the truth can very easily find out that such gossip contains only lies, even more so, since there are many people who have been to the places in question and can verify the truth.)

When I was almost nine years old, we became motherless; we did not fare very well, because our father was always at court, which was some five miles from home, and had appointed a schoolmaster's widow to take care of us. She had her own children in the village and would give them what rightfully belonged to us, depriving us of so much that we gladly accepted things that others no longer wanted. It also happened that she would leave us alone at night; and then people would appear, dressed in white shirts, their faces painted with honey and coated with flour. They would carry lights around the house, break open closets and cupboards, and take what they wanted. We were so scared that we would crawl behind the stove, trembling. This continued for a long time until the house became rather barren. But because our father was very strict with us, we did not have the courage to complain to him, but instead were only too glad to see him gone again. Thus we suffered for a long time until von Praunheim, who later married my sister, visited us. He was very young at the time and we poured forth our misery to him. He decided to hide in the house to see whether these ghostly creatures would come again. When they came and headed straight for the cupboard to break it open and take out its contents, von Praunheim jumped out and discovered that they were people from the village, the sons of a wagoner's, good friends of the widow who should have been with us. Because von Praunheim was alone, they were able to escape and never admitted to their deed. But the ghosts never came back and they left behind most of what they had dragged onto the kitchen floor.

The woman was dismissed by my dear father and then a captain's wife was recommended to him, who was well known for her housekeeping and other skills. So my dear father thought that his children would be well taken care of. But she was an unchristian woman, who had not yet laid off her mercenary ways. Once, when she saw a flock of calicut chickens, she had them chased into the house, grabbed the best one and had the others chased away. To prepare the booty, she needed dry wood, and sent me into the tower to fetch some. The tower was square and five stories tall. Underneath the roof, there had once been a dovecote, but all that was left were the dry boards, some loose, some still attached in places, which she sent me to fetch. I managed to throw down several boards but when I tried to pry one loose that was stubbornly attached at one spot, I lost my grip and fell backward two stories, landing on the stairs in so precarious a way that if I had moved, I would have fallen two more stories. I fainted and lay there unconscious for about half an hour, and when I came to my senses, I could not remember at first how I had gotten there. I was able to stand up and climb down a ladder. Then feeling very tired I lay down on a bed in one of the tower chambers where my father always slept when he was home. I slept for several hours, then woke up feeling rested and strong again. During the entire time, no one had asked about me, and when I told the woman that I had fallen down, she scolded me for not having been more careful. But I stayed away from the stolen meal. I was quite ashamed about the whole affair, but did not have the heart to say anything.

When I was ten years old and going on eleven, my dear sister, who was three years my senior, was sent to the pastor to receive instructions for Holy Communion. I badly wanted to go with her, but my dear father did not want me to, because I had only turned ten shortly before. But I persisted so long that he relented, on condition that the pastor would judge me capable. I was sent to the pastor who examined me by asking me not only for specific words but also for the meaning of those words. God graced me with such answers that the pastor admitted me wholeheartedly. But the devil again thought he could play a trick on me. A close relative, who was in the same instruction group as I, told the other children that I had said that when it was my turn to receive the blessed chalice, I would take a big gulp (insinuating that I loved wine). But such a thing had never crossed my mind, let alone passed my lips. I felt quite distressed by the rumors. When the pastor heard this allegation against me he believed it because of my youth. I was saddened when he confronted me with this allegation, which I denied. Then he realized the devotion which I bore toward the blessed chalice (which is the communion with Christ). Realizing that I was innocent, he accused the girl who had told the lie of making it all up. She then admitted that she had only projected her own thoughts upon me.

Some time afterward, my sister went to Stuttgart to live with our paternal uncle, and I had to manage the household and assume responsibility for everything. This was very hard for me because whenever my dear father would come home, he would be very harsh with me and scold me for everything that had been broken or that was not exactly to his liking. He would punish me severely even when I was innocent. Therefore, I had such a slavish fear of him that I would shrink whenever I heard a voice that even vaguely resembled his. I sent up many a tearful sigh to my Lord, and whenever my father left the house, I would be happy and in good spirits and would sing and dance merrily. Still I had a sincere aversion to whatever was unchaste, even if it was child's play, and wanted nothing to do with make-believe games of marriage, baptism, and other things that children play, feeling ashamed of such things.

When I was twelve years old, I was sent to the court of the Countess of Solms-Redelheim. After a few weeks, I noticed that she began to act rather strange at times. At first she was all right, but when she gave birth to twins, a boy and a girl, shortly thereafter, she grew worse by the day, even to the point that she would mistake me for her shaggy little dog, call me by its name, and beat me just like she beat the dog. In the winter, we often traveled by boat, because the land between Frankfurt and Redelheim would become flooded; whenever the water was so deep it came into the coaches, we would transfer to a boat until we reached dry ground and could board the coaches again. On these occasions she often wanted to throw me into the water and make me swim. But the Almighty protected me. Once I noticed that she took a knife in a sheath from a cupboard and hid it under her clothes. I told the chambermaid, who was much older than I. She did not want to listen to me and said that the Countess did not have a knife, that it was just child's talk on my part. Now, there was a door between our bedroom and that of the countess who had to go through our bedroom in order to reach her own. On the other side of our bedroom was the door leading to her husband's bedroom. When night fell and we all had to go to bed, I did not want to lie down because all I could think of was the knife. But the chambermaid scolded me and threatened to tell the Count that I was behaving childishly. So I just lay down on my bed and did not undress. During the night I heard a commotion; I got out of bed and woke the others. We heard the Count running out of his room and then saw the Countess with a night-light in one hand and the shining knife in the other running after him. When she saw all of us, she became scared and dropped the knife. I picked up the knife as if to return it to her, but instead ran with it out of the door and down the stairs into the dark. When I was on the stairs, I heard the Count call out: "Where is my wife?" I answered that I had the knife, but I was so scared I did not dare to turn around but went into a hall, known as the great hall, which was very spooky, and there I stayed. The chambermaid, a Bohemian who was a bond servant to the Countess's mother in Bohemia, returned to her mistress; and for a few weeks I had to dress and undress the Countess all by myself, which was very difficult.

But people told my dear father that I was in danger and he removed me from that court. When I was about fifteen, I was sent to the household of the Duchess of Holstein. She was herself a Countess of Hessen and had married Duke Philipp Ludwig from the House of Holstein-Suderburg, who had a daughter from his first marriage. The daughter was engaged to the Count of Zinzendorf, the Imperial Chamber President, and I was hired as a lady-in-waiting for this noble bride. She also had a chamberlady, a Lady von Steinling, who was already almost thirty. As soon as I arrived, they set out for Linz, where the nuptials were to be held. We traveled on the Danube and everything was merry; the drums and trumpets echoed over the water and everywhere we went we were well received by groups who had come to pay their respects to the noble bride. I had come to smile over all my former anxieties; my only fear was the recurrent thought: "I hope it won't harm my soul to go to a papist place." As soon as we would come to a resting place, I would look for a room where there were no people, kneel down, and pray to God to prevent anything from doing harm to my soul. These private asides were noticed by Lady von Steinling, who had secretly followed me to see what I was up to, for she considered me a child because I was very small for my age. When she found me on my knees, praying, she quietly left, so that I did not notice that she had seen me. Later, when my noble mistress once asked me whether I prayed, Lady von Steinling answered that there was no need to worry about me, that she had found me praying. Then I knew that she had seen me in my room. We arrived in Linz and the nuptials were held in the imperial castle; everything was arranged with great splendor. The next day, the noble bride had to go to the castle chapel, where she received a blessing and was given a golden chalice filled with wine. This is called St. John's blessing. She and the Count had to drink from the chalice, but I prayed to God that he would protect me from such papism. Now it happened that after the nuptials, when all the guests were about to depart, that a dispute arose involving me. The Count said that he could only seat chamberladies (as one calls the noblewomen there) at his table; the rest of the ladies-in-waiting, like myself, would have to eat with the governess. But the Duke did not want to accept that, because, as he said, the governess was a commoner, and everyone would consider me to be a commoner as well, even though I was descended from a very old family and no one's inferior. He could not allow a distinction to be made between me and the other women of noble rank, especially since I was his wife's godchild.

The dispute could not be resolved and so it was decided to send me home. When I was told of this and why, I was amazed that I would have to return for such a reason, since I would have preferred to have had my meals with the governess rather than at the table of the Count. I did not know then that God in His mercy had answered my prayers and had arranged it in this way; something I did not realize until years later, when I discovered that everyone in the nuptial party including the Duchess herself fell in with the papist religion. Then I learned God's holy ways with me, His poor creature, and learned to praise Him. At that time, however, I regretted that I had to return, for I feared that people might think that I had misbehaved. I was also afraid to come again under the harsh discipline of my father.

We reached Lissborg again, which really belonged to the Count of Darmstadt, and which the Duke only had in lien. Everyone was about to leave for Saxony, where the Duke had received Wiesenburg from the Elector, which is about ten miles from Leipzig and one mile from Zwickau. It so happened that the Duchess decided to keep me with her. I became very accomplished in all types of handiwork, was by far the best dancer, and well liked by everyone. This stroked my vanity so that I came to love dresses and similar vanities because they flattered my appearance and elicited praise. No one ever mentioned to me that this might not be right. Instead, such vanities were praised, and I was still considered pious since I liked to read and pray, went to church, remembered the sermons in detail, and could even recall what had been said about a particular text the year before. Thus I remained in everyone's good graces and was considered a pious young lady by religious as well as worldly people, even though I only sought the approval of the world and had not yet begun my true imitation of Christ.[. . .]

[*Johanna Eleonore became engaged to an officer, who was seldom around and eventually left her for someone else.*]

But I no longer cared. Here I had been worrying that I had misjudged my fiancé and had been wondering whether the things I was hearing about him were true or not. Now I realized that God had given my restless heart its liberty. The heavy burden was gone. I had been so strengthened by all of this that I no longer considered marriage at all; on the contrary, I believed that there were aspects of the life of the nobility that were totally against Christianity. First of all, there is more opportunity for drunkenness than among the people of other estates. Secondly, a nobleman has to wager body and soul every time he feels wronged or slandered, because he cannot afford to be slighted. This made me wonder how something this wrong could have befallen Christianity; how one could be considered a Christian and still live totally against the teachings of Christ. And no one urges these people either to better their ways or to leave the community of Christ. This rid me of any desire to marry. To be sure, I knew fine outstanding individuals who despised this kind of life, but one still had to take into account that our children would be exposed to such dangers. So I turned away from all thoughts of marriage, and I believed that there were no eligible men on this earth, for I thought that I would not be allowed to accept someone beneath my station because my dear father was so proud of his lineage.

But then it happened that a clergyman with a high position in the church took an interest in me. My heart was torn, because I could feel no inclination to marry. After a long battle I resigned my feelings to the Lord and decided to accept what my father desired. I wanted to see revealed in my father on earth the will of my Father in heaven. Before I did so, I wrote to two God-fearing men who were known to me to be truly pious. I asked them whether I should not look for answers in my own heart but they replied that I should resign myself to God's will, which I hoped to discover through my father's decision. My dear father, however, wanted my lord and lady to decide; they were for the marriage and informed the clergyman of this. But I insisted that my dear father should decide in this matter. I refused to answer yes or no, but maintained that his "yes" would be my "yes," his "no" my "no." It so turned out that my father was not of the same mind as my lord and said "no" and settled the matter. In the meantime, since we were forty miles away from my father and also from the clergyman, I was regarded as a bride at the court, despite my repeated protests. No one thought that my father would retract his previous decision to let the court decide. If the clergyman had persisted, it could have become a nasty situation. But such was not the will of God. The clergyman accepted my father's refusal. But I suffered a new humiliation because I noticed that many people wondered about this reversal.

However, these were only beneficial trials to enable my soul to be resigned to God. God was bestowing more and more grace upon me. Even before I had received this last proposal of marriage, I had become acquainted with two true men of God [Philipp Jakob Spener and Johann Jakob Schütz] in Frankfurt. Because the oldest princess was in ill health, the entire family traveled to Ems for the baths. Through God's amazing providence, this friend [Spener] was on the same ship on which we traveled to the baths. And through God's amazing providence, he chanced to sit next to me whereupon we had a religious discussion which lasted for several hours. The four miles from Frankfurt to Mainz, where he disembarked, seemed to take no more than a quarter of an hour. We talked without interruption, and it seemed as if he peered into my heart and all my doubts came to the fore. Indeed, his every word reminded me of the spirit of God, and how it could be put into practice. I found in him that which I no longer believed could be found in any person on this earth, for I had long searched in vain for someone who lived and acted according to the Word. But now I became aware that he knew how, that he could show me the depths of my own heart, and could help me find the way to truth through humility, tenderness, holy love, and earnestness. I felt truly consoled and strengthened and ready to break through and leave behind those worldly things that, out of ignorance, I had pursued until then. Those who should have encouraged me previously had only misled me by suggesting that what I had striven for with such great effort were only trifles. But I noticed in this friend that his intentions agreed with the Word of the Lord, and all doubts I had hitherto felt were dispelled. As I had known no one who lived according to the Word of the Lord in true simplicity, I had become convinced that it was not meant to be followed in all simplicity, that it was sufficient to know of it. But this friend convinced me that one should not look to the examples of others, but to the example of the Lord, and to the Word of truth, against which all men are liars.

I now had a divine conviction in my heart. I then met the second friend who also strengthened me in goodness. More and more I felt an aversion for this world and its ways. When the Lord made the words of 2 Peter 1 alive in my heart: "Thou shalt share in the divine nature, when thou fleest the transitory pleasures of the world," I said to myself: "Should I rob myself of this divine nature because of these contemptuous and transitory pleasures? No! I will push through with God's help, cost what it may." I wrote to the first friend, who had bestowed on me so many divine gifts by the grace of God, saying that I loved him like a father and that I intended to rid myself of the ways of the world. He worried that I would not be strong enough to endure that which lay ahead of me. He called upon me to begin wresting my heart away from everything. He said God would then send me the ways and means to free myself from all external things that burdened me. I should only trust in God and remain faithful to Him in love. However, the Spirit of God left me no peace, but convinced me in the strongest terms: "And be not conformed to this world, but be transformed" [Rom. 12:2]. "For the grace of God that bringeth salvation teaches us to deny" [Tit. 2:11–12]. "Work out thy own salvation with fear and trembling" [Phil. 2:12]. "Strive to enter through the narrow gate" [Luke 13:24]. "There are those that deny me before the people" [Luke 12:9]. "The devil goes around like a roaring lion" [1 Pet. 5:8]. The parable of the five foolish virgins and such useful passages of the Holy Scripture were always in my heart and drove me to cast off the ways of the world. Still I could not overcome fear of my masters. Thus I often danced with tears in my eyes and did not know what to do. I often thought: "Oh, that I could only be the daughter of a shepherd, then they would not mind if I lived in simple imitation of Christ; no one would even notice." But then I realized that no station in life would exempt me, because I would have to renounce them all to be a true disciple of Christ. Nothing would hinder me if I would just ignore the contempt of others and suffer it gladly in order to receive Christ.

67

So I decided with God's grace to pursue things in earnest from then on and that nothing would keep me from doing so. I went to my dear Duchess and submitted my resignation, which she categorically refused. But when she wanted to know why, I willingly told her that the life I led at court was against my conscience. My dear beloved Duchess wanted to convince me that this was not so; believing me to be suffering from melancholy, she said: "You are already living as a pious young lady: you read and say your prayers diligently. Just look at so and so; they are Christians, too, and yet they participate in festivities. This is not forbidden as long as we do not set our whole heart upon it." But I refused to hear her arguments and explained to her that the only true model was Christ and His Word as it had been pointed out to me. I did not mean to stand in judgment of other people, but I could not be satisfied with their example and needed a better foundation now that I had been called and chosen in Christ. When my dear Duchess saw that nothing could change my mind, she said to me that I could decline to do anything I found against my conscience, but asked that I stay with her and do my other chores as before. I pointed out to her that she would have to do without me on many occasions, especially when visitors came; and that it could very well happen that if the other ladies fell sick, she would be without any ladies-in-waiting because I wanted to stay away from all organized festivities to avoid giving ground for ridicule. But she persisted and sincerely promised me that my presence would not be required for frivolities. Afterward, she told the Duke. He did not like my resolve at all and was convinced that it was melancholy. He argued with me and said that the devil had inspired me to do this. I was a young lady, he said, who was loved by all but was about to throw herself into contempt, that everyone would hold me for a fool, and he asked me if I knew what my family would say. I answered confidently that my resolve was not my own doing, but based on the Word of my Savior, who was the Truth. I would accept gladly whatever happened now that I had heard His voice and was resolved to follow Him. He would give me strength to bear the world's humiliation. When all the arguments failed, some so-called men-of-God came to see me. They tried to convince me that I had misunderstood the words of Christ, that I was taking this far too seriously, and for no reason since I was already a Christian and virtuous, and that I should guard myself against such heavy thoughts. But I answered them according to the words of my Savior and asked them to tell me in good conscience which was the safer path, to follow in the footsteps of Christ or to follow the ways of a world that only talks of imitating Christ, that professes a love for it without acting accordingly. I said, "I have been ordered to choose the best part. I will let the Lord take care of how this is to be done. He has promised to grant me His Spirit. This Spirit is not weak but powerful in our weakness. If I were to do this of my own strength, I would be frightened and fearful because I know my shortcomings. But since I have made this resolve in the power of Christ in accordance with His command, I know and firmly believe that I will be able to do everything through Him. He who began this process in me is constant; He will continue and carry it through until His day comes." Then they let me go.[. . .]

[*When her stepmother died, leaving a young child, Johanna Eleonore was called home to care for the child. Upon arriving home she found that the baby too had died, and she was now free to take a position with the widow Baur von Eyseneck in Frankfurt. One of the daughters of her sister also came to live in the household.*]

After spending six years with dear Mrs. Baur, Almighty God saw to it that the man who was to be my dear husband, whom I had met a year before in Frankfurt, decided to marry me. He asked someone in Lübeck to contact me on his behalf, which that person only managed to do after some length of time. When the news reached me, I could think of no reason why I should marry. After I had addressed God in my prayers, I sat down and declined the offer in writing and suggested someone else, an excellent person. But my dear husband would not be deterred. He wrote to my father and also to a highly placed clergyman who was a dear friend. When I received the letter intended for my father, I did not forward it at first, but finally felt obliged in good conscience to do so, having no other purpose than God's honor. So I wrote this to my dear husband and sent his letter on and then I was very quiet as if the matter did not concern me, and as if all the negotiations had nothing to do with me. I did not think that my dear father would consent to the marriage, but he responded otherwise. He wrote that although he had many reasons not to send me so far away from him in his old age and although he was not inclined to let one of his children marry a commoner, he did not feel that he could resist the will of God. This touched me deeply and I became convinced that it was the will of God since my father's heart, contrary to expectations, had been moved. My father told me to do as I pleased, but I did not accept this, and assigned it to his will completely. My brother-in-law, von Dorffeld, a steward at the court of Hanau, was opposed to the marriage, but my dear father answered him in a very Christian manner, stating that it would be against the Lutheran religion to judge a clergyman inferior when those in the papal religion regarded their clergy so highly. Furthermore, he argued that his daughter was not inclined to accept a man of the world, and that everyone knew she was not marrying frivolously outside of her class. God had called me to this station. They had to be content with that answer, and the consent was granted. My dear husband traveled to Frankfurt and we were married September 7th, 1680, by Dr. Spener, in the presence of Her Lady von Phillipseck, my dear father, and a few distinguished people, around thirty in all. Everything took place in a pleasant and Christian manner which delighted everyone. Again the slanderous devil felt disappointed, since the wedding had not taken place in the ways of the world with eating, drinking, and ribaldry, and the devil chided those that were in cahoots with him. These people invented lies, namely, that the Holy Spirit had revealed himself in fire in the room in which we were married and had explained to us the Book of Revelation. (At that time I had not yet received the insight from Him, which I now have, about our judgment before God. I had also not recognized with great certainty the subsequent glory for His church here on earth, which is a compensation for the shame which we suffer for Christ's sake.) These lies were told in the presence of Dr. Heiler, but, unbeknownst to those that were telling the lies, he had attended our wedding. He took them to task and stated that he himself had been there and that everything had proceeded very nicely in a Christian manner. Then they were ashamed.

When we left Frankfurt, it was decided that the daughter of my sister would go with us because she did not want to leave me. As we reached Amsterdam, my dear husband became very ill. But his duties awaited him and he did not want to remain in Amsterdam. He wanted to be with his flock and with his lord, so we boarded ship; he was very ill for most of the trip. My little niece also fell ill, so that I was all alone with two patients, and I did not know anyone in the towns in which we stopped on the way. That was difficult for me and I thought: "Why is this happening to me? Why am I stuck here in strange places where I can get neither help nor advice? It was not even my idea to get married." When we went ashore one afternoon for dinner, I put my husband to bed and went into the meadow alone to cry before my Lord and I prayed for His help. I was completely consoled when I thought of the words in Hebrews 11:1, where it says in relationship to Moses that faith is an assurance of things hoped for, the conviction of things not seen. Then I thought: "Never mind that I am in a strange country, God is here with me and will not impose upon me more than I can bear." When we came to Lübeck, a doctor was called and he diagnosed that I, too, was deathly ill. I had not known this even though I had almost collapsed from exhaustion. The care of my dear husband had so preoccupied my mind that I had completely forgotten about myself, until the doctor came and told me. They put me to bed and I was very ill for some time, but I recuperated before my dear husband did. Several times I had to dedicate him to the Lord as Abraham did Isaac, and I was between fear and hope for nearly three months. Later many lies were told in that place and many reasons invented why I had married outside of my class. Some said I had misbehaved at court. Others spread evil gossip as if it were the truth. Indeed, some of these lies reached my dear Duchess and her husband, and she did something very nice and Christian; she wrote a letter to her sister, the reigning Duchess of Gotha, saying that they knew me well, and later gave very gracious testimony concerning my behavior at court. It was shortly before her death that she testified in such a noble manner about my innocence, which will not be forgotten before the Lord in all eternity. The Duchess of Gotha only spoke to my husband about this gossip after she had received the aforementioned letter concerning my innocence. Then new lies were invented and spread secretly, namely that the daughter of my sister was really my illegitimate child and this was the reason I had married beneath my station. It could never be determined where such slander originated, but I praised my Lord because I knew what He had done to my soul. He had given me a chaste heart from early youth, so that I could say with all humility that I had not only spent my unmarried state in maidenly chastity but also, through God's grace, was leading a married life with a chaste heart. Thus I suffered this slander gladly. It is hardly necessary to provide explanations here because it can be easily verified that the parents of my niece are still alive, living in Praunheim, which is situated about an hour from Frankfurt. Also the pastor who baptized her is still alive, as are the noble ladies of Solms-Redelheim who are her godmothers, all of whom live within half an hour of Redelheim. Any friend of the truth could also find out more about this, since the sister of the Duchess of Ratzeburg lives in Philippseck and is well acquainted with the father and the mother of young Lady von Praunheim, my niece, since my niece's older brother is a page at their court. The Lord may forgive them for their lies and grant that I may rejoice with my whole heart about everything inflicted by the world upon me through His will. I know that I am suffering for His sake now, whereas before I was praised when I only listened to His Word and did not act upon it. From the moment that I began to do what was pleasing to the Lord, I was vilified. Thus I can truly rejoice and I do rejoice in the Lord. However, it is not that I am glad that others are falling into sin and become guilty in the eyes of the Lord for the sake of their neighbors. No, I have often pleaded with the Lord to forgive them. So much goodness is happening to me that I have come closer to God, so His mercy should embrace them as well. Indeed, I have often experienced so much love toward the enemy through the grace of God that I could have taken them all into my heart and carried them in God. My love grew more ardent as I realized that my enemies had given me more than my dearest friends. However, not every hour is the same and it often happens that in the first moments of injustice, one does not experience such love, especially when all has been quiet for awhile and when some time has passed since the last suffering. Then I had to learn all over again how to love the enemy and accept everything from the hands of the Lord. Often I had to turn to the Lord and explore anew the benefits of this new suffering before I could accept it and bear it with joy.

After this first chastisement, I experienced much happiness in my marriage through the mercy of the Lord. Not only did I have a blessed and peaceful marriage and a dear husband who shows uncommon love and faithfulness toward me, I was also blessed with children. I bore my husband two sons. The oldest is still alive, and I hope that he will become a good servant of Jesus Christ, because he is a son of promise whose birth was accompanied by good omens. One year before he was born, when we were in Holstein in the house of a pastor, my husband opened the Bible in faith to Romans 9:9, and he saw that under his right thumb there were these words of promise: "About this time, I will return and Sarah will have a son." My husband accepted this proverb in faith and wrote on the table of the pastor: "In one year from this date, Johanna will have a son." But when half a year had passed, we had forgotten all about it; we thought that the words had been fulfilled by the pastor's wife who was with child. But one day about twenty weeks before the year had passed, when my husband spoke a blessing over me as we were about to rise, something stirred in my body as if something had jumped. I said: "The Lord has blessed me," and together we praised our Lord. We remembered the particular passage and made note that the birth of our first son would indeed occur one year after our visit to Holstein. We also knew that it would be a son because it happened in such a special way. Our son was born at the promised time and was very small. When he was only one day old, he raised his head in the cradle and looked around. There have been so many good omens that we hope that he will be a son of promise. Some people have taken offense at my words because they believe I claim to be someone special, but I merely claim for him what can be said about all of God's children, that they will be like Isaac, children of promise; as the apostle writes in his letter to the Galatians 4:28, referring to himself and his brethren saying: "Now we, brethren, like Isaac, are children of promise." This is what we hope our son will be.

In addition, the good Lord has done great things to my soul and has revealed His dear Word to me, especially in the writings of the prophets and in the blessed Book of Revelation. It is a key to the prophets and in turn is opened by the prophets. This refreshes my body and soul every day, so that I can truly say: "The Lord has done to me great things." It is good to rely on the Lord, because He is faithful and true. He will continue to protect me and will complete the work He has started within me until the day of Jesus Christ. He who has promised to do this is faithful and will see it to completion.

The above pages contain the biography which I wrote a few years ago at the request of good friends and which was included with the treatise "Conversations of the Heart with God" [*Gespräche des Hertzens mit Gott*]. It was written to show how God's guiding hand had led me from my youth and how the Lord had pulled me closer to Him in so many ways during those early years. Now I would like to add how our faithful Lord has disclosed to me one secret after another; how He has delighted me with this so often that I have been drawn ever closer from the love of the world toward

His divine love. In the remaining pages of this treatise I would like to discuss these disclosures but will refrain from describing the sorrows I experienced because of my ungrateful brother-in-law and other slanderers. Their lies will be my crown on the day of Judgment. My dear husband has already mentioned some of this in his biography. All the suffering which has been inflicted upon me has been very beneficial to my soul. Therefore, I do not want to complain about it here, but instead praise the Lord for it; I mention it only as an example of how God has looked with favor upon me.

From an early age, our faithful Lord had created a great conflict within me because I could not comprehend why He, who is love personified, could condemn so many to eternal damnation (as was generally believed at that time). Indeed, the idea that even the poor pagan children who had no opportunity to know God would have to remain for all eternity in such torment was something I could not comprehend true love capable of. I recalled the words: "He who does not believe will be damned," but I could not help but feel that this was hatred rather than love. I fought against this in my heart, saying, "My God is the very essence of love, and even though I cannot understand things that seem to me to be against love, I still have to worship and love Him as pure Love." Then in one of those hours of submission, the meaning of 1 Peter 3:18 and 4:16 was revealed to me, that those who were killed in body at the time of the Deluge had their spirits imprisoned because of their unbelief. Then the time came that Christ was killed in body on the cross and rose again in spirit. He descended to the dead and preached the Gospel to these imprisoned spirits, namely that their flesh was judged as human, while their spirits now live before God. Thereupon I realized that they must have become believers through the sermons of Christ who had gone to their prison and that they were saved from damnation through his redeeming sacrifice. Further were revealed to me the words of Zechariah 9:11–12. "As for you also, because of the blood of your covenant, I will set your prisoners free from the waterless pit," etc. But the words of Matthew 12:31–32 still troubled me, where Christ says: "Every sin and blasphemy shall be forgiven men but the blasphemy against the Spirit shall not be forgiven men, neither in this world, neither in the world to come." But the other passages completely assured me that salvation from hell was possible, that the blood of Christ also served in such cases, and that everyone would be saved from hell except the fallen angels and those who had trespassed against the Holy Spirit. At the time, the "return of all things" had not yet been revealed to me, because I had not come across that expression either in this world or the one beyond. I thought only of the word "eternal" and had not yet realized that eternal things only have their eternity in certain aspects. However, I had been delivered from my fierce struggle. I thought that the fallen angels and those who trespass against the Holy Spirit indeed deserved eternal pain, and I praised God that He had given us the Lord Jesus, our great Redeemer. Later God also relieved me of those scruples by letting me discover in the Scriptures that all creatures would praise God and that God, once everything will have been brought again under Christ's reign, will be all in all and that everything will be made new again (1 Cor. 15:22, 28; Apoc. 5:15, 21:5).

Another secret which was revealed to me before my marriage was the future conversion of Jews and pagans. This was revealed to me by our faithful God in 1664 through a dream. I dreamt that I was led into a beautiful square house which was supported by the twelve disciples. They were the foundation on which the house rested. In the middle of the house, on the middle floor, the twelve disciples stood again life-size, so that there were three on each side of the house, and each of them carried a strange musical instrument. When I entered the house they raised their voices in song, so that I rejoiced with all my heart. Then the roof of the house opened up and I found myself standing in the clouds. And I saw five suns in the heavens, two of which did not emit any rays, although they did appear bright. The other three looked as follows: one was bright, but did not emit any warmth, like the moonlight without heat; one shone brightly and warmly; and a third looked as pale as a sun in rainy weather but did have some warmth. In my dream I had my own explanations for these three suns. I compared them with the three religions, because at that time no sects were known to me other than the Lutheran, the papist, and the reformed. I thought: "The sun that emits no warmth is the papist religion, the one that looks bleak is the reformed one. The one with sunshine and warmth is the Lutheran religion." As I was thinking this to myself, I saw at my right hand a person in white linen, with a green wreath around his head and a golden scepter in his hand which he pointed toward the two suns that were not yet emitting rays, and asked: "Do you want to know the secret of the other two suns?" When I answered "yes" with a humble heart, he told me that they were meant to represent the two peoples who did not yet believe in Christ, but who would become believers; these were the Jews and the pagans, especially those who had sprung from Abraham's bond-woman. He disclosed such deep secrets to me on this matter that I realized in my sleep that this was something very special and tried to force myself to wake up. But the dream disappeared again quickly like a flash, and I only remembered as much as I have written down here. About the other three suns, he said nothing. Afterward I searched the Holy Scriptures to find more about the conversion of pagans and Jews; I had not heard nor did I know that such conversion was still to be expected. I was especially edified by Romans 2:25 and 4:13, where it is written that Abraham will inherit the world. I have related my dream to various famous teachers who have assured me that it was a divine dream.

My third visionary revelation was concerned with the article of justification from the writings of the apostle Paul. I saw in a dream the apostle Paul, small but of pleasant demeanor. He carried a large light in his hand, and when I looked at him intensely, he also handed me a light and told me that I should follow him. We came to a lovely green meadow. Many strings had been strung crosswise and I had to step over those as I followed him. I thought this procedure to be very tedious at first, but after awhile it became easier and easier until we had passed over all the strings. Then I saw on the meadow a beautiful green tree, and an angel hovering above it, who held a large gold-plated goblet filled with wine, which he gave me to drink. I drank it and received such strength that when I woke up I felt refreshed. From this I realized that I should read the letters of Paul carefully, which I indeed started and completed with God's help. And as I read and studied the letters to the Romans and to the Galatians, I learned that it is the pure Grace of God through which we become justified in our faith in Jesus Christ and gain eternal salvation. However, on this article of justification it is possible to err in two ways and thus miss the divine truth. On the one hand, one can do good works and attempt to deliver a saint to Christ before the justification through faith has been obtained; on the other hand, one can presume justification even while sinful and receive God's grace in vain and waste it. Then I realized that when we try to find grace in Jesus Christ and embrace Him, God will accept us, although we are as yet ungodly; but He does not leave us ungodly, but makes us just and holy, so that we will become dead to all sins and live in justice. This holy truth became very clear to me from Paul's writings and I also gained a love for the teachings of Luther, who is in unison with Paul on this point, and a true aversion for the papist dogma (for which I have had a fear and abhorrence since my youth because my relatives adhere to that religion) which runs counter to this holy truth.[. . .]

[*Eleonore began her studies of the Apocalypse, which she had previously avoided out of fear she would not understand it. The conclusions she drew from this reading coincided with those independently drawn by her husband. After reading Jane Leade's* The Eight Worlds, *she found in the Scriptures those passages that appear to point toward "the divine recollection of all things," that is, the notion that all creatures, even those previously condemned, would eventually be saved. The third disclosure was that of the "heavenly God-Man": Christ, in becoming Man, has enabled us to imitate Him (God), which would otherwise not have been possible.*]

In the spring of 1685, I dreamed that I was with a group of people in a large house like a prison. In this house there were twenty-four pictures with a profound meaning, because they held the key to how we could escape from this imprisonment. The meaning of these pictures was disclosed to me, and I learned from the first twelve pictures how one could descend into depths, while the other twelve pictures showed how one could rise up again from those depths. All the pictures carried strange markings, from which we could learn whether the descent or ascent was done properly, that is, when the procedure depicted was put into practice. As I made preparations to start on my journey, I chose others to accompany me although I did not reveal my plan to them as I was afraid that they would find it too difficult. Indeed, during the descent I found everything to be as I had learned from the pictures, and when we had accomplished what had been depicted in the first twelve pictures, I realized that the ascent would be even more difficult than the descent had been. But all went well because I vividly recalled all that I had learned from the pictures. However, after I awoke I had forgotten the details, except for the last task, which involved a nightingale whose voice I was supposed to imitate. It went like this: when everything had been accomplished successfully up to the endeavor depicted in the last picture, I came to a door that led into a chamber which contained a great secret. But when I stood before the door, I forgot what I had to do to open it in order to enter the chamber (in which there were a father, a mother, and a child) and discover its secret. Because I could not remember anything about the last picture, I was very sad and I thought to myself: "Now all my trouble has been in vain," and I sighed deeply. As I was raising a sigh to God, I suddenly remembered that I had seen a nightingale in the picture which meant that I would have to raise my voice in song like a nightingale. As I began to sing louder and louder, the door opened, and I felt so wondrous that I awoke. With respect to these pictures, I have found a possible explanation: in that same year, the secret of the Kingdom was revealed to my dear husband and me. For this we had to suffer greatly. It has made us descend in humility, but also made us rise up to the Lord, who has helped us mercifully in all our troubles. I was able to interpret the last picture, containing the secret of the father, mother, and child in the chamber, after the heavenly God-Man and heavenly Jerusalem were revealed to me as the dove-spirit in which we are born spirit from spirit. And this is how the secret of the Holy Trinity of the Father, the Son, and the Holy Spirit has come to be revealed: the Hebrew word for Spirit in its female form means fertile mother or breeding dove; its emanation into the central realm of power has rendered the invisible in God visible. When we see the heavenly God-Manhood truly and clearly, then the Holy Sciptures will become increasingly clear and distinct to us. May the Lord reveal His truths to us ever more clearly for His sake. Amen.

Translated from *Leben Frauen Johanna Eleonora Petersen . . . auf Kosten guter Freunde* (1718), reprinted in *Der deutsche Pietismus: Eine Auswahl von Zeugnissen, Urkunden und Bekentnissen aus dem 17. 18. und 19. Jahrhundert*, ed. W. Mahrholz (Berlin: Furche, 1921), 201–45.

Introduction, bibliography, and translation by
BRUCE DUNCAN

Luise Adelgunde Gottsched

(1713–52)

Luise Adelgunde Gottsched (1713–62)
with her husband Johann Christoph Gottsched
anonymous painting courtesy of Bildarchiv
preussischer Kulturbesitz, Berlin

The daughter of an affluent family, Luise Adelgunde Viktorie Kulmus received private tutoring at home, where her diligence and intelligence, combined with her father's personal involvement, served to make her education more rigorous than usual. While still sixteen, she was recommended as a learned young woman to her future husband, the twenty-nine-year-old Johann Christoph Gottsched (1700–66), who was about to assume a distinguished professorship in Leipzig. Throughout their six-year courtship, he tutored Adelgunde, as she preferred to be called, in the Enlightenment theories underlying the two great reforms he sought in German culture: a standardized literary language and a bourgeois theater tradition derived from French principles of Classicism. She meanwhile contributed to his projects by translating and adapting French and English plays and writing her own satires and comedies.

Adelgunde's dramatic writing, published anonymously in her husband's *German Theater Anthology* (1740–46), founded the tradition of the Saxon comedy, one of the few German literary movements based on Enlightenment notions of wit and satire. Her most notorious piece, *Die Pietisterey im Fischbeinrocke* [Pietism in Whalebone Corsets, 1736], attacked hypocritical piety within the now respectable movement of German Pietism. It created a furor in her hometown of Danzig, where copies were confiscated. Despite these criticisms of organized religious hypocrisy and the abuse of religious language, Adelgunde remained a believer. When Voltaire arrived in Leipzig to visit the Gottscheds, especially the learned lady herself, she refused to receive the man she regarded as a godless blasphemer, even though she valued his mind and had even translated several of his works.

By 1744, Johann Christoph's fame and influence as a reformer had reached their height; some of his disciples began to chafe under his often heavy-handed authority and broke away, founding their own journal, the *Bremer Beyträge*. He reacted with characteristic bad grace, alternating haughty condescension with petulant snipings. The evidence suggests that Adelgunde felt some sympathy for the revolt, although she remained publicly loyal to his cause. One of her contributions to the fray, *The Witling*, appeared anonymously in the last volume of the *Anthology*, but its authorship was never in doubt. The comedy demonstrates correct form by adhering to the current dramatic conventions, including the three unities and the naming of comic characters according to their characteristics. It also takes on a whole series of Gottsched's enemies: the ungrateful younger generation, poets who reject French models, writers of convoluted syntax, and speakers who employ regionalisms. The negative characters show disrespect toward their elders and benefactors, mix genres, and found a renegade linguistic society which—in contrast to Gottsched's own German Society—encourages bizarre tropes and Latinate constructions. They also use hyperurbanisms and ungrammatical dialect forms, rendered here in translation as improper verb declensions, pronouns, and negations. This exemplary bourgeois drama also criticizes the subordinate legal status of women, for whom marriages are arranged against their will. The remarkably fresh dialogue and the flowing action contrast with the play's conservative aesthetic aims and reveal a talented writer struggling to produce credible theater out of the primitive dramatic tools available in the early German Enlightenment.

In contrast to her dramatic work, which existed to support her husband's program of reform, Adelgunde Gottsched's private correspondence provides an individual statement of her own intellectual and ethical goals. Selected letters appeared immediately after her death, published by her best friend and lifelong correspondent, Dorothea von Runckel (3 vols., Leipzig, 1763). The freshness and emotional immediacy of her style are still striking today. The letters reveal her love of fervent religious language, as well as her attitude toward her own role as the childless wife and hard-working collaborator of a demanding and petulant husband. Appearing just as the first generation of women novelists was coming of age, these letters became a model for feminine epistolary style. Their influence has yet to be fully appreciated. The letters printed here—advice to an impoverished, but artistically gifted young orphan; a praise of friendship; a condemnation of war's destruction; and a refutation of religious enthusiasm—show the variety of Gottsched's interests and her control of language.

BIBLIOGRAPHY

Gottsched's Works

A substantial list of Luise Gottsched's works, her many translations, articles, and original creations, is provided by Ruth H. Sanders (" 'Ein kleiner Umweg': Das literarische Schaffen der Luise Gottsched," In *Die Frau von der Reformation zur Romantik*, edited by Barbara Becker-Cantarino. Bonn: Bouvier, 1980, pp.177–82). The following list contains only Gottsched's original productions.

Gottsched, Luise. *Die Pietisterey im Fischbein-Rocke; Oder die Doctormässige Frau*. In einem Lust-spiele vorgestellet. Rostock: Auf Kosten guter Freunde: 1736 (Leipzig: Breitkopf). Reprint edited by Wolfgang Martens, Stuttgart: Reclam, 1968.

———. *Horatii, als eines wohlerfahrnen Schiffers treumeynender Zuruff an alle Wolfianer von X. Y. Z.* N.p., 1740.

———. "Panthea." In *Die Deutsche Schaubühne*, vol.5, 1745.

———. "Das Testament." In *Die Deutsche Schaubühne*, vol.6, 1745. Reprinted Stuttgart: Metzler, 1974.

———. "Herr Witzling." In *Die Deutsche Schaubühne*, vol.6, 1745. ["Afterlude"] reprinted in *Der Witzling; ein deutsches Nachspiel in einem Aufzuge*. Edited by Wolfgang Hecht. Berlin: de Gruyter, 1962.

Briefwechsel der Frau Louise Adelgunde Victorie Gottsched gebohrne Kulmus. Edited by Dorothea Henriette von Runckel. Dresden: Harpeter, 1772.

Der Frau Luise Adelgunde Victorie Gottschedinn, geb. Kulmus, sämmtliche Kleinere Gedichte, nebst dem, von vielen vornehmen Standespersonen, Gön-

nern und Freunden beyderley Geschlechtes, Ihr gestifteten Ehrenmaale, und Ihrem Leben. Edited by Joh. Gottsched. Leipzig: Breitkopf & Son, 1763.

Secondary Literature in English

Becker-Cantarino, Barbara. "Outsiders: Women in German Literary Culture of Absolutism." *Jahrbuch für Internationale Germanistik* 16.2 (1985): 147–57.

Heitner, Robert. *German Tragedy in the Age of Enlightenment: A Study in the Development of Original Tragedies, 1724–1768.* Berkeley: Univ. of California Press, 1968.

Richel, Veronica C. *Luise Gottsched. A Reconsideration.* Bern and Frankfurt: Peter Lang, 1973.

Schreiber, S. Etta. *The German Woman in the Age of Enlightenment. A Study in the Drama from Gottsched to Lessing.* Morningside Heights, N.Y.: Kings Crown, 1948, pp.41–61.

Waters, Michael. "Frau Gottsched's 'Die Pietisterey im Fischbein-Rocke': Original, Adaptation or Translation?" *Forum for Modern Language Studies* 11 (1975): 252–67.

The Witling

A German Epilogue in One Act (1745)

The Characters in
this Comedy:

MR. PUREHEART
a rich merchant in Leipzig

MISS LOTTIE
his ward

YOUNG MR. PUREHEART
his son, a young lawyer

MR. FULLWIT
a young man who has
recently come to Leipzig
to study and lives at
Mr. Pureheart's house

MR. SMARTLY
a young scholar

MR. IAMBUS
a poet

PAUL
a servant

The setting
is Miss Lottie's room.
The action begins right after
lunch and ends about
five o'clock

FIRST SCENE

MISS LOTTIE (*sits on a chair, embroidering.* Enter MR. PUREHEART)

MR. PUREHEART: Well, how is everything, Miss Lottie? I wasn't able to eat lunch at home today. I met an old friend from Siebenbürgen at the Exchange and took him out to The Blue Angel, not wanting to burden my ladies with unexpected guests. Were you terribly bored during the meal?

MISS LOTTIE (*laughs*): Oh, not at all! At least, I wasn't! As long as we have an uncouth beast like young Fullwit at the table, I'm not likely to be bored.

MR. PUREHEART: Hey, what's that I hear, Miss Lottie? Young Fullwit uncouth? His father is such a rich man! Why, I'll bet that his fortune is as large as mine.

MISS LOTTIE (*laughs harder*): Wealth is no more a cure for foolishness than old age. I don't care how rich his father is: his beloved son is a conceited fop.

MR. PUREHEART (*astonished*): I don't know, the young man seems to me to be quite clever.

MISS LOTTIE: That's the root of his foolishness. Believe me, Mr. Pureheart, nothing makes a young man look more ridiculous than trying to look cleverer than everybody else. He is a great admirer of his humble self (*she laughs*); and, as far as I know, the only one.

MR. PUREHEART: It's true that he continually talks about himself and his learning; and at meals he almost forgets to eat, what with always incanting poems for us that he wrote at school. But that's just his youth. People outgrow such failings.

MISS LOTTIE: No, my dear Mr. Pureheart, this failing will most certainly

87

only grow with the years. The failings that youth is guilty of, and which disappear with time, generally result from an excess fire of passion. But in his case, it's a lack of reason, an inner arrogance of the heart, a foolish conceitedness, which will only grow with time.

MR. PUREHEART: Don't you believe it, Miss Lottie.

MISS LOTTIE: But I'm certain of it. Anyone who by his twentieth year doesn't have enough judgment to hide his love of self will stay a fool all his life.

MR. PUREHEART (*shaking his head*): Miss Lottie, I'm sorry to see that you're so set against the young man.

MISS LOTTIE: It's his own fault. If he had presented me with a better impression of himself, then I'd accept it.

MR. PUREHEART: But the man says and thinks such good things about himself.

MISS LOTTIE (*laughing*): That's just why I don't believe them, because he says them himself.

MR. PUREHEART: Now, now, he's been here only two weeks. After you've known him longer, you'll surely get to like him.

MISS LOTTIE (*smiling*): I assure you, the longer I know him, the more vapid he'll seem to me. That's simply certain people's fate: the more you see them, the more disagreeable they seem. And Mr. Fullwit is definitely that sort.

MR. PUREHEART: What a shame! To tell the truth, Miss Lottie, Fullwit's father is my very good friend; it's been over twenty years now that we've done business with one another.

MISS LOTTIE: That may well be. Does that mean that his son has to be intelligent?

MR. PUREHEART: Just let me finish. I only have your best interests at heart, dear Lottie.

MISS LOTTIE: I'm sure of that, and I'll be grateful all my life.

MR. PUREHEART: Your father was a good, honest, wealthy man; and he knew that I would have gladly given my life for his; that's why he made me your guardian, with one unusual condition, namely this: should you ever, while you are still a minor, marry against my will, I am not permitted to pay out a penny of your inheritance. Are you aware of that, Miss Lottie?

MISS LOTTIE: Yes, indeed, and I'm certain to receive my whole fortune.

MR. PUREHEART: That would make me very happy. But Mr. Fullwit should not strike you as being so ridiculous.

MISS LOTTIE: Why not? What does the young witling have to do with my father's last request?

MR. PUREHEART (*shakes his head*): You're normally so quick, but now you can't, or won't, understand me!

MISS LOTTIE: No, I don't understand you.

MR. PUREHEART: But I intend to make a couple out of the two of you.

MISS LOTTIE (*horrified*): Of us? Out of me and Fullwit?

MR. PUREHEART: Yes, indeed. He is respectably wealthy, and you are also respectably wealthy. You like to read and listen to and talk about intelligent things, and he also says that he is very intelligent. So it seems to me that you suit each other well.

MISS LOTTIE: Nothing could be further from the truth. Of all misfortunes that the world could offer, I consider the greatest to have a husband like young Fullwit.

MR. PUREHEART: What, such a rich man?

MISS LOTTIE: I have enough money to make even a poor man happy.

MR. PUREHEART: The smartest man in the world?

MISS LOTTIE: Heaven save me from the smartest man in the world, at least when he is a conceited fool.

MR. PUREHEART: Keep in mind the power that your father's will gives me!

MISS LOTTIE: That authorization befits a reasonable father. He merely wanted to protect me from the thoughtless impetuousness of youth. But he did not intend to make me the lifelong slave of another's caprice. When I have reached my majority, and have hopefully attained sufficient reason, then I can marry whomever I choose. It seems to me that that is what my father intended.

MR. PUREHEART (*reflects a moment*): That is no doubt the case! But will you be able to wait another five years?

MISS LOTTIE: Rather than accept Fullwit. For that, I could wait fifty years.

MR. PUREHEART: Don't provoke me like this! I'm as fond of you as if you were my own child! For that reason, you should be willing to do something for me in return.

MISS LOTTIE: With all my heart, anything you want. Except consider Fullwit intelligent.

MR. PUREHEART: But the man has so much learning!

MISS LOTTIE: I won't deny that. For such a young man, he knows quite a bit. But just because of that, he doesn't have to act so proud and clever, as if he could match wits with all the great scholars in Germany.

MR. PUREHEART: He'll outgrow that!

MISS LOTTIE: I'm certain that, if he didn't have such a high opinion of himself, I would be able to consider him a clever young man. But when he looks at his modest accomplishments through a magnifying glass, he becomes a fool.

MR. PUREHEART: Well, at least promise me, Miss Lottie, that you will be willing to have him come to coffee this afternoon, when you normally have a few other good friends in your room anyway. Do that for me!

MISS LOTTIE (*shrugs her shoulders*): What can I do?

MR. PUREHEART: I'm going to tell my son to scold him a bit about his pride. After all, they're good friends.

MISS LOTTIE: Your son is his good friend only out of respect for you, because you ordered him to be. Otherwise, he's far too reasonable to put up with him for an hour.

MR. PUREHEART: Well, well! We'll see. My son loves the fine arts, too, so he'll be able to talk with him all the more frankly. Are you expecting company today for coffee?

MISS LOTTIE: As far as I know, the only people coming are young Fullwit and your son. At lunch they started an argument that they want to finish here in my room.

MR. PUREHEART: Hm? What? An argument?

MISS LOTTIE: Yes, they were talking about Gottsched's *Theater Anthology*.[1] Fullwit ripped apart all the pieces in it.

MR. PUREHEART: Now, that I wouldn't know. I like to read in it a bit in the evening. Admittedly, I don't like all the pieces in it either, but some of them are very nice, and I always say, if I don't like it, maybe somebody else will.

MISS LOTTIE: That means, you think like a man of reason—but not like young Fullwit.

MR. PUREHEART: No! It isn't right to reject a book that way, not as long as it hasn't been written for just one person. (*He goes over to the table and notices a sealed letter lying on it.*)

MISS LOTTIE: But that's the way of these young gentlemen. They think that all authors should strive only to win the honor of their applause. Notwithstanding how meager the reward actually is!

MR. PUREHEART: What's this letter, Miss Lottie?

MISS LOTTIE: Oh, that! It's poems from young Mr. Fullwit. He sent them down to me this morning.

MR. PUREHEART (*pleased*): Hm! I like that! It's most likely a declaration of love. Why haven't you opened it yet?

MISS LOTTIE: Because I'm not interested in getting a headache today.

1. See "Biographical Introduction."

91

MR. PUREHEART: A headache? Why that?

MISS LOTTIE: I've already seen his poems. Arithmetic doesn't bother me as much as trying to understand the poetry he writes. You're used to racking your brains poring over your ledgers, Mr. Pureheart, why don't you open the letter and read it?

MR. PUREHEART: Huh! When I read my ledgers, it brings in money. From this, I wouldn't get anything. No, no! It's only right that you open your own love letters. (*He hands her the letter.*) There! Read it yourself. Besides, I have a couple of letters I have to write. (*Exit.*)

SECOND SCENE

(*The above.*)

MISS LOTTIE (*throws the letter onto the table in disgust, as* YOUNG PUREHEART *enters.*)

MISS LOTTIE: Your servant, Mr. Pureheart.

MR. PUREHEART, JR: Much obliged, Miss Lottie. Isn't Mr. Fullwit here yet?

MISS LOTTIE: No, but your papa was just here, and he assured me that he would give you the task of making young Fullwit reasonable.

MR. PUREHEART: What? Does my father think I can accomplish the impossible?

MISS LOTTIE (*laughs*): It looks as if he thinks you're capable of it.

MR. PUREHEART: If my father weren't my father, then we, Mr. Fullwit and I, wouldn't speak together very often.

MISS LOTTIE (*smiling*): Well, please be so kind as to make him a little smart. It would be to my benefit.

MR. PUREHEART: What? To your benefit?

MISS LOTTIE (*laughing*): Yes. You must know that I have in mind to become a Mrs. Fullwit some day.

MR. PUREHEART: You? You?

MISS LOTTIE: Yes, yes! I! There are good Christian hearts that desire this good fortune for me.

MR. PUREHEART: I can already guess what you mean by that, which is why I don't want to say my thoughts out loud. I might come into conflict with someone to whom I owe respect.

MISS LOTTIE: Oh, dear Mr. Pureheart, please help me prove to that person that the man is hateful!

MR. PUREHEART: Oh, we'll let him do that himself. Believe me, he will make himself so despicable to my father, and to everyone else, that we can spare ourselves any efforts in that direction. People who are that arrogant and pretentious never get very far in the world. I know that from experience.

MISS LOTTIE: Well, he's finished as far as I'm concerned. I already know what to think of him.

MR. PUREHEART: I do, too. At least I'll keep myself from such sleepless nights as the one I just had.

MISS LOTTIE: What? Why didn't you sleep?

MR. PUREHEART: Last night he invited me to come to his room, because it was too early for him to go to bed. In fact, I had a good book that I would much rather have read, but I went anyway, partly to be polite, partly to please my father. But! I'll be damned if I ever go a second time! I didn't get out of his room until three in the morning.

MISS LOTTIE: How so? You didn't start imbibing together, did you?

MR. PUREHEART (*laughing*): Hardly! It was all very dry! All that flowed was the Hippocrene,[2] for he greeted me with verses and entertained me with verses. First he recited from memory everything he had written in the

---

2. A spring flowing from beneath the peak of Mount Helicon, said to have been opened by a blow from Pegasus's hoof. A source of poetic inspiration.

last five or six years, until he was blue in the face and frothing at the mouth. After that, he thought of the poems from his youth, and he hauled out reams of paper, scaring me half to death. I suffered through it all until the clock struck three.

MISS LOTTIE (*laughing hard*): Why didn't you just fall asleep there?

MR. PUREHEART: Huh! As if I could have, with all the yelling. For some reason, young poets get overcome by raging enthusiasm when they recite their poetry or read it aloud. They shout worse than Stentor.[3]

MISS LOTTIE (*laughs*): Yes! That's good!

MR. PUREHEART: But I know what I'm going to do. Some evening I'll send young Mr. Smartly and Mr. Iambus up to his room. Those young gentlemen also admire their own poetry and like to subject everyone to recitations. That will be a regular dogfight! Either they'll all shout at the same time, or they'll have to hold each others' mouths shut. (*Laughs.*)

MISS LOTTIE: Oh, you'll have to let me know when you're going to do that. I'd at least like to stand outside the door and listen to the comedy.

MR. PUREHEART: In fact, you're going to get a little foretaste right now. To tell you the truth, I invited them here. I hope you don't mind.

MISS LOTTIE: What have you done? Am I supposed to have the whole poetical army in my room?

MR. PUREHEART: It'll be fun! And who knows what good it might accomplish?

MISS LOTTIE: I had hoped to hold onto my hearing to the end, and the —

THIRD SCENE

(*The above.* MISS LOTTIE, MR. PUREHEART.)
(MR. FULLWIT *enters with his hat on, not taking it off until he has closed the door.*)

---

3. An Achaian in the *Iliad* (5.785) with a voice as loud as fifty men.

MR. FULLWIT (*with great seriousness*): Your obedient servant, my dear mademoiselle! Your humble servant, Mr. Pureheart!

MISS LOTTIE: Your servant, Mr. Fullwit. Was it raining out in the hall?

MR. FULLWIT (*puzzled and smiling*): In the hall? No!

MISS LOTTIE: I didn't really think so. But I imagined something of the sort when you came in wearing your hat on your head.

MR. PUREHEART: That's the way his father always comes into his office.

MISS LOTTIE (*smiling*): Yes, his clerks sit there. But not here.

MR. FULLWIT: A different custom. Where me and my father live, a man does not take his hat off.

MISS LOTTIE: True enough! Rude customs are still customs. Please sit down. (*They sit down. Miss Lottie rings.*)

MR. PUREHEART: Have you perhaps been out, Mr. Fullwit?

MR. FULLWIT: Yes, this morning I attendanced various lectures.

MISS LOTTIE: Well, what did you think of our professors?

MR. FULLWIT (*shrugs his shoulders*): Just terrible! How I will miss my preceptors back home! No, I never expectated nothing this bad.

MR. PUREHEART (*astonished*): Really? Whom did you hear?

MR. FULLWIT (*contemptuously*): Oh, I'd rather not name the poor people. They have a certain respectedness in the world. (*Smiling.*) Let them enjoy their fame! I don't want to crush them.

MISS LOTTIE: Your opinion might not necessarily ruin them utterly, if, as you say, they have already made a name for themselves.

FOURTH SCENE

(*The above.*) (PAUL enters)

PAUL (*to Miss Lottie*). The lady rang?

MISS LOTTIE: Bring us some coffee. (*The servant exits.*)

MR. PUREHEART (*smiling*): So, you will have some difficulty achieving your purpose here, since you came to study?

MR. FULLWIT: I didn't come here to study, I only had in mind not to forget what I already learned at home. But before I would listen to that miserable stuff, I'd rather lock myself in my room for a year.

MISS LOTTIE: Hm! If I were in your place, I'd turn right around and go home, and then I'd set the people of Leipzig straight about the kind of professors they'd have to get before I'd study there.

MR. FULLWIT: In my hometown it is our habituation to go to universities for three or four years to forget what we learned at home.

MR. PUREHEART: That's a pity!

MISS LOTTIE: What a waste of such excellent learning!

MR. PUREHEART: But at least you can be of service to the world during this time by writing. There are many great minds who have barely left secondary school and can find nothing to do at the university except become writers right away.

MR. FULLWIT: Admittedly, I got some points on which to take issue about in Leibniz's calculus and Aristotle's poetics.[4] Perhaps I will applicate myself to that task. Ah, but how many grand reputations would be sacrificed! How many bunglers exposed, who till now seemed great, but who really just aped those two.

MISS LOTTIE (*smiling*): Well, I certainly wouldn't waste any pity on them. If they really were just a bunch of blind apes, they'll simply have to get dragged down with the others.

---

4. Gottfried Wilhelm Leibniz (1646–1716), the most influential philosopher of the early German Enlightenment, invented the calculus independently from Newton (see note 8, below). Later on, Pureheart refers to his major philosophical publication, *Essais de théodicée sur la bonté de dieu, la liberté de l'homme et l'origine du mal* (Amsterdam, 1710). Gottsched's aesthetics cited Aristotle's *Poetics* as the ultimate authority.

(The servant arrives, bringing a coffee table and service. Miss Lottie pours.)

MR. FULLWIT: When I'm finished with my commentary on that Aristotle fellow, where I take apart his rules, there won't be any more poetics, not for the French, not for the Germans, of which to speak about.

MR. PUREHEART: Are we to expect this wonderful work soon?

MR. FULLWIT: I can't say. To tell the truth, I actually completed its composition when I was still a junior in school, but you know how it is, when you got a kind a reputation . . .

MISS LOTTIE: Of course. You can't go risking it in a brawl. Especially when it's so new and fresh. *(She hands him a cup of coffee. Also Pureheart.)*

MR. FULLWIT *(drinks)*: Hey, that's good coffee! What'd it set you back, mademoiselle?

MISS LOTTIE: Oh, great scholars shouldn't have to know what petty household items cost!

MR. FULLWIT: Oh, yes, that's the way I am. I got to know everything. I can't help myself. I'll tell you. You paid at the most twenty *Groschen*[5] for it, 'cause at home it costs sixteen, cash.

MR. PUREHEART: Well, I'll be! I can taste that the coffee is very good, but to taste what it costs, there my palate is too ignorant.

MR. FULLWIT *(takes a lump of sugar from the bowl)*: And for the sugar? *(He examines it.)* If you paid more than twenty-two *Thaler*[6] for a hundred-weight, you got took.

MR. PUREHEART: You've learned prices from your father better than I have from mine.

MISS LOTTIE: No, Mr. Fullwit, I'm losing all respect for your future

---

5. A penny or tenpenny piece.
6. A silver coin (compare: dollar).

scholarly writings, now that I hear that you know the price of different foods.

FIFTH SCENE

(*The above.*) (MR. SMARTLY, MR. IAMBUS enter with ill-bred, wild expressions. PUREHEART *greets them.*)

MR. PUREHEART: Gentlemen, your servant. Here you see Mr. Fullwit, a young man from Lower Saxony who honors our university by wanting to study here.

MR. SMARTLY: Your servant, sir. I can't hardly say how nice it is to make your acquaintance.

MR. IAMBUS: It's a pleasure for my friend and I, too.

MR. FULLWIT: For myself, too, it's a delight to meet two such men, about who Mr. Pureheart has told me so much of.

MR. PUREHEART: Please be seated.
(*The two run over to a corner of the room and remove their hats and swords.* LOTTIE *is about to remonstrate with them, but* PUREHEART *signals to her to ignore it. They sit down at the coffee table. Miss Lottie pours each a cup of coffee.*)

MR. IAMBUS (*who continually bellows*): How long have we done had the honor of seeing you here amongst us, Mr. Fullwit?

MR. FULLWIT: Just two weeks.

MR. SMARTLY: Where have you been residing in?

MR. FULLWIT: I'm here at Mr. Pureheart's.

MR. IAMBUS: Ain't you planning to stay an extended period?

MISS LOTTIE: My goodness, gentlemen, you needn't discuss such trivial subjects with Mr. Fullwit. He's a great poet.

MR. IAMBUS: A poet?

MR. FULLWIT: At your service.

MR. PUREHEART: And a mathematician, to boot!

MR. SMARTLY: A mathematician? Then how could you lower yourself to being a poet?

MR. IAMBUS: Now, my dear Mr. Smartly, there were intelligent poets long before intelligent mathematicians.

MR. SMARTLY: Now, Mr. Iambus, we're good friends. But don't mess around with the longevity of mathematics; you'll just make an ass of yourself.

MR. FULLWIT: It is true: mathematics is the noblest thing that a thinking being can learn and know.

MR. SMARTLY: It is the only science that can reveal truths. All the others offer only uncertainty.

> Oh, art of measure, imagination's bridle,
> Thou art free from error, never idle.
> Who shuns your guidance, slips.

MISS LOTTIE (*contemptuously*): It's certainly true that two times two is four. That is a much more certain truth than that the sun shines brightly.

MR. PUREHEART (*laughing*): I would much rather have written a chapter of Leibniz's *Theodicee* than be the inventor of the multiplication tables, even if they do contain eternal truths. (*To Miss Lottie.*) I'll gladly stick with the analogy you made with arithmetic, even though that's only part of mathematics.

MR. SMARTLY: I don't dispute that Leibniz was a great man! By which I mean, he was a great mathematician.

MR. PUREHEART (*points at Fullwit*): There, however, sits a man who finds a great deal to criticize in the Leibnizian calculus.

MR. SMARTLY (*looks him over from head to foot*): You? In Leibniz's calculus?

MR. FULLWIT (*musters him in the same way*): Yes, my dear sir. I don't like to blindly admire great men. I like to examinate everything, and then I find that they're all in error.

MR. SMARTLY (*astonished*): And? What, for example, do you find to criticize in it?

MR. FULLWIT (*haughtily*): That will become clear when my work is in published form.

MR. PUREHEART: You should know that Mr. Fullwit wrote his work while still in high school, in his junior year. So it is already finished.

MR. SMARTLY: In high school? Did you go to school?

MR. FULLWIT: Yes, my dear sir. As far as I know, one isn't born with a knowledgment of Latin. Didn't you go to school?

MR. SMARTLY: It would have been better if I didn't. I didn't learn hardly anything from any teacher except in mathematics. That's the only teacher from who I learned anything.

MISS LOTTIE (*laughing*): Did you learn to read and write when you were a week old?

MR. IAMBUS: That could well be! At least, I can testify that he writes the way I would have wanted to write at the age of one year old.

MR. PUREHEART (*laughing*): Yes, Mr. Smartly, your sweetheart will first have to practice on Dr. Faust's magic signs before she'll be able to decipher your handwriting.

MR. SMARTLY (*proudly*): *Docti male pingunt!*[7] Meanwhile, to return back to the subject of schools: there one is plagued with ambiguities. With philosophical ambiguity, with legal, medical, rhetorical, historical, poetical, and a thousand other ambiguities. The only truth one encounters is mathematics.

MR. PUREHEART (*laughing*): Do you mean, Mr. Smartly, that everything you learned, except mathematics, is a lie?

7. "The learned paint [here: write] badly."

MR. SMARTLY: There may well be certain kinds of half-certainties, or probabilities, in the other disciplines. But any thinker who is born for eternal truths can arrive at them by himself, in any case. I didn't need any teachers for that.

MISS LOTTIE: Well, I'm just as glad I wasn't one of your teachers. I would find that a thankless task!

MR. SMARTLY: If you will do me the honor to become my tutor, I will gladly be indebted to you for all my knowledge.

MR. FULLWIT: You have, no doubt, already wrote something mathematical? May I ask to see some of it?

MR. SMARTLY: In about two weeks I can oblige you with a dissertation.

MR. FULLWIT: On what topic?

MR. SMARTLY: On the angle of divergence of the rays of vision of a cross-eyed man viewing an object.

MR. FULLWIT: That's a new subject!

MR. SMARTLY: What I have to say about it is totally new. The inventions are all myself's. I didn't hardly look at a single optical book, not even Newton's,[8] even though that's the only book you shouldn't be ashamed of having read.

MR. FULLWIT: I'm curious to read it.

MR. SMARTLY: I always close a proof with a line or two from a mathematical poet like Pope, Gebhardi,[9] or some such.

MR. IAMBUS: Aha! There we have it! First you insult poetry, and now you decorate your mathematical treatises with it.

MR. SMARTLY: Well, there's poetry, and then there's poetry. I don't mean

---

8. Sir Isaac Newton (1642–1727): *Opticks, or A Treatise of the Reflections, Refractions, Inflections, and Colours of Light* (1704).

9. Alexander Pope (1688–1744), English poet; Karl August Gebhardi (dates unknown), eighteenth-century writer.

any lullaby writers like Opitz, Canitz, Besser, Neukirch, Günther,[10] and those others; I mean the ones where you can find the true, the beautiful, the lofty, the profound, the dark, the contemplated, the roguish . . . in short, anything you could call abstract.

MISS LOTTIE (*laughing*): Abstract? Couldn't you call that the extracted?

MR. PUREHEART (*laughs*): Yes, yes! The extracted in poetry. That was said beautifully and extractly!

MR. IAMBUS: Now, Mr. Smartly, you have been entertaining Mr. Fullwit long enough. Now let me give poetry a chance. It's unnatural for a poet to remain silent so long and listen.

MR. SMARTLY: Fine with me! I will at least be able to join in, too, on the subject of poetry. You, on the other hand, had nothing to say about mathematics and had to let the rest of us do the talking.

MR. IAMBUS (*to Mr. Fullwit*): You have doubtless published much that is beautiful?

MR. FULLWIT: No, not really. But I am still sure that my work must be known here.

MR. SMARTLY: I don't believe I've read anything from yourself.

MR. FULLWIT (*astonished*): Didn't you hear the cantata last August in the Schellhafer Auditorium?

MR. IAMBUS: No. Did you write it?

MR. FULLWIT: Yes. The composer wrote and begged me to do him the honor and write a cantata for him.

MR. PUREHEART (*to the others*): My goodness, gentlemen, I wouldn't let the man get away with that. What? To have two such distinguished poets right at home and still turn to Lower Saxony when he wants something

---

10. Martin Opitz (1597–1639), Friedrich Freiherr von Canitz (1654–99), Johann von Besser (1654–1729), Benjamin Neukirch (1665–1729), Johann Christian Günther (1695–1723): German poets representing a variety of schools.

beautiful? I wouldn't put up with it! (*They shake their heads. Lottie laughs.*)

MR. FULLWIT: I didn't want to turn him down. I thought it could be the poor man's big chance. But if he was so stupid and printed it without my name, that wasn't hardly my fault. I can't help that.

MR. SMARTLY: No, we didn't know nothing about that here.

MR. FULLWIT: He's a stupid pig! Here a composer goes and makes his fortune with one of my cantatas. It was a beauty, too!

MR. PUREHEART: Oh, there's no doubting that!

MR. FULLWIT: In the meanwhile, the one I wrote here was beautiful, too. 'Cause, I said to myself, you got to show the Leipzigers something, give them something special. In one aria I put in something from algebra. That was real pretty. I worked hard on it, too . . . I why can't I remember it? (*He tries to remember.*)

MR. IAMBUS: Do you also make use of participles, Mr. Fullwit?

MR. FULLWIT: Oh, they're my strong forte! The cantata was loaded with them.

MISS LOTTIE: What sort of things are they, Mr. Pureheart?

MR. PUREHEART (*smiling*): It's like when I say to you: too cold for drinking, the coffee will have to be cleared away.

MISS LOTTIE (*laughs:*) Aha! and: not born to serving, I will have to call the butler. (*She gets up. The others and Iambus in full-throated laughter, so that Lottie covers her ears and exits.*)

SIXTH SCENE

(*The above.* MESSRS. PUREHEART, FULLWIT, IAMBUS, SMARTLY.)

MR. IAMBUS: I'm pleased to hear that you are fond of participles.

MR. SMARTLY: Me, too. One cannot hardly think without participles.

MR. FULLWIT: And a verse that has not been thought out is worthless.

MR. PUREHEART (*laughing*): Oh, indeed! And by "thought out," you mean phrased in a nobly un-German way.

MR. FULLWIT: Oh, you've got sucked in by the *German Theater Anthology*. That is why you lack the couth for clever verses.

MR. PUREHEART: Oh? Is that supposed to mean that the *Theater Anthology* has only stupid drivel in it?

MR. SMARTLY: Well, if it's watery poetic soup you're looking for, you'll find enough of it there.

MR. FULLWIT: My, gentlemen, isn't it a pleasureness to hear that we're in agreement! I except only one play there. Its author is my good friend. But the others are all worthless.

MR. IAMBUS: Do you mean the first piece in one particular volume? Yes, indeed! But as is sometimes said: *bonus dormitat Homerus*.[11]

MR. FULLWIT: Granted, not all the lines are thought out. After all, *ubi plura nitent in carmine*[12] etc. I usually don't utilize this rule with poems, but since this is my good friend . . .

MR. SMARTLY: The others're all infinitely worse than that one!

MR. IAMBUS: The flatness, coldness, improbableness . . .

MR. PUREHEART (*smiling*): The unable-to-be-readness? Isn't that right?

MR. FULLWIT: Indeed, I don't know nothing more awkward than Jean de France taking off his coat on stage. (*He laughs contemptuously.*)

MR. IAMBUS: And that idiot in *The Misanthrope*[13] who makes fun of participles!

MR. FULLWIT: No! I would have expected something better in a work

---

11. "Sometimes [even] the good Homer dozes off" (Horace, *Ars poetica*, 359).
12. "Where [or: when] many things glisten in the song [poem]."
13. *Le Misanthrope*, comedy by Jean Baptiste Molière (1666).

like that. Our own contemporary time won't get any value out of that.

MR. SMARTLY: Are those supposed to be masterworks?

MR. PUREHEART: Where did the editor promise that?

MR. IAMBUS (*with vehemence*): But we demand them!

MR. PUREHEART (*laughs heartily*): Fine. If he ever publishes an anthology just for you, maybe he'll try for some, or maybe even ask for your own works, which you claim to be masterworks. (*The servant enters and removes the coffee table*). But up to this point, he has only intended to provide plays that do not conflict too much with the rules, and to provide actors with material that is more tasteful and intelligent than the miserable stuff they have been playing everywhere up till now. You will have to admit that the pieces in the anthology at least do that.

MR. IAMBUS: (*The three of them all laugh contemptuously.*) No doubt you mean the *Banise*,[14] as well.

MR. PUREHEART: Yes, yes, that too! For it's infinitely better than the old, prosaic *Banise* that still gets played, no matter how stupid it is. But if you don't like it, sit down and write a better one. That won't bother the editor at all; it will bring him genuine pleasure.

MR. IAMBUS (*laughs uproariously*).

MR. PUREHEART: Oh, that's a clever answer! It seems to me that there is no better way to prove that something is bad than to sit right down and produce something better.

MR. FULLWIT: We, too, have a bit of cognizance about the theater, Mr. Pureheart.

MR. PUREHEART: Well, fine. Where are the masterpieces you have written? I don't see them anywhere.

---

14. Refers to a dramatic version of the Baroque novel, *Die asiatische Banise*, by Anselm von Zigler und Kliphausen, first published in 1689. Written in 1741 by Friedrich Melchior Grimm (1723–1807), the tragedy appeared in the fourth volume of *Deutsche Schaubühne*. Gottsched's introduction confesses to reservations about the play.

MR. FULLWIT: Then you must not have read the packet I gave you last night. I have indeed written some.

MR. PUREHEART: No, I've been very busy this morning.

MR. IAMBUS: But you've read enough of my things?

MR. PUREHEART: Yes. But I would certainly have as much to object to there as you find to quarrel with in the anthology.

MR. SMARTLY: And just what would you criticize about in my plays?

MR. PUREHEART: For one thing, that their language is not German.

MR. FULLWIT: Ha! ha! ha! Are you another one of them fussy pedants, who would strangle a beautiful idea just for the sake of grammar?

MR. IAMBUS: I don't write for people who are concerned only with conjugating and declinating.

MR. PUREHEART: But you do write for your readers, and you don't appeal to them with grammatical gaffes.

MR. SMARTLY: Oh, yes. I'd always rather read a beautiful idea than a proper expression.

MR. FULLWIT: And as for I, an idea doesn't hardly seem so beautiful as when the expression goes against grammar.

MR. PUREHEART: I'll tell you something else: sometimes the whole idea resides only in the grammatical error. When you put the words together correctly, the whole idea disappears.

MR. IAMBUS: Oh, that's just been made up by shallow people who can't hardly think.

MR. PUREHEART (laughing): Oh, my! Do you mean that it's such a great art to compose grammatical blunders? I can do that anytime, too, when it's a question of wit or magic. But why don't you do the same thing with Latin verse? Why do you confine yourselves to grammar there?

MR. FULLWIT: Oh, that's very different! German isn't Latin!

MR. PUREHEART: This isn't the first time I've heard that.

MR. SMARTLY: Latin, after all, has its rules. But you'd have to be blind to say that about German.

MR. PUREHEART: What? Doesn't German have rules, then?

MR. IAMBUS: No, you can say anything you want in German.

MR. PUREHEART: I don't dispute that. But you also can and must say it with good German formulations.

MR. FULLWIT: No. With that restriction, many a lovely thought gets lost.

MR. PUREHEART: I'm willing to bet that that isn't true two times in a hundred. For example: I recently read in a poem, where a lover is trying to gain his beloved's affections, the expression, "To us there will not always be spring." Isn't that just a Latinism?

MR. SMARTLY: Latinism or not—the thought is beautiful.

MR. FULLWIT: Don't it sound nice!

MR. PUREHEART: But wouldn't the thought stay the same if I were to Germanicize it: "We won't always be young?"

(*All three shout*). No! No! No! That's cold, flat, abstract!

MR. PUREHEART (*shrugs his shoulders and laughs*): That just shows that you only like the solecism. The thought is the very same.

MR. IAMBUS: In a pig's eye! "To us there will not always be spring." That's so picturesque, so pithy. The other way is just dishwater by comparison.

MR. PUREHEART: Is that so? "To me is spring." To me, that's just as if, with the *Epistolis obscurorum virorum*, I wanted to say, "*Habemus valde calidam aestatem.*"[15] (*They all laugh.*)

MR. SMARTLY: Now I'm delighted that we have gotten Mr. Fullwit here. Do you know what, Mr. Iambus? We ought to found a linguistic society together.

---

15. "The letters of obscure men"; "We are having a terribly hot summer."

MR. FULLWIT: Gladly. Count me in.

MR. IAMBUS: An antigrammatical one.

MR. FULLWIT: Yes! yes! So that we can dispel the prejudice that you can think and still have to write pure German.

MR. SMARTLY: Exactly.

MR. PUREHEART (*laughing*): Oh, you poor German language, quake! To you it will not always be beauty!

MR. IAMBUS: Now, now, don't mock us! Your poems will pay dearly, if in fact you write any that are pure German.

MR. PUREHEART: That martyrdom would be an honor for me! But it's not necessary. I am concentrating on my law practice, for a clever mind without bread seems to me to be a sad creature indeed. But I will still be attracted to the muses—and also to my mother tongue. If I ever want to read bad, distorted German, I can always look at my briefs or the newspaper! And if I ever want to bust my head over a poem, then I'll read Pindar and Persius[16] themselves, rather than their latest imitators.

MR. FULLWIT (*to the others*): He don't know a thing, and we won't ever convert him around. What shall we name our new society?

MR. SMARTLY: Yes, we need a name, of course. How would it be if we called ourselves the Participial Society?

MR. IAMBUS: No! no! That would emphasize only one feature. We have to simultaneously suggest at the same time that we are after pithiness and thought.

MR. PUREHEART (*laughing*): Well, then, call yourselves the Thinking Un-German Society, or else the Un-German-Thinking Society.

MR. FULLWIT: The thinking? That's not bad. But the un-German? That would be admitting that our poems weren't German.

MR. IAMBUS: Indeed. (*He thinks a minute.*) I've got it! We'll call ourselves the Solecistic Thinking Society.

---

16. Pindar (ca. 518–446 B.C.), Greek poet; Persius (A.D. 34–62), Latin poet.

MR. SMARTLY: Yes! yes! To spite the grammatical guilds!

MR. FULLWIT: Good! good! That expresses that we accept not only participles, but all the other solecisms.

MR. SMARTLY: Yes, as long as the poet thinks! For he must think! Nothing else matters.

MR. IAMBUS: So now we are the Solecistic Thinking Society. (*They all agree*): Yes! yes! (*and shake hands and embrace. Each says*): Your servant, my dear colleague.

MR. PUREHEART (*bows to them*): I heartily congratulate you on your new society, which will help the human intellect return to its former position of dignity. And commend myself to your charming pity, my worthy, thinking Messrs. Solecists! (*They shake their heads.*)

MR. SMARTLY: Where shall we meet in future, gentlemen?

MR. FULLWIT: Wouldn't my room be best for you two and I? A glass of wine and bit of smoked ham would always be available.

MR. PUREHEART: Well, accept the offer, gentlemen. Thinking always goes better when there's something in the offing.

MR. SMARTLY: If you don't mind, it's acceptable with me.

MR. IAMBUS: If it ain't too much trouble for yourself, Mr. Fullwit.

MR. FULLWIT: Not hardly at all. The pleasure'd be mine.

MR. IAMBUS: And there we'll consider all recent publications and examine everything about them that's shallow, dull, low, ponderiferous, extracetera.

MR. SMARTLY: Yes, yes. But so as not destroy our own taste with the miserable junk that other writers scribble, we should read one of our own works aloud each time, and make every effort to enrich our language with fractured expressions from English, which insipid poets commonly label Anglicisms and barbarisms.

MR. IAMBUS: Yes, and with time, we can take what we have read aloud, examined, and reworked, so that there is nothing left to criticize, and publish it in a little volume as an example for German poetry.

MR. FULLWIT: At the moment, I don't see that the world is worthy of reading anything by myself. Times will have to change a lot!

MR. SMARTLY: Well, gentlemen, when shall we have our first meeting?

MR. IAMBUS: If it makes no difference to yourself, Mr. Fullwit, we could begin tomorrow.

MR. FULLWIT: Yes, gentlemen. I have the honor to await for you.

MR. PUREHEART: Would it be possible for a simple German soul like me to have the pleasure of being present at your thinking gathering?

MR. SMARTLY: Yes, yes, but only as an observer.

MR. IAMBUS: Yes, he may not criticize, nor may he defend what we attack. Because he don't understand what goes into a really difficult poem.

MR. PUREHEART (*smiling*): Oh, I'll gladly be satisfied with that. I only want to free myself a bit from the grammatical urge that possesses me.

MR. FULLWIT: Who's going to read first?

MR. SMARTLY: I happen to have a mathematical treatise on Chloris's[17] knitting needles, although it's not quite finished. For it's going to be deeply ironical, taking a poke at more than twenty of my good friends and teachers. There are even a couple of stabs at my parents.

MR. PUREHEART: A fine bit of work! A mathematical satire!

MR. SMARTLY: Yes, a philosopher is related to no one, beholden to no one. He just plows ahead and speaks the truth to everyone. If you already have something finished, Mr. Iambus, you can begin.

MR. IAMBUS: I happen to have a tragedy at hand, with the first act finished. Probably nothing like it has ever been seen. It consists only of epigrammatical thoughts; two couplets each, or on occasion four lines to-

17. Either: one of Pierus's nine daughters (who challenged the Muses and were turned into magpies); the wife of Zephyrus; or the name assumed by Meliboea, daughter of Amphion and Niobe.

gether, make up each epigram. Every one of them probably cost me half a day's work. Now I just have to put them together and write the names above them.

MR. FULLWIT: You've done given me an idea. Couldn't we write a comedy the same way from Martial or Ovenus?[18] We wouldn't hardly ever run out of satirical ideas if every character came up with a delicious barb every time he opens his mouth.

MR. IAMBUS: Why not? It will just show off my piece to good advantage. Several places in it really came out marvelously. Sophocles and Euripides[19] are just so much cold water in comparison.

MR. PUREHEART: I do believe it! But what kind of audience would ever be able to follow such a closely written piece if it were performed?

MR. IAMBUS: I leave it to the poetic rabble to write for the rabble. I write only for cosmopolitans and mathematicians.

MR. PUREHEART: And I can promise that neither Wolff nor Bilfinger nor Euler[20] will read your tragedy.

MR. IAMBUS: One knows what to expect from the new prophets. Ain't you got something nice finished, Mr. Fullwit?

MR. FULLWIT: I have wrote a pastoral play of which I have given a copy of to Mr. Pureheart yesterday. Every bit of it is so waggish. (*He laughs to himself.*) Oh, it's simply incorrigible!

MR. SMARTLY: Can you tell me the name?

MR. FULLWIT: It's called "The Rape." A roguish, contorted piece!

MR. PUREHEART (*musters him from head to foot*): "The Rape?" A pastoral play?

MR. IAMBUS: That I'm curious to hear.

---

18. Marcus Valerius Martialis (A.D. ca. 40-100), Roman poet.

19. Sophocles (ca. 496–406 B.C.), Euripides (ca. 480–406 B.C.): Greek playwrights.

20. Christian Wolff (1679–1754), popularizer of Leibniz's philosophy; Georg Bernhard Bilfinger (1693–1750), a follower of Wolff; Leonhard Euler (1707–83), mathematician.

MR. FULLWIT: You'll enjoy it. It has cost a lot of effort to myself.

MR. SMARTLY: But for the sake of our collegial friendship, Mr. Fullwit, kindly stop using pronouns wrong. It hurts my ears.

MR. IAMBUS: Yes, I can't stand it no more.

MR. FULLWIT: And it's just as painful, gentlemen, to hear your grammatical constructions.

MR. SMARTLY (*laughs contemptuously*): Oh, I suppose we're going to learn German from the Lower Saxons?

MR. FULLWIT: And why not? German wouldn't be the only intelligent thing that you, sir, and your colleague could learn from Lower Saxony.

MR. PUREHEART: My, my, gentlemen! Is it possible that the founders of the Solecistic Society might come to a parting over their own solecisms? Each of you should contribute to the good of the whole.

MR. SMARTLY: I'll only accept Upper Saxon solecisms; they're the only valid ones here. The Lower Saxon ones might be fine in Lower Saxony!

MR. IAMBUS: Yes, but the Lower Saxon ones violate all reason.

MR. FULLWIT: I have met Upper Saxons who were just as unreasonable as their solecisms and needed to spend a couple of years in Lower Saxony in order to become halfway intelligent.

MR. SMARTLY: And just what's that supposed to mean, Mr. Fullwit?

MR. FULLWIT: I'm not naming any names, but I mean a couple of certain parties.

MR. IAMBUS: My dear sir, were you perhaps dropped on your head as a baby?

MR. FULLWIT: No, not at all! For it never occurred to myself to write a tragedy, or even a comedy, out of epigrams.

MR. PUREHEART: Why, gentlemen, I do believe you're beginning to think!

MR. SMARTLY: You certainly are conceit personificated!

MR. FULLWIT: But I never wrote a lampoon against my parents!

MR. SMARTLY: Sir, your approbation would be a real insult against my writings.

MR. FULLWIT: My thanks to your Solecism Society, but I don't never want to be a member!

MR. IAMBUS: The first thing I'm going to read aloud there is a satire on you.

MR. FULLWIT: And I'm going to write such a critique of your tragedy, that hardly nobody will be willing to even step on it.

MR. SMARTLY: Sir! Watch who you are dealing with; we are capable of making even the greatest scholar look ridiculous. We already intend to bring out a new weekly, called "The Joker." You might be featured in it.

MR. FULLWIT: Only ridiculous people would pay any attention to such ridiculous *criticos*.

MR. IAMBUS: Hey, why don't you say "to such *criticis* "? That would make a nice Lower Saxonism. (*Smartly and Iambus laugh loudly.*)

MR. PUREHEART: For heaven's sake, gentlemen! Stop thinking. Miss Lottie is coming.

SEVENTH SCENE

(*The above.* MISS LOTTIE.)

MISS LOTTIE: Well, there's certainly quite an uproar here in my room.

MR. FULLWIT: Forgive us, mademoiselle. I had thought I was among learned men, but I see they aren't hardly even students.

MR. IAMBUS: Yes, we give lessons in Latin declensions and conjugations. If you never got that far in school, Mr. Fullwit, you only have to say so.

MISS LOTTIE: Gentlemen, please! I beg you either not to quarrel in my presence, or, if you must, to pick some place other than my room. Mr. Fullwit sent me some of his verse this morning, which we might read together.

Mr. Iambus and Mr. Smartly know about poetry, so they will either be able to admire the work or criticize it.

MR. IAMBUS (*cries out loudly*): What? Am I supposed to sit here and listen to another poet's work? That's out of the question! That other people should listen to my poems at a six-hour stretch, that's only normal. But this way, I'm leaving! (*Rushes to the corner, gathers up his sword and cane, and runs out in agitation.*)

EIGHTH SCENE

(*The above.* MISS LOTTIE. MR. PUREHEART. MR. SMARTLY. MR. FULLWIT.)

MISS LOTTIE: What an ill-bred person! I'm amazed that all his friends aren't deaf. (*She sits down, and the others sit, too.*)

MR. SMARTLY: He no doubt feels that he possesses a clever mind.

MR. PUREHEART: He would do well if he felt not only his strengths, but his weaknesses, too.

MISS LOTTIE (*hands Pureheart the letter*): Here, Mr. Pureheart. Be so good as to read this aloud. I'll have my hands full just trying to understand it.

MR. PUREHEART (*reads*): "My dear, beloved father, . . ."

MR. FULLWIT (*leaps up in astonishment and tries to grab the letter from him*): For God's sake! What have you got there? If you've got a kind bone in your body, give it to me.

MISS LOTTIE: No, indeed, Mr. Pureheart! Or you'll forfeit all my goodwill.

MR. PUREHEART (*holds off Fullwit*): There you are! That is the greatest threat that a beautiful woman can utter.

MR. FULLWIT (*anxiously*): It's a letter to my father . . . It contains personal matters . . . I beg of you with everything I've got.

MISS LOTTIE: No! no! I must know what it contains. You surely couldn't have any secrets to write him from here. You aren't married, are you, Mr. Fullwit?

MR. FULLWIT (*falls to his knees before her*): Oh! oh! I beg you with all my heart, mademoiselle, make him give the letter back.

MISS LOTTIE: So that's it! You have a sweetheart at home? I have to find out about her! Read away, Mr. Pureheart.

MR. FULLWIT (*leaps up and holds his hand over Pureheart's mouth*): Oh, dear, wonderful Pureheart, my old friend, don't read it!

MISS LOTTIE: Then give me the letter. I'll read it quietly to myself.

MR. FULLWIT (*very agitated*): If you read it, I'm a goner, mademoiselle. (*He wrings his hands*). What a great blunder I've made in my haste! I must have sealed the verses to you in my father's letter and gived you the letter to my father. (*He throws himself onto the chair in utter dejection and wrings his hands.*)

MISS LOTTIE: If you didn't act so anxious, I wouldn't be half so curious. Just give me the letter, Mr. Pureheart. I'll at least read it to myself. (*She reads, now and then glancing earnestly at Fullwit, and making gestures of astonishment. Fullwit sits anxiously on his chair. Pureheart removes a sealed letter from his pocket and opens it.*)

MISS LOTTIE: Well, I never would have imagined that of you, Mr. Fullwit. After all the courtesy and respect that you received in our house; indeed, even more: after all the good that Mr. Pureheart senior had in mind for you—as I myself can attest—how can you write so contemptuously of him? Even if he did possess so little reason and wit as you claim, he does have a kind heart, and that brings about more good in the world than the greatest intelligence ever could, so long as that is coupled with a malicious, arrogant, and ungrateful heart. And I, for my small part, assure you that, however stupid I may seem to you, you did not appear so smart to me that I didn't notice two weeks ago that you are a fool. And as for what you say about young Mr. Pureheart . . .

MR. PUREHEART: What, am I in there, too?

MISS LOTTIE: Oh, yes! Your father will certainly let you read it. (*To Full-*

wit.) As for him! I assure you that the greatest revenge he could extract would be to withdraw his friendship, which he only offered in the first place out of respect for his father. And the great minds here in town, whom you condemned so contemptuously before even meeting them, will certainly avenge themselves, giving as good as they got.

MR. SMARTLY (*hotly*): What? What? Did he also speak badly of the great minds here?

MISS LOTTIE: Oh, yes! He portrays them so nicely, that all he can think of to call them is a pack of stupid children.

MR. SMARTLY (*to Fullwit*): Just a minute! Are you out of your mind? Wait till I tell Iambus! We'll write a satire about you that'll curl your hair! (*He runs to the corner, takes his hat and sword, and exits angrily.*)

MISS LOTTIE: I'm going downstairs to show Mr. Pureheart what kind of a fine guest he has been putting up in his house. (*She is about to go.*)

MR. PUREHEART: Say, wait just a minute. Here's another mixup. The verses that you were supposed to get were sent in this letter to me. Here, read them. (*He gives them to her.*)

MISS LOTTIE: Oh, I'm not smart enough to understand them. (*She throws them at Fullwit's feet and exits angrily.*)

NINTH SCENE

(*The above.* MR. FULLWIT. MR. PUREHEART.)

MR. FULLWIT (*horrified*): What? You got the verses to that girl in your envelope?

MR. PUREHEART: Yes, there they are. (*He gives them to him.*)

MR. FULLWIT (*puts his hands to his head*): Now I'm really done for! Yet another misfortune!

MR. PUREHEART: Why is that?

MR. FULLWIT: Oh, that means I sent my father that damn pastoral play!

What's the man going to think of me? He'll cut me off without a penny; he has a hot temper. I'm as good as dead!

MR. PUREHEART: I wish I could sympathize, but I'm afraid I enjoy watching stupidity and maliciousness get hoisted by their own petard.

MR. FULLWIT: I've got to send a courier right away to catch up with the mail and try to get my letter back. But my servant should reserve me a place on today's coach. I want to leave this academy right away, where everything gets so fouled up. (*Exit.*)

MR. PUREHEART: And I want to read those lovely words of praise that you wrote about me, so that I can wish you "bon voyage" with all my heart. (*Exit.*)

Translated from "Der Witzling, ein deutsches Nachspiel in einem Aufzuge," in *Deutsche Schaubühne,* vol.6 (Leipzig, 1750), 509–51.

Selected Letters

Mademoiselle,

Your beautiful handwriting astonished me. Each letter seems like a model from a master's hand; similarly, the manner of writing reveals the finest manner of thought. While I was reading it, something came to me that I want to share with you. Many of the great houses wish to find people to whom they can entrust their children; and just recently I was commissioned to look for someone who, admittedly, was supposed to be French, but who was also supposed to possess so many other qualities, that I could never find them in combination. The good pronunciation that we think to encounter in a Frenchwoman is lacking in many, and each province that yields up such people to us has its own particular dialect, which often deviates markedly from pure standard speech and can be excused only by the prejudice that states that a Frenchwoman can speak nought but good French. Your pronunciation, dearest Wilhelmine, and your intonation are so perfect that you could most certainly instruct young nobility. Your beautiful penmanship, your skill in drawing, your talent at the piano all qualify you for one of the best such positions, insofar as the perfections of the mind are concerned; and your good heart and irreproachable manners will surely inspire virtue and wisdom in the souls of your charges. May I make a suggestion to you? Accept such a position, dearest Wilhelmine. You will gain honor and advantage, just as your charges will receive greater benefit than from most native Frenchwomen. How many ill-bred people come to Saxony only to draw a high salary and to become a plague on their house, where their deficiencies are rewarded with a great deal of money. This lament is almost universal. I except those persons who carry out their duties with distinction and are worthy governesses. I know several who stand in contrast to the sort mentioned above, and who have provided conclusive demonstrations of their pedagogical skill, and for these I have as much admiration as I do pity for those young people who fall into bad hands.

Often I have wished that worthy preachers, merchants, or even scholars who do not accumulate any more than they require for their daily needs, and often leave behind a number of helpless daughters, would dedicate enough to the education of the latter so that they, when their fathers die, could earn their way in respectable fashion. This would bring about an extraordinary amount of good, and our own native daughters would be preferred to those foreigners who all too often instruct their charges in bad manners, bad pronunciation, and bad inclinations.

If you were to begin by taking such a position, then many would follow you in this admirable decision, although others may possess fewer perfections than you. Give careful consideration to my suggestion, dearest Wilhelmine, and if possible, do not let it remain just a wish. I embrace you and remain for the rest of my life your devoted

Gottsched

To: Mrs. von Runkel　　　　　　　　　　　　　　　Leipzig, Dec. 23, 1755

I have saved a copy of the Prologue for you,[21] here it is, my dearest friend. Oh, how happy humans would be if they could only follow the feelings of their hearts! But this must await a better world: in this one, we must now and again sacrifice that which we would most like to that prescribed

21. *The Best Prince*, an occasional piece written by Adelgunde Gottsched for the birthday of Princess Johanne Elisabeth, October 24, 1755.

by the duties of bourgeois society and the circumstances of the times. That is my excuse, dearest friend! Should it prove insufficient, then let your noble heart be my advocate; I know that I cannot place myself in better hands. As for the Prologue, there is much that I would like to change in it, if I could have it printed sometime according to my own ideas and if I had a free hand. The countess kept watch over this poetic child like a hen over her chicks. I shall soon let my poetic drive suffocate—poetry does not reward my efforts sufficiently. It is an ungrateful muse whom I have too often indulged. Now that a new fashion is emerging even in poetry, one with which I wish to have nothing to do, it is better for me to renounce this work entirely. Only friendship, true friendship, has the good fortune not to be disturbed by fashion and lose any of its value. Its pleasure is renewed in repetition, and we never grow tired of reading repeated assurances of it. These latter never seem dull in prose, and poetry cannot express them more strongly than our heart feels them. To friendship, all seasons, all occurrences are the same. Fortune and misfortune affect us with equal force: in short, I can imagine no more fortunate state than the happy concord of two friends who confide everything to one another, even the most hidden stirrings of their heart, and what great comfort, counsel, and support do they derive on all occasions from their shared affection! Wholly filled with this sweet emotion, I conclude the year that is hastening to its end, and may the same feelings bless the beginning of the next. Farewell, my dearest friend. I need not urge you to emulate me in feeling, but I will also certainly not prove your inferior.

Gottsched

To: Mrs. von Runkel   Leipzig, Oct. 13, 1758

Dearest friend,[22]

Gladly would I be the one to reproach me for my long silence, were not so many sad distractions the reason for my having been robbed of the pleasure of writing you.

---

22. This letter refers to events during the Seven Years' War (1756–63), during which Saxony was invaded by Prussia.

You have doubtless already felt compassion for your poor friend and our city of Leipzig in these terrible days, which have proved such a difficult trial for sensitive souls. Imagine the fearful tumult of the soldiers on a Trinity Sunday, the swarming hussars, the inhabitants' mute fear, the approaching threat of a horrible fate. With anxious hearts we witnessed the interruption of the public church service, the cessation of the bells, the barred gates, the awful preparations for burning down the houses outside the walls, the flight of so many miserable inhabitants into the churchyards, weeping children, inconsolable parents, trembling old people, all of them believing that they had seen their houses and possessions for the last time, having chosen to save their wretched existences at the cost of those goods. Imagine, dearest friend, that this is only a pale shadow of our suffering, and think of the painful anxiety of your friend, who feared and trembled for herself and others. For the most part, everything is now all right, God be praised, and our misfortune endured: but the possibility for the future, a perhaps more terrible future which might actually bring about that which we now had only feared and anticipated, this torments me and robs me of the few peaceful moments that my many tasks and domestic concerns and ruined health have left me.

Oh, if only the mighty of this earth would think of the variety of sufferings that accompany war, sufferings that extend into the succeeding generations and from which misery often flows for centuries; where virtues and art and science stand orphaned: they would, for their own benefit, willingly sacrifice the thirst of their ambition to the well-being of their lands.— How a prince, returning in triumph from the battlefield, would laugh if he were to read my pious dream, as he would call it; but you, dearest friend, you do not laugh. You weep with me at the widespread suffering, for which we have the ambition of a few mortals to thank. Oh! . . . Forgive me my sermon. I could not resist the impulse to write it down, any more than I can resist the urge to embrace you with all the affection and tenderest feelings of friendship.

Gottsched

To: Mrs. von * * *   Leipzig, Nov. 1760

My dearest little heretic,

Oh, yes, I am certainly not unjustified in conferring this title upon you. Your charming, seductive description of the Moravian Brethren could not help but lead me to the suspicion that Mr. von R. had turned you into a proselyte. How close were you to leaving me to stay in Herrnhut,[23] and I, I would have lost my only, best friend on this difficult pilgrimage of life. With all due respect to these good people, such a theft, through which the world and friendship would have lost so much, would have been anything but Christian. As far as I have heard, all ties of love, friendship, and affection are to be severed as soon as one joins these good people, since they recognize no community except among their own members. Even the strongest family bonds, I am assured, are loosed when they are not in agreement with the brotherhood's belief. In a certain sense, one is supposed to discover other fathers, mothers, brothers, and sisters there.—If this is so, what would remain for me, dearest friend? You could follow me, I hear you saying. Well and good: but I do not yet have so high an opinion of this brotherhood as you and am unlikely to have one. You say that the object of the Moravians' teaching is much too holy to you for you to offer a generally negative judgment of one or another of the members or of the whole group, even if certain of the former do not always write about it in a manner appropriate to the dignity of their subject. But do these good people always find listeners or readers who judge so kindly as you, whom I already suspect to be a novitiate? Everyone who hears or receives a speech, or who buys a book, pays simultaneously for the right to form an opinion about it. Therefore, whoever, especially in questions of religion, does not want to be judged harshly should neither write nor allow to be printed that which might offend and inspire a negative opinion. Tell your new friends that they should try to destroy all those writings which, for the reasons I have given, cannot help but offend us children of the world. For they surely write them not only for their brethren, but also to convert, to convince, us. But so long as we find in their books such sensual, indecent, ambiguous expressions, borrowed from the most vulgar speech and completely inap-

23. The center of the Moravian Brethren, a Pietist commune.

propriate to the holiest object of their teaching, then they will not achieve their purpose.

You are, I realize, quite taken with Mr. C***. This great orator will, if he continues to speak so convincingly in his community, create many proselytes, stirring not only children and laymen, but also such hearts as will help to defend his community against all arguments of malicious opponents.—And with this, keep the short, succinct, splendid speech of Mr. C*** in your splendid heart; it will, I am sure, bear fruit there a hundredfold. I imagine you all ears at the sound of the muted organ and the silver tones of the gentle voices which, you say, you prefer to any orchestra. But how glad I am that your wish at that moment did not come about. What? to die then and there? What would I have lost? Everything, everything that binds me to this earth. And Herrnhut, too, would have suffered. Your charming description gives this place a special value in my eyes. But just don't stop caring for me. No communities, no brotherhoods or sisterhoods, no orders anywhere in the world have a greater claim on your heart than does

Your Gottsched

Translated from Dorothea Henriette von Runckel, ed., *Briefe der Frau Louise Adelgunde Victorie Gottsched gebohrne Kulmus* (Dresden: Harpeter, 1771), vol.2, 37–40, 309–12; vol.3, 121–24, 141–45.

Introduction, bibliography, and translation of
the autobiographical letter by
JULIE PRANDI

Translation of poetry by
WALTER ARNDT

Anna Luisa Karsch

(1722–91)

Anna Luisa Karsch (1722–91)
etching by Daniel Chodowiecki
courtesy of Bildarchiv preussischer
Kulturbesitz, Berlin

Anna Luisa Dürbach was born on a farm near Crossen/Oder in northern Silesia. The poet's mother had been maidservant to the noblewoman who had raised her. Anna's father, Christian Dürbach, innkeeper, died in 1728, shortly after she had been taken to Posen by her great-uncle, who taught her to read and write, and with whom she remained until 1732. Before her uncle could teach her Latin as planned, Anna was summoned back by her mother who, having remarried, wanted ten-year-old Anna to care for the younger children. During the next six years Anna tended livestock and read novels and devotional literature borrowed from a neighbor. At sixteen she was married to a weaver named Hirsekorn, a man selected by her mother. Anna made her first poetic attempts in this period. After eleven years of marriage and three children she was divorced against her will by Hirsekorn, who had often beaten her and who finally drove her out of the house.

In 1749 she moved to the small town of Fraustadt (Posen) with her new husband, the tailor Karsch, an alcoholic unable to support the family. With her occasional poems, written to secure an income in view of her children's deprivation, she found patrons there and in the nearby larger city of Glogau, where she moved in 1755. As a favor to her one local nobleman arranged (illegally) for her husband's induction into the Prussian army (an effective termination of the marriage) while another, Baron von Kottwitz, enabled her to move in 1761 to Berlin, where she was celebrated as a great 'natural' poetic talent.

Of her seven children, only three lived into adulthood: one son was taken by Hirsekorn in the divorce settlement; another son and one daughter remained with her. Both this daughter, Karoline von Klenke (1754–1802), and a granddaughter, Wilhemine von Chézy (1783–1856), became writers.

Karsch earned her keep and spread her fame in Berlin by reading improvised poems at aristocratic parties. She was befriended by the poet Ludwig Gleim, who helped her publish her first volume of poetry in 1764, a tremendous success that secured her a modest income for the rest of her life. Karsch was romantically inclined to Gleim, but although he remained friendly and supportive, he did not reciprocate her deep-felt attachment. Major critics like M. Mendelssohn and J. G. Herder paid Karsch high tribute, yet they felt her poems were frequently spoiled by lack of polish or by the stilted rococo forms and imagery suggested by Gleim and others. In 1763 Karsch enjoyed an audience with Frederick the Great, who promised to have a house built for her. Not until 1789 under Frederick's successor was that house, in which the poet spent the last two years of her life, finally built.

Karsch's short autobiography and other letters, many to prominent people of her day, are written with verve and wit and provide a mirror of the times from the standpoint of a self-assertive lower-class woman. Though her first success was based on naive poems celebrating Frederick the Great's military victories, it is her autobiographical and nature poems that especially attract and still move the modern reader.

BIBLIOGRAPHY

Karsch's Works

Auserlesene Gedichte (1764). Reprinted Stuttgart: Metzler, 1966.

Neue Gedichte. Mietau & Leipzig, 1772.

Hausmann, Elisabeth, editor. *Die Karschin: Friedrich des Grossen Volksdichterin.*
    Ein Leben in Briefen. Frankfurt a. M.: Societätsverlag, 1933. Though limited
    basically to Karsch's letters to Gleim, this is the most extensive selection of

Karsch's letters published to date. It contains valuable historical background and very interesting historical illustrations.

Klenke, C. L. v., editor. *Gedichte. Von Anna Louisa Karschin geb. Dürbach.* 2nd edition. Berlin: F. Maurer, 1797. Karsch's daughter supplies a detailed biography of her mother (pp.3–127). She strives for objectivity and risks a number of criticisms of her mother's behavior and poems. Unlike Karsch's autobiography, this biography also covers the years from 1761 to the poet's death in 1791. Few good poems are included in the selections, but there are many that flatter the specific patrons who apparently financed this volume.

Wolf, Gerhard, editor. *O, mir entwischt nicht, was die Menschen fühlen; Anna Louisa Karschin: Gedichte und Briefe; Stimmen der Zeitgenossen* (Berlin: Der Morgen, 1981); also (with different subtitle) Frankfurt a. M.: Fischer, 1982. All in all, this is by far the most important volume on Karsch to date. The substantial interpretive essay by Wolf (pp.267–307) sees her in the context of her age and evaluates her poetry and letters positively. Included here are: Karsch's autobiography and other letters, an excellent selection of her poems, critical essays on her poetry by famous contemporaries, and an extensive bibliography.

Secondary Literature in English

Becker-Cantarino, Barbara. "Outsiders: Women in German Literary Culture of Absolutism." *Jahrbuch für Internationale Germanistik* 16.2. Bern: Peter Lang, 1985, pp.153ff. Introduction to Karsch's poem "Belloises Lebenslauf," which is read as "real" or "inner" biography tying personal experience to artistic expression.

Autobiographical Letter
to
Professor Sulzer[1]

Magdeburg, September 1, 1762

No one sang at my cradle about great ancestors or riches. My grandfather, in his rural cottage, was content to be given the title of an honest man. His master and fifteen or so of the surrounding towns joined in praising him furthermore as the best beer brewer in Silesia. He trained his son, who afterward would become my father, in this very same art, and that son redoubled his diligence in preparing the malt in order to equal the fame of his father. The years of his youth had already passed when he first became acquainted with my mother. She was the grandchild of a former bailiff and had been reared by a magnanimous country noblewoman. From her tenth through her twenty-seventh year my mother, in gratitude to this lady, attended her as maidservant, occupying in addition the posts of cook and controller of the pantry—three offices at once. My father redeemed her from these several posts; the lady provided her dowry, which my grandmother, since she was a poor widow with seven

1. Johann Georg Sulzer (1720–79) was a Swiss-born aesthetician, teacher, and critic who lived the latter half of his life in Berlin. As one of the editors of Karsch's first poetry volume he requested from her a short autobiography which he then used to write the introduction to the book. Her life story up to 1761 was set down in four letters to Sulzer, the first of which is translated here.

children, was unable to provide. My grandmother had reason to believe that her daughter would be happy, and she was not deceived. My father obtained a position as innkeeper at a dairy farm. The lord of the manor granted him certain emoluments in consideration of my mother. My father prepared the beverages required by travelers and was in charge of the kitchen so as to furnish meals for hungry wanderers; my mother was engaged at his side. He supported her in every task, and she often told me that I had the best and most affectionate father to thank for my existence.

Through no fault of my own I displaced my brother, the firstborn, from the maternal bosom. He did not live to see my arrival on December 1, 1722, and my mother refused me her kiss when she gazed upon me for the first time because I seemed to peer at her from behind a sullen brow. I was never the darling of her heart, and I think that her lack of attentiveness to me is to blame for the fact that I passed through the first years of life without being conscious of my existence. I must have survived six springs when my grandmother's brother visited our home to console himself for the loss of his wife. He asked that his sister come to manage his household for a year. My mother could not deny him his request though she also needed the services of an older woman who was a frugal housekeeper. It was resolved that my grandmother would make the trip. One day my great-uncle asked about the measures that were being taken to educate me. "Oh," said my mother, "the naughty child is supposed to be learning things, but I cannot seem to knock anything into her head."

My uncle proved to her the impossibility of such an undertaking in the loud din of the tavern. So he took me along. He lived in Poland. In his little abode he enjoyed the peace of old age and supported himself with the sum he had saved while employed as a bailiff. A most loving soul spoke in his every word of instruction, and within a month I was reading to him, with all fluency, Solomon's Proverbs. I began to consider what I read and, aflame with an indescribable eagerness, I pored incessantly over that book from which we acquire the basic precepts of our religion. My good uncle secretly rejoiced when I did so, yet he often tore me away from the book in order to take me for a walk through a thicket or flowery field. Both were on his property and gave him occasion to speak to me of the beauties of nature. I recounted to him everything I had read and asked him to explain those passages which were beyond my grasp. He was delighted to interpret for me, and I rewarded his gentle labors with a thousand little compliments. He himself had no children and his heart was all the more open, having been empty, as he took over the duties of a teacher. I expressed the desire that he might teach me to write; my grandmother set herself against this and employed all the eloquence at her disposal to destroy this resolution. But she did not succeed. I searched out a blackboard from some corner of the room and brought it to my kind uncle. He drew letters for me upon it, and I copied them after him. Soon I had taken up the pen, and when my parents once visited us I dashed toward them with paper in hand and exclaimed full of feeling: "Father, I know how to write!" My good father kissed me; I saw him no more, for he died but a few months after this visit. My mother did not long remain a widow. She gave her heart to another man and came in his company to visit us. "Dear Uncle," she said, "I have come to fetch my daughter! I will need her soon in the nursery and I fear her brains will be unsettled if she continues to pore night and day over books. She knows how to read and write; that is all a girl needs to know." "Yes," said my uncle, "that is true, but did she not want me to teach her as much Latin as I myself know? She displays a genuine desire for it and has already learned a great many vocabulary words by heart!" "That may be so," said my mother, "and I thank you for your goodwill, but she will not be going to a university." All my designs and dreams were in vain. My great-uncle gave me his blessing and I traveled away with his tears on my cheeks. My mother gave her second husband a son and I obtained the office of nursemaid.

I was ten years old; caring for my stepbrother was my sole occupation. I was miserable sitting at his cradle without any books, for in my birthplace at the dairy I found none. Finally the stormy disposition of my stepfather made it necessary for us to leave the dairy. We moved to Tirschtiegel, a small town in the principality of Glogau, not far from my birthplace. My parents became tenants at a manor farm and I began to herd cows. Early, before the sun had drunk the dew, my old economical grandmother milked three cows, which I then drove before me, proud of the contentment I felt as the lark proceeded with her continuing song above me. I enjoyed all the wonders of summer, and often invented little stories for myself, stories similar to the biblical tales. I built sandcastles, shored the walls up with pebbles and then razed my castles to the ground with wooden missiles. In my right hand I bore a staff, and in conversing with myself I became the head of an army! All the thistles were my enemies and with martial valor I slashed all their heads off. The feats of David and the Maccabees were my models and triumph was as sweet for me as it had been for them. After many important battles I was sitting one autumn day on the edge of a narrow stream when I caught sight of a boy on the other side of the water who was surrounded by several other herder children. He was reading to them and I flew to his side to augment the number of listeners. What good fortune for me! During the following days I drove my cattle in a roundabout way, through the river where it was shallowest; and I discovered the rapturous joy I had missed so long—books. I found Robinsons, errant knights, dialogues in the realm of the dead, ah, there were new worlds for me! Autumn passed far too quickly. I cried, thinking winter would provide no occasion to meet; but soon we resumed our meetings. As often as my mother sent me on errands I slipped into the house of the herder boy.

Our meetings did not long remain secret. My stepfather thundered at me because of my passion for reading! I hid my books in the discreet shadows of an elderberry bush and tried from time to time to steal into the garden so as to give sustenance to my soul. These clandestine pleasures lasted almost one year.

My mother delivered me into the service of a middle class girl so that I could practice sewing under her guidance. I was an apt pupil, for in one summer I had command of the various skills of the seamstress. My teacher however proved unfaithful to me; a propertied widower from Poland found his way into her life and married her. How indignant I was at my fate! Beloved books became my sole refuge and I had again forgotten that I was a girl when one day a splendid hunting sled stopped in front of our house. I recognized my sewing teacher despite the crimson taffeta-lined fur she was wearing. She jumped down from the sled, came toward us with the sprightliness of an Amazon, embraced my mother, and said that she desired to employ me as her companion. I will leave her eloquent plea unrecorded; suffice it to say that she was convincing and I had to prepare myself for the journey that same afternoon. I, who like a young Spanish damsel had a head full of adventures, agreed to everything. I kissed my mother and was proud to ride off in such a magnificent sled. Two hours before nightfall we arrived at our destination. During the first weeks my provisions were more than ample. After that, however, I suffered scarcity in all things. Famine had descended on the land due to flooding in the fields. People were apprehensive of impoverishment; my share of bread was parceled out to me in small bits. My mistress, provoked by bad treatment from her husband, took her revenge upon me. I was to act the part of servant, yet my twelve years did not supply me with sufficient strength for the task. Drawing water and pushing a wheelbarrow of grain up to the mill—these were my daily labors. It pleased the benevolent Creator to train me early in the school of patience so that I would submit myself in the future to more harrowing trials without a murmur.

My mother did not trouble herself about me; she had once again changed her place of residence. My dear old uncle was no longer alive; his sister, my grandmother, inherited his farm, which my parents then acquired by purchase. An unfortunate brother-in-law to my mother chanced to come by and deliver us this news. I seized this excellent opportunity and resolved to leave my mistress in order to appease my hunger at my mother's house. My mistress wept feigned tears at my departure. She had forebodings of my stepfather's wrath which, as it turned out, she had good reason to fear. I left all my remaining possessions with her and strode off keeping pace with my guide. In biblical times young Israelite girls walked in like manner and carried upon their shoulders the unleavened bread; I however carried in my expectant heart the hope of a better future and forgot all my miseries!

We put the first day's journey behind us as a rising thunderstorm brought on the night even before the sun had turned toward other earth dwellers. We took shelter under the roof of a fir tree. The following day found me brisk enough for another day of travel on foot. We were halfway into the forenoon when we found ourselves in a small forest. My traveling companion walked several steps ahead and brought out on his arm my aunt, a lean unhandsome woman who was half dead from fatigue and distress and who, because of the smoke the hut emitted, resembled a fortune-telling Egyptian [gypsy]. She welcomed him with good grace and brought out some warm goat milk in a wooden bowl for breakfast; we sat at the entrance to her cottage. This man was living like a second Robinson, secluded from all his fellow men. His house was half-submerged in the earth and roofed over with planks and patches of sod. His entire wealth consis-

ted of two goats and a few acres of land, which he worked with great difficulty, sowing one-half the acreage with barley and the other with kitchen
vegetables. In his younger days he had been something of a coxcomb; by
occupation he was a papermaker and in his imagination a prince. Pride
and ingratitude had made him poor, yet not docile, not humble. My good
aunt had to suffer with him the penalty of his imprudence. She seemed to
suppress her sighs so as not to displease her husband. He was continually
interjecting Charles XII[2] into his conversations. I do not know whether he
was born in Sweden or not; suffice it to say that he had convinced himself
that this inimitable warrior was still alive in some corner of the world and
would reappear at the proper time to mortify all his enemies.

We walked together to my parents' residence; it was hardly more than a
quarter mile away. My stepfather met me in the yard; you must permit me
to repeat his welcoming salutation: "Where the devil did you come from,
girl?" he howled with a savage laugh. I briefly recounted the recent events
in my life and he led me by the hand to my mother. So many words were
exchanged, so many reproaches regarding the all-too-hasty yielding to the
woman on the sled. My mother lamented my fate with her head shaking in
amazement and brought me the noon meal. I ate with the appetite of the
Prodigal Son and thanked Heaven that I would now be receiving unra-
tioned bread again. A few weeks later my mother presented her husband
with a third child, and I took my appointed place at the cradle once more.

My passion for reading seemed to be completely stifled here. All opportunity was lacking for it and my complaints were fruitless. My stepfather
believed I had changed for the better and heaped praise upon me. He went
so far as to begin to prefer me to my mother since the humble, adulatory
fashion in which I treated him appeased his haughtiness. Bitter quarrels occurred daily and I often cowered in mortal fear. Heavens, I was not aware
of what other great hardships awaited me in the future. Quivering with
fear, I implored my mother to hold her peace in order to prevent the misery
that would have resulted if this man had ever struck her. He had a propensity for sudden rage and I feared nothing less than murder. Nonetheless, in

2. Charles XII of Sweden (1682–1718), whose representatives had helped secure the Prot-
estants of Silesia some rights during the period of Habsburg (Catholic) rule, was famous for
his stern, uncompromising character and his overly ambitious wars.

all his malice he listened to reason, which dissuaded him from ill-treating his best friend, my mother. The underlying cause of most of the quarrels was the severity of those times of warfare and famine. My stepfather's affliction combined with the bogs of the region produced in him a raging fever. He felt an unbearable burning, demanded fresh water day and night, and then became bloated from drinking so much water. Complaining bitterly that he was to find his grave in such an obscure landcape, he expired.

Meanwhile my mother was not in the best of circumstances; a woman with five children, without provider, and unable to earn her bread is pitiable. Moreover, she was constantly ill. I was fifteen summers old yet I had not been instructed in things a woman ought to know. I was kept busy as a nursemaid, but was neglected as a young woman; a misfortune that will make itself felt all the days of one's life. My mother's disposition was as disagreeable as her body was infirm. There was not one day in the entire year when she was free of fever. I was to take charge of rearing the three children when I myself had need of rearing. The area we inhabited was poor and supported no one whose company could compensate me for that which was wanting in my upbringing. Blithely unconcerned about my future fate, I grew apace like a wild, uncut grapevine.

No one could ever have considered me beautiful; still, there appeared among the youths of the country one who sought my hand. My mother approached me one day with unusual cheerfulness and told me of a young man recently arrived whom she would present to me as my bridegroom. "He is handsome, of fine stature, and agreeable," she proclaimed. "My friends in Tirschtiegel had already informed me some time ago that he intended to become my son-in-law, and I have no objections." I marveled at this unexpected news. She ordered me to receive the stranger warmly. I obeyed and noticed indeed so many ingratiating things about him that I began to believe my mother's claims. I shall not detain you with any lengthy descriptions. He won my favor, and on the second visit undertaken for my sake, I obeyed my mother and him. He asked for my hand; my mother objected on account of my tender age; he countered her arguments. He moved my mother's heart; and she wanted to secure me a means of support. In a polite manner he presented me with two rings, which I cordially accepted. We thus became engaged, and in one month we were wed.

I became a wife knowing no other role to play than that of a nursemaid.

My husband did not inquire before the marriage about my paternal inheritance. He had refrained from doing so out of an affected high-mindedness, but in time I perceived that my dowry had been too small for him. Our natures did not harmonize at all; my tenderness, my overflowing heart and his greed for wealth made us far too dissimilar for a happy union to be possible. My only comfort lay in the books with which the herder boy still supplied me; for I was once again living in that town where cows had walked before me in the fields. This time, however, my days were full; either I was tugging at a board, carding prickly tufts of wool to prepare them for spinning, or I was incessantly winding yarn by hand for the swiftly turning weaving spool. Hundreds of religious songs were stored in my memory; my work did not prevent me from singing the loveliest of them. My selections were chiefly hymns of praise. I felt content singing them and wondered: would it be possible for me to compose a poem? I was not familiar with any poets except Johann Frank,[3] who had immortalized his name with a number of church hymns. His lyrics were favorites of mine and remnants of his secular poems floated through my mind at times. I found these as a child in my great-uncle's loft, covered with dust and pulled all asunder. There were wedding poems and a lot of mythology. I did not understand the contents but the poems struck me as beautiful nonetheless.[. . .]

I now decided to write poetry myself. I chose the melody of a given hymn, while seated at the murmuring spinning wheel, and repeated the verses I was presently composing until they were fixed in my memory.[. . .]

There was always a book lying under my child's pillow. I took it out whenever I performed the duties of nurse or acted as maid. I read the *Asiatische Banise,*[4] the Arabian stories in *A Thousand and One Nights,* and the Syrian-set novel *Aramena.*[5] Poems were scattered throughout these, but I did not care for their unnatural, constrained manner. I proudly resolved to invent something better than these novelists had invented. Then I found a volume full of rhapsodic poems. The rhymes flowed easily

3. 1618–77, author of several Lutheran hymn texts, such as "Jesu meine Freude" (Jesus my delight), which was used by Bach in his third motet.

4. The heroine of this gallant Baroque novel (1689) by Heinrich Anshelm von Ziegler (1663–97) is the historical Asian princess Banise.

5. A courtly Baroque novel by Anton Ulrich, Duke of Brunswick (1633–1714). The actual title is *Die durchlauchtige Syrerin Aramena* (Her Highness Aramena of Syria), 1669.

and helped give me courage. It was said that the author of the book was first inspired to compose poetry during the height of a fever. He had been destined for the pulpit, but when this rhyming enthusiasm fell upon him, his conversations and sermons were all transformed into poetry. [. . .] But my spirit was even more animated by the poems written by a young scholar who lived across the way.

I longed for more books and fewer tasks to occupy me. I had heard of Frederick's heroic deeds[6] and burned with ardor to sing them. The mere pronouncement of the King's name seemed to inflame me, but my thoughts did not soar high enough. My genius lay buried under a pile of stones, my arduous daily labors. Nothing, however, could completely extinguish the divine spark within me. My former life's companion might have encouraged me if he had been allowed to see into the future. A glance into that future would have instilled in him more indulgence and fair-mindedness regarding my passion for reading. Perhaps he would even have loved me, since the prospect of my fame would have flattered his vanity and made me more deserving in his eyes. It is very difficult to recall unpleasant events. I am going to maintain a discreet silence regarding all of them. My husband's character was not without its better side. He kept his affairs in order and was an enemy of all intemperance. He had the gift of being able to endear himself to everyone, but lacked the ability to be master of himself. It was not possible for him to know and understand my heart. Our partnership was not the gently corresponding trust and intimacy of two human beings created for each other.[. . .]

Translated from *Zeitgenossen. Ein biographisches Magazin*, volume 3, series 3 (Leipzig, 1831): 3–49.

6. The Prussian King Frederick II, the Great (1712–86) seized most of Silesia from Austria in 1742. During the Seven Years' War (1756–63) he kept Austria from reconquering it. Karsch, influenced by local worthies and noble patrons who were Protestant and enthusiastically pro-Prussian, composed many poems later in Frederick's honor.

Zorn auf den Krieg, als er zu lange währte (1764)

Mein ganzes Herze zürnt auf den, der in den Tagen
Der erstgeschaffenen Welt den ersten Mann erschlagen.
Mein Geist erschüttert sich für den, der einst zur Schlacht
Den ersten Pfeil gespitzt, das erste Schwert gemacht.
Schwarz ist aus Plutos Reich die Seele aufgestiegen,
Die es zuerst gewagt, zu morden und zu siegen.
Den zeugten Furien, der mit ergrimmtem Trieb
Die erste Kugel goss, das erste Pulver rieb,
Der hat die Menschlichkeit bestritten und bezwungen,
O, der hat die Natur selbst mit dem Schwert
    durchdrungen,
Der mit grausamer Müh den ersten Stahl gewetzt
Und an des Bruders Brust blutdürstig ihn gesetzt.
Du Geissel für die Welt, Krieg! Den die Gottheit sandte,
Weil der verblendete Mensch die Tugend frech verkannte,
Verlarvte Raserei, dein Fuss ist rauh und schwer,
Und wo er niedertritt, da wird von Blut ein Meer!

From Herybert Menzel, ed., *Das Lied der Karschin. Die Gedichte
(. . .) mit einem Bericht ihres Lebens* (Hamburg, 1938), 130–31.

Anger at War,
When It Lasted Too Long
(1764)

I loathe with all my heart the first of men who slew
A human fellow-being when the earth was new.
My spirit shrinks from him who for primeval raids
Made sharp the world's first arrow, honed the first of blades.
For sure that soul rose up from Hades black as sin
That first conceived the thought by murdering to win.
He was by Furies nurtured who with savage lust
First ground gunpowder, first a bullet cast.
He waged his war against all human kind and won,
Oh, he has maimed all Nature with his baneful gun.
He who was first to hone with evil toil the steel
To hold against his brother's throat with barbarous zeal.
Thou scourge, War, for the world! which the Almighty shook
When in his willful blindness Man the Good forsook;
Masked lunacy, thy foot is rough and weighs like lead,
And where it treads, a sea of blood is shed!

Lob der
Schwarzen Kirschen
(1792)

Des Weinstocks Saftgewächse ward
Von tausend Dichtern laut erhoben;
Warum will denn nach Sängerart
Kein Mensch die Kirsche loben?

O die karfunkelfarbne Frucht
In reifer Schönheit ward vor diesen
Unfehlbar von der Frau versucht,
Die Milton hat gepriesen.

Kein Apfel reizet so den Gaum
Und löschet so des Durstes Flammen;
Er mag gleich vom Chineser-Baum
In ächter Abkunft stammen.

Der ausgekochte Kirschensaft
Giebt aller Sommersuppen beste,
Verleiht der Leber neue Kraft
Und kühlt der Adern Äste;

Und wem das schreckliche Verboth
Des Arztes jeden Wein geraubet,
Der misch ihn mit der Kirsche roth
Dann ist er ihm erlaubet;

In Praise of
Black Cherries
(1792)

The grapevine's luscious fruit has known
The praise of bards in ardent throng;
Why has the cherry not been shown
Loud voices raised in song?

O fruit in lustrous ruby's guise,
You must, in ripest bloom unfaulted,
Have first been tried by Eden's prize,
Whom Milton once exalted.

No apples so the palate scent
Or flames of thirst allay,
And should they even claim descent
From orchards of Cathay.

Boiled juice of cherries is the giver
Of much the best of summer soups;
Endows with youthful strength the liver
And cools th' arterial loops.

Let him who has been barred from use
Of wine by snarling doctors
Dilute it with red cherry juice,
And banished are the proctors.

Und wäre seine Lunge wund,
Und seine ganze Brust durchgraben:
so darf sich doch sein matter Mund
Mit diesem Tranke laben.

Wenn ich den goldenen Rheinstrandwein
Und silbernen Champagner meide,
Dann Freunde mischt mir Kirschblut drein
Zur Aug- und Zungenweide:

Dann werd' ich eben so verführt,
Als Eva, die den Baum betrachtet,
so schön gewachsen und geziert,
Und nach der Frucht geschmachtet.

Ich trink und rufe dreymal hoch!
Ihr Dichter singt im Ernst und Scherze
Zu oft die Rose, singet doch
Einmal der Kirschen Schwärze!

From *Gedichte von Anna Louisa Karschin,
geb. Durbach. Nach der Dichterin Tode nebst
ihrem Lebenslauff herausgegeben von Ihrer
Tochter C. L. v. Kl[enke], geb. Karschin* (Berlin: gedruckt mit Vitericischen Schriften,
1792), 125–26.

However sore his stricken lung,
His breast ploughed up so deep.
Still from this drink his languid tongue
May healing solace reap.

If golden wine of Rhenish flood
And silvery Champagne I shun,
Then lace them, friends, with cherry blood,
Delight to eye and tongue.

Then am I lured from Virtue, much
As Eve the Wisdom Tree embraced
(So wondrous fair to sight and touch)
And longed its fruit to taste.

I drink—and thrice my cheer I raise!
Too often did you poets, merry
Or grave exalt the rose; now praise
The blackness of the cherry!

Introduction, bibliography, and translation by
JEANNINE BLACKWELL

Sophie von La Roche

(1730–1807)

Frau von LA ROCHE
geb. von Guttermann

Sophie von La Roche (1731–1807)
engraving by Brekenkamp, 1787
owned and reproduced by Schiller-
Nationalmuseum/Deutsches Literaturarchiv
Marbach am Neckar
courtesy of Schiller-Nationalmuseum

Sophie von La Roche, the first recognized and acclaimed woman novelist in Germany, was both a pioneer in the establishment of an independent women's literary public and a conservative monarchist opposed to full independence for women. The contradictions in her own literary and personal life embody those of her era: although she was considered the sentimental novelist par excellence until the end of the century, she rejected the love match as a basis for marriage and tried to arrange financially advantageous situations for her own children; a renowned author and part of the new nobility, she—as a widow with no pension—used her writings to support herself and her children from 1787 until her death; and last but certainly not least, although La Roche spoke and wrote French as her first language, the language of the educated court lady, she had to learn German orthography slowly and painfully in later life in order to reach the middle-class audience to whom her novels were addressed.

Marie Sophie Gutermann was born the first of thirteen children in an affluent and respected family. Little is known of her mother, Regina Barbara von Unold, who died when Sophie was seventeen. By age five, Sophie, her father's "little librarian" and a *Wunderkind*, had read the whole Bible; yet in spite of her keen intelligence and intellectual motivation, her father, Georg Friedrich Gutermann, a physician and later dean of the medical faculty at Augsburg, did not allow her to engage in serious studies. Instead, she was to perfect herself in traditional female accomplishments: French, dancing, sewing and cooking, painting, and music. After her engagement to an Italian physician was brutally ended by her father and her involvement with her distant cousin, the author Wieland, came to a sudden end, Sophie Gutermann was married off to the private secretary of the Duke of Stadion in Mainz, Georg Michael Frank (who later assumed the name La Roche). They received the nobility patent in 1774, well after both husband and wife were famous. As a courtier's wife, Sophie was to lead salon and dinner discussions and to learn the role of mediator and propagator of French, British, and, to some extent, German culture. In the course of their years in the Stadion entourage (1753–68), she bore eight children, five of whom survived infancy. Georg Michael La Roche's later career as chancellor of the principality of Trier was ended abruptly by political intrigue in 1780. His fall meant a withdrawal from court life in the turbulent years before the French Revolution; it also launched Sophie La Roche's career as self-supporting writer.

As early as 1771 Sophie La Roche published her *History of Lady Sternheim*, the first epistolary novel in German, and, according to some critics, the first German novel of Sentimentality. The book became a bestseller. La Roche was lauded as maternal muse by the fiery young Storm and Stress authors; *Sternheim* was noted for the adeptness with which the heroine fused Pietist introspection with bourgeois sentimentality, creating a heroine with a beautiful soul in an attractive body. "Sophia von Sternheim" was later to become known as "the female Werther."

While *Sternheim* assured La Roche of the continued support of her female readers, the enthusiasm of Goethe, Schiller, and Lenz was more short-lived. Their ideal of free love and freedom from tutelage clashed with La Roche's concept of rational happiness and reform through education. In fact, all of La Roche's twenty-eight books and her moral weekly, *Pomona for Germany's Daughters*, were designed to serve as tools for women's education that aimed at self-knowledge, self-love, and self-improvement. This supposedly conventional concept of "Bildung" caused La Roche to be cast into several confining roles that ignore or underrate her contribution as author: for literary historians, she has become one of the aging "beautiful souls" who inspired Goethe; she is known as mother of Maximiliane, one of Goethe's romantic interests; as the grandmother of

Clemens Brentano and Bettina von Arnim (whose book *Goethe's Correspondence with a Child* so shocked the literati of her time); and as inspiration for Wieland's pastorals. Only recently has a reevaluation of popular literature in the eighteenth century begun to do justice to La Roche's oeuvre.

Her thirty-year career as a self-supporting writer begins with *Rosalie's Letters* (1781). Here, as well as in her series of *Letters to Lina* and in most of her moral tales of the 1780s (including "Two Sisters"), La Roche creates a tension between the abuses of authority within the bourgeois family in the city and the idyllic countryside where class and religious dispute, as well as the subordination of women, are suspended. Behavioral reform rather than revolt, flight to the country rather than social conflict are her themes. The careful architectural, horticultural, and decorative detail of her country setting underscore her belief in the concrete possibility of this vision. All her narratives are in a sense practical guides for the creation of a female utopia.

The country idyll extends into her travel literature of the 1780s and 1790s. As one of the few upper-middle-class women traveling without male companions, La Roche opened a wide literary field to German women authors (see the travelogues by Johanna Schopenhauer, Therese Huber, Fanny Lewald, Luise Mühlbach, and many others). Her trips to England, Switzerland, Holland, and within Germany not only allowed her to do research for her works, they also promoted her writings and gave her a chance to meet the cultural leaders of her day. She overcame the geographic limits of her travels by writing travel fiction, for example in *Visitors to Lake Oneida* (1798).

In establishing so firmly the notion of a female sphere that was rural, domestic, and caring, La Roche not only created a space for women's fiction; she also indirectly contributed to the confinement of women authors to that sphere throughout much of the nineteenth century, a confinement she herself tried to subvert by describing her own intellectual growth in *My Writing Desk* (1799) and in the autobiographical essay in *Melusine's Summer Evenings* (1807). She also promoted the works of younger women authors, whom she found particularly vulnerable to questions of status: she published works by Karoline von Günderrode (in *Autumn Days*, 1805), Caroline von Wolzogen, Philippine Gatterer Engelhard, Sophie Albrecht,

Luise von Göchhausen, and Wilhelmine von Gersdorf (in *Pomona*), and she edited the autobiography of her deceased friend Friderica Baldinger (1791).

As influential as La Roche was in developing a German women's literary culture, her significance faded as she and her loyal reading public aged. While she continued to write works portraying sentimental yet enlightened characters inspired by virtue, charity, and noble self-interest, the female intellectual avant-garde gradually abandoned her. It was above all her rejection of the love match that distanced her from the younger "Romantic" generation, for whom romance, and no longer virtue and education, was the organizing principle of women's fiction. Yet her belief in the educability of humankind remained firm until her death in 1807—which went practically unnoticed in the turmoil surrounding French occupation.

BIBLIOGRAPHY

La Roche's Works

For a full list of La Roche's works and letters, see Jeannine Blackwell, "Sophie von La Roche," in *Dictionary of Literary Biography: The Age of Goethe*, edited by James Hardin and Christoph Schweitzer (New York: Bruccoli Clark and Gale, 1990).

Geschichte des Fräuleins von Sternheim. Von einer Freundin derselben aus Original-Papieren und anderen zuverlässigen Quellen gezogen. Leipzig: Weidmanns Erben und Reich, 1771. Recent editions have been published by Günter Häntzschel (Munich: Winkler, 1976) and by Barbara Becker-Cantarino (Stuttgart: Reclam, 1983).

Translations

The History of Lady Sophie Sternheim: Attempted from the German of Mr. Wieland. Translated by J. Collyer. London: T. Jones, 1776, which also appeared under the title: *Memoirs of Miss Sophy Sternheim.* 1786.

The Adventures of Miss Sophie Sternheim. From the German of Mr. Wieland. Translated by Elizabeth Harwood. Dublin: J. Beatty and C. Jackson, 1776.

Britt, Christa Baguss. *Sophie von La Roche's Sternheim: A Translation and Comparative Study.* Diss. Texas Tech Univ., 1985.

Rosaliens Briefe an ihre Freundin Marianne von St * *von der Verfasserin des Fräuleins von Sternheim*. 3 vols. Frankfurt and Altenburg, 1779–81.

Moralische Erzählungen im Geschmack Marmontel's. Mannheim, 1782.

Pomona für Teutschlands Töchter. 24 issues, Speyer, 1783–84. Reprint edited and with a preface by Jürgen Vorderstemann. 4 vols. London: Saur, 1988.

Die zwei Schwestern. Eine moralische Erzählung. Frankfurt, 1784.

Briefe an Lina. Mannheim, 1785. Continued as *Lina als Mutter*. Mannheim, 1795–97.

Neuere moralische Erzählungen. Altenburg: 1786.

Tagebuch einer Reise durch die Schweiz, von der Verfasserin von Rosaliens Briefen. Altenburg, 1787.

Journal einer Reise durch Frankreich. Altenburg: 1787.

Tagebuch einer Reise durch Holland und England, von der Verfasserin von Rosaliens Briefen. Offenbach: 1788. Part reprinted as *Niederrheinisches Tagebuch*. Edited with an introduction by Günter Elbin. Duisberg: Mercator, 1985. Translation of the England segment of the journey: *Sophie in London 1786: Being the Diary of Sophie von La Roche*. Translated with an introductory essay by Claire Williams. London: J. Cope, 1933.

Friderica Baldinger. *Lebensbeschreibungen von Friderica Baldinger, von ihr selbst verfasst*. Edited by Sophie von La Roche. Offenbach: 1791.

Erscheinungen am See Oneida. 3 vols. Leipzig: 1798.

Mein Schreibetisch. An Herrn G.R.P. in D. 2 vols. Leipzig: 1799.

Herbsttage. Leipzig: 1805.

Melusinens Sommerabende, von Sophie von La Roche. Edited by C. M. Wieland. Halle: 1806.

Recent Secondary Literature in English

For a full bibliography of secondary literature on La Roche, see the thorough study by Bernd Heidenreich, *Sophie von La Roche; eine Werkbiographie* (Frankfurt, Bern, and New York: Peter Lang, 1986), the well-organized selection of letters by Michael Maurer, *Ich bin mehr Herz als Kopf: Sophie von La Roche. Ein Lebensbild in Briefen* (Munich: Beck, 1983), and the biography by Blackwell mentioned above.

Craig, Charlotte. "Sophie von La Roche's Enlightened Anglophilia." *Germanic Notes* 8 (1977): 34–40.

Mielke, Andreas. "Sophie von La Roche: A Pioneering Novelist." *Modern Language Studies* 18 (1988): 112–19.

Petschauer, Peter. "Sophie von La Roche, Novelist between Reason and Emotion." *Germanic Review* 57 (1982): 70–77.

Lange, Victor. "Visitors to Lake Oneida: An Account of the Background of Sophie von La Roche's Novel *Erscheinungen am See Oneida*." In *Deutschlands literarisches Amerikabild: Neuere Forschungen zur Amerikarezeption der deutschen Literatur*. Edited by Alexander Ritter. Hildesheim: Georg Olms, 1977, pp.92–122.

Two Sisters

(1784)

Gentle Lady Birch[1] felt her health gradually declining. This did not disquiet her, though, because in her fullest years, whenever she had seen others carried to their graves, she was always reminded that once it would be her turn as well; and also because her life was such that she had nothing in the least to fear from death and eternity. For in her father's house she had been the model of a good daughter, and after her marriage the model of a wife and the most excellent of mothers. Her happy days, her good fortune, her joyful moods she met with thankfulness to God, with charity and modesty; the days of her sorrow, on the other hand, she bore with calm resignation and wisdom. Beauty and a good education had won her the love of Royal Privy Councillor Birch, a polite gentleman

1. In German, the "von" with a surname indicates the status of recently knighted lower nobility. Following Jane Austen's example in *Mansfield Park*, we decided to translate "Frau von Birke" and "Herr von Birke" as "Lady Birch" and "Sir George" or just plain "Birch." Like Austen with "Mr. Knightley," La Roche invents names with pastoral/gentrified connotations: Birke (=Birch); Goldbach (=Goldbrook), Adelwald (=Noblewood or Sterlingwood), Adelinde (=Noble Linden), or Einhausen (Lonehaven, which suggests a reduced space, a community of minds, a religious retreat, and is therefore a proper name for La Roche's pastoral idyll/utopian community). A similar desire for the utopian or the idyllic is apparent in names given by North American colonists to their new settlements: New Haven, New Harmony, Springfield, and so on. We have, whenever possible, tried to find a proper English equivalent for the German names.

of much intelligence and large fortune. She gave him several children, most of whom died; however, the youngest, a daughter whom she raised herself, could rightly be considered the most delightful of girls. The eighteen-year-old Laura was her father's pride and the joy of her mother, who hoped that her own beliefs and values would be passed on to her grandchildren through this daughter.

Lady Birch had postponed her trip to take the waters until after Laura's betrothal, since her daughter was to accompany her there, while her husband, their two sons, and Lord Goldbrook, beautiful Laura's fiancé, set out for the Prince's palace. For a long time Laura had been noticing that her mother often looked at her earnestly, was moved to tears, and pressed her hand or kissed her. To Laura these were forebodings that she would soon be losing her mother.

Some days after their arrival at the resort, Lady Birch gave her daughter a bundle of papers that she said had been sent to her by a friend. They were of interest, because the story and the painted miniature enclosed were the work of a seventeen-year-old who had described in them the life of his parents. Laura was immediately taken by the lovely picture of a small house and little garden that stood all alone on a wooded hill; and the four children who sat under a walnut tree reading books pleased her even more than the beautiful brushwork of the young artist. Eagerly she read the following story:

"For generations, beginning with one of our forefathers, all the sons of the Hahle family had been carpenters, because the father had always been able to instruct his sons himself, and thus train them thoroughly. Only my father did not want to become a carpenter; he wanted to study theology instead. Yet his mother, who loved him dearly, had great difficulty obtaining permission for him to attend Latin school. He studied so diligently that he was sent to a university at the town's expense and there became a learned and respected man. After his return home, his father died, and his mother had to feed her other children with a journeyman's help and could give little support to her beloved Heinrich; there was no employment in the town and she had no powerful friends. Then one day, when she was delivering a nice letterbox to a rich and distinguished man, the good woman resolved to take the diploma and references which Heinrich had brought home from the university and show them to the gentleman. Motherly love made her eloquent; the reports were very complimentary and, as it happened, the distinguished gentleman needed a tutor for his sons just then, and had Master Hahle called. My father's respectable appearance, his scholarship and his mastery of languages, his great skill at the piano and at miniature painting won him the praise of the wealthy man, who then hired him immediately as tutor, paid him well, and treated him with respect. That was a great stroke of good luck for my dear father under the circumstances, and it also gave him good prospects for the future. He fulfilled his duties so well that he was loved by the parents and all the relatives of his young charges. He noticed, however, that the father took exaggerated pride in his recently acquired aristocratic title, that he honored only those who shared his rank, and that his emotions were most vehement. The young boys told their tutor that they also had an older sister who was not loved by Papa, because she was so ugly and so headstrong—but that Mama always caressed her and visited her whenever Papa was away from home.

"When my father had worked in this position for some months and Sir George was away on a trip, he was summoned to the garden by Lady Birch, who expressed her satisfaction with his education of her sons and added that his character had won her complete trust. She then revealed to him the sufferings of her daughter and of her motherly heart:

" 'Adelinde is growing up; she has a good mind and much energy; I have taught her all the domestic feminine skills to sweeten her loneliness; but this is no longer enough to entertain her. I would therefore like you to arrange my sons' lessons so that whenever my husband is absent, you can teach my poor Adelinde piano and painting and provide her mind with other knowledge. I hope to accomplish two things by this: first, my sweet child might be happier in her lonely hours, and second, if she develops any of those brilliant talents that are now valued in young ladies in polite society, she might possibly gain her father's love, and both of them would be better off for it.'

"My father readily agreed to her request. He bought a beautiful piano and a set of paints with all the materials for sketching and painting, because the mother was willing to try anything to awaken Adelinde's interest in music and art. She succeeded, for Adelinde was delighted when she saw the small paintings my father had completed and heard him playing the piano. With tears of joy and thanks she kissed her mother's hands. Her industry was astonishing. My father admired her considerable achievements and rejoiced, together with the mother, in the certainty that Adelinde would win her father's heart in spite of his unfortunate pride. My father also taught her languages and history, and she made extraordinary progress in the arts and in anything else she undertook. She no longer had the slightest complaint; on the contrary: she was filled with such gentle good spirits and looked so cheerful, that when she was playing the piano or singing, her mother and my father often thought her beautiful. Years passed, and there was probably no one on earth happier than Adelinde's mother with her hopes for her daughter, and Adelinde with her acquired gifts of knowledge, her talents, and the quiet enjoyment of her teacher's sweet friendship. He seldom saw her alone, for the mother was always present at her lessons; neither did he seek it—least of all when he felt affection for Adelinde growing in his heart and when he noticed how much he now meant to her. He trembled for the poor girl and for himself because his soul was noble and virtuous. He did not want to kindle in Adelinde's heart a love that would bring her no happiness and her family no satisfaction. The thought that people would accuse him of having ensnared a rich man's daughter was repugnant to him; and/after Adelinde had given a demonstraton of her singing and playing and had shown them the many miniatures she had painted, he told the mother that it was now time to execute her plan and to present Adelinde to her father as a young lady who would grace any rank. The mother heeded his advice, and when she thought the right moment had come, she spoke about it to her daughter. Adelinde responded with a flood of tears; her mother could not stay with her until her weeping ended and therefore asked Mr. Hahle to go to her, to tell her the whole plan and to convince her to accept it. He found her quietly reading a book, but her piano was closed, the sheet music put away, her sketches and paints removed; and Adelinde looked at him with an expression of pain and ill-humor that he had never noticed in her before. He acted as if he had not seen it, and asked her softly why the piano was closed.

" 'Because it has become hateful to me, and because I wish I had never seen it.'

"My father was alarmed: 'My dear young lady—what is it?'

" 'An intense feeling of injustice suffered. I cannot bear the thought that nature and religion have no hold over my father, nor that the one thing that consoled me for his harshness and for the deprivation of every pleasure in life that a good child of tender parents is entitled to—that now this has become nothing more than an artful device for endearing me, his daughter, to my father, as a painter and a singer. Any stranger who had mastered these talents could achieve the same. And who? Oh who promises me that my skills, acquired through such bitter tears, that my long-lasting pain will receive the rewards which my mother hopes for?'

"My father struggled to remain calm, for he had never guessed that Adelinde had this adamant vein in her. He did not directly contradict her; he did not chastise her feelings, but he told her that prejudice had driven even the best people at all times to unjust actions, and that there was no other means to make them recognize their error than by showing them, through a gentle detour, the object of their hate in a light that is favorable to their own inclinations: he insisted that if goodness were to be achieved, it was even a duty of wise and good people not to confront the weaknesses of others and generously to overlook their shortcomings.

" 'Think, gracious Adelinde, of your joy when your father realizes all the accomplishments of his worthy daughter, when he drinks in the tribute that everyone who recognizes true learning and virtue will have to pay you! Should you not prefer to receive fatherly affection combined with respect because of your hard-won achievements, rather than because of a blind natural instinct? And your mother!—Oh, think what this happiness will mean to that worthy woman!'

"Adelinde wept: 'Oh, Mr. Hahle! all this is true for a heart open to justice and kindness. But I feel it will not affect my father. My learning, my talents, and the idea of my suffering will seem to him reproaches for his own unfairness. A proud man cannot bear reproach. Just wait: I will be made more miserable than I am now—but my mother,—and you, my friend and benefactor—you will perhaps suffer for it as well.'

"Her gaze, the touch of her hand at the words 'friend' and 'benefactor,' pierced my father's heart with foreboding. Yet he tried to show her the better side of the possible consequences saying:

" 'Your father's very egotism will protect you: it will flatter him too much to have such a daughter; he will love you as your mother does now.'

" 'Oh my dear teacher! You have more knowledge of humankind and of books than I, but I think that my intuition is sharper than yours in this matter. For you, for my mother, I was the object of sympathy and magnanimity. From your books I have learned that people love those to whom they do good, as we love the mirror that reflects our figures in full beauty,—yet at the same time, we tend to hate the person whose presence shows us the ugly, sinful side of our souls. Ask nature, ask humanity: does man love the witnesses of his flaws? My father has no ennobling pride, he has but vanity.'

"My father was surprised at the use Adelinde had made of his books, and he now valued her mind as he had valued her gentle heart and her artistic talents. Her mother appeared and, trembling with joy, embraced Adelinde as she said:

" 'Come, my child! Come! Give me your paintings, the beautiful selections you made from the books you have read! and you, my dear tutor! have the piano brought into the garden room. Adelinde, my dear! Your father is in a good mood and inclined to see and hear you.' With these words she took the paintbox and seized Adelinde's hand to lead her away.

" 'Oh, mother! what have you done?' Adelinde cried out and fell at her feet. 'Leave me here forever, both of you, and visit me, as you have done before: I want nothing else on earth. My father and the world can give me no greater happiness.'

"Her mother moaned and pleaded; my father tried to persuade her. Finally she gave in, gave both of them her hands, stood up, and said:

" 'I will! yes, I will follow you. You have both done so much for me, you deserve a sacrifice. But I am leaving a prison I loved because you made it beautiful for me—to encounter death. I feel it—weep for me, my friend! Weep! Adelinde will be in misery.'

"She leaned on my father, who really did weep. Her mother pulled her away, she turned, threw a kiss toward her room; my father stood, his hands folded.

" 'Pray for me!' she cried.

"Her mother went into her husband's study and Adelinde's heart pounded as she heard the abrupt sounds of her father's voice. Finally her mother beckoned her from the door. Her father sat to one side at a small table, where he had placed her miniature case and paintings in front of him, and glanced at her obliquely. She slowly approached leaning on the arm of her trembling mother, who beckoned her to kneel. Adelinde knelt down, her father's face reddened, and he grimaced precisely at the moment when Adelinde's heart was about to melt in tears. Her father's expression stopped her tears and stifled her breast; white as a sheet she sank onto her father's arm.—Her mother cried with fright, and the servants who were just then bringing the piano into the room, ran over to help the mother who was kneeling by Adelinde's side. Raging and angry the father looked up, pushed Adelinde's head away, overturned the table, and cursed the servants out of the room. Maternal tears revived Adelinde again, and then she was forced to hear from her father that he would never forgive her for this farce and that she should get out of his sight.

"Adelinde left, wringing her hands and looking about wildly. In the hall she ran into my father, who, called by the servants, was hurrying forward; he supported the swaying Adelinde and gazed at her with pain and tenderness. Fear, born of pride, drove her father to see if she would speak with anyone and possibly complain. When he saw the unfortunate girl with my father, he cried with the voice of a madman: 'Preacher! pack up and leave my house—or I will throw you out!'

"Adelinde locked herself in her room; my father wanted to speak and explain the situation as it really was. But the haughty man, who minutes before had been ashamed that the servants had seen his wife and daughter prostrate at his feet and who had feared their adverse conclusions about his harshness, was relieved to find here an excuse that would justify his behavior. He used his wife's revelation of his daughter's education and achievements against my father, whom he accused of having secretly seduced his child, and he let the servants know that this was the reason his wife and daughter had knelt before him.

"Adelinde fell severely ill and was taken to the country.

"My father immediately left the city, hoping he could appease the rage of unjustified pride after he had written down the truth of the whole affair and presented his own view of it. But hearing the truth simply proved to the harsh man that he had judged too quickly and unjustly. He tore my father's letter to pieces and even threatened my father's good mother until my father finally realized how much better Adelinde had understood the situation.

"Unfortunately, it was not an unfrequent occurrence that a tutor, hired to teach wisdom to the sons, would lead the daughter to folly. Therefore the story was believed. People of course thought that a girl kept in seclusion would easily be seduced by the flatteries of a man, and that a private tutor would then assume that the nobleman would have to give him a high position and wealth in return. People thought that Adelinde's father must have known her very well to keep her locked away, and the respect that he had always shown to Master Hahle served to affirm his actions. What were the wronged innocents supposed to do? Should the mother—should the daughter rise up and vindicate herself with long-winded stories to prove the father a liar?! Should my father do it? Oh no, he forgot about himself and his own unhappiness. Adelinde's and her mother's destiny were his sole concern. He wrote once more to that fearsome man:

" 'You have saved your own honor by destroying mine.—But in your lonely hours, you must admit my innocence in your own heart. I don't blame people if they think that a father cannot make his child miserable without a reason. I also forgive everyone who considers an apparently kind man of intellect incapable of mistreating his sons' tutor, whom he has respected, unless he has a significant reason,—all of this only proves that there are many people who could not act that way and who believe in fairness. I forgive even you. Passionate pride rules you in a tyrannical fashion, and as soon as you fear that something might dim your long-sought fame, then all your charitable feelings are stifled and you sacrifice truth and other people without further thought, but certainly not without eventual remorse. I tell myself that if the servants had not entered that room by coincidence just as your unhappy daughter lay at your feet, none of this would have happened.—Be assured that I will never contradict your version of the story. Innocence and kindness reside in my heart. As far as I am concerned, do me but one favor, for your own peace of mind. Make your deserving wife and your admirable daughter happy, and be satisfied with the misery of one family, my own.'

"This letter produced a mixed effect. Every syllable of truth outraged the man, but the quiet, firm character that he saw in it, and the impression that the letter made on him, made him fearful; he thought that other people would eventually believe a man who wrote in that way. So he treated his wife with much kindness and gave her the inheritance that Adelinde had received from her godmother, under the one condition that no one would ever mention Adelinde to him again.

"Adelinde was ill and pensive. She became indifferent to life; she only asked her mother to give her, before her death, news of the honest man who had been made unhappy for her sake. My father had not been heard from for some time. Finally he wrote to his mother that he had been employed as a village schoolmaster and was pleased to live far, far away from the haughty and so-called fortunate few of the upper class. Adelinde's health was so precarious that her mother thought it would be cruel to deny her anything that could alleviate her last bitter days. She therefore wrote to my father about her daughter's illness and dejected state, and asked him to inform Adelinde of his peace and well-being, so that the good child could end her days without grieving for him—and not hating her father. She received the following response:

" 'If reassuring Adelinde about my well-being can comfort her good heart, oh, please tell her that one could be happier than I only among the blessed souls of eternity, where she is going. The innocence and simplicity of my pupils makes them angels on earth compared to other people. My solitary house, the dear old mother of the deceased schoolmaster and her two grandchildren who live with me, my field, my meadow, the lovely birch grove and the small brook that flows past my vegetable garden, all of this harmonizes with the purity and grief in my heart. I was born in the house of a poor but pious craftsman, and will die in the cottage of a poor, pious schoolmaster.—No brilliance—no glory—no gold will lure me away.—I rejoice in the approaching death of the noble, mistreated Adelinde.—Her heavenly father will receive her with love!—Her memory is the sweetest thought that I brought here with me from the ranks of the genteel. A recounting of her fate and virtue will be the last work of my pen, and I want to live through the few days left to me after her death in such a way that this cherished martyr to prejudice will be glad to share her crown with me.—Along with the news of her departure for a better world, please send me her paints and her piano. I want to paint her ethereal figure, and my lonely little refuge will often echo with the songs she loved.'

"This letter, given to Adelinde, was to her like dew to the thirsting flower. She answered him herself:

" 'The assurance of your well-being and friendship are the last drops of joy I could taste. The thought of your suffering and possible indifference was the bitterest thing I ever experienced. Here is my piano, which I am giving you myself. May every touching and serious tone remind you of Adelinde's tender thanks for the edifying hours in which you shared your talents with me. May they remind you of my pure and virtuous love for you!—Blessed be the cottage in which you live! Blessed be the lonely refuge where you found peace from evil!—Oh, if only my fate had allowed me to share that cottage with you, as I will share my long-sought crown with you!!—'

"My father's pain was deep, but gentle. This last letter from dear Adelinde, her piano, her excerpts from great works—the wish that she could have shared his cottage with him—the images that he drew from this letter cannot be described, only felt. He grieved, and wished to live just long enough to visit her grave.

"It seemed to him that he had not heard from Adelinde's mother nor his own for a long time, when his brother-in-law, a respectable citizen in a small town, wrote him that his mother would like to see him once more before she died; that he should come to their house, where his mother was staying. He hurried, not only to fulfill his filial duty toward a good mother, but also because he hoped to find out something about Adelinde's death. He found his mother very ill, but happy to see him. After awhile she had everyone leave the room, to speak with her son in private. She asked about his affairs. He assured her that he lacked nothing.—About his health.—'I hope to die soon.'

" 'Oh, my son! And I wanted to secure your happiness through a good marriage.'

" 'God save me from that, dear mother! My heart has already gone on to eternity, and my hand will not touch any other woman's hand than that of my dying mother.'

" 'Dear son, I know where your heart is! Give me your hand.'

"He did, and she said: 'dear daughter, come!' A plainly dressed woman appeared from behind the curtain, weeping and faint. My father had anticipated something unusual, but not this: that he would see his Adelinde here, alive. But it was she, and she handed him an open letter that her father had written to her after her recovery:

" 'You are still alive—I wish you were at the end of the earth with your schoolmaster. Here is a marriage certificate, and this is the last word you will ever hear from your wronged father.'

"My father sank down onto a chair, worried and shocked. Adelinde supported him. He composed himself and took the trembling Adelinde by the hand:

" 'My God! what changes! Did you want . . . ?' Resolutely she answered:

" 'Yes! I will share your cottage—take me in, friend of my heart! Take one under your wing who has been rejected by pride and scorn, and let me forget all my sufferings and the world.'

" 'Come, Adelinde! Come into my arms, for you have long been in my heart. Virtue and moderation will make us happy.'

"His sick mother wept, and gave them her blessing. My father then said, pointing at her:

" 'Adelinde! My mother has now come to the end of all human disagreements and differences. As Klopstock says, before God, happiness and virtue are the same. With this one advantage, we will continue on our path, until we meet my poor pious mother again.'

"After this Adelinde explained that she had sent her mother this note and had written to her that if Hahle would accept this sad union, then she would be happy. Her mother had answered, that she was certain Adelinde's father wanted it so, and had let her know that they would speak about it with each other. There she had assured Adelinde that since her father had gone so far on the wrong path, a change of heart was now inconceivable.

" 'I would not want that anyway,' was Adelinde's reply. 'I am the innocent victim of an unjustified and cruel prejudice, but my father's peace of mind depends on it. Oh! may he find peace in his soul, as I will in the poor cottage of my virtuous friend. Love and the blessings of my good mother go with me. You have counted and shared the days of my troubles. My heart and my life will be happy now, because, dear Mother, my love has been devoted only to you and my dear teacher.'

"Her mother wept long and gave her her inheritance; when she heard that Adelinde would tell no one other than Mr. Hahle's mother, she was relieved that her husband would be spared public humiliation. She went to Adelinde, brought her the necessary plain dress of a middle-class girl, and led her to the town where the carpenter's widow lived. Adelinde went to her, revealed her identity, and was taken in and comforted warmly by this sensible woman. Adelinde asked the widow right away to tell her daughter that Adelinde was the betrothed of her brother, and that she wanted to nurse her future mother-in-law, which she did with more love and devotion than the woman could expect from her own child. Adelinde was sent mattresses and linens. She selected everything that the poor sick woman could possibly use and the daughter's husband had to write immediately to my father.

"Adelinde was married at the bedside of my pious grandmother, with whom they stayed until God took her away. Afterward they moved to the school, where my dear mother practiced with diligence and joy all the skills necessary for a commoner's household, skills she had learned in caring for my grandmother and working with the respectable old woman she met at the schoolhouse, who taught her how poor country folk keep house. Her mother visited her once, and wanted to die of grief when she saw her Adelinde in the small cottage. She demanded that my father seek better employment, but neither he nor my mother wanted it. The mother had a wing built onto the house, and thereafter they lived comfortably, and we children were instructed by the best of parents in everything one need know in order to be good and happy in any station.

"My father taught us children that the highest merit in the eyes of God and of society was to employ one's mind, one's virtue, and the work of one's hands usefully, and he thus showed us all the stages through which both the mighty and the lowly must go to acquire these merits. He particularly taught us what would be required of us by the station to which we would one day belong. He taught us boys the value of reputation and the satisfaction we might gain through knowledge and skill; he painted us pictures of the true happiness that we would encounter along the path, just as he showed us that most complaints and the greatest danger of losing the joy of life lay among people of the upper class. I am seventeen years old, and have now read for myself those books from which our father taught us, and I find that he had more wisdom than his books. For the natural history that he gave us was transformed in our souls to a deeply felt admiration and love of God; religious instruction became the knowledge of divine love for us and the thankful desire to show ourselves to be His worthy creations, by loving our neighbors as ourselves. He taught us languages together with the history of the lands in which they were spoken. The beauty

of the country surrounding our home made me a good student of miniature painting, as our nightingales made my older sister Lucie the best
singer. I have mathematical and philosophical knowledge and an honest
heart, like my father; I play the piano and I write like he does.

"Oh, if only this would move the beautiful and gracious bride of Lord
Goldbrook to hear the request of a boy of seventeen: that her husband's
uncle appoint my father to the position of village vicar, a position that will
become vacant after the impending death of our preacher. Then I would
continue running the school until the old schoolmaster's grandson reaches
the age of twenty, when my father could install him with the approval of
the whole community."

Laura dissolved into tears when she saw from this request that the story
was not a fictional one. She hurried with the notebook in hand to her
mother.

"Oh dear Mama! what have I read here? Are there really such men in
the world? What if Goldbrook turned out to be like that?" In speaking she
embraced her mother.

"No, no my child! I do not feel that you were meant to undergo such trials."

"Oh, but I want to put Goldbrook to the test," said Laura, "he must do
with his uncle's gift what I want, without asking why, and if he concedes to
this willingly, then I will love him with all my heart."

"What will you do with the money?"

"Once his good uncle has granted me the vicarage, I will give all the
money to the family, so that they will have something for the children in
the future and so that the excellent young man who has set all his hopes on
me can attend the university. When he returns, I will have more credibility
with the Goldbrook family and also with Papa, and then I will ask them to
find the young man a position, and perhaps—"

"Perhaps what, my dear? What?"

"Perhaps I can save enough of my pin money that I can give the daughter
a dowry and marry her off. For I would like to elevate Adelinde's children
once more: for that would console their mother about the loss of her birth-
right."

Lady Birch pressed Laura to her breast:

"Oh, my child! How happy your good heart makes me!"

"I am glad, Mama! But now I want to write quickly to my uncle, and you should lend me the servant who can ride so well. The one that Goldbrook gave me can serve you in the meantime; for I fear that other people will request the vicarage as well."

How happy this mother was over the yearnings in Laura's soul! Laura returned joyfully saying that the servant was already on his way and that she had promised him a good reward if he hurried. She counted on her fingers the days until he would return with the decree about the vicarage. "But," she continued, "then I want to see the young man himself. He must have a good and noble face and an air of innocence about him, for I see in his descriptions the spirit of a refined young man, yet also whole passages of touching simplicity."

She read to her mother those passages, and showed her the beauty of the miniature.

"Why didn't you send this painting to your uncle as well?"

"Oh, Mama! I was afraid he would treat the young man as an artist, possibly even commission a work from him or something like that; for I don't know Lord Sterlingwood very well as yet."

"But if you had included the story that touched you so deeply, something fortunate for the youth might have come out of it."

"But dear Mama! If Lord Sterlingwood had said it was just a sob story, as Papa sometimes does when he hears people talking, then he wouldn't even have a chance at the vicarage, and it might have wounded the poor people to know that their story was known to everyone. It might be that Adelinde's parents are still alive, and then they would have new sorrows."

This sensitivity to the peace of mind and good name of an oppressed family in the soul of her young Laura was the best reward for the efforts expended on her upbringing. Lady Birch embraced her with great tenderness, certain that she could depend on the benevolence and discretion of her daughter:

"Laura! Now I am the happiest mother in the world; I have a daughter who will use her happiness and wealth in the noblest way, just as my daughter Adelinde bears her undeserved misery with steadfastness and virtue."

Laura fell to her knees and clasped her hands: "Eternal God! Adelinde—your child?—my sister?—and my father hers?"

"Yes, my dear! It is all true—every syllable of the story is true."

Laura sobbed on her mother's lap. Finally she took her earrings off, pulled the diamond hairpins from her hair, and, full of noble rage, removed from her arm the bracelet which bore her father's image and placed it face down on the table. Her mother first watched her silently, then asked why she had done it.

"Oh, Mama! How can I see myself surrounded by diamonds and know my sister to be in such misery? How am I supposed to be able to look at my father without feeling my heart in a vise? I will keep your picture—and the picture of my Goldbrook—alone."

"To express your pain and your sympathy is certainly good, my child! But you must also do as your sister and her worthy husband did. In the midst of their troubles they sought out all the reasons that would excuse her father's great harshness. You, my dear Laura, are carried away and at this moment hate your father, who loves you so much, because you have learned of an act committed by him which goes against every inclination of your heart. Think, my child, that even the wisest and best person is always imperfect, and does something in passion which he later regrets. You have now forgotten everything good about your father and punished him as much as you could with his picture. You see, that is how he felt when Adelinde and her tutor had displeased him. He went as far as his powers could take him and—unfortunately!—they took him far."

Laura sighed and asked how long Adelinde had been banished from her paternal home:

"Soon it will be nineteen years, my dear! When I first visited them, you lay under my heart, and I think that the great sympathy in your soul grew from what I was feeling for Adelinde then. I was sad to become a mother again—I did not know that I was carrying an angel of mercy in my bosom. For Laura, my dear, you will some day be more for Adelinde and her children than I was able to be. I was poor and had no access to most of your father's wealth; I was constantly in submissive fear of my husband. But you are rich by birth; that in itself gives a woman much respect. Your Goldbrook has a soft, noble heart; he loves you tenderly and also has great wealth. You will be able to do much good."

"But dear Mama! How is it possible that an otherwise exemplary man like Papa can torture another person for nineteen years? Papa went to church and throughout all this he was reading scores of good books. What effect did religion and philosophy, which are so esteemed by men, have on him?"

Lady Birch had to smile when Laura raised this objection.

"My dear! You must always remember the weakness that clings to us all. For if this were not so, then all religion teachers would have to be angels, all lawyers just, and all philosophers wise. No beautiful soul would ever commit an ugly deed, and all who called themselves Christians would be good. But as we are, most of us are like certain families that have inherited titles from their forefathers and have the best prospects and claims to large estates, without actually owning a foot of land. Nothing pains me more about men than the great fuss they make over their philosophy, where they describe the beginning, process, and effect of great passion, and then condemn a poor overwhelmed man who can no longer control himself—as if he had strayed into error with calm and cold deliberation.—Oh, how many unhappy people would be saved and brought back to the path of goodness and beauty, if everyone acted like Hahle and took into account the effect of the passions on humanity, if people felt it a duty to forgive others as they forgive themselves."

"But there is something else I must say, Mama! You are so gentle, so endearingly good in everything you say and do. Papa loves you: couldn't you have found a moment in nineteen years, where you could have spoken movingly to Papa of your poor Adelinde?"

"Yes, my child! If your father's action had been caused by a drunken rage, or fury, or anger at an outside person—oh, I would have risked it and would have won. But how was I supposed to step up and prove how unjust vanity can make us, when facing the kind of haughtiness that never deserts a man once it has taken control? And then, what man thinks that he owes anything to his subjects? My Laura, you have a good mind that will improve, you will make observations, and some day you will find that your mother could not act in any other fashion.—Since your father was calmed and Adelinde content, since we are all equal before God, I no longer worried about the elevated station that Adelinde had lost, but rather about the welfare of her children. I put away everything I could save from my pin money and sent it from time to time to Lonehaven. But when my health began to give way, my worries for the dear creatures were doubled and I decided to leave them your heart and your love as the best legacy from their poor grandmother. And if death does not take me by surprise, I will speak for Adelinde on my dying day. If I can no longer do this, your father will find the story written in my hand along with a request that he take care of her family."

Laura wept softly but intensely at the thought of her mother's death and her sister's fate. She had the miniature before her. The small home, the family under the walnut tree affected her much differently than at her first glance that morning, when the landscape attracted her heart as pictures of simplicity and innocence always did. But now the woman who sat there spinning was her sister; the man who leaned against the tree was the honorable, unhappy father of her sister's children, and the young man sitting on a stump opposite him, with a sketchbook in his hand, was the youth who had asked her today to improve his parents' lot.

"Is Lonehaven far from here, dear Mama?"

"Why do you ask, Laura?"

"I would like to see my sister, and embrace her, weep with her, and assure her, before God, that as soon as I receive my inheritance I will share it with her. For now I am certain that Papa will give me my inheritance with the dowry, so that I will have a double portion because my sister is excluded."

Her mother embraced her: "Thanks and blessings on the heart of my sweet Laura! Yes, my child, you shall visit your sister with me, as soon as the servant returns. Meanwhile I will buy a few pieces of linen and good woolen cloth, the kind Adelinde loves for her children. I already have new music and flower bulbs for Lucia, and good vegetable seeds as well."

Thus passed the five days they had to wait for the servant's return. Laura had worried a thousand times that the vicarage would already have been given away, and how would she be able to look her sister in the face with those disappointed hopes? But she received the guarantee deed right away, together with the promise of a pay raise of 100 guilders and much praise from the congregation for their schoolmaster. Laura almost jumped into her mother's bath with glee. That same afternoon everything destined for Lonehaven was packed up, and Lady Birch began her journey with Laura the next morning. Laura had dressed very simply to avoid as much as possible all appearance of difference in wealth between her and her sister. She was deeply moved when her mother showed her the church spire in the village of Lonehaven and when they stopped silently at the edge of the forest to let the servants drive their carriage on. Laura and her mother walked to the schoolhouse on foot, just in time to see the farm children come swarming out. The poor girl could not go any farther: her knees trembled and big tears rolled down her cheeks. Suddenly Adelinde and her children came running through the garden that led to the forest. Speechless with joy, Adelinde embraced her dear mother, whom she had not seen in four years. Laura watched them, reached out for the hand of Lucia, an exquisite young girl, and fainted into her niece's arms. Hahle caught her, they carried her to a nearby bench beneath the walnut tree; as she recovered, her mother and her sister were crying over her, and Adelinde was astonished and touched when Laura embraced her, held her close, and cried out in a flood of tears:

"Oh, forgive me! I am innocent, I didn't know, never—nothing—"

"Dear child! what should I forgive you for? You have not done me any harm. Compose yourself, my angel, and let me enjoy the pleasure of seeing my sweet sister cheerful in my home!"

Laura, sobbing, said with folded hands: "Oh, thanks to God that I was not yet alive when my dear sister was banished from my father's house!"

"Dear, gentle Laura!" said Adelinde and kissed the tears of sisterly love from Laura's eyes and cheeks. "You have my thanks, dearest, for everything that you feel for me. But do not be disturbed: look at me—do I not enjoy the great gift of good health? Look at my husband, at my children— do not wisdom and innocence dwell in my home? The love of the best of mothers accompanied me here, where I came to make a simple, but real happiness my own, not without the approval of our Eternal Father. As long as I have lived in this little cottage, I have felt no pain in my soul and have enjoyed the delights of nature and virtue every hour. But this day has become one of the most hallowed ones, since I can embrace you, good, pure-hearted soul. Oh, my Laura! May God pour out his peace and blessings on all the years of your life, as He has done onto me! Believe me, you are embracing in me a happy sister!"

Then Laura looked up and smiled through her tears at Adelinde's children, on whom she was still leaning. The oldest son then said to his grandmother:

"Oh, I would like to paint my beautiful aunt and my good mother like this!"

Laura stood up, embraced the youth and gave him the vicarage deed: "Here, you worthy son of your parents, is the answer to your request."

The joy of that excellent young man lightened her mood and she walked around with Adelinde, who showed her all her possessions inside and outside the house and explained how content she was with her daily routine in the small, rural household:

"Today you will eat vegetables that I planted—these lovely fruit trees were raised by my husband—these flowers by the children, all of them magnificent creatures who have their father's heart—my three sons, who drink in his intellect like healthy plants drink in heaven's dew. And my Lucia—Laura, haven't you already noticed that she looks like our mother? Laura, someday I will pass Lucia on to you. Be a mother to her, when I no longer can! She is beautiful, and a child of the purest love. When you know her through and through, you will be happy that her heart is so close to your own."

Then they came back to their mother, who was in the mulberry arbor they had planted along the stream, under whose branches the young Hahles bathed every day. Then Adelinde's husband said that he had been appointed vicar, and that the wishes of the congregation and his son's request had accomplished it. He embraced his wife saying:

"My dear Adelinde will now be able to enjoy more wealth in her later years, and rejoice that the respect of our honest farmers and the childlike loyalty of our George were the cause of it all. Come, George! Let your mother give you her blessing as well! And Laura! Your heart—oh may God keep it pure and benevolent until it stops beating!"

How modestly and yet how delighted the upright youth stood there as he saw joy shining in the eyes of his parents, since their every glance at him was pure blessing and love—oh, only a mother, only a father who wish for such a son, only a youth who thinks but of his parents, can feel like that! For George Hahle had only been asked by his grandmother to write an excerpt of his parent's story and bring it to her secretly, because she had counted on Laura being moved by it and had wanted to use this feeling as a means to reveal the sisters to each other. George had seen Laura and had found her countenance so full of goodness that he appended the request for the vicarage without saying anything about it to his parents because the outcome was so uncertain. When his father asked him why he had given away the school, when the former had wanted to run it himself for three years, George blushed, but admitted immediately that he and his brothers were too young and spirited to spend their days alone. Therefore he had thought that within three years his worthy father would be known to the patron of the vicarage, who would then respond kindly to the request of an excellent father's good child. And then he would perform so very well that everyone would want to have a young Hahle from Lonehaven, and that way his brothers would find positions as well.

"Dear Lord," said Adelinde, "give every father of three sons a firstborn like our George!"

He kissed her hand and said, smiling: "Dear Mother! Your wish will be in vain, unless you can give that son my two parents as well."

Adelinde asked Laura: "Isn't Lonehaven a paradise, where hearts like this can grow?"

They ate lunch on a beautiful lawn in the small courtyard shadowed by the house, from which they could see the herd grazing on the other side of the brook. It delighted Laura to see the lovely fowl picking up the crumbs around the table and to see each of her sister's children call a chicken, let it perch on their hands, and feed it from their plates. Afterward they all strolled back to the walnut tree. Adelinde's piano was there. She played the last piece that she learned in her father's house, which she jokingly called her marching song. Laura played excellently as well, and then George played improvisations but soon began an aria which Lucia sang with a most graceful voice. Laura embraced and admired her. George and Lucia sang a duet, and finally father, mother, and the two younger boys joined in the chorus.

Before they had actually finished they heard applause and a shout of "bravo," as two gentlemen and a lady emerged from behind a bush. Laura and Lady Birch recognized Lord Sterlingwood and his sister Lady Goldbrook, but they did not recognize the attractive young man leaning on a tree some distance away. Laura and her mother were very shocked by this visit. Lord Sterlingwood smiled at the Hahle family gently and thoughtfully, and then went into the house with the teacher. Lady Goldbrook, however, sat down with Laura and her mother, telling them that

four men from the Lonehaven congregation had come to visit Lord Sterlingwood on the same day that Laura's eager plea had arrived. "The love
and respect that the people expressed for their schoolmaster had touched
him: for they could not stop talking about his fine sermons, his instruction
of their children, his goodness, diligence, and (dear Frau Hahle, do not
take this the wrong way!) about your poverty and your good children.
They insisted that you were such a smart woman and that you held the ancient schoolmaster's widow in great respect and called her mother. All this
they said without any order, but my brother found truth in the eloquence
of their hearts and all indications of extraordinary merit in Master Hahle.
One of them added at the end that it was certain that since Mr. Hahle's arrival, all the children had become better and the old folks smarter. My
brother assured them of the position of vicar. But they also asked for a salary raise: the congregation would contribute toward it, too. Naturally, my
brother thought he would find an extraordinary man: and since Laura
seemed to know him, he decided to visit her at the baths and then go on to
Lonehaven. We found she was no longer at the resort, and we followed you
here. The lovely singer and everything we saw aroused our deepest admiration and I now understand why my dear Laura intervened so eagerly on behalf of Mr. Hahle."

Adelinde and her mother were happy that the affair was seen in this
light. Laura asked about the stranger. "He is a young Englishman of great
wealth who had met my son during his travels and is now visiting him. He
was in my study when my brother told about the meeting with the peasants, and asked that I travel here. He wanted to come along, too, and when
he saw you, he was quick to point out that Mrs. Hahle and her daughter
dressed like pretty Quaker women in England."

Adelinde listened with inward pleasure to the praise given to her beloved husband and herself by their good country neighbors. Lucia went off
with her brothers into the garden where they were busy with the flowers.
Mr. Kent, as the stranger was called, walked there slowly and watched in
silence. Adelinde stood up and approached him, and he congratulated her
on her children and the beautiful setting of her house, observing her reflectively all the while. She asked him what he liked best about this rural solitude? He answered with gentle earnestness: "If I were a good friend of
yours, dear lady, I would tell you." "I imagine," she said pointing to the

stream and the forest, "that an Englishman might like to build a country home in that kind of landscape." "I would, not only for the landscape," he said, looking at Lucia. Adelinde was a bit too embarrassed to continue the conversation and signaled Lucia to leave. At that moment Lord Sterlingwood returned from the village with Adelinde's husband. Both of them looked pleased, and Sterlingwood embraced the three sons with much kindness:

"Good children! You shall all become my children, too, just keep following in the footsteps of your venerable father." He grasped Hahle's and Adelinde's hands:

"Worthy couple! I thank God for having planted your virtue in my own soil. I will see you again soon."

At that the carriages drove up. As they were walking toward the tree, Sterlingwood said: "Where is your enchanting daughter?" Hahle told George to look for her. It was a beautiful sight to see the magnificent pair of children approaching: George was carrying a green varnished coffee tray with glasses full of milk, each decorated with a charming garland of small meadow flowers, and Lucia a shallow basket full of bouquets from the garden. The two younger sons offered the strangers delicately cut sandwiches on plates surrounded by roses. Sterlingwood said softly to Adelinde, looking at Lucia: "This is the loveliest flower I ever saw." Upon farewell, she was embraced by the departing ladies, who all promised to return soon. Sterlingwood sat in the carriage alone with Lady Birch and Kent with the two ladies.

"Our Laura, my dear Lady Birch, has given me one of the happiest days of my life. For without her I would not have come here so quickly, and this family is as curious as it has become dear to me."

Lady Birch tried to hide her emotions saying: "You are not displeased with the man?"

"More than pleased—I admire him for living according to his principles, not just teaching them, and for his great knowledge and the steadfastness with which he denied me an explanation that I wanted very much—at the very moment when tears of gratitude for some improvements in the parish were rolling down his cheeks. Surely, this man and this woman who possess such noble, sublime morality, and yet are so simple, so content, so dear to the peasants, by their own testimony—these people came here from a different world and truly represent a model of human perfection. I freely told him what I had surmised. He answered: 'Yes, I came here with my wife in an unusual way, but virtue and innocence came along in our hearts. More than that I cannot and will never tell, because the story of our lives does not belong to us alone: for twenty years we have kept the secret in order to spare a fellow human being. We are at peace and I hope that a just man will forgive me, if I remain silent with him as well.' I embraced him and assured him that I would never ask again, but that he should make me his friend and put his oldest son, that magnificent youth, into my care—and either you or my sister Lady Goldbrook must take his daughter under her wing. She is a second Laura and if she one day falls in love with a worthy man, I will give her a dowry as if she were my own child. My nephew already knows that I have kept one-half of my wealth uncommitted. He is magnanimous and I am sure that he himself will do much good for this family."

Lady Birch wept—what else could she do? All this kindness had been brought about by her children for her children. Every virtue that she heard praised touched her deeply. Sterlingwood asked: "Have you known these people long? Do you know any details that I might learn or any way that I can serve these worthy people better? Oh, do tell me!" She cried harder and made a gesture with her head and hands that indicated: "please, spare me," and the noble man understood. "You know the secret, alas, keep it, because it is so sacred—but I would not have abused your trust." Both remained silent until their arrival at the baths, where Lady Birch stayed alone with Laura for the whole evening, telling her about the conversation. Laura was pleased with Sterlingwood's plan and also said that Lady Goldbrook had spoken of nothing else but those parents and those children; the young man had, however, not said a syllable. At dinner Sterlingwood spoke about it as well, and his sister seemed to be very pleased at the idea of taking Lucia into her care. Kent continued to be taciturn and distracted. Sterlingwood repeated the conversation with Hahle saying that he wanted to take the oldest son into his care. Breakfast the next morning was spent going over the events at Lonehaven, except that Mr. Kent did not join them. He appeared at lunch and sat deeply absorbed in pleasant thoughts. The following two days they saw him only late in the evening.

The fourth morning Lord Sterlingwood rode to Lonehaven and was very surprised to find Mr. Kent's servant standing with two horses in the forest. He asked him about his master. "He is with the shepherds in the meadow in peasant clothing and he won't be back until dark, sir." Sterlingwood was taken aback, and hurried toward the schoolhouse. George met him with a letter that he had meant to deliver to him at the baths. In this letter Hahle asked him to confront Mr. Kent about his spending time in the forest and in the meadows, as it was very painful to him and his wife to have to worry about their Lucia's possible seduction. Sterlingwood became angry and assured the parents of his total support. From the yard he himself noticed the young peasant on the bank of the small stream across from the school, and in the evening he met Mr. Kent on the way home. They rode along for some time without speaking. Finally, close to the resort town, Sterlingwood suggested that they dismount and walk the rest of the way. Kent agreed, and Sterlingwood told him straight away what he had just promised Lucia's parents. Kent admitted that the splendid girl had made an extraordinary impression on him, that he had only wanted to see her more often in her rural innocence and freedom, but that he decided yesterday to ask for her hand in marriage when he saw her sitting on the garden steps between two peasant children whom she was teaching the alphabet. Never would he have noticed this gentleness, this expression of her charitable heart, never would he have believed it, if others had been present.

Sterlingwood stared at him: "You—Lucia as your wife?"

"Yes, for I come from a country where virtue and beauty count as much as title and dowry. If you will help me to win the affection of the parents and their daughter, you will make me a happy man. I am independent and can therefore live where I choose. Give me the land around the schoolhouse! I want to build a house there for myself and my Lucia."

Sterlingwood was happy beyond belief at this declaration. He promised him right away to go to Lonehaven the next morning and to speak for him but insisted that Kent should not return there until the parents had been reassured. Kent agreed to everything. Sterlingwood went to Lady Birch:

"You are concerned about the Hahle family. It will be a pleasure for you to learn that Mr. Kent has asked for our charming Lucia's hand, and that I will go to Lonehaven tomorrow as his mediator. He wants to build a house there and in the meantime I will give him my own to live in."

Lady Birch dissolved in tears of joy. "Is this possible? Is it not a dream?" Laura, on the other hand, knelt before her uncle and kissed his hand: "Oh my noble, good uncle! If you will do this for my sis . . ." but she went abruptly silent and looked fearfully at her mother, who appeared highly embarrassed and shaken.

Sterlingwood observed them silently a few moments. Finally he said: "Dear Laura! The overflowing joy of your good heart has revealed to me a secret that I already sensed yesterday from the tears of your worthy mother. Dear noble and excellent lady! Open your heart to me! Is Mrs. Hahle not your daughter, who was banished from her paternal home? Let me assure you that every syllable of your secret will be sacred to me."

Lady Birch took a packet of papers from her secretary and gave them to Lord Sterlingwood: "You deserve my trust. Read what my husband is supposed to read after my death, and what Laura did, before she could hope to open up her heart to the most honorable of husbands."

Sterlingwood took it: "I will leave immediately, dearest lady! One can never discover soon enough that truth which will help rescue innocence."—In his room he read through everything and was full of respect and sympathy.—He thanked God for having been chosen to end the misery of these worthy people, and immediately devised a plan to use this very desirable marriage to Mr. Kent to make haughty old Birch realize the injustice of his hatred. He gave the story to Mr. Kent to read, too, because he sensed from the young man's noble heart that he would then stand by his union with Lucia all the more firmly. And that is what happened, for Kent wanted to go immediately to Lonehaven to apologize to the parents and, with their permission, seek to win Lucia over.

They came quietly into the schoolhouse just as the family was eating a small breakfast. Lucia stood next to the old woman and held the tea saucer to her mouth with so much childlike love and care in her lovely face that even Sterlingwood admired her, while Kent, younger and faster, hurried toward her, knelt down, and kissed the hem of her skirt. Lucia looked at him with deep feeling, her father, in contrast, with serious preoccupation. Kent saw it: "Oh, forgive me! What else could I do but kneel in front of this angel!"

Lucia turned, blushing, toward her mother who took her by the hand and led her away. Kent went into the garden to the tree that was his first friend in Lonehaven. Sterlingwood asked to speak with Mr. Hahle in private and revealed to him the honest young man's intentions. Hahle became very pensive and was deeply moved, opened a window and looked at the heavens with tears in his eyes: "Eternal Father! What a gift, what a blessing for my child! Lord Sterlingwood! It is of course impossible that you are deceiving me. Please accept the blessing of a faithful, burdened father—for everything that you have done! I can say no more—for—oh! twenty years of worry concealed inside—to be lifted up, such a wealth of goodness!—Oh, Adelinde, this is the reward for your sufferings!"

He bent toward Sterlingwood, who embraced him.

"Dear friend! Do you know how happy I am to be the instrument of your consolation? Bless Laura for a heart so soft that she let slip the name of her sister!"

Hahle drew back, shaken, and sighed.

"Be calm, noble sufferer! Rest assured that God wanted to put an end to all this. Grant me the joy of being the means by which it will happen and now come, let us comfort and calm Lucia and Adelinde! Go to them—I will go to Kent, he is a worthy young man."

He found him leaning against the tree, embracing it. Sadly he looked at Sterlingwood who offered him his hand and gave him hope. They sat down to talk about everything, until they saw Mr. Hahle hurrying toward Sterlingwood:

"Thank Heaven," said the first, "that Mr. Kent is an honest man: otherwise my Lucia would now be miserable, for she loves him indeed."

Joyfully, Sterlingwood asked: "Is that true?"

"I went to her and found her crying at her mother's breast as she had never cried before. She would not speak until I said: 'Oh, I wish I had never seen this young stranger!' She answered quickly: 'Oh, Father! that man who loves goodness so much?' Blushing, she looked at me and embraced her mother again. Tell me, Lord Sterlingwood, what besides true love would make her defend the stranger to her father? Oh, how quickly the sweet poison of admiration and praise takes effect!"

"You good, understanding father! I respect your principles in this as in other matters. You are right: great praise is just as dangerous to the innocence of our daughters as to the modesty of our young men. But now that you are convinced that a virtuous and rich young man has won Lucia's affection, and since love brought you and Adelinde here in the first place, then let your daughter indulge in love as well."

"Yes, since the young man's love is pure, I give it my blessing with peace of mind. But tell me: how in the world could the honest denizen of this cottage have thought that his daughter could love a noble, wealthy man without encountering misery?"

"That would be true for thousands among the rich, but Kent is an exception among them, just as you were among the young men of your station. Now let a just reward go to the efforts of a rich man, as it is due to the virtue of your cottage as well."

"Kent! Come here and reveal your soul to Lucia's father."

Kent jumped up from his chair and hurried to take Mr. Hahle's hand:

"Forgive me! I realize that I neglected to show in front of your whole family that love of which I had not yet spoken, and which I had not yet tested. But since the day before yesterday Lucia has been my chosen bride. I felt and thought nothing else and when I saw her in the full brilliance of beauty and youth, holding the cup for a poor weak woman to drink, like an angel—oh then—Mr. Hahle! even in the midst of the splendid, seductive world my heart has remained open to every virtuous emotion. You do not know how tiring splendor and luxury can eventually become for a good soul. I met young Goldbrook while he was traveling and found in him a kindred spirit. I promised to visit him after the death of my father; his uncle's excellent character held me there longer than I had anticipated. I was present when Lord Sterlingwood explained with deep feeling everything that he had heard of you and how eagerly he wanted to see you and your family. Lady Goldbrook had the same desire to see this model of active virtue. My heart and good luck drew me here as well, but your venerable age, your serious occupations, the daily habit of seeing this cottage and its delightful environment, your distance from the world of artifice— and, I might add, a father's eye kept you from understanding the overwhelming delight that made me beside myself with love as I stood here at the tree, looking at the countryside and at you all and hearing Lucia sing— oh, dear father, you cannot feel what was happening inside my heart! Ask your wife, ask Sterlingwood—if you could only see here how I responded! (He bared his breast.) I wish I could show you the musings of my conscience as they lie bare before God's eyes!—You would take this poor stranger into your home, you would permit Lucia to regard me above all as a friend of her father and her virtue and then, if she found me pleasing, I would be made happy through her love."

Hahle had listened with deep contentment. He thanked God that He had directed the pure love of an unspoiled youth to his Lucia. He marveled at the path his own fate had taken.

"A coincidence that led Sir George's servants into the room at an inopportune time made me and Adelinde unhappy for so many years; a coincidence led a stranger into the Goldbrook home, just at the moment when I was being spoken of favorably. An excess of the passion of wounded pride caused my sudden misery; an excess of the noble passion of benevolence and love caused my sudden good fortune. Steadfast manly virtue! You have led me through care-ridden trials, to you I owe thanks for their resolution!"

He embraced Mr. Kent and said to him:

"I will take you into my paternal heart and my cottage, as you desire. God witnesses our union and I shall praise His Providence forever. I want to speak with Lucia, my son! She is crying. She is crying because of you—oh, if you were not so honest, how unhappy my child would have become!"

Kent embraced him. He could not speak. Hahle went quickly into the house and Kent said to himself: "She is weeping because of me? Oh, Lucia, never, never again will you need to weep for me, except for when I die, die with our love still strong."

He put his arms around the tree where he had leaned when he saw the family for the first time. Sterlingwood came and called to him: "Good tidings, young man! For us both! We are the object of the blessings of these worthy people, and Lucia loves you. I went to her and her mother. I asked gently why she was crying, and added that you were terribly sorry for having given her and her parents disquiet and that she should not be angry at you. 'Oh, I am not angry, I saw all too clearly that Mr. Kent praised me only because of my good heart, but the alarm of my dear parents broke my heart. They were afraid of Mr. Kent, and that hurt me.' I reassured the daughter and her mother that you loved virtue above all else and honored it in every station and every form. I then had us invited to lunch, and Lucia flew into the kitchen like a bird. This distraction will do her good. And while I was still discussing a few things with her mother, her father came in and I hurried here to share my thoughts with you. As early as yesterday, I sent an order to my home to have bedding and household items brought here and today I had the old castle cleaned out and scrubbed. My sister, you, and I will want to live here for some time. Then you can continue your courtship of Lucia. Goldbrook will return soon as well, and Lonehaven will become a paradise that we have earned."

Kent was perfectly content and he, in turn, described his plans to Sterlingwood. Hahle's sons brought a table and set it. Their father and mother came out, and Kent was introduced to Adelinde as their son. Only Lucia and her brother were not supposed to know it yet: the enchanting girl served the soup and her father told her that Mr. Kent was their friend. The simple country food was eaten with great joy.

Toward evening, the two friends departed. Kent asked for permission to return the next day, and it was given. Lady Birch had been uneasy the whole day; now she was much relieved when Sterlingwood told her how the visit had ended. He departed early the next day, and George appeared with a long letter from his parents to Lady Birch, who no longer felt the least ache or pain from her illness. Sterlingwood immediately visited Laura's father, who had returned from court, and told him that he wanted to spend a few days in the country before the betrothal of his nephew, so that in the meantime the preparations for the betrothal ceremony could be made in both houses.

"You should come along, Birch!"

"When?"

"In two days."

"But then I will be finishing the paperwork—don't you want to see how I am taking care of my Laura's dowry?"

"I am certain that you will do it magnanimously.—But don't do any harm to your other children by giving her too large a share!"

Struck by this statement and by Sterlingwood's serious tone, Birch collected himself and said:

"There, read this as well, it is a kind of last will. You will see that my sons have enough and that my wife, should she survive me, will be provided for as suits her rank."

Sterlingwood read and acknowledged that everything was well done and in the best order. "But," he said, while moving his chair closer to Birch and taking him by the hand, "doesn't your otherwise fair heart speak on Adelinde's behalf at all?"

Birch pulled his hand away and rose:

"Oh! Do not mention her name!—She has what she deserves."

"Certainly not—for then she and her magnificent children would not be poor."

Birch glowered, ready to speak heatedly about Hahle. Yet Sterlingwood remained cold, saying: "Listen to me. Nature has given you many noble qualities: you are a highly respected man—but your vehement temper is a heavy counterweight. Because of it you have condemned Adelinde to misery, during which she was miraculously maintained only by her virtue and the support of the Almighty. I honor Adelinde and her husband as the most virtuous people I have ever met. I esteem you as well, you know that, but you must clean this stain from your life: the greatest man can err for awhile, but the noble man lifts himself up, and acts justly toward his fellow men, even toward his enemies. Birch, look into your heart and become my relation through your principles, as you will be through your Laura!"

Birch was somewhat taken aback, but his pride found support in the thought that a great man can also err, and he said with true nobility: "Yes, I was on the wrong path. Do not scorn me! I want to get back: I want to be just toward my Adelinde—just tell me, has she complained about me? Has her husband?"

"No, neither of them has said a syllable—I swear it."

"So how then do you know her story?"

"I had to hear about it when I requested that Mr. Hahle give his lovely daughter in marriage to our young Englishman."

"What? Mr. Kent is marrying Adelinde's daughter?"

"Yes, and he would take her even if he were a duke. My sister wants to take her in as a daughter and I wanted to give her a dowry."

"Where then are they living? Where did you see the family?"

"At my estate Lonehaven, where I will be going with my nephew next week; don't you want to come along?"

"Certainly! But now I have to write another will!"

"That is not necessary, for Goldbrook will share Laura's dowry with Adelinde."

At that Birch tore up all his papers. Sterlingwood observed him in silence. Birch said: "Is it not true—you respect me as an honorable man, and believe that I keep my word even if the papers are torn to pieces?"

"Of course, and all the more, since you have now returned once again to nature and just kindness. Consider my reproaches as the greatest proof of my friendship, I know the joys of benevolence, I would like to have enjoyed my Hahles alone, but a father should experience and grant the joy of reconciliation."

They traveled to Lonehaven on the designated day. Sterlingwood arrived at the castle that had been made ready for them and then they took a shortcut to the schoolhouse.

Sterlingwood left Birch at the moss-covered bench. He hurried into the house to fetch Adelinde, whom he led to her father. Birch rose, but fell back again trembling—Adelinde embraced his knees, and he kissed her, speechless. Hahle, along with his three sons and Lucia, stood watching. Birch glanced up, and said in a broken voice:

"Oh, children! Forget everything—everything!"

"With all our hearts!" was their answer.

Adelinde showed and named for him her children; Birch said that he was not surprised that the daughter was named Lucia, after his wife, "But the first son George after me?"

"You were still my father!"

Touched, he said: "No, Adelinde! I was not—but I want to be—believe me, children," and he extended his hands to Adelinde and her husband, who kissed them.

"Adelinde, were you here all the time?"

"Yes, father, and it is a happy piece of earth." With tears streaming down his face, he wanted to interrupt her. "My children grew up healthy for that reason, and you, my father, have come here."

Soon afterward the others came from the baths to visit them. Birch walked toward his wife with Adelinde on one arm and Lucia on the other. She rushed with wide open arms to him and embraced him:

"Oh, now I can die happy. May God reward you, my dear, for your noble deed."

Kent kissed Lucia's hand and Sterlingwood led him to Sir George as the bridegroom of his granddaughter. Everyone was happy, and toward evening they all went to the castle, where the main hall was beautifully lit. Birch embraced Sterlingwood and thanked him for awakening the desire for reconciliation in him: "a stone has been lifted from my breast. For only at the beginning did revenge make me happy. Often, very often, it weighed me down here—but for the last hour I have been genuinely happy. My Laura loves me twice as much as I thought, and Adelinde seems to as well. She is a proper wife."

Sterlingwood and Hahle withdrew for a few moments. Laura and Lucia were gone as well, but soon Sterlingwood returned to the hall. Everyone felt that he was the source of their joy, and surrounded him, as if drawn by an invisible power. He enjoyed at this moment the bliss of a true friend of humankind who has made others happy. A tear shone in his eye. Everyone was silent as he began to speak: "I look with unspeakable satisfaction on your friendship for me and your contentment. Let us make this day fully sacred. Kent! Goldbrook! You love your worthy brides. You have your paternal blessings. Come, my dear young men! I want to lead you to receive the blessings of the church as well."

He took them both by the hand and went to the double doors which were opened instantly. Mr. Hahle, in his ministerial garb, stood on a raised platform covered with a beautiful carpet; Laura and Lucia, wearing white dresses and pearls, stood next to him. Everyone was surprised. The two mothers pushed forward to their daughters, who knelt down and asked for their blessing.

"Father Birch!" Sterlingwood called out, "will you give your daughter Laura to my nephew?—and I give my—daughter Lucia to his friend."

And so the lovers were united before anyone could even give it a thought. After the embraces and congratulations had been exchanged, the noble, dear man said:

"Now children! We have passed beyond all the thistles and thorns of ceremony and splendor. Tomorrow we will give to the poor of the church the same amount we would have wasted in vain display."

Everyone was absolutely happy; Adelinde received the same dowry as Laura; Birch took George Hahle with him; Kent bought Lonehaven for himself and his Lucia, and every year Laura came with her husband to celebrate the anniversary of that memorable day that had united her with Adelinde and with Goldbrook. Sterlingwood spent his later years with Hahle, on whose sons he bestowed part of his possessions.

Virtue! Active virtue! You can be found in all stations and circumstances. One can be an Adelinde in misfortune, and a Laura in good fortune.

Translation of "Zwei Schwestern," in *Moralische Erzählungen*, vol.1, 3rd improved and expanded edition (Mannheim: Bender, 1850), 169–236.

Introduction and bibliography by
RUTH P. DAWSON

Translation by
WALTER ARNDT

Philippine Gatterer Engelhard

(1756–1831)

Philippine Gatterer Engelhard (1756–1831)
painting by Johann Heinrich Tischbein
courtesy of Sächsische Landesbibliothek, Dresden

hilippine Engelhard née Gatterer was one of the best known and best loved German women poets of the eighteenth century. Her poetry often constitutes a celebration of herself, though in conventional and complacent terms that make her writing very different from the eccentric and expansive egotism other writers demonstrated a century later. She wrote frequently about her own experiences, fitting them into the framework of her times. Notes of protest occur often in the poems but are not followed by ideas on how to promote change. In fact, the very characteristics that made her a favorite among women readers of her day—her endorsement of conventional morality, her satisfaction with her station, and her self-righteousness—detract from the readability of many of her poems in ours.

She was born on October 21, 1756, the third of fifteen children. While she was still an infant, her father, Johann Christoph Gatterer (1727–99), moved his family to Göttingen, where he became a famous professor of history. Her mother remains a dim figure, unnamed and rarely referred to. As she was growing up, Philippine and the sisters close to her in age received an education—partly at a "French school"—that was considered good by the usual standards of education for girls but not distinguished. It included no study of literature, for example, so that even after her first poems were published Philippine did not know what iambic verse was.

During her times, Göttingen was home to a cluster of extraordinary young women. Thus Philippine knew Therese Heyne (later Forster, then Huber); Caroline Michaelis (first Böhmer, then Schlegel, and finally Schelling); Dorothea Schlözer (later Rodde), the first woman to be awarded a degree from the University of Göttingen—without being allowed to attend classes there; Friderica Baldinger, and Dorothea Wehrs, all of whom eventually became noted at least in part for their writing. Years later Engelhard was still cultivating connections with distinguished women such as the writers Sophie von La Roche, Elise von der Recke (after whom she named one of her daughters), and Sophie Mereau.

Gatterer-Engelhard's career as a poet follows a pattern similar to that of other women of her time. After several years of secretly writing poetry, the young woman shared some of her work with a friendly editor who promptly published several of the pieces under a female pseudonym. When rumors of her authorship began to circulate, she confessed the truth to her family. Her father was pleased and her mother worried, because being a published writer was so audacious for a woman that it could jeopardize her chances of marriage. Still, Philippine, who was proud to be an untrained and unaided "natural poet," decided to publish her first collection, which was well received. Her mother's fears proved unfounded. Philippine's second collection appeared two years after her marriage at age twenty-four to an official in the bureaucracy of Hesse.

Gatterer-Engelhard's literary productivity did not prosper in marriage, especially once the poet was bearing and rearing ten children (all of whom survived to adulthood). In 1787 and 1789 she published short collections of verse for children. By 1790, even the act of submitting work to periodicals had become too difficult. Finally, almost a decade later, Engelhard began to publish again. Despite tremendous changes during that time in the literature around her, especially the appearance of German Romanticism, she continued to write in exactly the same mode as before. Her range of topics was almost unchanged; she still preferred four-line stanzas; she was still self-satisfied, though now a little more aware of decorum and less willing to examine anxious or unpleasant experiences. Significantly, she waited until after the death of her husband (1818) to publish another serious volume of poetry, although it contained work that had been written over the course of four decades. Little is known of her old age. She continued living mostly in Kassel, published her translations of the French poet Béranger at the age of seventy-four, and died a year later on September 9, 1831.

The poem presented here belongs to the small but important body of her protesting poems. Written before Engelhard's marriage, it is witty, playful, crafty, and although—even in its form—it represents the poet's giving in to convention, it freely vents the young woman's frustration and anger at her confinement.

BIBLIOGRAPHY

Gatterer-Engelhard's Works
(There is as yet no secondary literature in English.)

Gedichte von Philippine Gatterer. Göttingen: Dieterich, 1778.
Gedichte von Philippine Engelhard geb. Gatterer. Göttingen: Dieterich, 1782.
Neujahrs-Geschenk für liebe Kinder. Cassel, 1787.
Neujahrswünsche. 1789.
Neue Gedichte von Philippine Engelhard geborne Gatterer. Nürnberg: Georg
    Eichhorn, 1821.
Lieder von Béranger. Translated by Philippine Engelhard geb. Gatterer. Cassel: J.
    J. Bohne, 1830.

Mädchenklage

(1779)

Oft hab ich mit Thränen
Und innigem Sehnen,
   Verwünscht mein Geschlecht!
Es fesselt fast immer
Mich Arme ins Zimmer—
   Wie frey gehn die Männer! selbst Knabe und Knecht.

Wie um sich zu schauen
Ist Mädchen und Frauen
   Vom Schicksal vergällt.
Als Diener, als Lehrer,
Als Held, als Bekehrer,
   Als Kaufmann, durchreisen die Männer die Welt.

Dann forschen sie Länder,
Durchschauen behender
   das menschliche Herz.
Sehn Kronenbeehrte,
Und grosse Gelehrte;
   Und glückliche Völker und Völker voll Schmerz.

Girl's Lament

(1779)

How oft with damnation
And tears of frustration
My gender I curse!
Its ban ever dooms
Us girls to our rooms;
How freely men move! Even youngster and serf.

How Fate did imprison
The scope of their vision
To women and girls!
As servant, as teacher,
As hero, as preacher,
As merchant, a man may encounter the world;

Audaciously cruising,
More shrewdly perusing
Folk mind and belief;
See wearers of ermine
And pillars of learning,
And prospering nations, and nations in grief;

Sehn glänzende Heere—
Und brausende Meere,
   Mit Schiffen bepflanzt,
Sehn fruchtbare Felder,
Und schauernde Wälder;
   Und Klippen von silbernen Quellen umtanzt.

Sie klettern auf Höhen
In Wolken zu stehen,
   Auf ewigem Eis.
Sie fahren in Schachten
Das Erz zu betrachten;
   zu sehen des Bergknappen fröhlichen Fleiss.

Und vielerley Sitten,
Paläste und Hütten,
   Erblicken sie dann;—
Ich traure fast immer
Im einsamen Zimmer
   O wär ich ein freyer und fröhlicher Mann!

Wenn strahlende Seen
In Heiden nur stehen;
   Was spiegeln sie wohl?
O könnt es mir glücken
Die Welt zu erblicken,
   so säng ich oft hoher Begeisterung voll!

Zwar könnt ich entfliehen
Und Länder durchziehen
   Im männlichen Kleid;
Doch Weisheit und Feuer
Erkauft ich zu theuer,
   Denn weh mir!—Die Sittsamkeit hätt ich entweiht!

View armies in motion,
A blustering ocean
With men-o'war strewn;
View bounteous harvests
And glowering forests
And boulders besprinkled with silvery spume.

To summits they climb,
Stand clouded in rime
On the ice-covered crest;
Deep pits they explore,
Inspecting the ore,
Observing the mining-men's spirited quest.

The customs and habits
Of castle and cabins
They contemplate then;
I languish in gloom
Alone in my room—
Oh, were I a lusty and fancy-free man!

If lakes in their brightness
Can mirror but blightlands
What can they reveal?
Oh, could but the world
To me be unfurled,
I'd carol, exalted to rapturous zeal!

Indeed, I might wander
Through homeland and yonder
In masculine dress;
But wisdom and cheer
Would cost me too dear:
Morality would have been flouted, alas!

Wie stürmen die Wellen,
So thürmen, so schwellen
   Oft Leiden mein Herz.
Verlösche, mein Leben!
Dann dort werd ich schweben
Auf Flügeln des Windes—und Traum wird mein Schmerz!

From *Gedichte von Philippine Engelhard geb. Gatterer*
(Göttingen: Dieterich, 1782), 157–59.

As salt breakers tower,
So griefs overpower
My senses and rake.
O flame of life fail!
For then I shall sail
On wings of the wind, and a dream is my ache!

Introduction and bibliography by
DENIS SWEET

Correction and expansion of George Soane's
1826 translation of "*Der Mantel*" by
JEANNINE BLACKWELL

Benedikte Naubert

(1756–1819)

Benedikte Naubert (1756–1819)
with her nephew and foster son Ernst Eduard Wilhelm Hebenstreit
pastel by Daniel Caffe d. Ä., 1806
reproduced from: Albrecht Kurzwelly, *Das Bildnis in Leipzig vom Ende des*
18. Jahrhunderts bis zur Biedermeierzeit, Leipzig 1912, plate 98.
Widener Library, Harvard University

Christiane Benedikte Eugenie Hebenstreit was born into an academic family in Leipzig noted for its doctors and university professors. Her father, Johann Ernst Hebenstreit, a well-known physician, died of typhus when she was an infant. Her mother, Christiane Eugenie née Bossek, also from an academic family, played no active role in Benedikte's upbringing. Since the biographical sources tactfully refrain from mentioning the concrete cause of the mother's "withdrawal," but allude to her "frailty," the nature of her malady is open to speculation. Benedikte's education fell to a much older stepbrother and a brother who taught her subjects not normally part of a woman's education in the eighteenth century: philosophy, history, Latin and Greek, French and English. She was said to be proficient at the piano and harp, and later learned Italian. Her life was sedentary and reclusive. When her two older brothers died, the burden of maintaining the family passed to her. An almost frenzied writing activity ensued. The decade between 1785 and 1795 was her most prolific period, when she published at least one novel a year, and in one year even four.

In 1797, at the age of forty-one, Benedikte married a wealthy Naumburg merchant and vineyard owner, and her book production enjoyed a brief respite. Two years later her husband died. In 1802, Benedikte remarried on the advice of her relations, this time to a man below her station who could tend the estate, one Johann Georg Naubert. The couple moved to Leipzig in 1818 where Benedikte Naubert was to undergo eye surgery (she had earlier been blind for a six-year period). A short while thereafter, Benedikte died of pneumonia.

Benedikte Naubert was one of the most prolific and widely read German authors of her age. Her publications—family novels, the first historical novels set in the Middle Ages, and fairy tales—extend to some fifty titles, eighty if one includes her "free translations" from the English. Many of her fairy tales and novels were reprinted time and again. Indeed, the public had become so well acquainted with her steady stream of novels that the advertisement on the title page "by the author of *Thekla von Thurn*" or "by the author of *Walter von Montbarry*" sufficed to promote the sales. Or rather: it had to suffice, for all of Benedikte Naubert's books up to one year before her death were published anonymously. She herself vigorously maintained this anonymity, referring to it as her "vestal veil." As a consequence, many of her works were ascribed to other authors, or theirs to her. The confusion surrounding her authorship persisted into the 20th century.

Her historical novels exerted an important influence on Walter Scott, who adopted her two-level technique of creating a fictional family/love story on a carefully researched, historically "true" background. The extent to which she influenced women authors has not yet been studied.

Three years after Musäus's fairy tales (*Volksmärchen der Deutschen*, 1782–86) had appeared, Naubert began publishing her own *Neue Volksmärchen der Deutschen* (1789–92). Written in the earlier part of a very prolific and long literary career, the fairy tales represent some of Naubert's most successful texts. Rather than simply continuing on in the rationalistic path struck by Musäus, Naubert's tales combine the marvelous with the everyday, the delight in supernatural occurrences with candid accounts of "real" problems: coming of age, the relation between the sexes, loss of work, poverty and old age. The juxtapositions and collage techniques, the framing, foregrounding, and backgrounding she exhibits in *The Cloak* (and in many of her historical novels) serve to create both ironic distance and profound emotional involvement with the characters. Before publishing *Grimm's Fairy Tales,* Wilhelm Grimm went to Naumburg in 1809 to interview Benedikte Naubert. Readers will note the parallels between passages in *The Cloak* and *Frau Holle*—yet the Grimm tale does not exhibit the psychological insights into female development contained in Naubert's tale. The Romantics, even more than her own generation, came to appreciate Naubert's fairy tales for what Achim von Arnim called their "fullness" and "primordiality." For Arnim, the husband of another female storyteller, Bettina von Arnim, Naubert's tales were a "delight in tortured nights."

BIBLIOGRAPHY

Naubert's Works
For a more extensive, if not complete list, see Gerhard Sauder's afterword to Benedikte Naubert's *Heerfort und Klärchen. Etwas für empfindsame Seelen.* Hildesheim: Gerstenberg, 1982.

Geschichte Emmas, Tochter Kayser Karls des Grossen und seines Geheimschreibers Eginhard. 2 vols. Leipzig: Weygand, 1785.
Walter von Montbarry, Grossmeister des Tempelordens. Leipzig: Weygand, 1786.
Amalgunde Königin von Italien oder das Märchen von der Wunderquelle. Eine Sage aus den Zeiten Theoderichs des Grossen. Leipzig: Weygand, 1787.
Herrmann von Unna. Eine Geschichte aus den Zeiten der Vehmegerichte. Leipzig: Weygand, 1788.
Elisabeth, Erbin von Toggenburg. Oder Geschichte der Frauen von Sargans in der Schweiz. Leipzig: Weygand, 1789.
Neue Volksmährchen der Deutschen. 1789–92. Available on microfilm, from Rare Books, Univ. of Cincinnati.
Barbara Blomberg, vorgebliche Maitresse Kaiser Karls des Fünften. Eine Originalgeschichte. Leipzig: Weygand, 1790.
Alf von Dülmen. Oder Geschichte Kaiser Philipps und seiner Tochter. Aus den ersten Zeiten der heimlichen Gerichte. Frankfurt und Leipzig, 1790.
Wallfahrten oder Erzählungen der Pilger. Leipzig: Schäfer, 1793.
Velleda. Ein Zauberroman. Leipzig: Schäfer, 1795.

In English Translation
Feudal Tyrants, or The Counts of Carlsheim and Sargans. n.d.
Alf von Dülmen. Translated by Miss A. E. Booth. London: Bell, 1794.

Hermann of Unna: A Series of Adventures of the Fifteenth Century in which the Proceedings of the Secret Tribunal under the Emperors Winceslaus and Sigismund are Delineated. 1794, 2nd ed. 1794/95.

Walter de Monbary (sic). Grandmaster of the Knights Templars: An Historical Romance. Translated by Mary Julia Young. London, 1803 and 1808.

Lindorf and Caroline or, The Danger of Credulity. Translated by Mary Julia Young. London: W. S. Betham, 1803.

"The Mantle." Translated by George Soane. In *Specimens of German Romance,* London: Whittaker, 1826.

Secondary Literature in English

Blackwell, Jeannine. "Fractured Fairy Tales: German Women Authors and the Grimm Tradition." *Germanic Review* 62 (Winter 1987): 162–74.

The Cloak

(1789–92)

T he Britons, time out of mind, have fabled so much of their King
Arthur that a portion of these wonderful tales have echoed across
the sea, and been repeated by the neighboring people. Of course
the legends, when told by such various tongues, have not always remained
the same: here, something has been added; there, something has been
omitted; hence the many variations of the old English legends, and hence
so many romances, the fruit of British soil, to which posterity has given the
name of a Gallic or German hero.

The Emperor Charles the Great was particularly fortunate, in that the fab-
ulous histories of King Arthur were so frequently set down to his account.
Like him a hero, like him a friend to love, and like him a member of the society
of Saint Gangolph,[1] the most of those wonderful adventures fitted him very
passably; and, were it not for our conscientious honesty, we might aptly
enough, in compliance with the German tradition, set down this legend,
which really belongs to the court of the old Briton, as having happened under
the eyes of the son of the great Majordomo. But to show you, gentle reader,
that you may rely upon our word, we freely confess it is not Charles the Great
and his countless wives or mistresses, but King Arthur and his lady Guinevere
that are the hero and heroine who are to figure here.

1. The patron saint of all cuckolded husbands. [Author's note]

The court at Carlisle had, besides the Queen, many a blooming, and many a fading beauty, who still maintained their rank on the score of seniority. Some of these we must name to you, as they have their parts to play in the course of the story. The loveliest amongst them was Iselda, the beloved of the brave Hector; who for fifteen long years had let her knight sigh for her love, without having as yet granted him any other favor than the liberty sometimes of kissing the hem of her veil. After her came Rosalia and Isabella, the wives of Sir Gawain—whose name cannot be unknown to you—and of the bold Iwain, the King's son; these ladies were sisters, and while the one had adopted Pride as the guardian of her honor, the other one took up Piety as her watchman. Next on the list is Sir Ydier's bride, the Lady Agnes, who, notwithstanding her sleepy watery blue eyes and her rather stupid dove-like looks, yet maintained her rank amongst the British goddesses. The wild Britomarte follows, who used to punish with one, or two, years' banishment every presumptuous glance of her knight, the bashful Girflet. Below in charms, but, according to age and their own estimation, in the very first place, come the lusty wife of Sir Guy the Seneschal, and Lady Eleanor, the wife of Peter the Holy, Count of Brittany, who herself was itching for a halo and in the meantime neglected nothing to maintain that rank in the British court which she expected one day to hold in the court of Heaven.

Two beauties we have omitted to mention—the one because she could in no respect be said to belong to the court of Queen Guinevere, being mortally hated by her—the other, because it was only from her extreme loveliness that she was placed upon a level with the rest, for neither by birth nor by property had she any title to rank amongst the high court-ladies.

The first of these two, as yet unnamed, beauties, was the Princess Morgana, the sister of King Arthur. The second was little Genelas from Wales, who came to court an orphan, and made the Queen an indifferent return for her kindness by completely eclipsing with her simple loveliness all the splendor of the royal beauty. The little maiden, however, should be forgiven; she did not desire any of the admiration which was lavished upon her; but one must have been blind not to have preferred Genelas, unadorned, to the proud British Queen in the splendor of her diadem—especially after taking into account innocence, simplicity, and goodness, of which Queen Guinevere possessed very little.

Although we have coupled Genelas and Morgana together, the reader must not imagine that they were of the same stamp; as little inequality as there was in their beauty, yet they differed a whole world in manners and thinking, and not less so in wealth and rank. The Princess sought for conquests, pleased, loved, and was beloved; the little Welsh girl knew nothing of conquests—after which she did not strive—pleased without wishing it, and was beloved without replying to it, or even being aware of it. Morgana was a wise and deeply learned lady, well versed in all the mysteries of nature, a pupil of the great Merlin, and, to say all in one sentence, an enchantress of the second rank. Genelas, on the contrary, knew no magic but that of her needle and spindle, which she was skillful in using, notwithstanding she was a court-lady. Besides, she willingly remained within the narrow limits then prescribed to female knowledge, and was on that account so much the sweeter.

The Princess was on the point of bringing to a conclusion her seven-and-twentieth love affair, while it was only within the few last days that Genelas had gained a dim awareness of her first. Sir Carados—surnamed the Armbreaker, because this sort of damage was the least with which his opponents could normally reckon—a hero, as mild in peace as bold in war, had at the last court-festival passed over all the other ladies, and led her out to dance; at parting too he had tenderly squeezed her hand, a point which she did not clearly comprehend, and yet which her heart told her was not without meaning.

Amongst all the inequalities between the two ladies whom we have thus coupled were also the causes of the low esteem in which they both were held by Queen Guinevere—that is, Genelas, on account of her humble manners, was despised; and Morgana, on account of her arrogance, detested.

We have often observed that the sisters of married men stand at best on a footing with stepmothers. These good creatures are always peculiarly jealous of their dear brothers' honor, strict censurers and inexorable judges of every error of those whom love has converted into their relations; and if they happen to be young and handsome enough to rival their sister-in-law in their conquests, then war at once is declared, and not unfrequently they proceed to open hostilities.

Through all these circumstances King Arthur's sister was destined to be Guinevere's enemy; the scenes of overdone courtesy and friendship, which are generally used in the commencement of such hostilities as the cover of real feelings, had long ago been played out between them, and they had got to the second act, namely, that of conscious avoidance and occasional little sarcasms, which often degenerated into earnest, and led people to anticipate the conclusion of the tragedy, a public rift.

The Princess was never at a loss for biting sallies; once, when King Arthur held his *cour plénière* at Christmas, she seized the cup—with tolerable boldness for the manners of the ladies at that period—and drank to Arthur, Guinevere's cuckolded husband, and to the health of all his brothers, warning him at the same time to drink moderately, that a drop might remain for each of them. Queen Guinevere, as well as the rest of the company, saw perfectly well that her allusion was to all those who had shared the honor of the regal bedchamber; it was only the good-natured King who betrayed by a simple question that the real meaning of the words was a mystery to him, and his crafty wife took care not to open his eyes and ears by the bitter answer which yet trembled upon her lips. She swore in her heart, however, the direst revenge against Morgana, and watched her opportunity so well, that, before the moon had filled her bow with new light, the detested sister-in-law would have fallen into her snares.

We have said, my dear friends, Morgana was a fairy of the second order, and we will not fancy you so ignorant as not to see what the name means. It cannot be unknown to you that this designates only those spiritual beings who dwell about us without being perceived by our grosser senses, those confidantes of holy nature, whose mysteries are not covered from them by any veil—that it is only those who deserve that significant name of fairy in its real and important meaning. The mere earthborn, who only by art subdue the secret powers of nature, are much their inferiors, and are often violently persecuted by them for their presumption in endeavoring to elevate themselves to their level. The former—so fabled the legends of old—by immortality, by comprehensive power, and a sort of omniscience, were exalted almost to demigods; the latter always remained weak, mortal creatures, subject to chance and misery, could only secure life and fortune by secret means, were far from being able to do all they wished, and knew nothing but what they gained by laborious inquiry.

This too was the case with the disciple of the wise Merlin; how else could the schemes which were brooded against her in Guinevere's brain have remained a mystery to her? A peep into the great book of the stars would no doubt have shown Morgana the snare laid for her, and she would then have found the means of avoiding it; but at present she read in no book but the eyes of her twenty-seventh lover; nothing existed for her in the world except him; for his sake she sank into the weakness of a common mortal, and, to confess the truth, after so many intrigues, behaved in the whole affair very like a little girl who, for the first time, hears from a young man's lips that she is a sweet little thing.

Oh, how Queen Guinevere rejoiced at the way in which her enemy laid herself open! She pretended to be blind to the love of Morgana and Guiomar, to make them the more secure, watched all their motions in silence, and looked forward to the moment when it would be in her power to expose the weakness of the enamored damsel to the whole court, and by this striking proof of his sister's moral laxness either persuade the King to be deaf forever to her covert slanders, or else to make him banish from the court a hated informer, whose watchfulness laid such hard restraints on the Queen's private pleasures.

That she not let this desired moment slip by, strict injunctions were given to the female courtiers of the third order; all were to seek, to peek, to creep, to sneak, and to repeat, that the slippery forelock of Occasion might not elude their grasp, and all were ready enough for such an occupation. By nature light, crafty, supple, and inclined to little malicious tricks, they found pleasure in that which was imposed upon them as a duty; Genelas had always behaved so very awkwardly in such matters the few times she had an inkling of the subterfuge, that she was now left alone, and the development of the catastrophe was reserved for her, either as a punishment for her dullness, or to put the truth in so much more striking a light through the mouth of simplicity.

That which made the little Welsh girl so stupid now—particularly now—in one of the most fashionable points of female education, was not so much her own pious simplicity, not so much the modest lessons instilled into her from childhood by her nurse, as—a love affair of her own. At the last court-festival Sir Carados had again led her out alone to the dance, had again squeezed her hand, met her for several days after at various times as if by chance, and latterly, when she was surprised by a storm as she traveled on the Queen's affairs, had wrapped her up in his cloak and brought her safely home. So many sweet speeches had passed in these short journeys that no one but a naive girl like Genelas could have doubted the knight's real intentions; she, however, was so astonished, so confounded, that she scarcely knew what she said, or what she heard, and that—that—we can scarcely write it without blushing—that she not only received a kiss from Sir Carados, given in the dark, but even returned it.

Genelas was beside herself at her own recklessness; she wept her eyes red, expected the contempt of her lover for this breach of maidenly manners, and endeavored to regain his respect by assuming prudery and diligently avoiding his company altogether. But all this found her inexperienced heart with so much employment, that she had no senses for anything else, committed a thousand blunders in her duties, and, above all, showed very little inclination to interfere in Morgana's matters.

As the court had no lack of other, more effective, agents, the time came on without her aid for the catastrophe of the tragedy in which Morgana and Sir Guiomar were to play the principal parts. Queen Guinevere had assembled her privy council, in which all the above-named ladies had a seat and voice, and opened the sitting with the question—"What should be done to her who watches with an eye of censure over the actions of others, and at the same time abandons herself in secret to the grossest excesses?"—and all had unanimously voted for death or a public exposure.

"You all know," continued the Queen, "that heroine of virtue, Morgana, and I must tell you I am on the point of tearing from her the veil which has preserved to her that title."

"She a heroine of virtue!" said Iselda, bristling up; "I know ladies, who, by the fifteen years of subjection in which they have kept an adored lover, much more deserve it."

"And I," exclaimed the Seneschal's fat wife, who was in possession of an ample court chronicle, "I could quote more than twenty testimonies to Morgana's virtue, of which she would not be very proud."

Rosalie and Isabella blushed; Agnes gawked; the spouse of Peter the Holy sent up a pious sigh to heaven; and the wild Britomarte, jumping up, begged the Queen to be more explicit, and to use her aid, if she needed any, in withdrawing the veil from Morgana's illicit love affairs.

"A request," said the Queen, "which I must deny; I have chosen for this office a person whose simplicity, should my project succeed, would make her evidence much less suspicious than yours, and who, if it should fail, will alone bear all the blame, and screen us from the vengeance of the malicious enchantress."

Eleanor and Isabella vaunted that they could annihilate all Morgana's magic with a single Ave, while Iselda and Rosalie doubted altogether the Princess's possessing any such knowledge; but the Queen, who feared the loss of the favorable moment, paid no attention to the advice of her councillors; she ordered little Genelas to be called, and, feigning a desperate hurry, dispatched her to Morgana, desiring her not to be stopped by anything, but to press on into Morgana's chamber, and if she found that princess not in a state to comply with the Queen's request of coming to her, that then she should steal away quietly, and bring back an exact account of the condition in which she had seen her.

Guinevere had taken care to stage things so that, immediately upon the dismissal of Genelas, the King with his nobles should be in her chamber, so that he might be present at her return, and witness the unmasking of his sister.

King Arthur knowing nothing of all this, had, as usual, not the foggiest notion, and came into the room at this moment, only because it was the customary time for his visit, which, as a very punctual gentleman, he never missed.

"My dear lord," said the Queen, approaching him with that respect which artful women ever use to conceal from their husbands that they in fact command them, "my dear lord, you find us all assembled here to beguile the remainder of the day in play or dance at your pleasure. Two persons only are wanting to our circle, whom we cannot do without; I mean your noble sister and the hero Guiomar. I have sent after the first myself, and to the latter you will be pleased to dispatch a messenger."

The King had already turned round to the Seneschal to give him the commission requested by the Queen, when little Genelas, half out of breath and blushing like Aurora, entered the room, and quietly took her place.

"Have you executed my commission?" said the Queen.

"No," replied Genelas, blushing still more deeply.

"Did you not find the Princess then?"

"Yes—no—yes," stammered the maiden.

"Oh!" said Lady Seneschal, "I will lay anything that our absent little maiden forgot your message along the way, and now does not know how to extricate herself from her embarrassment. Recollect, my child; you were to request the Princess to grace this company with her presence, and you have not spoken to her?"

"No, indeed."

"And why not?"

"I think she was in the bath."

"And where?"

"In truth I do not know; I listened through the trees, and saw—saw that her maidens were around her, amusing her with dance and song."

"What nonsense the child is chattering!" exclaimed the Queen; "she looked, and knows not where, saw, and knows not what."

"Allow me, your highness," said Britomarte, "to go and fetch you more accurate information. The bath scene is probably in the Princess's garden."

"That is not necessary," said Guinevere; "we will all go and see whether Genelas has told us the truth."

"Indeed, indeed," said the maiden, "I think I have not lied; that much at least is certain: the garden was closed, and, had I not been ordered to press on without stopping, I should hardly have forced my way through the bushes to see what I saw."

"Fool!" cried the Queen; "you know not what you say; you contradict yourself at every word. Come, my lord; we will go and see ourselves."

"But only consider," said Genelas, throwing herself at the Queen's feet, "the Princess is in the bath."

"Very well," replied the Queen, "we will go, and you shall be our guide."

The fat Lady Seneschal here seized the weeping Genelas by the arm, pulled her up, and dragged her along the well-known way to Morgana's garden, the whole court following them.

Morgana availed herself of her magic only to enjoy the pleasures of life in full measure. By means of that her palace was the most splendid, her attendants the most numerous, and her gardens comprised all that the earth has most alluring; and even her own beauty, as her enviers maintained, was so irresistible only through the power of magic. "All deceit and vapor!" Guinevere would often say in a philosophical mood, "born from a breath, and just as easily destroyed again by a breath; a void, as it was formed by the Creator."

Adorned with all the attractions of a goddess, the Princess would often give splendid festivals in her magic gardens to King Arthur's court; but her most splendid celebrations were in the arms of a confidential friend, surrounded by no other witnesses than a part of her own court, who owed their existence to her wand, and at a touch from it would again melt into vapor; these of course were the zealous servants of her will as long as she left them life and, as may be supposed, silent, unimportant witnesses of her secret pleasures. It was in this circle that the innocent Genelas saw the fair enchantress; she had found, as she told them, the palace empty, the garden closed, and had made a way for herself through the bushes and hedges until she got into the center of an orange grove, which concealed a broad plain in its bosom; in the middle again of this, lofty cedars, interwoven with low myrtle shrubs, shaded a marble bath, where Morgana delighted to refresh herself in the heat of the day.

Genelas had spied through the myrtle hedge, and seen the princess in the bath, surrounded by her shadowy attendants—a heavenly sight even for the eye of a maiden, who was herself not deficient in charms! But the Princess was not alone; upon the green bank, where her suite reclined in picturesque groups, lay the arms of a knight, who was sharing with her the coolness of the limpid waters. The eyes of the modest little Welsh maiden were instantly turned away in terror upon seeing Morgana's bathing companion. She, who grieved so much about a kiss too boldly returned, and who deemed the maiden veil that covered her lovely face to be so indispensable—it may be guessed what she thought of the boldness of one of her sex in admitting a man into the very sanctuary of her evening toilette, into the bath itself. She hid her face in her dress, flew back quicker than she had come, and in the greatest confusion entered the hall where Guinevere with her court were waiting for her. The Queen had learned beforehand from her spies that Guiomar had a private interview with Morgana, knew the Princess's improvidence, which had not made the place of meeting inaccessible to the Queen's envoy, and had purposely chosen simple Genelas for that office, to crush the offender so much the more heavily by the innocent way in which the maiden would tell the story.

As we have seen, the project did not altogether succeed. Genelas was too much ashamed at this impudence in one of her own sex, and felt too much repugnance at owning she had witnessed it, to speak with frankness now. She was as much confused as if she had been the offender; her words, her tears petitioned them so earnestly to leave the veil upon Morgana's mysteries, that those who know not how real innocence behaves—and there were few such innocents at Arthur's court—must have been quite mistaken in her.

Genelas was compelled to show the company the way to Morgana's bath, or rather they knew it already, for they might conclude pretty well where it was from the broken speeches of the abashed maiden.

Morgana was so blinded that she had not taken the least measures for her security. She had imagined the court was absent on a hunting-party, settled long before, had forgotten to place any shadowy terrors or spiritual guards at the entrance of the orange grove, and held herself safe under the simple protection of a few locks; great, therefore, was her surprise, when all of a sudden a thousand witnesses appeared at the edge of the marble bath, some speechless with horror, and others with malignant delight, and gazed on her and her companion of the bath, without knowing how to express their feelings.

King Arthur lifted up his eyes and hands to heaven; the knights exerted all their powers of sight to lose nothing of the surprising spectacle; the ladies beat their breasts with averted eyes; and the Queen alone had enough presence of mind to break the silence.

"Really, Princess," she exclaimed, in a tone such as only triumphant malice can form from lips distorted into bitter scorn, "really, Princess, we surprise you here in a singular condition. Genelas, who brought us hither, said nothing of the state in which we were to find you, or we should have spared our eyes this spectacle."

Vexation, wrath, and shame fettered the tongue of the surprised Morgana. Sir Guiomar at first hid his face in his hands, till a sort of instinct, which makes every hero grasp after his arms upon an insult, drove him to the edge of the bath to fetch his sword. In the meantime, Morgana's eyes were so far from being fixed to the earth by any modest confusion that they flashed fire on the surrounders. Revenge was seething in her heart, and doubtless, if she had possessed the power, she would have punished the gazers in the same way that Cynthia once punished the presumptuous huntsman; indeed, she did fill both hands with water, which she scattered about her in a thousand glittering drops; the whole effect, however, of this maneuver was that the bath scene of the new Diana, together with her Endymion and her nymphs, disappeared from the eyes of the spectators in a thin mist, and even the surrounding grove with the whole of the magic country was enveloped in a bluish fog that by degrees passed off, and let the curious company see where they really stood—namely, on a wide plain of yellow sand, scorched up by the burning sun, with a few dusty bushes that spread out their thin withered foliage. In fact, it was precisely the same desert spot that Morgana had originally found here, and by her magic wand converted into gardens.

It may be imagined with what confusion the assembly looked about them, and with what discomfiture they made their way back again under the heat of the midday sun. But at the same time, Morgana had not been able to effect with her wand that which she had probably intended—causing all to forget these events, or at least, to doubt their reality. All present knew perfectly well that they had been awake and not asleep, and all, to the infinite delight of the vindictive Queen, protested that while they looked upon Morgana as the greatest of magicians, they at the same time deemed her the most frivolous and shameless creature upon the face of God's earth. King Arthur betrayed his thoughts only by a troubled silence and angry looks; and it was well that the Princess had taken herself off with all her entourage, or else banishment or death would have been the inevitable punishment of her offence. In fact, she had left nothing of hers behind. In the spots formerly occupied by her extensive palaces, nothing was now to be seen but empty spaces, and even the presents which she had made to the King and Queen in gentler hours had vanished from their jewel chests.

Guinevere's project had thus succeeded; she had revenged herself upon her enemy, and had removed her from the court, perhaps forever, but still she was not quite satisfied: it seemed to her that her revenge and triumph might have been yet more complete; many little circumstances might have been omitted from the whole adventure, and as she was accustomed, in the manner of great ladies, to make others suffer for her discontent, and had just then no other object on which to pour out the cup of her wrath, the storm burst upon poor little Genelas; she was that very evening called before the great council of the ladies, tried, and condemned. A thousand sins occurred, which on this occasion were all brought forward to her account; but the most important charge, or at least that which possessed a little semblance of truth, was that she had a secret understanding with the enchantress, and probably participated in her excesses. From the very beginning she had so reluctantly mingled in the plot against the Princess, had at last, when others had imperceptibly involved her in it, behaved so simplemindedly, had so earnestly sought to hide the offender's shameful trespasses, sparing neither prayers nor tears to keep the rest of the court from the way which she had first taken, that her judges deemed it could not be otherwise than that she was a creature of Morgana, an enemy of the Queen, and consequently as wicked and as vicious as those whose part she had so solemnly and simpleheartedly taken.

We, however, know the motives of the little Welsh girl; at least we can swear that sympathy with Morgana's excesses was far from having any place in her innocent heart, though they could not, and would not, see this at Arthur's court. The sentence pronounced upon her case in the Queen's private chamber soon communicated itself to every heart, however much interested in her favor before; she was with general consent banished from court, and abandoned to poverty and misery. Poor creature! To complete her wretchedness, it was only wanting that she should know the fortune which had that day awaited her, and which had by this fatal event alone been thwarted.

Sir Carados, whose heart cleaved to the beautiful maiden, had already spoken of his passion to King Arthur, and intended this evening to make a formal application to the Queen; but now his beloved appeared in so hateful a light!—What his own eyes could not find was supplied by the opinion of others; no one was there to defend the accused, and thus it happened, that, if not his love, yet all his designs in her favor vanished, and he saw her banishment, not without secret tears, but without any effort to defend or save her. "I loved beauty without virtue," he said to himself mournfully; "I loved a deceptive hallucination that I must now forget. But there can be little virtue in women since Genelas is sinful." So saying, he girded on his sword, mounted his horse, and set out to kill the feelings of grief and love in the tumult of warlike adventures.

In the meantime, Genelas left the court of King Arthur as poor as she had entered it, or rather much poorer; then she had possessed a total freedom from care, ignorance of human necessities, and all the evils arising out of them, together with an abundance of joyful hopes; but, alas! these inestimable goods are only the property of childhood, which we must entirely leave behind on entering the age of manhood or womanhood.

Robbed of every means of honest subsistence, driven out into the wide world, alone and friendless, the poor wanderer could not be without care, and could hardly possess any great stock of hopes for the future. She wandered many a day and many a night, living sparingly on that which she had saved up in happier times, and which was hardly worth naming. It is true, indeed, that King Arthur had sent after her a traveling gift, but her enemies had taken care to intercept it. Genelas was too beautiful to have many women friends; it was no secret that she had pleased many eyes, and above all, the sparkling black eyes of brave Carados—reason enough for most ladies, even for Queen Guinevere, to hate her mortally, and to rejoice that this feeling could just now be so admirably concealed under the mask of the love of virtue.

It was late one evening that the pilgrim, on reaching a village, felt an excess of weariness which made her apprehend the end of all her travels. She had wandered for many days with scanty nourishment, little rest, exposed to the sun's heat and the chilling rains; what wonder then that at last her strength failed, and she sank down almost senseless before a cottage which stood alone by the roadside, about twenty paces from the village? Her dying moans excited the attention of the person within, who opened a little window in the door, and asked, "Who's there?"

"Alas !" sighed Genelas, "a sick wanderer. Help! Help! Or it is all over with me."

The inhabitant of the hovel seemed for a long time to be taking counsel on what was to be done in this case. At length the door opened, and a female figure came forth, whose appearance was unremarkable, and whose manners evinced anything other than hospitality.

"What do you want?" asked the peasant woman in a rough voice.

"Alas! Everything!" replied Genelas, who was scarcely able to speak any longer.

"What?" cried the woman, who now held the light more closely to her guest, "So young, so lovely, and in such a plight! You are a pretty one indeed! Away with you! Get away from my door! My cottage is no place for such creatures."

It is impossible to say what idea the woman really entertained of the young pilgrim, but she hastily turned her back upon her, and, hurrying into the hovel, slammed the door with violence.

"Have pity! Pity!" cried the deserted Genelas; "by hospitality some have harbored angels."

"Pity! Hospitality!" grumbled the old woman from within, "I should gain much good by that! Formerly, indeed, I was such a fool, and well I was rewarded for it!"

The poor little traveler continued to weep and implore, till at length the woman handed her a draught of water through the opening in the door, and she raised herself with difficulty to receive it.

"Is there no other place here in the village where I could find refuge?" asked Genelas, when she had drunk the water.

"Oh, yes," replied the peasant, "besides the public-house, we have here a very rich lady who harbors all beggars and finds great pleasure in it: see the great red mansion yonder with the two large linden trees, and try if you can drag yourself to it; she will not turn you away."

Genelas opened her weary eyes to look for the great house of the rich lady, but could see nothing more than a neat little cottage, which only envy, ignorance, or scorn could have called a mansion. She nevertheless thanked the woman for her information, and slowly raised herself to creep to the place which had been pointed out to her as the abode of hospitality.

At the first knock, after a little preliminary inquiry through the window, the door was unlocked. The person who opened it—to all appearance the only inhabitant of the cottage—was a friendly old woman, whose neat clothing did, indeed, evince a sort of rustic prosperity, but whose looks were too kind and accommodating for Genelas to fancy her the rich lady she had been labeled.

"Come in, come in, my child," she exclaimed, on seeing that the pilgrim hesitated to cross her threshold, "the night is unkind, and I see you are weary."

"Oh, yes; so weary I could die!" said Genelas, clinging to the wall to keep herself from falling. But the hospitable old woman shoved a stool over and had her sit down; then she fetched milk from the cellar, brought a cooling bath for her sore feet, and stood before her ready to serve, as once Abraham had stood before the angels.

Genelas enjoyed the refreshment prepared for her, without being able to show her gratitude. It was only her tear-filled eyes and her arms stretched out from time to time toward her benefactress, that testified how fully she felt comforted.

The kindhearted peasant treated her with the greatest tenderness, spared her all unnecessary talking, ventured no idle questions, gave her supper quietly, and as quietly put her to bed. She wrapped her in clean linens that served as a blanket, and promised to cage the rooster in the coop, so his crow would not wake her too soon. In short, she played the part of a mother, when that part is played most affectionately.

It was almost midday when Genelas awoke, and even then she could not resolve to leave her bed; she saw her hostess many times stealing to the half-opened door and peeping in to see if her guest needed anything; this told Genelas it was time to rise, that she might not fall into the ill repute of laziness.

She found Frau Rose seated at her spinning-wheel, and was received by her as if she had been an old friend. Genelas was now prepared for the questions: "who?—whence?—and whither?" but the old woman asked nothing, and only seemed occupied with the care of the weak pilgrim, without minding who the object of her benevolence was. On the third day, Genelas, having perfectly recovered, began with a trembling voice to talk of going on further, and when this idea was contested on the plea of her continued weakness, she asked on the fourth day for work.

"My child," said the old woman, in answer to this request, "I know not how you may be situated, but to judge from appearances, you may as well stay with me as with anyone else, and that without further thinking on the matter. If this be your opinion, you must in truth have some occupation; for idleness brings no good. But, as a guest, I cannot burden you with work, and you may stay as long as you choose, provided that you take care of your own needs."

These words, spoken with a half-laughing, half-serious mien, touched the heart of the young Welsh maiden. She folded the old woman in her arms and called her "Mother," and it was agreed between them that the name of guest should be dropped forever. The wanderer declared she would sooner live here than anywhere; and thus she was installed in the right of sharing the labors of the house and spindle, and enjoying the profits with her hostess.

Weeks had thus passed, when one day, in an hour of their common labor, Genelas asked: "My dear Mother, am I so utterly foreign, so utterly indifferent to you, that you do not once ask me who I am?"

"My child," replied the old woman, "you have told me your name, nor are you otherwise unknown to me. I perceive you are quiet, pious, modest, and grateful; the other points are trifles, which you will tell me when it seems necessary to you, and after which I should not inquire, though we should remain together till the day of our death."

Genelas saw that her new friend well understood the minutest points of hospitality, and did not hesitate to reward such forbearance with a circumstantial narrative of her adventures at King Arthur's court.

The old woman listened attentively without interrupting her, and at the conclusion said, "Only one question—allow me only one question. Are you really innocent of the suspicion of having made common cause with the sinful Morgana?"

"I can give you no other surety for my innocence except my words and my condition," replied Genelas, with a melancholy glance at her wretched garments.

"You are right," replied Rose; "vice generally rewards its adherents better, and your poverty is an honorable pledge that I do not overlook: indeed I threw out these doubts only to see what weapons you would use to defend your innocence. Your eyebrows were not wildly elevated, your face was not covered with an angry glow, your looks continued mild and friendly, and even these trials you have stood with honor. Know then, that from all I now have learnt of you, I form great expectations for you in the future; only wait the course of time, and all will be made manifest."

Rose and her adopted daughter spent their time in quiet industry without any adventures. One thing only troubled them—the neighbor in the house a few yards from the village, who had repulsed the wandering Genelas so roughly on her first arrival, began to visit their cottage more frequently than she had done before. Genelas could not look upon her enemy with favorable eyes, and Rose seemed to have yet other reasons for disliking her company. One day she said to the young maiden: "This woman is my cousin, but when I have told you my story, you will see I have little cause to be fond of her. This much is certain: envy and avarice are her leading passions, and she visits us for no other purpose than to spy out the mysteries which she suspects exist with us, and to turn the knowledge to our injury."

Genelas had never heard her hostess speak of anyone in this tone before, and believed her; but Rose, who desired no blind belief and knew no better mode of convincing Genelas of the truth than by the promised narration, put fresh flax upon the distaff, and began as follows:

Rose's Story

"I am by birth a German, and first saw the light in a little village in the depths of the Harz forest. While yet a child I lost my parents, and left the peaceful hut, which now fell to their creditors, for the cottage of an aunt, who was at the same time my godmother, and who, therefore, could not avoid taking charge of me. I and her daughter—the very neighbor against whom I have just been warning you—together with an old maidservant made up her whole establishment; and we might have lived quietly and comfortably enough, if stubbornness, avarice, and quarrelsomeness had not got the mastery over my godmother. She had taken me into her house unwillingly, grudged me every morsel of bread she gave me, required of me things I had never learnt, and scolded incessantly at my awkwardness, without telling me how to do things better. Her dislike increased as I grew up and by gentleness and natural good humor gained more affection from her friends and neighbors than her own daughter, a spoiled child, who was much clumsier than I would ever be and who had malice and obstinacy inscribed upon her features.

"The old servant died, and they freed me from the finer labors of the needle and spinning-wheel, to put upon me the dirty and toilsome household-work. Willingly could I have submitted to this aggravation of my lot, if it had not proceeded from so melancholy a cause. I missed the deceased at every turn, for she was the only one in the house who gave me a friendly look; she had taught me moreover the little that she knew, and in the evening, before I went to bed, would tell me a tale of entertaining, terror-filled import.

"My toils and my grief had no cessation but on Sunday, when my godmother and her daughter went to church. Never one to be idle, I would take up the maidenly work of the spinning-wheel, a labor I had been kept from doing; I always deemed myself nobler and better when working at this cleanly occupation. But the threads that I drew out were coarse and unequal; I had seen the delicate girls of the village fill the spindle with white yarn fine and delicate as silk; and I wept over my own awkwardness.

"My seat in these sweet hours of melancholy solitude was generally under the lindens in front of our cottage by the side of a well, which was no longer used and was more than half choked up with moss and bushes. It was natural enough that the vicinity of this well should bring to my mind certain legends that the deceased, whom I here so often lamented, had in other times related for my amusement. 'Know,' she would often say to me when admonishing me to industry and order, 'know that, for unthinkable ages, a spirit has dwelt in these parts, called by the people the Frau Holle or Hulla; she ascends from the side of yonder well, steals through the houses, and sees whether the young women have done their work properly; should she find any uncleanliness in chamber or kitchen, at table or hearth, she pinches the lazy maids, strips off their nightgowns, and lays them naked on the stones; or, should she find on holy eves, or at the end of the week, unspun flax or unfinished needlework, she either dips them in the mire of the duck-pond, or sets fire to them, so that at times barns and houses have suffered by her love of industry. But, then, order, diligence, and cleanliness never remain unrewarded by her, and not unfrequently the tidy maids, when they carry water at sunrise into the clean kitchen, find silver pennies in their pails, with which they buy ribbons and shoes, and trim themselves out on holidays.'

"Such were the tales of my kindhearted old teacher, and I believed her with all my heart. I had never, indeed, found any of Hulla's silver pennies, notwithstanding all my industry and struggles after such a reward, but I was so much the oftener pulled and pinched for any little neglect by my godmother, who was perhaps the spirit's substitute on such occasions. I had sometimes too found dirt in unfinished work; and once, when I fell asleep over flax-combing, the flax caught fire, and, upon awakening in a fright, I was scarcely able to put it out, and so escape the well-deserved punishment.

"Things of this sort taught me to believe in this rigid judge of order and industry, and made me extremely conscientious in the performance of my duties. The punishments I had experienced, and from the rewards I promised myself much in the future.

"I took care never to sit down to work by the well till the house was swept from garret to cellar, my face and hands had been seven times washed in the neighboring spring, and I had put on my cleanest everyday clothes. Then I would spin and grieve that I could not spin better; and when at times I succeeded more than usual, I would look about me proudly, and my eyes would rest upon that corner of the well, where, according to the legend, the spirit used to rise, as if I meant to challenge her to witness my good conduct.

"One day, after I had been spinning for a long time and the place of the sun told me that my tormentors would soon return, I was seized with a sudden sadness at the idea of what I might then have to suffer from them. Their sky had not been very clear that morning; what had I to expect then from their afternoon, knowing, as I did, that they always returned in a bad humor from their devotions? I expanded on these notions, thought on the past and the future, and burst out into tears. My hands sank into my lap, the reel broke from the spindle and tumbled into the well, so that I heard it rebound once or twice from the sides and fall to the bottom. Full of terror I awoke from my dreaming. If with the consciousness of having committed no fault I had trembled at the idea of their bad temper, what must I now fear, after the loss of this valued utensil? I was so poor that I possessed no spinning implements of my own; the wheel at which I had been spinning with all its accoutrements belonged to my young cousin, who had no objection to my hiding her laziness by my diligence, though without rewarding me with a single kind look for it; and there was no doubt she would reckon with me for misplacing the little leaden reel as if it had been of solid gold.

"Full of despair, and quite uncertain what to do, I jumped up and bent over the edge of the well, in whose depths I thought I perceived my lost treasure. At the same time I heard the voices of my cousins, who were coming home over the next field, and I cannot tell whether it was fear of them, or anxiety to regain the lost reel, that brought me to the desperate resolution of plunging into the abyss.

"Just as little am I able to give any account of the thoughts which followed this rash act; it seems to me as if I had ceased to think, and had no other sensation than that of uninterrupted falling, which, from its length, might, I fancied, have brought me to the very center of the earth. About me was utter darkness; my senses now utterly failed me; and I did not recover till I received a violent blow upon coming at last to the solid ground. My eyes were still closed; for a time I thought, as I felt no pain from the fall, that the whole adventure was a dream, and was not convinced of the contrary till I had recovered, and, upon looking about me, found myself in an unknown country.

"It was a lovely, astonishing place, illumined by a gentle twilight, most grateful to the eyes. Here were soft, flowery banks to rest on; there, rustling leaves and running streams; in the distance, an extensive ornate edifice and blue mountains on the horizon: but the outlines of all I saw were so soft! every murmur I heard so gentle! the perfumes I breathed so fine! and all things I touched slipped so gently from under my hands!—that I fancied myself in the land of shadows, where the objects retreat from the grosser senses.

"I collected myself, and went on to the mansion, where I hoped for an explanation of the doubts which were every moment increasing with me. At the same time I felt an unspeakable delight within; the calmness which rested on the silent country around seemed to have passed into my inmost soul. That which had hitherto disquieted my soul now lay as if in the distance behind me, while before me spread an interminable plain, rich in the fairest prospects.

"In this manner I wandered a whole summer's day, as it seemed to me, and without reaching the object of my travel, or feeling any disquiet at its continued remoteness. Judging from the quiet, holy feeling which then possessed me, I should have deemed myself a being of a higher order, if hunger and thirst had not convinced me to the contrary. No sooner was I conscious of the desire for nourishment, than the means of satisfying it presented themselves. Trees, laden with sweet cherries and odorous pears, inclined their boughs to me; they seemed ready to break with their burden, and invited me to enjoyment. My hand was already stretched out to break off what they offered, when I was suddenly restrained by the doubt whether I was permitted to plunder the property of another; for the castle, now close beside me, was a proof I was in no uninhabited wilderness. I therefore curbed my appetite and contented myself with a small portion of the fruit shaken off by the wind upon the grass, and in gratitude for the refreshment set up the fallen props under the heavy branches, that they might not lose any of their sweet burden.

"I was not so moderate with a fresh fountain by which I had to pass; I took as much as I could drink, though not with the golden vessel that stood there, but with the hollow of my hand. The quenching of my thirst increased my hunger, and the objects of excitement grew more and more powerful, for I had now reached the fore-court of the castle. Wide cool halls extended along the side, from one of which a bright fire gleamed most alluringly, and here I entered, expecting to find some of the inhabitants. All, however, was solitude, though the delicious scent that came from the saucepans convinced me that a supper was preparing for some people—who perhaps were not so hungry as I was.

"I looked everywhere for the cook, and now ventured boldly to the fire; but it was not greediness to taste any of the cookery that made me so free and easy; I saw, with the distress of a good housekeeper, that the spits were standing still, and the ragouts burning, and I hastened to set the spit back to motion and fought down the flames, though not without secret exclamations against the cooks' carelessness. I went to the hearth oven and turned the bread which had just browned. This being done, I hurried away, that I might not yield to the suggestions of hunger; but the conquest cost me a deep sigh; I could not help turning back and sweeping off a few crumbs from the clean kitchen table, which I swallowed hastily, and then went on.

"I now approached the double steps that led to the entrance of the house, and ascended them without further thought. When, however, I had continued my way, and found on all sides more magnificence than I had ever witnessed before, I began to suspect that I was approaching very exalted people, such as I had not been accustomed to meet with, and from whom, therefore, I could not expect the best reception. 'After all,' I said to myself, 'what are you doing here, and what brought you to the desperate resolution of plunging into the well? A lost trifle. Will you find it here? Dare you ask for it? Yes, indeed, won't it sound nice, when you come before the owner of this castle, and say, "Gracious sir—or gracious lady—have you seen a spinning reel that tumbled into your well?"—For shame, Rose! Scorn and contempt will be the reward of your boldness and simple-mindedness; it would be better to turn back and see how you can re-ascend the well, and to be satisfied with what fate has decided for you. But then how shall I come before my cousin with her orphaned spinning-wheel? If I had but the lost lead I should be contented, and go back again without fear.'

"Such were my thoughts, and I looked disquietedly about me, as if seeking for that I had lost. In a moment my eyes were struck by an open door, leading into a bright, neat room, filled with all manner of spinning instruments, a sight that attracted me irresistibly. Heavens! what splendors I perceived there! The spinning-room of the empress could not be better outfitted. Flax and wovens of the finest kinds, distaffs and spindles of the most costly materials and finest workmanship, and above all, a whole army of neat little reels, formed after all the rules of art to give motion to the most awkward spindle.

"'Yes,' I exclaimed, clasping my hands, 'here is a storehouse! Had I but one of these beautiful things, I should be contented. But some of them are of gold, and some of silver; no, they are not for my purpose; mine was of lead, covered with green varnish. But stop: these resemble the lost one to a hair; I must see if I cannot find mine amongst them.'

"Upon this I sought amongst the twin-brothers of my lost reel, which I knew accurately by a little mark, but without finding it, and I went away in melancholy, saying to myself, 'I could, indeed, make good my loss here, for my cousin does not recollect her spinning utensils so very accurately; a little resemblance would be sufficient for her—but then you must not steal.—Oh, if I could only find my own.'

"'What are you doing here in my spinning-chamber?' exclaimed a fearful voice behind me, just as I was crossing the threshold and shutting the door to avoid any further temptation. I turned round full of terror and saw a tall female figure, swathed in a thousand veils, who repeated her question, threatening me with her long, bony, curved finger. This costume told me at once whom I had before me. The apparition answered exactly to the description of the well-spirit as I had it from my old instructress, and a cold shuddering seized me.

"'Gracious Lady Hulla!' I exclaimed, falling upon my knees—

"'Call me not *so*,' she cried, 'you see I do not deserve the name.'

"'Lady of the Veils,' I continued—

"'Call me not *so*,' she exclaimed in a still more terrifying voice: 'that is a bad name, borrowed from my dress, and I will not suffer it. Above all, seek for no excuses, but tell me in few words what you want, although I know it all without your telling.'

"'Then you must know,' I said with trembling voice, 'that I had no intention of robbing you; I only sought amongst your goods for my own property, and, as I could not find it, was going away again.'

"'It is well,' she replied; 'tomorrow you shall have it and be dismissed. For the present, follow me; you shall eat with me.'

"At the word *eat*, my heart jumped with joy, for fear and terror had not been able to drive away my hunger. I followed into the innermost of the many beautiful chambers, where she ordered me to set the table, finding fault with me the whole time in the most vehement manner; I was, however, used to this with my godmother, listened in silence, and did as she desired.

"'Have you shaken my trees?' she demanded.

"'No, lady; I propped up the bending branches.'

"'And have you forborne from picking?'

"'I tasted a few pears that lay upon the grass.'

"'Have you stolen the gold-cup from my spring?'

"'I did not touch it, but drank much and often out of the hollow of my hand, for I was thirsty.'

"'How are things going on in the kitchen?'

"'I basted the game and stirred the ragouts, for the cooks were out of the way; I turned your breads too in the oven, because they were on the point of burning.'

"'Did you taste any?'

"'No, I scraped together a few crumbs to appease my hunger.'

"'That you should not have done; but it is well, and you may serve up supper.'

"Thus I found myself suddenly, without any previous discussion, in the service of a wondrous mistress, and accommodated myself to it as well as I could. I went into the kitchen, got everything ready, served up the meal, and placed myself behind her chair to wait upon her; but she bade me, in a rough tone, to sit down opposite her, and eat with her. 'Do you think,' she grumbled, helping me at the same time very plentifully to food, 'do you think I do not know what I am saying? I asked you to be my guest, and that's the end of it.'

"I ate and drank as moderately as a hungry person could do, and answered her few questions with brevity, promptness and truthfulness. Upon rising from table she said, 'Undress me,' and I applied myself with trembling, but without impatience, to the arduous task of shelling, as it were, a thin, and almost ethereal, body from a world of veils. Nature had wasted little that was material upon the visible part of her and seemed to have been lavish only in an abundant mass of hair, which was as entangled as if no comb had passed through it since the first day of its growth. All this was to be put in order, and a silver comb with a golden brush was given me for this witch's task.

"I set to work with the greatest care and patience, and had the pleasure of seeing the lady smile approvingly, when, after four hours' toil, the locks curled under my fingers, and shadowed, not ungracefully, the pale thin face. Upon the whole, the House Mistress—for so I would call her—was now much more friendly than at first, and, when I had put her to bed, addressed me as follows:

"'Rose, you have conducted yourself well, yet not wholly without fault. You must remember the feelings that delighted you upon your first entrance into my realms; they were the feelings of the blessed, and such you might have enjoyed forever, if you had been able to resist the appetites of the body. You did, indeed, restrain hunger and thirst within the bounds of moderation, but you did not wholly subdue them; had you been able to do so, you would have never returned to the upper world, but remained here in the kingdom of shadows, where, as you may easily believe, I would have appeared to you in another form than now and talked to you in another manner. As it is, you must return to the life of wretchedness; but your visits to me are not forbidden, whenever you find courage enough to plunge into the well. The trials which you have today experienced are for your benefit; I love you and would like to see you perfect; whether you will be so rests with yourself. But, not to leave you without some recompense for all you have endured here today, see what I give you.'

"With these words she pressed something into my hand, and bade me go to sleep at the foot of her bed.

"I could not forbear examining the lady's gift by the light of the bedroom lamp, and, to my great astonishment, found nothing but the lost reel. 'But it is well,' said I to myself, 'and in fact it is the best thing she could have given me, for, without it, how could I appear before my cousin?'

"With these thoughts I fell asleep. Soon after I was awakened by sundry thumps and pinches, which, as I could tell with eyes yet closed, must come from the hands of my aunt. I looked about me, and saw that I was still sitting by the brink of the well, the distaff at my side, the spindle and reel in my lap, while before me stood my aunt, together with some neighbors, who were falling upon me without mercy.

"'Lazy sluggard!' cried my godmother, 'we have looked for you over the whole house without finding you; nay, we have even been here at the well without seeing you, and now after all we meet you in the very same place. I suppose you can make yourself invisible, or else have some lurking-places of your own. Away with you to your work; Monday has not the same privileges as its predecessor.'

"I obeyed, but knew not what to make of the language of these women, or of my adventures in the country of the House Mistress. It seemed impossible for me to consider the latter a dream, and yet I had not the least circumstance to prove its reality. Nor could I reconcile the time which I thought I had passed below, with that in which they had in vain sought for me upon the earth; the first appeared to me to be longer than a day and night; the latter, scarcely the duration of morning till evening. The whole week long I pondered upon this while at my household chores, and longed for the Sunday, when I might better meditate in my solitude by the well.

"All my reflecting and composing, however, served no other purpose than to convince me I had been dreaming. I grieved much at this. Notwithstanding all the little vexations I had met with in the twilight realm of the underworld, they were yet so delightful to me, the mistress of them was at last so friendly to me!—and then she had professed love for me, and invited me to visit her, things which were unusual to me, and the recurrence of which I most fervently desired. My longing at length got to such a pitch that I was many times upon the point of descending into the well to convince myself whether all these pleasant things had been dreams or reality; but a glance at the peril I was going to expose myself to at random always frightened me back again; the descent itself, setting everything else aside, was by no means agreeable; the mud, the toads and frogs in the well, made the mere looking down into it terrible, and thus the desperate deed was never carried into effect. Still, however, the seat by the well continued to be my favorite resort, and the thoughts of the shadowy realms and their mistress a feast of thought. Often I would intentionally go to sleep on the spot that was so sacred to me, hoping to dream again that sweet dream, but never were my hopes fulfilled.

"Now came a time when the thoughts on my subterranean friend were joined to another subject that did not less interest me. Soldiers were quartered in our village, and though I was not beautiful, I was young, gentle, and neatly dressed, things which drew many eyes upon me, notwithstanding the care of my aunt to prevent it. However, none of my admirers pleased me but tall Martin, a young fellow who united to a well-made figure a heart full of goodness and benevolence that entirely won my affection. He was billeted in our cottage, so that it was impossible I should not sometimes see him, unless I was actually locked up. He began in all earnestness to speak of love and marriage, and although it had not come so far between us as that I had answered him with the one emphatic syllable, my heart had spoken for him the more decidedly; Sundays, in particular—when he went to church with the others, and I was left at home alone—were dedicated so entirely to a conversation with him in my fancy that Frau Hulla became only a secondary idea, which I was too simple to connect with his to any advantage.

"But my cousin Magdalene, my godmother's daughter, saw our lodger with as favorable eyes as he saw me, and played precisely the same part with him that he played with me. She followed his every step and made him proposals of love and marriage, which he as little answered as I answered his. It must have struck her that I was more fortunate than she, and the hatred which she had always felt for me now reached its highest pitch. She daily sought occasion for attacking me with words and blows; one Sunday, instead of going to church, she hid herself in the house fearing I might use this opportunity of a secret interview with lanky Martin, and fell upon me so furiously, as I sat spinning by my dear well, that, in my despair, I plunged into it without any consideration. 'I must die,' said I to myself, 'under the hands of this fury; it is better, therefore, to perish here!'—'Or,' whispered something within me, 'find again the place where you were once so happy.'

"This was my last thought as I fell; for the thickening air and the incessant plunging soon robbed me of all recollection, and I did not recover till I reached the ground, or rather was received by a pair of soft arms.

"'So!' said a friendly voice, 'Were such violent means requisite to bring you back again to me?'

"I opened my eyes, and saw myself in the arms of my good friend, the spectral House Mistress. She was not now so fearfully thin as upon our first acquaintance, was much less enveloped in veils, and wore a countenance of good humor.

"'I bade you,' said she, casting at me a glance of assumed severity, 'I bade you visit me again; why have you not done so?'

"'Gracious Lady, I held all the good I experienced with you for a dream, and did not like to set my life in hazard.'

"'It is well. That you may not again think you have been in a dream, and that you may not again be compelled to risk your life in leaping into the abyss, take this leaden ring, which, when you stand upon the brink of the well, will bring you to me as often as you choose. But now go. They are anxiously seeking for you in the upper world. Or would you rather remain with me?'

"'No, gracious Lady,' I replied; for the thought of lanky Martin quickly recurred to me, and I certainly could not expect to see him down here.

"'Or,' continued she, 'have you any other favor to ask of me?'

"'No, gracious Lady. At least I cannot recollect anything at the moment.'

"'Go then and bethink yourself, and return to me soon to let me know your wishes. Now go and cheer those that are seeking for you.'

"Hereupon she led me along a dark ascent and brought me into a cave, which had an outlet in the middle of the well; so short was the time of our walk that I could not at all reconcile it with my long falling. Above, I heard the voices of Magdalene, my godmother, and many of her neighbors, but none sounded so sweet to me as that of Martin, who by a few words expressed the despair into which the news of my loss had plunged him.

"'I will leap into the well myself,' he said , 'if I do not find her. Yet, hold; let down the bucket, and I will place myself in it to seek her below; perhaps she is hanging somewhere by the clothes and may yet be saved.'

"'For heaven's sake, Martin,' I cried below, 'do not risk your life; for here is nothing save mud and poisonous reptiles; but lower the bucket, and draw me up; I have sustained no injury.'

"A cry of joy from Martin replied to my exclamation. My cousins remarked that they had thought from the first it was of no consequence, and the leaping into the well was merely a malicious trick of mine, to cause them alarm and anxiety.

"After such a prologue, it may be easily imagined what my reception was from my tormentors. From Martin it was so much the more cordial; but I drew back gravely, for his turbulent joy offended my modesty.

"This adventure, however, had brought us nearer to each other. I knew how dearly he loved me, and he might form a tolerable guess at my feelings toward him; but we had no further opportunities of conversing together, for I was watched with all the eyes of Argus and could no longer stay at home on Sundays. Hitherto I had not been able to go to church from want of a cloak, but now my cousin Magdalene willingly lent me hers, that she might get rid of me and have a pretext to stay at home and brood projects against Martin and me.

"Strong objections, too, were shown to my sitting by my well, and I was for a long time forced to defer my promised visit to the House Mistress, till at last I hit upon the idea of hazarding a visit to her in the night. For this I made all my preparations beforehand in secret. I baked a cake, a thing for which I was renowned; for I said to myself, I must do something to honor the good House Mistress, and at the same time show her my accomplishments. That delicacy, I thought, would certainly taste better than her white bread, which—the truth be told—left something to be desired.

"I now crept out of the house and took my way to the well, when it suddenly occurred to me that I had forgotten one thing, and I sat down by the brink to meditate upon it.

"'Suppose,' said I to myself, 'suppose she should ask if you have thought what favor you would request of her. Silly creature, not to have reflected upon this before! Which would you choose of all the things you wish for? Rose, Rose, choose wisely, that you may not repent.'

"After a few minutes' reflection, I exclaimed, 'Now then I see it. Martin loves me—that is certain—and would marry me, but that we both are poor, and cannot therefore even think of it. Even if he should get enough in war to buy a farm, and marry me, still I should be a poor girl without a dowry; besides, I am awkward and should bring him little profit with my labor. I will ask the Frau Hulla to make me the most skillful spinner in the land; then Martin will cultivate the fields, while I work at home and make money, and we shall be well off.'

"My resolution, which bore the mark of the greatest simplemindedness, was now taken. I turned the ring as I had been taught, and in a moment found myself with my subterranean friend. I gave her the cake with a deep curtsy; she consumed it with a benevolent smile, and upon her request I expressed my wish.

"She looked at me with eyes full of wonder and smiled, as she said, 'Poor simple soul! And this then is all you request? Your wish shall be granted, yet that does not exclude you from making others; but first go and attend to my affairs. Prop up my trees, water my flowers, and get my meal ready, that I may eat, and we will then see further.'

"I did as I was ordered; and the friendly House Mistress condescended to seat herself at the spinning-wheel to instruct me. Afterwards I combed, undressed, and put her to bed, and then laid myself at her feet. She said, 'Sleep well, awake in the upper world, and return soon, that I may go on with my instructions.'

"'Yes, gracious Lady,' I replied, 'but I am afraid that my aunt will use me ill when I awake, for I have been long absent.'

"She bade me be without fear, and I fell asleep.

"My slumber was short and invigorating, and, when I awoke, the morning was beginning to look gray upon the windows. I got up in terror, and set about my household chores, for, after the multitude of things I had seen and learned in the lower world, I feared that I must have been absent a whole day and two nights. I was, however, convinced to the contrary, and perceived that more could be done with time in the place where I had been than in the upper world.

"I burned with desire to try my newly acquired art, and, as soon as I dared, sat down at the spinning-wheel. Magdalene, who for some time had been learning to spin in the city, mocked my awkwardness as usual; but how great was her surprise when she saw me load the distaff with the greatest neatness, and fill my spindle in a moment with the finest yarn! Everyone came to see me spin, and I had the honor of remaining this and the following days at the wheel, for my aunt saw plainly that I should bring her more profit by my spindle than by doing the coarse work of the house, which was now turned over to a maid.

"In a short time I was so famous for the fineness of my work that my aunt gained by it considerably. This, however, did not improve my situation; my two relations were still avaricious and cruel to me, and I was obliged to sit up half the night, because, with all my industry, I could not do enough in the day to satisfy the avarice of my hard taskmistress.

"This deprived me of the opportunity of visiting my benefactress as frequently as I wished, and of being fully initiated into the mysteries of the spinning-wheel. At times, however, I managed it. But I never went without carrying a cake, which she seemed to enjoy, and never left her without acquiring some new skill, for upon her allowing me a second wish, I thought of the loom, the knowledge of which she imparted to me as well, thereby considerably increasing the profit I brought into my godmother's house.

"As I grew more intimate with the House Mistress, our conversation became at times unreserved, and she never dismissed me without asking if I had not a secret to disclose to her? Upon my always answering 'no,' she would admonish me to be as cautious toward others as toward herself. Ah! Whenever she looked into my heart so, I always thought of my Martin; but how could I venture to mention his name to her?

"Owing to the incredible quantity of work imposed upon me since my dexterity had increased, I had almost ceased to see him; in the grief which this caused me, I had no consolation but my visits to my subterranean mistress, who seemed to grow fonder and fonder of me, and in her quiet realm every tormenting passion was lulled to rest.

"One day I found her melancholy; our repast and shared work were dispatched almost without a word, and she dismissed me with tears in her eyes. Again she urged her former questions, 'Would I remain with her? — had I any secret to communicate?' —then followed the usual admonition, and the parting kiss with which she now often honored me.

"'Alas!' she said, 'I fear I shall not see you again. Be cautious, and, for fear of the worst, take, in memory of me, this golden spindle; it will make you rich; but be carful not to part with it, for, in losing it, you lose all claim to my beneficence.'

"I kissed and wetted with my tears her soft white hand which was now no longer a fleshless skeleton, as in the beginning of our acquaintance. 'It grieves me to my heart,' I said, 'to see you weep, but surely you have no reason. This dear ring can bring me back again to you in the very next hour after I have left you. Oh, it is dearer to me than that which my bridegroom will one day give me at the holy altar.'

"'Rose! Rose!' she cried with a threatening gesture, 'that is saying much. Ask your heart whether it would not readily sacrifice my friendship to passion for a lover? Yet why should you need such sacrifice? I am not so hard as to deny you love, if you were only candid toward me. As to the ring, keep it well, but beware of its falling into strange hands; I should not like to see unbidden guests breaking into my quiet realm.'

"The sadness of the lady changed at the end of her speech into partial anger, and I went away less cheerful than on former occasions. I said to myself, 'What must she think of me with these strange speeches? Certainly she has found out my love for Martin. I know that I talk at times in my sleep, and she must have overheard me. Fool that I am, not to have told her of it long ago! She is so good, so condescending, she would not have scolded me! But did not my dear mystery hover a thousand times upon my lips, and yet I could never speak it? Away, Rose, with this foolish bashfulness! Consider the lady your mother, and speak boldly to her. There is no evil in loving and marrying, and besides I cannot and must not do anything without her, since she has shown so much kindness to me.'

"Such was the way in which I conversed with myself upon my return to the upper world, and resolved not to draw down upon me the anger of my friend by a longer silence. It was late on a Saturday night, when I fully made up my mind as to what I should do, and I urged on my spindle more rapidly, that I might finish my task, and not, as it sometimes happened, have to work on a Sunday, and so be hindered in my design.

"My cousins, who had got fine clothes, and burned with desire to show them, did not fail to go to church, but I stayed at home under the pretext of indisposition, and, as soon as they had turned their backs, hastened to my beloved well, to turn the ring and carry out my design. Before I could get there, however, I suddenly heard myself accosted by a gentle voice, 'Shall I never find you inclined to listen to me?' It was Martin, who stood beside me.

"'For shame!' I exclaimed with glowing cheeks; 'how you frightened me! Go, I cannot talk to you; you see we are alone.'

"'It is for that very reason I want to speak with you. I have so much to say, good Rose, and your spies never leave you for a moment.'

"I blushed still more, pressed his hand, which had seized mine, and cast to the ground my tear-filled eyes.

"He took my silence for consent. We seated ourselves at the edge of the well and began a conversation that might never end.

"'O my benefactress!' I exclaimed with folded hands and a glance at the well, when Martin had finished the confession of his love, and the detail of his plans for our happiness, 'O my benefactress! you hear the oaths of this man! Be you his judge if he ever should break his faith with me! Be you my judge if I ever should break my faith with him! For I love him more than ever maiden loved a youth! And now, Martin, farewell—I am going to obtain her consent to our happiness, and perhaps tomorrow I am yours. Fool that I was not to ask the good lady for it before.'

"'What are you about?' cried my lover, who understood nothing I had said, and saw with terror that I got upon the edge of the well, with the intention of descending into the lower world by the help of the ring. 'Leave me!' I replied, 'Our happiness depends on the step I am about to take.' But Martin, who knew nothing of my purpose, embraced me with vehement gestures, nor would he desist till I had again seated myself by him to explain to him the mystery.

"My narration lasted long, for I resolved to conceal nothing from him, and his exclamations of joy and wonder, with the thousand questions interposed, made it still longer. I had just ended when I saw my aunt coming over the fields, and now knew that the time for the visit to my benefactress had passed in the conversation with my lover. Another embrace, a few more words of delight at our approaching happiness, and then we separated.

"My scolding aunt found me, when she came up, unusually red, and bade me go away from the well to my work. Not knowing what else to say, I asked after Magdalene, and received for answer that she had gone over to the neighboring village, and would not return before night. This troubled me but little; I worked hard the whole day long, that I might go to bed so much the sooner, and then wake again after midnight to execute my important commission with my protectress.

"Soon after I had fallen asleep I was awakened by the voices of my two relations, who were talking together very loudly in the next chamber, and, upon hearing my own name mentioned, I listened more attentively. 'She will wake,' said the mother, 'speak softly.' 'Let her wake,' answered Magdalene with her accustomed roughness, 'the time is coming when all must be explained. For the rest, you would do well in believing me more for the future, since you see that I am right in all things. We now see that her sudden dexterity was not acquired by fair means, and I found out today her secret understanding with my Martin. Heavens! what it cost me not to burst forth at once from my hiding-place and strangle the impudent wretch with my own hands! but my moderation was well rewarded; I now know her whole history—know what I have to do to visit, like her, the old woman in the well, and, like her, become dexterous and beautiful; for, believe me, the red and white of her cheeks are not natural; they are a gift from the old witch. Oh, I will go and get from her all that she has done for that idiot—and then Martin shall love me—yes, he shall love me, I assure you—for I will be fairer and better than Rose is, if my project succeeds.'

"As she spoke thus Magdalene clapped her hands, and screamed so loudly that her mother again bade her be silent.

"'Still! Still!' she whispered, 'I entreat you in Heaven's name! You forget that, for our project, we need the ring, which she never takes off her finger, and which we must try to get away secretly. Oh, I had observed this little thing before, but without guessing its value, because it was of lead, or else I wouldn't have let her wear it so long.'

"With terror I heard this conversation without knowing what to do; but the moment the ring was mentioned, I recollected that my friend had strictly bidden me not to let it fall into other hands. I was here the weaker, and thought that I could not otherwise save it than by letting it drop behind the bed. This I endeavored to do gently, but its fall rung loudly, as if metal had fallen from a great height into a rocky abyss. I heard the sound for several moments; it bounded twice or thrice, as Magdalene's reel had done before, when I let it fall into the well.

"I felt strange on hearing the sound, as if something within me cried out, 'Good night, my true benefactress! The bond between us is for ever broken!'—but I had no time to examine my thoughts, for my tormentors, who had probably agreed to lay aside craft and kindness and proceed by violence, stormed in, found me awake, and without further preface, demanded the ring from me. I pretended not to understand their meaning, and it came to an explanation, which, mixed as it was with abuse and poured forth by two yelling female voices at the same time, would have been absolutely unintelligible, if I had not been informed of everything beforehand.

"My hesitation and denial availed me nothing. They laid hands upon me and used me most cruelly; and when at last I was forced to confess that the treasure they sought had fallen behind the bed, I was dragged out and everything turned topsy-turvy to find it again. They did, indeed, find an old iron ring, which had probably been broken off from some piece of furniture and would have fitted a giant's finger rather than mine. This, they wanted me to confess, was the one they were looking for, and without paying any attention to my denial, they dragged me to the well, to teach cousin Magdalene how she was to manage in visiting the subterranean kingdom.

"The mother stayed with me, regaling me with blows, while her daughter ran to put on her best things that she might appear properly before the Lady of the Well. I employed my utmost eloquence to persuade her that it was all over with Magdalene, if, trusting to this ring, she plunged into the abyss, for I was not wicked enough to wish her to meet with any accident. But my cousin now appeared in formal dress, leaped upon the edge of the well without listening to any suggestions, turned the ring, as she had learned from my talk to Martin, raised the right foot, then the left, and tumbled with a dreadful crash into the abyss, where no hope remained for her but that her clothes might be caught by some protruding stone or branch, and she might thus be saved.

"This, probably, was the case, for we heard her whimpering below, and calling out for help in a faint voice. I was the first who hurried off to call Martin and the neighbors that they might assist in getting her up again, but

I was not fortunate enough to be present at her rescue; my aunt soon followed me and locked me up in my room, with the assurance that I should not leave it again until Magdalene had reappeared, or she had been revenged for Magdalene's death.

"After I had tolerably recovered in my solitude—for everyone had gone to the well—and made myself a thousand reproaches for the fault which had drawn upon me this misfortune, my first care was to look for the ring which, to my great joy, had not fallen into the hands of my enemies. I had flung it behind the bed and could point out with a needle the precise spot whereon it ought to lie—but I sought in vain. Alas! I recollected only too soon the sound of its heavy fall, and I exclaimed, bursting into tears, 'O kind mistress of the house! You have taken it back again, for I was not worthy of it; but could I act otherwise if I did not wish your gift to become the property of an unworthy creature, who by means of it would have forced herself into your kingdom and disturbed its quiet?'

"Worn out with continued weeping, I at length fell asleep on the bare floor, where I was sitting, and a multitude of confused images floated darkly before my fancy. When I awoke I was unable to separate and define them, nothing remained distinct upon my memory but the image of my benefactress, with her long, thin finger raised up to menace, and her warning voice, with which she spoke the words, 'Candor, circumspection, and prudence'—Ah! the dear voice, ever admonishing rightly! I can still fancy that I hear her! She laid before me my errors only too plainly, and told me what I had to do for the future.

"I followed her directions, and recollecting the golden spindle, my only remaining possession, I hastened to look for it, and when I had found it, sewed the treasure in the lining of my underfrock that no one might rob me of it. But this last gift of my benefactress was secured to me by another circumstance, which is the best security for all treasures—namely, no one knew that I possessed it. By chance I had forgotten to mention it in my unlucky narrative to Martin, and thus the listening Magdalene had not the slightest suspicion of my riches.

"I spent the whole of the following day in solitude, without eating or drinking, and in the most painful disquiet. I heard nothing but the groans of my aunt and the curses and vituperations that she poured out against me toward the neighbors who had gathered for the purpose of comforting her.

Martin too came in for his share, having shown himself careless in the measures taken for Magdalene's rescue. She laid it to him that the unfortunate girl had not been found; he had besides vehemently urged my release, and, when all he could say was fruitless, had left them with a declaration that he would find the means of righting both himself and me, since, before God and man, I was his bride, whom he would lead to the altar as soon as I was in his hands.—O Martin, what transports did I feel at heart from your zealous ardor! It was my only consolation, and I seated myself joyfully at the window to await the end of my sufferings in the fresh air that breathed upon me through the grating.

"It was about the time of evening twilight that I heard from the neighborhood of the well a hollow moaning, like the sound of Magdalene's voice. I was just rising to call for help through the door, when I saw a figure at a distance, which, I know not why, I took for hers, although it was scarcely human, and which the nearer it came, grew the more horrible. Face and hands were hardly to be recognized from bruises and swellings; the high headdress and the long garments were drenched in mud and drew along a great part of the mire and bushes of the well; her pace was rather a creeping than a walk, and her voice broke out from time to time into fearful shrieks echoing frightfully in the mountains. She would have excited pity, had not rage and malice burnt upon her distorted features, and all her actions betrayed an impotent spirit of revenge. As she passed beneath my window, she held up her hands with furious gestures and immediately afterwards beat violently at the door with balled fists; my aunt, who had chanced to see her through the window, would no doubt have opened to her directly, but the fearful apparition had so terrified her that she could not in her hurry find the key, so that for a long time Magdalene served as a laughingstock for the passersby. No doubt, however, her greatest vexation was that Martin, who happened to come that way, could not forbear approaching her to be convinced of what he saw and then hurried off with every sign of abhorrence.

"Magdalene was now admitted, and I crept to the door to learn from her conversation what had brought her into this miserable condition; but her discourse was a howl, and it was not till after many hours, when she had been cleaned, salved, and put to bed, that I learned what had happened, less from her mouth than from her mother's discourse with her neighbors.

"I caught fragments only, and as I have never, since that time, asked her any questions on the subject, I can give you nothing more than a broken narrative. She had reached the bottom of the well, covered with wounds and swellings and with her dress in the most miserable plight. From the unconsciousness—which I too had twice experienced—she recovered in the same country and went through the same adventures as I, but acted in a manner quite consonant with her usual character. She trod down the fruit and flowers, plundered the kitchen and cellars, and replied with rudeness and falsehood to the House Mistress, who received her with ironical politeness. Frau Hulla had her own peculiar way of taming her enemies; she called up half a dozen of her subordinate spirits—with the sight of whom she had never alarmed me—the black brood of lasting night! images which few mortal eyes could see without dying with terror!—and these she ordered to try their arts upon the unruly Magdalene.

"Magdalene did not, indeed, die, but before evening she grew quite tractable and crept imploringly to the feet of the indignant House Mistress from whom she obtained her pardon. Her gratitude for this was shown by getting up in the night, stealing the gold and silver implements from the dressing-table, and secretly escaping, not forgetting to carry off the golden bowl from the fountain. A hundred spirits were bound to the enchanted vessel, who would not suffer their treasure to be taken from them; the whole shadowy kingdom was awake behind her; they fell upon the poor wretch to torment her, as only spirits can torment a mortal, and at last hurled her from one point to another up the well, on the brink of which she lay unconscious for hours, without being sought or found by anyone, till at length she revived, and crept back, howling, to her maternal cottage.

"However little Magdalene had deserved my pity, the description of what she had suffered moved me to tears; nothing consoled me but her mother's opinion that the greatest part of these frightful adventures had been only a dream, or pure fancy, and that she had in reality suffered nothing more than the contusions from her tumble into the well. Magdalene, however, found little comfort in this interpretation of her story; she did not like to be robbed of the honor of having been actually ill-treated, and, from her bed, roared out repeated assertions of the truth of what she had uttered.

"'It is true!' she cried, 'it is all true! and, if you won't believe me, feel in my pockets. Of all my booty, at least the old witch's comb and brush have remained; they are of gold and will make my dowry so considerable that Martin must take me.'

"No sooner had the mother heard of golden treasures than she ran to her daughter's clothes to get them, when two hideous toads leaped out upon her, and, fastening themselves upon her neck, would have killed her, if one of the neighbors had not had courage enough to tear them off and fling them into the fire.

"This scene ended with execrations, insults, and threats against me, who was looked upon as the cause of this misfortune. I thought I should die of fear and exclaimed wringing my hands, 'Good God! what will become of me, if I remain in the power of these furies?' But at this moment the voice of my lover sounded throught the grating, 'Come, my beloved, let us fly! The hour of your deliverance has struck.'—I flew to the window, and, by the pale moonlight, saw Martin upon a ladder, armed with tools to break the iron bars of my prison. The loud screams in my cousin's chamber drowned the noise of our escape. Martin received me in his arms, and, before the next day was over, the priest's hand had made me his wife.

"The persecutions of my enemies were now fruitless, for the officer with whom Martin served took us under his wing. In a short time too I should be entirely free from the danger of their malice, for, after a few days, the army was to break up from my birthplace for a distant country.

"Oh! I was happy in the arms of my husband and nothing grieved me but that I should be forever separated from my benefactress, the good House Mistress. I heeded not the loss of my ring and went one night to the well with the intent to plunge into it, let the consequence be what it might, and once again see my insulted friend; but, alas! the well was filled up! My story and that of Magdalene had excited general attention; everyone passed with terror the spot that was so dear to me, and the magistrates, if they would not have the country quite depopulated, saw themselves compelled to block up the passage with stones and rubbish, both against mortals and ghosts. I wept over this destruction till the rising of the sun, and invoked my benefactress by her most hateful as well as her dearest names, that I might see her again, even if it were in anger; I rubbed, too, and pressed her last gift in a thousand ways to awake any secret power it might have, but all in vain. My husband found me bathed in tears on the spot, which was so dangerous to me from the vicinity of my persecutors, and with some anger led me home whence in a few days we began our march to the country where you now find me.

"With the profits from his occupation Martin bought this little farm and left me here while he went off to war, consoling me with the hope of peace and of his return. I, however, employed my first quiet hours in setting my golden spindle in motion, which I vowed to use till death in memory of my benefactress.

"It was with good reason that she had told me this gift would make me rich, for it was incredible how much I could accomplish with it. In three hours I did as much as could be done in a day with any other, and—what was the strangest part of the story—when I left it overnight hanging at the distaff with scarcely a single thread upon it, I found it in the morning full and heavy with a yarn so fine that even my fingers, skillful as they were through the lady's kindness, could not spin anything like it, and which I sold at court as dear as gold.

"I never saw this wonder without heartfelt gratitude toward the occasion of it. But a greater delight was reserved for me: one sleepless night—and the absence and peril of my husband caused me many—as I raised my eyes to the distaff, which stood at the window in the clear moonlight, I saw Frau Hulla hard at work spinning. I uttered a loud cry of joy, and, calling her by name, rushed out of bed to throw myself at her feet, but as I came near to her, the beloved spirit melted into air, and I held nothing but the spindle that was only half filled.

"In the following nights, notwithstanding this disappointment, I endeavored to see my benefactress again and embrace her knees; in the first I always succeeded; in the latter, never. Sometimes her looks seemed to rest upon me in the distance kindly and smilingly, but she still remained intangible to my arms and made no reply to my lamentations. In the meantime my wealth increased by her aid, but I kept it a secret, that I might surprise my husband with it on his return. In truth I lived happily in this quiet middle rank of life and rejoiced in my treasures solely upon his account. Still I did not let them lie quite idle. Charity toward the poor and hospitality were two of the most agreeable lessons I had learnt at the Lady's spinning-wheel, and her instructions were much too sacred to be neglected. My treasures flowed in silence to the needy, and many an eye was brightened by me that did not know me.

"That I might be able to attend to the duties of hospitality as well as those of quiet benevolence, I bought the little cottage, about twenty paces from the village, where our wicked neighbor lives now, and in this I received the sick and the weary—a blessed occupation, for the practice of which the continuing war afforded me a thousand opportunities. A battle was fought in these parts and my house was filled with the wounded who sought to be healed, and the dying, who wished to breathe their last in quiet. I could tell you many instances of this kind, but hear only one, the most essential.

"A young man who, in spite the care and attention I had bestowed upon him, fell a victim to death, and before his end commended his wife to me telling me the place where I should find her sick and nearly dying. 'She has not,' he said, 'deserved this care at my hands; she almost forced herself upon me, and during our short marriage has been a torment to me, but she is a helpless stranger, and I must not leave her entirely without comfort; she came over with me from distant Germany to find a grave here. Take her to you and let her die in your arms; perhaps your intercession may open to her the gates of heaven which her own sins have closed against her.'

"The young warrior died, and I delayed not to fulfill his last wishes. A sick and deserted creature of my own sex, a native of my fatherland, a sinning woman at the gates of eternity—what demands this made on me to practice my most sacred duties! The wretched creature who was brought into my house was to me an object of real pity, but she never could be an object of love and goodwill, for her appearance was as hateful as her conduct. Her face, covered with scars, was an image of her impure soul. In her illness, scorn and furious impatience against me who nursed her were poured out alternately with feeble lamentations and creeping humility; a cold shudder thrilled through me whenever I saw her, and great was my joy when her recovery allowed me to remove so unpleasant a patient from my cottage.

"I procured for her a little habitation in the village and gave her work for which I paid her double, for she, like myself, was a spinner. Unfortunately our common occupation gave her many opportunities of tormenting me with her presence, which became to me the more intolerable the more I thought I discovered something familiar in her voice and features. I therefore gave her a small sum that she might begin for herself, and do without me, but still she would creep after me every day as I sat at work, peep into every corner of my house, criticize everything, and find fault with my domestic arrangements. A trifling sickness that attacked her one day when with me gave her an excuse for passing the night in my cottage, and I had reason to suspect that it was more curiosity than illness that detained her with me for many days.

"I did not conceal my thoughts from her, and she left me with murmurs and threats. 'There are people,' she said, 'who drive good luck out of their houses and who then find misfortune at their heels.' I paid no attention to her raven cry, for I did not reflect that the wicked have the fulfilment of their prophecies in their own hands.

"Only a few days had passed, when the wishes of my enemy were gratified; a fire destroyed my house at the entrance of the village, together with my stores of flax and thread. All the treasures that I had collected for myself, my husband, and the poor were irretrievably lost, and I saved nothing from the flames but my spindle.

"In my distress no one appeared more ready to assist me than my enemy, and, deprived as I was of all other support, I was compelled to accept the refuge which she offered me in her cottage. To add to my misfortune, on the third day of my abode with her she brought me the news that my Martin had been made prisoner, and that, according to the custom of the time, he, with others who had fallen into the hands of the enemy, would be killed, unless someone was found to pay the ransom set upon him. The sum demanded was exorbitant; even with the secret help of my benefactess, I would have had to spin for months to get together so much money, and his deliverance must take place in a few days at the farthest.

"I was in despair; no expedient occurred to me but one, at which I recoiled, and yet which I was forced to adopt at last, because it was the only one. I set out, sold my golden spindle, swept up the money with tears, and flew to the camp to ransom my husband. 'Ah, love!' I cried on the road, wringing my hands, 'Love! What a sacrifice have I made to you! Now the bonds of union between me and my old friend are forever sundered!—The loss of the ring only robbed me of all intercourse with her; but the loss of the spindle deprives me of her sight, too, of her care, of her blessing. What did she say at our last parting? Take good care of it, for in losing it, you lose every claim to my goodwill and protection.'

"Such were my lamentations; but the sight of Martin who was waiting for me and my joy at having saved him, never again to part from him, soon chased away all melancholy thoughts. He agreed to follow me to the country where the ruins of our house lay, and I managed to gain so much by my industry in a short time as to be able to make it habitable. Alas! I did not consider what I was saying! My connection with her, who so supernaturally blessed my work, was broken up; henceforth I was nothing more than a common spinner, and consequently the profits of my labor were hardly sufficient to support us. Still, could I seriously think that my benefactress would be angry at an unavoidable act, springing out of duty to my husband? I had not sacrificed her gift out of capriciousness or frivolity, and in truth she was kind enough to restore it; a short time only and the golden spindle again hung at my distaff, and I saw the dear spinner sitting by it at night and finishing my task for me.

"My joy and gratitude were inexpressible, and the hope of advancement certain. Our house again rose from its ashes, our fields no longer lay waste, and Martin himself plowed the land or brought its rich produce into our new-built barns.

"We were happy through our shared labor, and nothing vexed me but that for some time Martin's eyes had not dwelt upon me with the same affection as formerly. Still, I comforted myself by saying, 'Martin is no longer your lover but your husband; besides, you are not the same blooming Rose, nor he the same eighteen-year-old youth as when he swore eternal love by the well. The toils of the war and the labors of domestic life have deprived him of his cheerfulness; he feels for you as formerly, but he cannot show it in the manner that once used to enchant you.'

"At last, however, his coldness betrayed not only a diminution of love but of confidence. From the very commencement of our reunion I had hesitated to reveal to him the mystery of the spindle and the inexhaustible source of our wealth; and now that Martin no longer cast upon me those looks which had been wont to draw every secret from my inmost soul, now it was so much the easier for me to keep my little mysteries to myself. 'Silence—silence,' thought I, 'is the best guardian of my treasure. My mysterious friend will love me so much the more for my not communicating to anyone what has passed between us.' Alas! I practiced this clever rule in the wrong place and soon found that the reserve exhibited in almost all my actions had only more estranged my husband. Alas, I said to myself, it is enough if my friend distances himself a few steps from me, at the crossroads; I do not need to do the same from my side, anticipating an eternal separation. Let me wait patiently at the spot where he tore himself from my side, let me follow him begging—if the space that lies between us is not to become immeasurable. Martin began to be absent from me for days in a row, and what most vexed me was that the time thus robbed from me was spent in the house of my odious neighbor. With her ugliness jealousy was out of the question, but the suspicion of her poisoning his mind against me was only too well founded. The bitter reproaches with which he now began to attack me and the hateful coloring he gave to my conduct during the time of his absence in the wars all showed me that I had not without reason dreaded the whispers of this venomous viper. My care of the poor and the homeless was extravagance and a cover for secret excesses; my wealth was ill-gotten property; and my continued connection with my secret friend was no better than witchcraft and intercourse with evil spirits. At the last accusation I thought I would sink into the ground and asked with trembling what he could know of such things.

"'Rather let me ask, why you conceal such things from your husband?' he replied. 'At the time when you were yet young and innocent, you hid nothing from me, and I was too inexperienced, too much blinded by love, to find a crime in anything you did. Now you are a hypocritical sinner, and I am sufficiently aware of my duty to give you the choice of two things—either eternal separation from me, or from the abominable specter that sits at your distaff every night and tears the flax with her clawlike fingers.'

"'Martin, do you slander the benefactress who has made me yours, who has blessed our labors and saved you from death?'

"'I curse my alliance with a witch!—curse the gain that has been made by prohibited arts!—curse even my life, since you bought it by the sacrifice of the instrument of your sins, the magic spindle!—Oh, if I could once find it, I would hurl it into the deepest abyss, and fling myself after it.'

"'Martin! You are mad! Why do you talk of things which you have not heard from my lips, and which, therefore, may be false?'

"'Oh, there are kind folks who have opened my eyes—folks who have seen and heard, and have made me see and hear, till my senses well nigh failed me.'

"This fearful dialogue was the prelude to an explanation, which showed me I had to thank my wicked neighbor for all my misery; she had by degrees spied out all my mysteries and had imparted them to my husband in a way best calculated to raise in his fiery soul the storm which now burst over me. I wept bitterly; anger at the furious conduct of Martin was subdued by the most lively compassion for his unhappy error, an error which made him so wretched and which I in vain endeavored to dissipate. The image of his former love and of his present wrath stood in dreadful contrast with each other, and I exclaimed, 'O Hulla, what do all your benefits avail me, if I am to purchase them so dearly? Take back your gifts, take back your blessing, but restore to me the same Martin, who swore eternal love to me by the side of your well.'

"Martin stood with folded arms and eyes fixed steadily upon me, as if waiting for my decision.

"'Are you decided in offering me such a choice?' I asked, drying my eyes.

"'Yes, Rose; duty, religion, and even love command it.'

"'Love!' I cried, and, jumping up, I loosened the dear spindle from the distaff, 'Oh, if you still love me, take it all—take it all—but be wholly mine again. Take your own supporter, the savior of your life! Take the true bond that linked me to one of the most blessed of the heavenly spirits! I willingly sacrifice it, if in so doing I can only buy back your heart.'

"Martin took the treasure, gazed at it for a few minutes, then at me, then pressed me to his heart, and hurled the unlucky cause of our dissension through the window into the river below, which swallowed it instantly.

"With the loss of my spindle the fountain of all our prosperity had vanished; our wealth no longer increased, and all we possessed soon disappeared. We were poor peasants, like our neighbors; my spindle was filled only with the common yarn, laboriously procured and badly paid, and the earth was iron under my husband's plow, giving now only a simple return, where before it had yielded tenfold. But do you think this disturbed me? No, my mind had never hankered after riches; that which gnawed at my heart was the eternal separation from my benefactress, whom I no longer saw in bright nights spinning my spindle, and smiling on me with affection.

But this was made up to me by the perfect love of my husband, who was now quite reconciled to me and grew again the same as when I had first known him. I succeeded in convincing him of the injustice he had done me and in making the disturber of our peace suspicious to him. Nothing more effectually contributed to his dislike of our evil neighbor than the realization, which we gradually came to, that she was the same worthless Magdalene, who from the first had viewed our happiness with envious eyes and had not rested till she had destroyed a part of it, though, Heaven be praised, not the better part. Eventually her own confession confirmed our belief; she put on the appearance of a repentant sinner and under that guise kept the door of our house open to her.

"Still we disliked her society and tolerated it only from compassion, while she was trying partly to ameliorate, and partly to deny the plots of which she stood convicted. In nothing was she more eloquent than in defending her hatred of the woman of the well. 'Could I,' she would say, 'see my enemy be the companion of my friends?—she who punished my youthful presumption so cruelly?—she who robbed me of my beauty, and covered my face with scars that prevented even you from recognizing me? Thank Heaven, my friends, that I have freed you from this monster, who sooner or later would have shown you her claws and destroyed you.'

"To such language I was silent; my husband too said nothing, but I believe that he suffered in his heart more than I did. I had resigned myself to my fate, while he, who with time had come to sounder thoughts and had reason to look upon himself as the destroyer of our prosperity, grieved in silence, pined away, and—died.

"Please allow me to sketch the greatest catastrophe with a few words. I was now a poor, helpless, deserted widow and began to realize for the first time what I had lost in my separation from my old friend, who certainly would not have left me uncomforted in my affliction. But I had in a certain measure given up the connection with her voluntarily and did not deserve that she should give herself any more trouble about me. Still she did not abandon me; her kind hand was not to be mistaken, and I should even now be enjoying the fruits of her benevolence, if my enemy had not always contrived to rob me of more than half the benefit of it.

"In the course of time age and tears had weakened my eyesight, my earnings were scanty, and want and poverty stood close at my door. I thought of selling my goat, which till now had supported me with her milk, so that, once I got money into my hands, I might try to do something better for myself. With this view I went into the field to get her some food for the last time, when a shepherd whom I had never seen before passed by with his flock, at the moment when I was weeping bitterly at the idea of the approaching separation from my poor goat. 'Why are you weeping, Mother?' said he, and I did not hesitate to tell him the cause of my lamentation.

"'Nonsense!' replied the shepherd; 'do as I do; singing, I drive my flock out; singing, I drive it home again, and all my work prospers.'

"'Alas! I too did my work with song and with cheerfulness; but now I wet my spindle with tears.'

"'Are you a spinster? I too—Heaven be praised for it—can spin, but I do not wet my spindle with tears, and therefore I thrive in my occupation. Take this wonderful ball of my own spinning; I give it to you; perhaps it may bring you profit, as it was spun amidst mirth and laughter.'

"I looked at the speaker, a stout young man, and took the yarn he offered me with a smile, as he said, 'Wind off as much as you please from it; your fortune will last as long as the thread, but do not look for the heart from which it springs.'

"These were mysterious words, the explanation of which I would fain have heard from him, but just then my collection of grass fell out of my apron, and, when I had gathered it together and got up, sheep and shepherd were gone.

"I hastened home, gave the fodder to my goat, and began, with the expectation of some miracle, to wind a thread from my ball, such as no shepherd is like to spin. I wound and wound this and the following days so much from the ball that I no longer needed to sell my goat. My yarn supply was inexhaustible and my fortunes again began to flourish. I paid strict attention to the donor's warning, was cheerful over my easy labor, and thanked God for the blessing that followed all my actions; I was soon the same woman of substance that I had formerly been; the homeless and the poor again found a mother in me, and even Magdalene shared in my prosperity.

"One evening, as I sat in my chamber and by moonlight was drawing out a whole host of threads from the inexhaustible ball, I heard Magdalene's voice behind me of a sudden, exclaiming, 'All things considered, neighbor, there must be something singular in this ball of yours, and I would lay a wager that the golden spindle makes the heart of it; only dig with the needle into it, and you will see if I am right or not.' I started up full of terror. From no one had I so anxiously concealed my mystery as from my unworthy cousin, and now I found myself so completely watched by her. I drove her away with violence and reproach and closed the door, as indeed I thought I had done before her appearance, but I could not drive her words out of my memory. 'Is it possible,' thought I to myself, 'that the devil can for once speak truth? It is beyond doubt that the source of my fortune is the gift of my old friend; what if with this endless ball the dear spindle lies concealed, and by means of this she would renew the bond between us?'

"This idea haunted me incessantly; at last I got up one night after having dreamt that my fancy was true and between waking and sleeping dug with a needle into the heart of my ball, till the end which came from it broke, and no skill of mine could find it again.

"I now began to wind it off from without, and saw that in this way I should soon come to the end of my wealth, for the ball grew thinner and thinner, till at last I got to the core, which, instead of being the treasure I sought, was only a pebble.

"Whoever has suffered as much as I cannot be utterly inconsolable at a blow from fate, and I saw the ruin of my fortune with a sort of melancholy calmness; but my most painful feelings were indignant scorn at my folly and an increasing hatred toward my tempter. Still, I could scarcely be angry with her; this time it might be that she had spoken only from the impulse of chance and not from any evil intention, so that I alone must be blamed.

"I had found, and lost, too much good fortune in the world to expect anything more in my old age; I, therefore, collected the proceeds from my yarn adventure, which now had abruptly ceased, and husbanded it so that I might hope to gain a tolerable subsistence from it till my death. The spindle and the weaver's spool continued to be my darling implements, and I kept them constantly in motion, till I met with a second adventure, which convinced me I was under the protection of a higher power, and which filled my heart with the peace and cheerfulness that you now see in me, and that I want so much to transfer to you.

"I was sitting one evening, as usual, at the door of my cottage, looking out into the twilight to see if I could find any poor traveler to share in my humble repast, when a man appeared before me in the dress of a pilgrim from the holy sepulcher; that holy garb, however, could scarcely be recognized, so much was it worn out by the long journey. The snow of age covered his head, and his trembling limbs were supported by a knotty stick. I stood up before him respectfully and invited him into my cottage, where I treated him as I treated you on your first appearance—that is, I refreshed him with bread and milk, gave him water to wash his feet, and made up a bed for him. But I could scarcely sleep for thinking of him, so much was I moved by the sight of his misery. I reflected upon the means of helping him, but found myself too unprovided to do it thoroughly, and I had already in vain solicited him to make a longer stay in my cottage, for he had vowed, he said, to be a pilgrim till the day of his death. Of a sudden his wretched clothing struck me; it was indeed but a poor defense against the rain and cold, and I rose hastily to supply the want while he was yet sleeping. I found in my provisions enough cloth to make him two shirts, and set quickly to work, yet the morning star still found me at the task. I pulled out Martin's Sunday cloak—the only thing of his I had not traded in for money. Having completed my preparations, I packed up the clothes in a bundle with a loaf of bread hidden inside, together with half the money I then possessed, and laid the whole by his bedside.

"Soon afterwards he awoke, took up his staff and bundle, and went away without any particular expression of gratitude; only at the door he turned round to me with such strange words, that they seemed rather a curse than a blessing, and at all events I did not know what to make of them.

"'Let him mutter what he will,' said I to myself as I returned to my room, 'I did what I could for him, for the sake of God, and not to gain his praise or blessing.'

"The haste which had driven me to my nightly project caused my work to be still lying in disorder upon the table. I took up the remnant of linen from the piece I had used for the old man and began to measure it, not well knowing what to do with such a fragment; but the cloth seemed to extend under my hands on the rod; there was no end to the measuring. Behind me appeared the end of the linen, and yet before me was a mountain of the finest material, so high that I could not see over it. My breath failed me, I ceased to count, and would have willingly rested, but an invisible power compelled me to go on measuring and augmenting my wealth. The hours fled; already by midday I stood in the midst of a mountain of snow-white linen, and by evening my wealth would probably have half stifled me, if on a sudden Magdalene's voice had not sounded at the open door. 'Heaven help us!' she cried. 'What are you doing? I have looked on at this work for an hour already; is the measuring to have no end today?'

"I looked back in terror. The end of the linen slipped from my hand, and I measured the last yard, sinking back upon my seat and gasping for air.

"'Thanks, my dear neighbor,' I cried, 'thanks for your having interrupted me. Oh, the bounty of Heaven is too excessive, and I am almost sinking beneath the weight of it.'

"Magdalene fancied that, in such a case, she would not say it was excessive, and asked after the source of this strange blessing. Joy had opened my heart; I told her all and dismissed her with rich presents.

"I now began to reflect upon the last words of my guest, which darkly hinted a wish that I might not end before night the first work I should take up in the morning. This wish would probably have been fulfilled if the eternal disturber of my fortune had not forced herself upon me, and she was too disagreeable to the powers that befriended me for them to continue any longer the spectacle of their benevolence.

"The more I thought upon the subject, the more I regretted my frank narration to the enemy of my invisible benefactors. Oh, if I had but kept to myself a part only of the secret upon which my wicked neighbor formed the plan for my destruction!

"I had mentioned to her that my guest promised to return in a year and a day; this was enough to make her strive after the possession of my house, which stood by the road and consequently could not be missed by the benevolent saint upon his return. She thought, if she could drive me out, and settle herself in my house, she would succeed in attracting him to her and, by giving him a much more splendid reception than he had found with me, obtain a still more striking wonder to her advantage.

"It was easy for her to effect what she wished, for she had long ceased to be the needy person whom I had known in the commencement of our renewed acquaintance. Want and idleness are the mother of the strangest projects. Magdalene occupied herself with the spindle unwillingly in spite of my efforts to make it advantageous to her, for she felt concealed talents in herself that would support her still better. A portion of the year she employed in wandering about the country and telling fortunes, and the strange sort of ugliness which she possessed gave her the appearance of that she wished to represent. She had, besides, profound cunning, perfect knowledge of the human heart, skill in sounding those who came to be instructed by her, and some experience; these ingredients made her what she was, namely the oracle of the surrounding country. People came from miles away to ask her advice, and rewarded her counsels splendidly. In her travels she had even gone as far as the court, where, if her boasts might be trusted, she was received by the Queen herself with approbation and presents. Nor does this seem to me improbable; people of Guinevere's sort are inclined to every species of folly and have always a particular curiosity about the future, which they seek to satisfy at any price. It is possible too that the snares which Morgana laid for the Queen were so multiplied that supernatural wisdom was requisite for their prevention. Little, however, can be said upon such subjects, and, therefore, let me go on with my story.

"With such means, and, above all, with such powerful friends as Magdalene possessed, it was an easy thing for her to get from me the house in which I had spent the happiest days of my life, and entertained angels.

"As I was now a trader in linen and in good circumstances, I could manage to oppose her claims for a time, but eventually I lost my cause, built this cottage from the shipwreck of my fortune, limited my expenses, and commenced the life which you now see me leading. I was, indeed, well contented to be no longer plagued by the importunities of Magdalene, who—God knows why—has begun again to show her face here since you have been with me.

"In the meantime, the year drew to a close, and with every day I might look for the return of my benefactor. Alas! it was only to express my gratitude that I wished to see him yet once again, though my neighbor made preparations for his appearance with very different motives. He came on the day appointed, entered her cottage without asking after me, his old hostess, was splendidly entertained by her, and dismissed in the morning with ostentatious presents. He left her with the same blessing with which he had before left me, while Magdalene would scarcely allow him to finish it, so much did she burn with desire to hasten to her chamber, that she might begin the work which she had proposed to herself and which she did not wish to end before the evening. A short time previous, Morgana's generosity—Heaven knows wherefore—had supplied her with a quantity of gold pieces, and these now lay ready to be indefinitely augmented by counting and turning over. She was already on the point of crossing the sill and commencing the profitable labor, when she saw that a great spider had been busy, while she let out the pilgrim, spinning her web between the doorposts, as if to prevent her entry. She raised her hand to sweep the impotent obstacle out of the way, but no sooner was the odious doorkeeper killed and her web destroyed, than another appeared in her place, far surpassing her predecessor in size and loathsomeness. This too was killed, when, lo! from the fragments of her crushed body twenty other spiders arose, and more and more webs thickened amidst the broken threads, till all was life and motion with the eight-legged monsters, and the light was darkened by their nets. Magadalene's hand was incessantly raised to kill and destroy, and yet her disgusting task was no nearer to its end. Then she thought about the blessing, or rather curse, uttered by the pilgrim, which she had forced from him by prayers and presents. She cursed her hard fortune, exclaiming, 'I shall die! I shall die! The breath of these monsters will stifle me!—Help, help! Neighbor Rose! Come in and save me! Remember that I saved you when you were on the point of being smothered under the burden of your wealth.'

"It so happened that I was just then passing her window. I had gone out to thank the beneficent pilgrim and had actually seen him, but his frowning looks stifled the thanks that were upon my tongue. His eye seemed to say, 'Go, chatterer; your folly has lost you my friendship; now, go, and learn to be content with little.' Alas! I had only too well seen through the whole year, that a sort of curse followed me even in the midst of all the advantages derived from his benevolence. Had I been wiser, I might have had more. I was content, however; but it is always sad to think that you have yourself trifled away half of your prosperity.

"Amidst such reflections I had lingered for several hours in the fields and was now passing Magdalene's house in the way to my own, when I heard her voice calling me for help. Accordingly I entered, and my appearance as quickly ended her distress as her appearance before had checked the growth of my fortune. A quantity of boiling water from the kettle on the fire destroyed the last of the disgusting insects that had crept out from all corners for her torment, and I raised her up from the floor without inquiring any further into the matter; appearances and a few broken words from her told me nearly all, and I had no inclination to enter into long discourses with her.

"Alas, Genelas, you have not been so prudent; I guessed yesterday, when she stole to you during my absence, that you had let her partially worm out of you the story of your adventures at the king's court; I know the way she has of winning from everyone his dearest secrets, and I have told you my history to show you who it is that would gain your confidence, and how you have to guard against her."

"In truth," answered Genelas, "I know not how I came to give even the show of satisfaction to her pressing questions; I hate her heartily; the mere sight of her must needs excite distrust and abhorrence; but you are well aware of her art; she seems to know already everything she is asking about, and thus learns all that she desires."

"This is precisely why I warn you," replied the old woman, "and to save your frank inexperience from this unequal war with cunning, I will lock you up for the future, when I go to the city to sell our work."

Genelas consented to be a prisoner once every week and would laugh in her sleeve, when at such times her neighbor came pulling at the door-latch and tapping at the window. What, however, was her surprise one day when she thought herself secure against all intrusion and fancied nothing was near her except the social little mouse, who here lived on the most friendly footing with the house-cat—what was her surprise on hearing steps in the front yard, and, directly after, seeing the door open and a person enter, who was ony too well known to her! She started up from her seat in terror, exclaiming, "Heavens! Princess Morgana!"

"Yes," said the visitor, "I am Morgana. I have sought you out that I may snatch you from the misery in which you are living, and revenge you on your enemies."

"Gracious Lady, I know nothing of misery and desire no revenge."

"Genelas, you distrust me; you mistake me, because I abandoned you to exile and wretchedness which fell upon you on my account. But know that I also was mistaken when I considered you as conspiring with my enemies; hence my indifference to your fortunes. But an error cannot long exist with me; I now know the whole truth of the matter, and am come to be your friend. What can you see in a gloomy hut and the society of a cross old woman? The spinning-wheel is no employment for these hands; come with me; far other recreations await you. No pleasure, no happiness, shall be wanting to you in my court, in requital of what you have suffered for me; even the society of Carados shall not long be wanting; from the remotest corner of the earth, whither he has been driven by despair, I will recall him to make you happy."

Genelas blushed; the name of the beloved Carados raised a strange tumult in her innocent heart, but her better self quickly regained the ascendant. She was silent, hesitated, and finally stammered a few words, which Morgana could only consider as a refusal.

"It is well," she said; "you may bethink yourself; I will forget what you have said and will again come to repeat my offer. I hear footsteps approaching and will depart; it is only in the hour of solitude that you will see me."

Soon after, the kindhearted hostess of the young maiden entered, but Genelas said nothing of the temptations she had endured in solitude, nothing of the consent of her own heart to Morgana's projects, and which she had with difficulty subdued. But at last the temptations grew stronger; Morgana brought with her Carados, who flung himself at her feet, and with the voice of love entreated her not to reject the offers of their protectress, and this time nothing saved her from yielding to the dangerous prayer but the unexpected arrival of Rose, which made the whole vision disappear. She now broke her silence.

"Mother, I must request you not to lock me up for the future, when you go to the city. Let Magdalene steal upon me in your absence; her company is not so dangerous as this solitude."

A full relation of the past followed this introduction, and after a thoughtful silence Rose replied:

"My child, you have done well in not entering into any league with the vicious Morgana. The slightest interaction with her would fix a stain upon your good name and confirm all the slanders against you at court. As to the Carados that she has presented to you and your denial of his pressing suit, do not give yourself the least trouble: Morgana is a mighty dreammaker who can present any image she pleases, and, beyond doubt, your lover was nothing but one of those shadows with which she is accustomed to deceive everyone. Her present abode is on an island near the Sicilian coast, where she constantly mocks the passing sailors with her illusions. In the mist, which perpetually rests upon her domain, the inexperienced seaman fancies seeing castles, cities, men, and strange forms of animals; but, when curiosity or necessity brings him closer, he finds himself deceived and only meets with a poisonous blue vapor, from which he is not unfrequently greeted with malicious laughter, for Morgana's island is inhabited by none except Morgana and her court, and is visible to no human eye but from a distance."

The prudent old woman said much more of the deceitful arts of the enchantress, and by her conversation so confirmed Genelas in her resolution of giving no ear to Morgana that henceforth all these apparitions made not the slightest impression upon her. In her hours of solitude she was always busily employed and scarcely lifted her eyes, when Morgana raised her opulent display, till at length the seductive visions ceased altogether, and Genelas began to breathe freely again.

But one day, upon Rose's return from the city, her young friend met her with exclamations of delight: "Oh mother! all our cares from lack of work and poor prices are over now. I have again had a visit with locked doors; this time, however, it was no deceitful shadow but one that incited me to good. See this provision for my spindle; he who brought it was a man resembling your pilgrim, and promised double wages for my work, promised that I should never lack material for my industry till my fortunes changed, and said that with my spindle I laid the foundation of my future fortune."

Rose went to the table at which she and her friend used to work, and saw piled up a great heap of reddish, purple, sky-blue and golden wool; she shook her head, and with a thoughtful mien pronounced the name of Morgana; but when Genelas described the form and manner of the stranger, and when, upon reckoning, she found it was precisely the time of year that the pilgrim paid his visits, she became at once contented, thanked God for this new blessing, bade the young spinner be industrious and leave the rest to Heaven.

The spindles were quickly filled with a web which might shame the threads of Arachne in fineness and the rainbow in brilliance of color. The mysterious donor came regularly once a week in Rose's absence to fetch what was spun and never forgot to say, "Spin, maiden, the stuff for your cloak of honor; spin, maiden, spin the threads of your fortune!" But when he took away the last of the spinning, and brought no fresh materials with him, terror and sadness fell upon the poor Welsh maiden, and she exclaimed to Rose: "Ah, Mother, some change of fortune is at hand with me, since I lack the wool to spin; and what change can it be that will not snatch me from your arms, and how can I be happy without you?" Rose endeavored to comfort her, but tears stood in her own eyes at the thought of being separated from the child of her heart.

At length that which she had feared from the pilgrim's prophecy really happened. A message came from the King, summoning Genelas to court, and she was obliged to obey. "Ah!" she exclaimed, folding her kind mother in her arms for the last time, "must I then exchange your society for the motley crowds of folly?—give up my dear spinning-wheel for the business of idleness and luxury, and the peaceful silence of this hut for the persecutions that await me at court?"

Such were the lamentations of Genelas, and she would have found still more reason for lament had she known the real cause of her recall to court.

Great ladies have ever in the execution of their secret affairs made use of very subordinate agents, who, in recompense, possess much influence with them and can speak many a word to the advantage or disadvantage of their friends or enemies. Such was the relationship, as we have already mentioned, between Lady Guinevere and Magdalene; the latter, therefore, who grudged Rose any pleasure, even the company of sweet Genelas, needed nothing else to remove her than to give the Queen a hint of Morgana's visits, and these she had learnt with her usual curiosity by listening at the window to the conversation of the two spinners.

Guinevere could not bear the idea of an alliance between Morgana and the young Welsh maiden; she hated both and had an indefinite fear of mischief to herself if they should make common cause. To prevent this, an order from the cabinet was hastily issued, and Genelas was obliged to submit to the journey which gave her so much pain. As she followed the royal envoy, Rose stood at the door and wept; Magdalene, too, stood before her cottage and bade farewell to the traveler, but the tone of the farewell betrayed the heart which uttered it.

Genelas arrived at court and did not even enjoy the favor of being presented to the Queen, but was immediately set about menial offices, which were hardly suited to a servant of the wardrobe. For her part she could not conceive why they had torn her from her beloved solitude, when they seemed so little to need or value her. She surely would have seen that her presence was required only for the sake of watching her more closely, if her innocence could have acknowledged its own value; but she had soon occasion to imagine another cause for her not being allowed to remain any longer in the quiet of obscurity. The hero, Carados, had come back again to court after many victories to receive his reward from the hands of King Arthur, and it was strongly suggested that, in lieu of all other recompense, he would demand the hand of one of the Queen's maids of honor.

"Ah!" sighed Genelas, "that is the reason of my being called hither. All these women hate me, as is evident from their haughty, scornful glances whenever they pass by me; they know that Carados loved me before the loss of my good name made me unworthy of him, and now they want to triumph over me, to make me the witness of a good fortune which, in truth, belongs only to her whose virtue no one can question."

Whitsuntide was approaching, when the King was always wont to hold open court, and this time it was to be kept with more than usual splendor, as, owing to Arthur's indisposition, the preceding Christmas festivities had been canceled: for you must not imagine that the court of the old monarch was like the courts of our days, when every morning brings with it a fresh scene of pleasure. No, it was three, or, at most, four times a year, on high holy days, that the monarchs of the olden days unveiled the splendor of their courts; the rest of the year they led a happy private life amidst their family and their household in the obscurity of their castles. At these times of quiet, if war did not call upon them, the men occupied themselves with state affairs and the chase, while the ladies, even such as Lady Guinevere, found themselves obliged to have recourse to the needle and the spinning-wheel, if they were not to die of boredom.

It may be imagined with what eagerness the lovers of pleasure, after so long an abstinence, looked toward such a festival, where all was industriously collected that could gratify the senses. Great and early bustle was made with the preparations for the important day, that they might amuse their minds agreeably in the tedious interval and unite the retelling of past adventures, which never failed on such occasions, with the hope of those that were to be. The preparations for this feast were particularly grandiose and boisterous, for King Arthur, who wished to exhibit his splendor upon this occasion, sent messengers to kings, dukes, barons, and all who held only an acre of land in liege, commanding their attendance with their servants, children, wives, and mistresses, to adorn his festival, and partake of his joy. Accordingly, on Whitsun Eve there was gathered in Karduel, the capital, as fair an assembly as can be imagined, but the ladies of the Queen's court had the advantage of all the provincial ladies in beauty and manners, or at least fancied they had, notwithstanding that the eyes of many a knight were fixed with more ardent longing upon the charms of a simple country squire's daughter, who now for the first time cast a timid glance at the great world, than upon the faded beauty of the haughty ladies in Queen Guinevere's suite.

Genelas saw the splendid preparations for the feast, saw the influx of strangers from afar without the hope, without the wish of partaking in it; how, indeed, could she hope for such a thing in her present state of degradation, or how could she think of wishing it, when she had taken it into her head that Carados was going to celebrate his marriage with some lucky stranger, and that all King Arthur's preparations were only made to show him the greater honor?

She kept herself apart, partly because she shunned the sight of a fortunate rival, partly because she thought she could not show herself before any of the splendid assembly with eyes on which a deep melancholy rested, or in such homespun garments; yet these garments, the fruit of her own industry, were fine and white as snow, and the glance of those mild eyes was rendered still more alluring by the sadness of love; nor need she have blushed at being led to the altar just as she was—advantages which were all the more striking since their possessor was not conscious of them.

During all this time Genelas had kept eyes and ears closed against the joy which glittered and resounded about her on every side. But early on

Whitsun morning, when the solemn church procession began, she could no longer forbear looking out of the window of her little prison to see the knights and ladies pass by in their splendor. They went in pairs; each knight led the lady of his heart, and Sir Carados—a maiden, slim as a youthful Hebe, and blooming as the goddess of the spring. At this sight she slammed the window shut and flung herself upon the bed to weep. "Ah!" she cried, "it is just as I expected. It is indeed true that the fascinating creature who hung on his arm seems almost too young to follow him to the altar, but in a few years she will be so no longer. He has chosen her today intending to make her his own at some future time, and that is as good as if it had already happened, for Carados is true and constant and would not break his oath to a maiden whom he loves."

Tears streamed from her eyes as she thus thought of the virtues of her former love that were now to advantage another, and at the good fortune of her rival; a fever-frost shivered through her, and she really felt so ill that she was obliged to lie down.

In the meantime Queen Guinevere had her cares in the midst of her splendor, just like little Genelas in her dusky chamber. "You know," she said to her women, "how many evil tricks Morgana has played us for a time past, how many a feast she has spoiled by her malice. Sometimes the pleasures were thwarted by the sickness or whims of my old husband; sometimes the country ladies wore finer clothes than we, or were more admired than ourselves; sometimes the meat was burned that I myself wished to serve up; and sometimes the defenders of our beauty were laid upon the sand during jousts—all tricks of the malicious enchantress, and I should really feel surprised if she suffers us to enjoy the present pleasure without interruption. Heaven knows what misfortune is now hanging over us! To avoid anything of the kind, we should have done well in inviting her to our festival, and then perhaps she might have treated us more kindly, but, alas! It is now too late."

"Why too late?" asked Eleanor, duchess of Brittany, "if Your Majesty thinks proper, I can, with a few grains of incense scattered on live coals, call the Princess hither, even if she were in the center of the earth. You must know that in inviting enchantresses to a feast, the same ceremony is not requisite with them as with common ladies. Their senses are infinitely more refined than ours; an alluring odor, a few mysterious words, spoken under the fitting circumstances, will bring Morgana into our circle more certainly and rapidly than the most splendid embassy."

All the ladies wondered at this knowledge of black magic in the wife of Peter the Holy, and one who herself also aspired at being canonized; with eyes wide open they saw her throw a handful of incense on the brazier at the Queen's command, and draw up her mouth to words that were as unintelligible as they were efficacious, for no sooner had she finished than Morgana entered in her usual free and laughing manner. Guinevere colored slightly at seeing her look so handsome, but quickly recovered and greeted her as a sister. Morgana answered the hypocritical salutation as warmly as it was given and remarked somewhat sarcastically that the invitation was of the latest.

"Why, sister," said Guinevere smiling, "do you think we would treat you as any common mortal, who must be brought to court with carriage and horses? We know your rank and act accordingly; nor have you come too late, for no part of our festival is over except the procession to church, and of that, as I remember from former times, you are not particularly fond."

"It is well," replied Morgana, and placed herself at the right side of the Queen to follow her to the banquet, which was already set out.

The sinister clouds which had gathered upon her brow at the last malicious remark were dissipated in a moment, when, upon entering the hall, she perceived the immense crowd of handsome young knights assembled there, and who now came forward respectfully to meet the cavalcade of ladies. She had always entertained a peculiar goodwill toward the male sex, and it was the hope of meeting the handsomest and bravest at this festival that had more particularly inclined her to appear so suddenly at this impromptu invitation. The sight of her too made an advantageous impression upon the knights; she was really beautiful, and the rumor that she was not one of the most virtuous only made her more interesting to the greater part of the men.

The admiration which the fair enchantress read in every eye put her into an exceeding good humor. In the joy of her heart she gave the Queen a thousand caresses, and as Guinevere and the other ladies, notwithstanding the great circle about Morgana, still found admirers, the two first days went off happily, and the third, the most splendid of all, was eagerly awaited.

King Arthur had appointed this day for the celebration of the peacock-festival, of which, my dear readers—knowing your experience in the manners of other times—I need not say anything, except that the first course at dinner was opened with a dish in which was a peacock floating in an aromatic sauce. This dish had to be prepared and served up by the lady of the house, even if she were a queen, as in the present case. The regal bird which was now to decorate the table stood forth in all the splendors of his tail, a golden crown circled his head, and from his beak blue flames incessantly fell into a silver dish, a display invented by the complaisant enchantress Morgana to give a still more splendid appearance to the dish, which was to be served up by the Queen, for at this time both parties conducted themselves as sisters.

The King, the Princes, and the knights were already assembled in the lofty banquet hall, and every moment expected to see the Queen enter with the dish in her hands, followed by her ladies, and preceded by the minstrels and harpers; but a delay took place from a little quarrel for precedence amongst the actresses in the ceremony. In the meantime King Arthur had retired to a window with his favorite, Sir Gawain, when, lo! a handsome page came trotting up the street on a snow-white palfrey, dressed in sky-blue velvet, and carrying before him on his horse a purple-colored portmanteau. At the great castle gate he dismounted nimbly from his horse, tied him to the railings, took his portmanteau under his arm, and ascended the stairs into the royal banquet hall. Upon entering he uncovered his head, bent his knee before the King, and said, "I am sent to you, sire, by a lady of the highest rank in another land, who through me begs a favor at your hands."

"It is granted to her," replied Arthur, bending his head with a gracious smile. The page thanked him, arose, and placed his portmanteau on a side table, that he might undo it and take out its contents.

O ye men! boast not that nature has given more curiosity to the weaker sex than to yourselves! Never did a company of ladies press forward with more eagerness to peek at a novelty produced from the portmanteau of a stranger than did these heroes of the British king.

"Gently! gently, good sirs!" cried the page; "allow me air to breathe, and room to show my curiosities."

At this expostulation all drew back a little, and from every mouth came an exclamation of wonder, for a sight met their eyes, beautiful beyond what any lover of finery could imagine. This was a cloak as large and broad as the coronation robe of an emperor, adorned with all the colors of the rainbow, transparent as a jewel, and of a web so fine and delicate, that it was only with the help of the green spectacles of some old gentlemen that the sharp eyes of the younger ones could discover the threads.

"This garment," continued the page, as he kept back the intruders from incautiously touching the wonderful web, "this garment was spun by maiden hands, of materials more precious than silk, and woven in an elfin land, and so prepared by the most profound magic that it can only fit one person in this court, and for her it is intended. The favor, sire, which my noble mistress begs of you, is, that she may be permitted to present this garment to that woman amongst your ladies who has never committed any infidelity to her husband or her lover, and who, besides, surpasses all her contemporaries in virtue and inward excellence."

"And who is the happy one," cried all with one mouth, "who is to receive this wonderful garment of honor?"

"That will show itself," replied the stranger; "for, by virtue of the royal promise, every lady must try on the cloak, that we may see what virtue and fidelity dwell in the hearts of British women."

"That will be a glorious exhibition!" cried Sir Gawain, rubbing his hands, and laughing, "permit me, sire, to fetch the ladies, for I can scarcely wait for the things we are like to see."

Without waiting for an answer, Gawain ran to the ladies, who had just commenced the procession of the peacock, with the court minstrels playing and singing lustily before them. With difficulty he suppressed his laughter as he said, "Ladies, I entreat you to quicken your steps; presents have come from a foreign land, which the King destines for her who shall be recognized for the fairest amongst you."

At these misleading words the cheeks of the Queen began to glow more warmly, her heart beat in the victory, which she thought undoubted, and her hands trembled so much that she was scarcely able to hold the heavy peacock-dish. The others too felt their share of unquiet sensations; only

Morgana was somewhat pale, and stepped a few paces aside, as if she meant to leave the procession, but she suddenly bethought herself and followed the rest, who, without time or order, quite contrary to the custom of the peacock-festival, hastened into the hall and found the King and his nobles employed in admiring the wonderful cloak. During this the King, from certain misgivings, had endeavored to persuade the page from the public trial of the cloak, or at least to exclude the Queen from so dangerous a test, but all was in vain; the page insisted upon the royal word and proved beyond contradiction that this too was contained in the allowance of his request.

"My friends," said the King, as the ladies rushed in, "here is a priceless cloak, which I deem a gift for her who is fully entitled to it."

"Oh, I see already," said Queen Guinevere, giving her dish into the hands of a chamberlain, "I see that it will fit me as if made for me, and I will try it on first. But, tell me—I understand this is a trial of beauty; is it true that she, whom this gown fits, is the fairest?"

"Oh, yes!—the fairest!—undoubtedly the fairest in the world!" cried the King and his knights with one voice.

Guinevere, who did not perceive the double meaning in this speech, hastened to throw on the cloak and gain the prize, which, as she imagined, belonged to her before all others; but what were the feelings of the bystanders, when instead of flowing about her in proper ample folds, and fitting closely about the waist only, the mantle suddenly shrunk up to so small a size that it could scarcely pass for a three-cornered neck-kerchief, stretching itself out on one side to a narrow point, while on the other it lost itself amidst the headdress! The worst part of all this was, that from the wriggling of the mantle the rest of the dress fell into disorder, and revealed more of her person than was agreeable to the decorum of the age.

"Well!" said Guinevere, who alone seemed to be blind to this spectacle, "well, what is your opinion? Shall I win the prize?"

"For Heaven's sake, Madam, throw it off," exclaimed the King, blushing up to his ears and hiding her naked figure with his own robe, "for Heaven's sake, throw off the abominable thing that was not made for you; remove yourself as quickly as possible, and do not show yourself again for some time to come; for there is more in this matter than you imagine."

"Remove myself!" cried the Queen, half ashamed, half angry, for she was now partly sensible of her situation, "remove myself! Certainly not, till I see whether these ladies are more fortunate than I have been."

Upon this Sir Iwain, the King's son, took the cloak from her with stifled laughter and presented it to fair Iselda, the bride of the brave Hector, saying, "Fair Lady, who keep your lovers pining in your chains for twenty years, perhaps this costly garment was intended for you." The fair one instantly put it on, proud of seeing it flow down so decorously to her ankles; but behind her arose a loud laughter, and as the spectators did not feel it requisite to use so much forbearance with her as they had done with the Queen, she soon found out in what a singular way she appeared to them.

With looks of profound contempt the faithful Hector took the treacherous garment from his strict mistress and brought it to the proud Rosalia and the pious Isabella, whom he almost compelled by force to put it on. "It is but just," he said, "that your husbands, who are so ready to laugh at others, should see their own darlings put to the proof."

Great was the triumph of honest Hector, when he saw that these ladies were caught with their virtue down as had been his own cruel Iselda, who had seated herself on a distant couch in shame, and did not dare to lift up her eyes.

"Ah, woe! Ah, woe!" cried the Seneschal, upon seeing that the Lady Agnes and the wild Britomarte met with precisely the same fate as their companions had done. "Fidelity of British ladies, what has become of you?"

"Fidelity!" exclaimed the Queen, "What do you mean by that? Is this a trial of beauty or of virtue?"

"Of virtue, gracious lady," replied the Seneschal, laughing immoderately, "of virtue; and one might almost congratulate you for being at least the best amongst your ladies, for, compared to what we have now seen, what happened to you was nothing."

"Insolent jester!" exclaimed the Queen, "you deserve to be severely punished. But it is not enough that you laugh at the fate of these poor ladies; we will see how it is with the fidelity of your own wife."

At the Queen's command the fat Lady Seneschal was compelled, notwithstanding all her protests, to try on the treacherous cloak. Luckily for her, she had the pious Countess of Brittany, Lady Ellinor, for a companion, or her shame else would have been intolerable; for the garment fitted her so ill and presented such strange sights to the spectators that they averted their eyes.

"Take comfort, ladies," said the Seneschal, "you are not the only ones liable to this misfortune, nor am I the only one amongst the deceived husbands. However, that there may be some order amongst the tried and untried ladies, you, who have already tried the virtue of the cloak, will be pleased to seat yourselves by the side of the distressed Iselda, who is lamenting her mishap in the corner yonder."

The countess and the Lady Seneschal followed, their heads drooping, to the bench on which Rosalia, Isabella, Agnes, and Britomarte had already arranged themselves of their own accord, all with downcast eyes and none venturing to address a single syllable to their neighbors.

Now that the real nature of the trial of the cloak was thoroughly known amongst the ladies, there was not one who did not wish herself a hundred miles away from King Arthur's court. All were sweating with fear and sought a thousand excuses for not putting on the abominable garment; even the compassionate King, when he saw their distress, turned to the bearer of the unlucky present and said, "My friend, it seems to me that you had better remove yourself with your cloak, for it is made clumsily, and will certainly not fit any of these ladies, married or unmarried."

"Great King," cried the page, "where is your word?—No; you have pledged yourself once for all, and I will not stir from the spot, till, amongst the ladies of your court, I have found her for whom this prize of fidelity and virtue is destined."

The ladies were now forced to submit to this ticklish trial, and the Seneschal came again and again to those who were sitting on the couch in the corner, exclaiming, "Room, room, my beauties; I bring you fresh companions."

Sir Perceval, the giant-killer, had a mistress whom he deemed too worthy to be exposed to the gapers of King Arthur's court, and who was not present on this occasion; but when the hero found that such a recompense and such glory were to be gained, he held it against his conscience to exclude his beloved from the possibility of obtaining them, and hastily ran home to fetch her. "Here, my beloved," he exclaimed, as he led her into the royal hall amidst the crowd of terrified women and of knights, some of whom were smiling, some distressed, "here is a jewel to be gained that has come from fairy hands, and for you only; take it and give me, in addition to the name which I bear of being the bravest knight, that of the happiest lover of the fairest and truest maiden that ever lived."

"By no means, my dearest," said the trembling fair one, who, from some words of the bystanders, had just then gathered what was the point in question, "do not let us be in such a hurry. I should be accused of intrusion, being as I am the lowest amongst these ladies. Let us at least wait till I am called for."

"That is not necessary," cried the Seneschal, casting the cloak over her in spite of her struggles. "I know the time when you set yourself up above ladies of far higher quality than yourself, and now we will see which has most cause to laugh at the other."

In fact she was one of the numberless mockers and scorners of the Lady Seneschal, as the Seneschal himself had suspected. But he was amply avenged now, for the fair one found herself put into such a condition by the mantle that with a loud cry she cast herself at her knight and attempted to escape, but the Seneschal caught her, led her away past the deceived Perceval, who looked at her over his shoulder, and bringing her to the general assembly in the corner, said, "There, my dear, seat yourself by my wife, for I think the one is as good as the other."

More benches were brought for those tested and all were quickly occupied. The bearer of the cloak looked around for fresh subjects, but perceived that there were none remaining who had any pretensions to the trial.

"Sire," cried the page aloud, "where is your royal word? There is still wanting one of the ladies of your court, who must try on the garment of virtue. Let her be brought hither, that the matter may take its fair course."

"I know of no one," cried the Queen, indignant at the disgrace of her ladies, "I know of no one, except the virtuous Morgana, who, I suppose, has played us this trick."

"Oh," replied the page, "the mere sight of my cloak has already shown its effect upon her; she disappeared the moment she saw it, and we should seek for her in vain."

"Perhaps the missing lady is my sister, Edda," said Sir Carados, who had been a silent spectator of all that passed. "I will hasten to fetch her, for she has recently left the cloister, and I cannot think she will cause me any shame in the trial."

Edda was the very girl whom Genelas, with so much unnecessary jealousy, had seen going to church in the morning with Sir Carados, and it was now probable she would carry off the prize of innocence, but all the ladies protested—and the cloak-bearer agreed with them—that a maiden of ten years ought not to be admitted to the trial with mature women. Carados thought of Genelas with a sigh, secretly thanking fate that she was not present to increase the number of the disgraced, for he still loved her and would not willingly have seen her exposed to shame. But the Queen, who at this happened to recollect the deserted Welsh maiden, and who from old pique grudged her the good luck of being exempted from the common humiliation, called out her name aloud and ordered her to be summoned to the meeting immediately.

Genelas was found lying upon her bed, still indisposed, but she was used to obeying and followed the Queen's messenger without questions and without opposition. A few paces from the royal apartment Sir Carados was waiting for her; from the Queen's words he had learnt her presence, and hastened to meet her with trembling, that he might warn her of the impending misfortune.

"Lady," he said, "I come to lead you back to your chamber, or wherever else you may think proper; my heart still speaks for you, notwithstanding the scenes with Morgana, and I should unwillingly see you taking a part in the things which are now going on in the royal hall."

The terrified Genelas drew her hand away from his and asked what he meant. He explained as well as he was able, but still she did not comprehend him and left him with an angry look, occasioned by jealousy of his companion on the day of the church procession. Carados followed sadly, while she entered the hall with all the ease of conscious innocence, and with a modest curtsy asked what they wanted of her?

"Nothing, child," said the Queen with a malicious laugh, "but that you should try on this cloak. It shall be yours if it fit you."

Genelas stared mightily at this liberality of the Queen's, for the cloak waved toward her in the bearer's hands in all its splendor, and with each moment discovered a fresh brilliance in the wonderful web. What maiden is there, whose heart would not beat faster at the sight of a new garment? Genelas blushed with delight at this regal present and exclaimed, "For me? This costly garment for me? Oh, how have I deserved such kindness? I, who imagined myself obliterated from the memory of my Queen?"

Genelas fell upon her knees, and in the most captivating manner kissed the hands of the malicious Guinevere, who only bade her rise and set to work immediately. The delighted maiden tripped joyfully to the page, to take from his hands the miraculous gift, still ignorant of its real nature, but Sir Carados was close behind her and whispered in her ear, "Suffer anything rather than put on this cloak." Genelas could not at all comprehend this strange importunity of the knight; moreover, since the first day of the festival she had entertained a peculiar aversion to him, which made her inclined to put the worst construction upon all he said or did. She looked upon him as the disturber of her happiness, made as if she heard nothing of his admonition, and boldly flung the magic garment over her shoulders. Carados turned away his face, the knights drew nearer, the ladies on the couch began a malicious whispering, and the Queen collected all the evil of her heart in a single look to beat to the earth the chastised girl in the state in which she soon hoped to see her. But what were the Queen's feelings, what were the feelings of all who envied the young maiden, when the cloak quietly arranged itself about the slim figure of Genelas, without leaving a single tuck, and when from the mouths of the collected knighthood resounded a loud exclamation of "She is the maiden! She is the maiden of rare virtue and fidelity, for whom the wonderful garment was made!"

Genelas stood there in all her splendor, without being able to comprehend why so slight a matter as the putting on of a cloak should be accompanied by such loud acclamations. Her inquiring looks wandered around from one to the other, but the clamor continued, and it was not for some time that Sir Carados—who could scarcely speak from transport at the unexpected outcome of this ticklish affair—found an opportunity of explaining in few words, that by this very putting on of the cloak, which to her seemed so trifling, she had accomplished a feat which concerned the happiness of her life.

Ashamed, confused, confounded at the praise which poured in upon her from all sides, the charming girl stood in the midst of a circle that grew thicker and thicker around her. Her cheeks glowed, her eyes were sunk to earth, her right hand lay in the hand of the delighted Carados, who murmured a thousand words of joy, which she only half heard, and in her confusion still less understood, while her left played with the folds of the billowing garment.

"Pray, put an end to this farce," cried Guinevere, who could scarce contain herself for envy. "Why do you intoxicate the poor fool with your admiration, before you know whether she more than half deserves it? Let us examine her first on all sides, before you trumpet forth her praises."

With these words she turned the trembling maiden round before the assembly twice or thrice to spy out any defects, but, lo! the cloak floated about the girl in such graceful folds on all sides that the male spectators unanimously exclaimed, "She is without reproach!" Genelas, however, did not think so; she suddenly recollected an adventure, which, she imagined, rendered her unworthy of the general approbation, and when with these repentant thoughts she cast down her eyes upon her bosom, and found it more exposed than the decorous manners of that period allowed, she was covered with deeper blushes and her eyes swam in tears.

"Treacherous cloak!" she cried, and with her hands covered her bosom, which was as beautiful as the heart that beat within it, "Treacherous cloak! Fold yourself more closely about me; I will willingly confess the fault I once committed."

"There, you see!" cried Guinevere; "she is like the rest of us. Confess, you godless creature, confess your sin this moment and put off the garment, which does not belong to you."

"Gently," cried the page; "gently, fair Lady: one must be blind not to see the difference between you and this innocent soul; we have not yet forgotten certain things. The mantle is incontestably her right, and if she choose to render herself yet more worthy of it by the confession of a peccadillo, it is for no one to prevent her."

"Ah!" said Genelas, "I will confess—willingly confess, so that this shame may be taken from me. I once had a lover—I loved him more perhaps than I ought to do, and thus it happened, when he kissed me in the dusk, that I—that I was so bold as—as to return his kiss."

"And the fortunate man," asked Carados, "the fortunate man, who led you into this mighty fault, was—"

A glance, cast at the speaker from the soft dove's eyes of the fair one, replied to this question.

"Oh, heavenly girl!" cried Sir Carados, "it was I then!—I!—Mine was thy heart, mine the first kiss of thy love, mine the fidelity which distinguishes thee from thousands of thy race!"

No sooner had Genelas made her confession than the cloak fitted decorously about her snowy bosom and left her at liberty to give up to her lover the right hand, which he was endeavoring to possess himself of, although she did not yet well know what to think of him, for the church procession was still fresh in her mind.

But the Queen, to whom this scene was for many reasons intolerable, gave orders to the attendants that they should sound the dinner gong, complaining that the peacock paté was getting cold over the farce. All accordingly placed themselves at table, the knights unanimously protesting that Genelas should yield precedence to no one but the Queen and should sit between the King and Sir Carados. It was, however, by no means Guinevere's intention that Genelas should be introduced to the royal table; she objected that the Welsh maiden held no place at court entitling her to such an honor. But to these objections no answer was made, and the matter remained as it had been settled.

During the whole dinner-time the knights did not cease to lift up the praises of fidelity, while the ladies repasted in sad silence, not one of them venturing to raise up her eyes, and indeed it was as if they had not been present, for no one spoke to them; all attended to Genelas only, who sat by the side of her lover, splendid as a queen and modest as a nun. The only person that sought to give a turn to the conversation was the page, who had been invited to sit at the dinner-table. He brought forward all manner of jests; they were, however, of such a nature that it was easy to see he was laughing at King Arthur's court. Thus toward the end of the meal he drew a boar's head from the middle of the table to his own place, and swore a lofty oath that no knight who had an unfaithful wife or mistress would be able to cut a morsel from it. Herewith he got up to present it in his own person to the knights and nobles, but all recollected the spectacle with the cloak and very gravely begged to be excused. Some, who were too hard pressed by the knavish boy, flung their knives under the table, or protested that they had no knives, while others had, as they said, made a vow never to carve for themselves at dinner. But Sir Carados gracefully cut up the boar's head, presenting a piece to each of the company, and the first and daintiest piece to Genelas.

The knights, however, fell more readily into the snare when the page requested a golden horn, and, having filled it with wine, presented it to the King, with the assurance that only he could empty the cup without spilling a drop who had never been faithless to his beloved. It had been hitherto believed that the fidelity of men was not of so delicate a nature as the fidelity of women, and the knights and princes therefore drank boldly, in the hope that a few trifling gallantries would not be reckoned against them. But, oh heavens! what a sight was there! King Arthur, indeed, spilled the least, but amongst the rest were many who could not bring a drop of the precious wine to their mouths, but missed the way thither in the most ridiculous manner imaginable and soaked themselves and their mistresses.

The ladies now began to lift up their heads a little and to gaze at the knights more boldly. Some even ventured a slight titter and a few words of mockery, when the page commanded silence, for the turn had now come to Sir Carados, who confidently took up the brimming goblet and drained it to the health of the truest and fairest maiden in the world, without spilling a drop.

"Lady! Lady!" said the page to Genelas, "Happy is the man who calls you wife; but happy also is the wife of such a man."

Genelas was silent, not altogether believing in the veracity of the horn, for she still dwelt upon the fair companion in the church-procession. But little Edda, who was present, had only once to call Sir Carados brother, and every doubt was removed.

All now got up from the table, and still Genelas could not keep her eyes for a moment from the page, who again solemnly declared her to be the rightful owner of the magic cloak. She endeavored to get a tête-à-tête with him, and succeeded before the party broke up.

"Tell me, pray, who you are," she said, "I am puzzled by your appearance. The whole assembly calls you a young page, yet to me you seem the very reverse. I discover in you the form and features of a venerable old man, who once provided me with work and hope during the time of my poverty."

"Do not ask too much," replied the stranger with a smile. "Know me, or know me not, it is all the same to me, but never forget that the threads of which your garment of honor was woven, were spun by your own hand in the time of your adversity."

Genelas had perhaps gone on with her questions, but the cloak-bearer was sent for to the King, who drew him aside, saying, "Tell me, pray, who is the high and noble lady that sent you to us with your wonderful present?"

Before the page could answer, the Queen drew him to the other side to ask the same question. And now the questioners, male and female, increased so much about him that he found no better way of helping himself than by vanishing altogether.

"It is Morgana who has played us this trick," said the Queen, as her way was lighted to bed.

"It is Morgana!" exclaimed all.

But Genelas was much happier in her guess that the page was no other than the kindhearted German household spirit, the friend and protectress of female virtue, for whose favor she was indebted to honest Rose.

The next day Sir Carados solicited the hand of fair Genelas of Wales and obtained it without any opposition. She brought him nothing but her well-earned cloak and a heart full of loyalty and virtue, a dowry with which in those simple times people were wont to be contented. Soon after he hastened away with her from Arthur's seductive court to his lands in Scotland, where they were accompanied by Genelas's old friend, Rose, who willingly left her cottage and the neighborhood of Magdalene to lead a life of heaven at the side of the child of her heart.

Adapted from the translation of "Der Mantel," in *Specimens of German Romance*, ed. and trans. George Soane, vol. 3 (London: Whittaker, 1826), 95–259.

Introduction, bibliography, and translation by
JANICE MURRAY

Caroline
Schlegel-Schelling

(1763–1809)

Caroline Schlegel-Schelling (1763–1809)
lithograph after pastel by Friedrich August Tischbein, 1798
reproduced with kind permission of the owner

Athough Caroline Schlegel-Schelling published little under her name, she is undoubtedly the most outstanding letter writer of German Romanticism. More than any of her women friends, "Caroline" was able to translate her longing for a fulfilled emotional and intellectual existence, her profound personal sufferings, and her frustration with bourgeois narrow-mindedness into a passionate language that deeply affects us even today. In fact, both her untiring search for self-realization and her at times shocking outspokenness make her the most "modern" among her Romantic sisters. Many of her contemporaries, particularly women, were intimidated by her and resented the unconventionality of "Madame Lucifer," as she was known among the associates of Friedrich Schiller.

Caroline Michaelis was born in Göttingen on September 2, 1763, and died in Maulbronn on September 7, 1809. She was the eldest daughter of the well-known orientalist and theologian Johann David Michaelis (1717–91) and his second wife, Louise Philippine Antoinette Michaelis, née Schröder (1739–1808). Except for two years (1775–77) in a small boarding school in Gotha, Caroline Michaelis spent her childhood and youth in Göttingen, an intellectual center of the Enlightenment, and was educated primarily by her father and by private tutors. By the age of fifteen she had learned French, Italian, and English and was well-versed in European literature and theater. In Gotha Caroline Michaelis became acquainted with Luise Stieler (later Gotter) who remained her lifelong friend and correspondent.

Following the wishes of her half-brother, Friedrich, Caroline Michaelis married the physician Johann Franz Wilhelm Böhmer on June 15, 1784. During this first marriage she bore three children: Auguste (1785–1800); Therese or "Röschen" (1787–89); and Wilhelm who was born in 1788 but only lived for a few weeks. After the sudden death of her husband in February 1788, she attempted for several years to live independently and devote herself to Auguste's upbringing and her own intellectual interests.

She spent the years 1792–93 in Mainz with Georg and Therese Forster, taking an active interest in the political events in this city which had just been declared a republic. As Prussian troops were advancing in 1793, she left Mainz but was arrested and imprisoned along with Auguste in the fortress Königstein. While there, she discovered she was pregnant, and since the father was a young French officer stationed in Mainz, Jean Baptiste Dubois-Crancé, she considered committing suicide rather than allowing her pregnancy to become known. Before this was necessary, however, her release was effected by August Wilhelm Schlegel and her brother Philipp Michaelis. In November 1793 her son Julius was born in Lucka near Leipzig. She left him with foster parents in the country, where he died in 1795. In Lucka, she met Friedrich Schlegel and made such a lasting impression on him that he later devoted a section of his novel fragment *Lucinde* to a characterization of her.

Mainly out of thankfulness and friendship, Caroline married August Wilhelm Schlegel on July 1, 1796. Shortly afterward they moved to Jena where, until 1800, the Jena circle of Early Romantics gathered with Caroline Schlegel at its center. During these years Schlegel also worked with her husband on translations of Shakespearean plays and contributed essays to the *Athenäum* (1798–1800), a journal published by the Schlegel brothers.

The greatest crisis in Caroline Schlegel's life came in 1800 with the death of Auguste, her fifteen-year-old daughter and closest companion. After this loss she attempted unsuccessfully to renounce her love for the philosopher Friedrich Schelling which had become ever more apparent since 1798. With the intervention of Goethe, the marriage between August Wilhelm and Caroline Schlegel was dissolved in 1803 and Caroline and Schelling were married the same year. From then until her death in 1809 she wrote reviews for the *Neue Jenaische Literatur-Zeitung,* some of them in collaboration with Schelling.

Caroline Schlegel-Schelling's extensive correspondence with friends and family members began in 1778 and continued until 1809 shortly before her death. These letters not only present a detailed and extremely moving picture of Caroline's personality, her times, and the essence of the Early Romantic movement, they also stand in the eighteenth-century tradition of the letter as a consciously artistic form of personal narration, a form chosen particularly by women. The exchange of letters was considered by the Jena Romantics to be both a continuation of discussions conducted in the group as a whole (what Friedrich Schlegel termed "symphilosophizing") and a "spontaneous," "authentic," and therefore particularly desirable form of literary expression.

ANNOTATED BIBLIOGRAPHY

Schlegel-Schelling's Works

Caroline: Briefe. Edited by Georg Waitz. 2 vols. Leipzig: S. Hirzel, 1871. The first selected edition of Caroline Schlegel-Schelling's letters collected by Friedrich Schelling's son-in-law, Georg Waitz.

Caroline und ihre Freunde: Mitteilungen aus Briefen. Edited by Georg Waitz. Leipzig: S. Hirzel, 1882. A collection of letters to and from Caroline Schlegel-Schelling not included in Waitz's first edition.

Caroline: Briefe aus der Frühromantik. Edited by Erich Schmidt. 2 vols. Leipzig: Insel, 1913. Complete edition of the letters with explanatory appendix and register. Also includes a novel fragment, a parody of F. Schlegel's *Habilitationsthesen* and a review of A. W. Schlegel's *Ion.*

Carolinens Leben in ihren Briefen. Edited by Reinhard Buchwald. Leipzig: Insel, 1914. A selection of letters from the E. Schmidt edition with an introduction by Ricarda Huch.

Caroline und Dorothea in Briefen. Edited by Ernst Wieneke. Weimar: Kiepenheuer, 1914. A selection of letters written by Caroline Schlegel-Schelling and Dorothea Veit-Schlegel.

Begegnung mit Caroline: Briefe von Caroline Michaelis-Böhmer-Schlegel-Schelling. Edited by Sigrid Damm. Leipzig: Philipp Reclam jun., 1979. (A slightly shortened edition was published in the FRG: *"Lieber Freund, ich komme weit her schon an diesem frühen Morgen": Caroline Schlegel-Schelling in ihren Briefen.* Darmstadt: Luchterhand, 1980). A selection from previous editions of letters with a biographical and critical introduction by Sigrid Damm.

Athenäum: Eine Zeitschrift. Edited by August Wilhelm Schlegel and Friedrich Schlegel. 3 vols. Berlin: Frölich, 1798–1800. Caroline's review of Johannes Müller's letters to Bonstetten and "Die Gemälde" by Caroline and August Wilhelm Schlegel were published in volume 2 of the *Athenäum.*

Schlegel, August Wilhelm. *Kritische Schriften.* 2 vols. Berlin: Reimer, 1828. In the table of contents Schlegel marked essays which he wrote together with Caroline. In later editions her contributions are not noted.

Frank, Erich. *Rezensionen über schöne Literatur von Schelling und Caroline in der Neuen Jenaischen Literatur-Zeitung.* Sitzungsberichte der Heidelberger Akademie der Wissenschaften 3. Heidelberg: Winter, 1912. A selection of reviews by Caroline and Friedrich Schelling with a critical introduction.

Secondary Literature in English

Kahn, Robert L. "Caroline and the Spirit of Weimar." *Modern Language Quarterly* 20 (1959): 273–84 Rather than viewing Caroline Schlegel-Schelling strictly as a Romantic literary figure, Kahn argues that her personality and aesthetics represent a synthesis of Storm and Stress, Romanticism, and Classicism.

McCullar, Sylvia Yvonne. *"Ideal" versus "Real": Womanhood as Portrayed in the Literature and Correspondence of Early German Romanticism.* Diss. Rice Univ., 1979. Ann Arbor: Univ. of Michigan Press, 1979. This dissertation treats the conflict between Romantic male and female concepts of womanhood by comparing the works of Friedrich Schlegel, Novalis, Dorothea Veit-Schlegel, Caroline Schlegel-Schelling, and Rahel Varnhagen von Ense.

Sidgwick, Mrs. Alfred [Cecily Sidgwick]. *Caroline Schlegel and Her Friends.* New York: Scribner and Welford, 1889. A biography of Caroline Schlegel-Schelling based on the letters published by G. Waitz.

Selected Letters

To Meyer[1]   Göttingen, March 1, 1789

If there were anything unexpected I could encounter in a world which I find more wondrous every day and which can therefore surprise me less and less, for *l'Admiration est la fille de l'Ignorance*—as Mad. Schlegel always told me—then it was your letter. It did not, however, displease me, for you could and surely must have known that I would have gladly requested tidings of you? How often have I not enquired about you whenever I had any occasion to do so. Yes, my sister and I had the bold idea more than once—I call this bold since much that is natural is so named—of sending you, without any reason, a missive that would repeat my last words to you: "You will never be estranged from us." In Göttingen you seemed to be so, but wherever I may find you and wherever you may be in the future, I know you will not be so to me. Taking interest in your fate is perhaps a thankless task, but insofar as you and your whims are the creators of your fate, I cannot help but follow it. However, you should concern yourself little with my fate and only not deprive my person completely

1. Friedrich Ludwig Wilhelm Meyer, writer and librarian in Göttingen, friend and correspondent of Caroline until 1794. She had returned to her parents' house in Göttingen after the death of her first husband in 1788. Her son, Wilhelm, died the same year a few weeks after he was born.

285

of that interest you promised—I do not greatly concern myself with it, I do not worry nor do I make plans, there is only one aim I believe I must firmly pursue: the welfare of my two small girls. All else lies before me like the surging sea and if I reel at the sight, then I close my eyes and entrust myself to it without fear. I do not know if I can ever be completely happy, but I do know that I will never be completely unhappy. You knew me in a situation in which I, being closed in from all sides, sank down under the pressure of my own weight; I was cruelly pulled out of this, yet I feel that I am saved, for it has become so light around me, as if I were living for the first time, just like a sick person who returns to life and gradually regains strength and breathes the fresh, pure spring air and rejoices in an awareness never sensed before. One veil falls after the other, nothing is very important to me any more—experience reduces the value of things since it deprives them of their originality—I do not value anything more than what my heart gives me and acquire nothing but what I have myself prepared. You boast a little about your poverty, and mine, at least, does not offend me. It seems to me as if I had never needed other people less and never looked down at them from a higher vantage point than since they have begun to think that I would become attached to them more firmly. We are proud beggars, my dear Meyer, and I know several more of our kind; let us form a group one day, a secret society, which reverses the order of things and, just as the *Illuminati* wished to replace the fools with the wise, so may the rich step down and the poor rule the world. I found your idea of marrying Bür-ger[2] excellent, but Lotte thought you would not make a good match and it is certain

> In the world far and wide
> There is no altar
> Where your love is sanctified.

He told me that you will probably go to Berlin together—but what if I tried to make you professor of aesthetics in Marburg, where I am probably

---

2. Gottfried August Bürger, poet and friend of Meyer and August Wilhelm Schlegel. Bürger was in a state of emotional despair since the death of his second wife, the "Molly" of his poems, in 1786. The idea of the marriage is a joke and probably reflects the close personal and literary friendship between Meyer and Bürger.

going?[3] Indeed you only exclude Schweinfurt and have presumably not renounced all ties. I wish you could remain in London, for a large city would be your element; here you could lose yourself in the throng but not in your own circle, and in the evening at a festivity or in the theater, you could cast away the weight borne during the day and forget yourself in the bustle of diversity. Are you not one of those who must be enraptured in order to be happy, and if the terrible void between one rapture and the next is not filled with some external object—what do you do then? It is a sad alternative to feel this emptiness completely or to fill it in an everyday way. May your good spirit then lead you! A straight path this will surely not be. Father and mother thank you for your greetings, and my sisters return them. Lotte is happy, Louise is happy, one of them is writing at present and the other is at a ball. You spoke of Feder in your letters to T[atter],[4] I heard him speak about you recently, and never has an honest man spoken so advantageously about you as this one: it pleased me to hear this for the sake of both of you. Once again I wish you well and may no harm come to you!

Caroline Böhmer

To Philipp Michaelis [?][5]

[The beginning of the letter, a double sheet, is lost]
[Marburg, Dec. 1789]

. . . she seemed to see something in silent visions toward which her lovely arms extended so that even her fingers seemed to stretch out. Then she grasped tightly hold of my hair—once she pressed my hand firmly to her heart—she plucked at the bedcover in gentle spasms—and I was still blind to this sign. All the while she was completely conscious—she still under-

3. Caroline Böhmer lived from 1789–91 with her brother, Friedrich, who taught medicine at the University of Marburg.

4. While in Göttingen, Caroline became acquainted with and probably fell in love with Georg Tatter, the son of a gardener in Hanover and companion of three English princes who were studying in Göttingen.

5. Gottfried Philipp Michaelis, Caroline's younger brother. The letter refers to the death of Therese (Röschen), Caroline's second child in the marriage with Böhmer.

stood me when I told her about the Christmas [present] her grandmother would send—she still answered—"to Guste too." In order to ease her spasms, Fritz ordered a warm bath in which I placed her with inexpressible fear in my heart. I was delighted that she seemed to feel so well in the bath and she herself said: "Good! Good!" with the heartfelt tone in which she said "Yes"; and after I had laid her in bed again and she seemed so much better—it was nearly four in the afternoon—I *could* not doubt that she would be saved. . . . Toward eight o'clock. . . . a second warm bath—into which I placed her with the greatest effort by summoning up all my strength, whilst everyone trembled for the life of the dear child, and Lotte lay unconscious on the floor in a violent attack of sobbing and convulsions—strong doses of musk—everything was tried—without expectations on my part—nor presumably on the part of the others either. Her spasms were not convulsive, but rather a quiet stretching which was followed by stiffness.

I was active until I found nothing more to do—then I sat down next to Lotte on the sofa—my Rose fell silent—Mmes. Malsburg and Breidenstein knelt before her bed—none of the maids were present—everyone fell silent—and I wished ardently that this silence might never be interrupted. I trembled before the moment when I, motionless and with a leaden heart, would have to move again. Where are you, spirit of my little one? This question occurred to me amongst images, amongst ideas of which humanity in its limitations only has a dull sense—and even though this numbness combines with a yearning for clearer knowledge—and even though in these same notions the sense of loss is also awakened—my heart resisted with a power—which I had known of—but which I had not yet experienced in this way. In the end I was alone with Lotte—and I now called people that they might hold vigil with the departed one during the night. They came and did not yet know that she was dead. Whether I slept afterwards or remained awake, I do not know. I remained silent—I was concerned about Auguste—she did not seem to realize—she went into the room alone—she came out again without any further comment, finally I told her that Röschen would no longer be able to play with her now. Then it burst out—she screamed in an almost sickeningly violent tone: "You *must* not tell me that, mother!"—as if she had wanted to hide it from herself until then. I cannot decribe the strangeness of it to you—it seemed to be depth of feeling combined with such a singular thoughtlessness —I was not able to discern that something was fermenting within her—and still, when it later came to tears again, it seemed to be an outburst of concealed feeling. Now she blends much childish frivolity into her memories, which come very often. She calls Röschen by her name—she says: "I can see her, she does not want to come, she is with her father."

I spent the rest of the day in an apathy which I may have prolonged unconsciously—exhaustion dictated it to me. In the evening I was so weak that I could not walk and when I went to bed I felt ill and I coughed blood. This continued all night and was followed by extreme exhaustion. But I soon regained my strength and was, at least, not idle. Since then my health has been what you would imagine with my constitution—just that my chest caused me pain and contracted so that I could not sit up straight, and from time to time some blood came which was probably caused by its gathering in the abdomen. I feel tolerably well now—I have been out walking twice—and the coughing is only spasmodic—the fresh air strengthens my lungs again. . . .

Farewell, I can write no more. La Roche[6] wrote today that she was expecting you—so I presume you were there. Tell Therese[7] that I will probably write to her on the next post day—because I would like to. May God preserve for her that which I no longer have and the loss of which I feel all the more since I feel it so consciously. Only one more child—and the lovely one for which I had so many sweet hopes—gone—with all that I could have done for her.

To Meyer   [Lucka] August 15, 1793

I am glad I had made my decision and had already carried it out eight days ago, when I received your letter the day before yesterday. I also real-

6. Sophie von La Roche, one of Germany's first professional women writers. See her biography in this volume, p.149.

7. Therese Heyne, Caroline's childhood friend in Göttingen, who later married Georg Forster.

ized that Göschen[8] knew so much and that he and his wife could guess so much that it was safer for me to confide in them. They have supported me so actively and sincerely that it would be very wrong of me not to thank them now and ever more. Göschen appears as honest as he is assiduous, and she is certainly a good woman acting [?] out of kindness. Through his mediation I am in a small country town, silent as a grave, three miles from Leipzig in the Altenburg region, in the house of an elderly, unmarried, ailing doctor who is said to be skilled in the profession in which I need him and who often accommodates sick persons in his house. Göschen did not know the man beforehand—he claimed that I was his stepsister, was here to appease relatives, the man not yet being able to declare a marriage etc. I left the fiction up to him. Your advice is so excellent that the Marquis von G[rosse][9] would be pleased by it, and it is so judicious that I would have followed it had it not been too late, and if I knew at all how to lie to someone other than on a mischievous impulse. I have said nothing more than that it must remain a secret now because I would estrange my family and grieve them, and because public opinion would be so affected by my imprisonment, that people would not acknowledge the truth, and I would lose a pension which I cannot *yet* forgo[10]. Indeed this is very true. The Göschens may guess that there is someone, perhaps they assume a secret or at least a future marriage—but through no fault of *mine*.

My child is provided for in case I should not be able to care for it myself. The father is alive and demands to have the child, but if it lies in my power in any way then the baby shall remain *mine*. I have never believed that Auguste would lose anything by what the child would take away from her—I was only convinced that the shame, yes even scandal, involved in the discovery of my situation would cause a negative turn in the fate of the eight-year-old girl, and would forever embitter everyone far and near who took

8. Georg Joachim Göschen, publisher. After her release from Königstein, Caroline was brought to Lucka by August Wilhelm Schlegel where she bore her son Julius under a false name. Caroline had appealed to Meyer for assistance during her imprisonment; he had, however, chosen not to compromise himself.

9. Karl Grosse, a former suitor of Caroline's sister Louise, who had returned to Göttingen from his travels and claimed the titles of Marquis von Grosse and Count of Vargas.

10. Caroline was in danger of losing custody of Auguste and her widow's pension if her predicament were to become known.

interest in me. For this reason, I was able to form the idea which I myself held to be loathsome, but necessary, within the walls enclosing me.[11] I sense all too much how little you know me when you think it your duty to scold me for overreacting, which would fill me with self-contempt, were my heart and mind capable of it. I know my duties and I hope I am fulfilling them now to the full extent by attempting to make good the offense I have committed and by losing neither courage, patience, nor cheerfulness.— You can hurt me for I am more vulnerable than usual, and you could have done good for me, but my composure remains the same, even if you change your tone toward me. I would not have to be suspicious but rather blind if I did not notice this change. I have only one speculation as to the cause— Chancery Secretary Br.[12] answered you and reprimanded you concerning a woman whom he knows sufficiently through vulgar rumors. You became suspicious because you are acquainted with the way of the world. Words, letters are *nothing*. This is my belief, too. We have not seen each other for four or five years, what can have become of me since then?

This much is certain: we must misunderstand each other from now on until chance should cause us to meet again. Recently, I thought I would see you within the next three months; however, you notified me of a long stay in Berlin. What can happen after that is at the very least doubtful.

My brother wrote that he has sent Voss[13] a letter for me within an envelope addressed to you. It must have already arrived—could you not enquire of Voss about it? When you send it to me, take an envelope addressed to G[öschen], for his people suppose me to be in B. and a letter would therefore surprise them. My friends in Gotha believe me to be near B. in the country. So much about the letter, so that you may not inadvertently cause me harm.

11. While in prison Caroline had planned to commit suicide using poison provided by August Wilhelm Schlegel, in order to prevent the discovery of her pregnancy.

12. Cannot be identified.

13. Christian Friedrich Voss, bookseller in Berlin.

To Julie Gotter[14]   [Jena] February 18, [18]03

If you thought my silence bodes no good, either in that it indicates a physical indisposition or inner discontent or a lack of concern for old friends—then, my child, you were mistaken on all three points. To be sure, I was hindered from time to time just when I intended to write. I am, however, in good health and have much affection for those few close to me, so that I was happy to read in your last letter about your mother's altogether correct and worthy decision. What she is planning to do is just what I often wished to suggest to her, only with regard to Dresden, but which I considered impossible to carry out especially due to the sick aunt. Your mother's excellence is yet again proved to me, in that she is undertaking something for her children which, as I can easily imagine, must seem extremely difficult to her. When all hindrances have been removed in Gotha, then there will be nothing wanting in Kassel, least of all a good lodging . . . The area will please you greatly, the theater will accord you some diversion, and regarding acquaintances you would probably have found fewer still in Dresden. Cäcilie[15] must now be commended to her guardian spirit, she must help herself—she knows that Nahl is not right for her. May she find her own way now.

It is also time that I give you an account of myself. In May or June I will leave Jena for some time and will go first to a spa in Swabia and then in autumn to Italy, and winter will be spent in Rome, God willing. In order to have complete freedom to undertake this and also not to hinder others in their freedom, the bond of marriage between Schlegel and me will be, or rather, has already been dissolved—the bond of cordial friendship and respect will, I hope, remain always. I doubt that these tidings are new to you at this moment. Let us put everything else about this matter aside, and just concern ourselves with what I tell all of you directly. I do not have, nor do I need to have, the least misgivings about addressing it to you, my young friend, since all is the truth and stems from my heart. Although Fate has often showered me with its greatest gifts, at the same time it has been very

---

14. Daughter of Luise Gotter, née Stieler, Caroline's lifetime friend. Julie's sister Pauline later became Friedrich Schelling's second wife.

15. Cäcilie Gotter, Julie's and Pauline's sister.

painful for me and has thus also poured over me its most carefully chosen sufferings, so that whoever looks at me cannot be enticed to stray onto unknown ground through bold and capricious acts, but must beseech God for a simple fate and make the solemn promise not to do anything to forfeit it. Not that I would accuse myself; what I am forced to do now is perfectly justified in my own case, but cannot serve as an example to others. I have now lost everything, my treasure, the life of my life is gone,[16] I would perhaps be forgiven if I were to cast off the last mortal frame in order to free myself, but herein I am bound—I must continue in this existence as long as it pleases Heaven and the only certain thing I may still wish for is peace, true peace and harmony in my immediate surroundings. This peace I can no longer find in the marriage with Schlegel; many disturbances have come between us, and my heart has turned away from him completely; from the very first moment on I did not conceal this from him, I was completely honest. Since then some matters could have been changed, but other people—and as you know not the most praiseworthy—gained influence over him when I retreated. So I saw ever more reason to decide on a definite and public separation—not without a struggle, for it was dreadful for me to have to experience this too, but I finally decided it was my duty. I could not and no longer wanted to be everything for Schlegel and would only have impeded him, a man standing at the zenith of his life, in his search for happiness elsewhere. In addition, my health leaves me no hope of becoming a mother again: and thus I did not wish to deprive him of that which I was unable to give him. Certainly children would have made our marriage—which we never regarded as anything other than free—indissoluble. These are the aspects of my fate in which doom plays a part and in which there is no question of guilt. On the other hand, I should have been more careful than to agree to this marriage, which was decided more at that time by my mother's insistence than by my own will. Schlegel should always have remained just my friend, as he has been so sincerely and often so nobly throughout his life. It is excusable that I was not more steadfast in this conviction, and that the fearfulness of others, as well as the wish to provide a protector for myself and my child in my ruinous situation at that time per-

16. Here she is referring to Auguste's death in 1800.

suaded me; for this, however, I must now atone. In so far as *you* know Schlegel, Julchen—I must appeal to your impartial feeling—do you believe that he was the man to whom I could have given my love wholly and absolutely? Under other circumstances this would not have changed anything once the choice had been made; however, as things developed, this fact had to influence me, especially since Schlegel reminded me several times of the freedom existing between us by his frivolities which, even though I did not doubt the continuation of his love, did still displease me and at the very least did not contribute to binding my affections. Now that no other person's fate is entwined with mine, I am surely entitled to do what is right and true for me and not to ask at all how this, which is in its essence good, may appear to others. I intend to live and to die with the knowledge that this is true. I reached this decision in Berlin, where everything displeased me and where Schlegel intended to remain, but my mother's illness postponed its implementation. When you were here the last time all necessary steps had been taken—I do not wish to, and may not, tell you who aided me almost paternally in this matter[17]—enough, the Duke proved willing to preserve us from all long and adverse formalities in this affair and very soon the last word will have been spoken in it.

I cannot tell you how calm I have become since the moment when we made our decision, I can almost be considered happy and my health has improved considerably.—All slanders which the matter might further bring with it, spoken or written pasquinades, and whatever else belongs to this cannot harm me. I have only requested of my loved ones that they not injure me with opinions taken from a different world from the one in which I exist. I desire nothing from that other world, and besides, I am so well acquainted with it that I could renew my claims on it whenever I should so desire. It is strange that I, once drawn into the turbulences of a great revolution with my personal affairs, am now in this situation a second time, for the movement in the literary world is as strong and fermenting as the political one was then. The rogues and infamous scoundrels

---

17. The divorce was approved on May 17, 1803. Goethe had been instrumental in gaining support from Duke Carl August of Sachsen-Weimar and in sparing Caroline a personal appearance before church leaders.

seem to have the upper hand at present. Beginning with Kotzebue,[18] who almost became minister in Berlin, there is a divine connection of baseness in the world, I say divine, for Providence will certainly come to glory by disposing of it. Schlegel is not so inconsistent that he would allow himself to be challenged in the least by anything which is happening, and he has just declared this attitude emphatically in a letter to Schelling, which has fortified me completely in my composure.

If my present situation were to allow it, I would see you in eight–ten days around which time Herr v. Podmanitzky is traveling to Gotha, but since the last ruling has not been passed and I was supposed to avoid a personal appearance under the pretext of my indisposition, I am not able to leave. Podmanitzky will visit you and will tell you much about me and Schelling. Tell Minchen as well to expect a visit from him, for Manso gave him a card for her in Breslau. In addition I would also ask that you inform her, if the content of this letter is made known to her, that she alone caused me to waver regarding the divorce. I would not have wished to prove her wrong after she had once so boldly declared herself as my guarantor and said to the other women, "If Mme. Schlegel is divorced, then you will all be divorced." She should not vouch so far for someone again, one never knows what will happen and what a person will be forced to undertake—only one thing can be vouched for, "This man or that woman may do what they wish; they will, however, retain something which is worth all friendship and which I do not wish to rend from my heart."

Please greet my dear Chanoinesse.[19] She will learn nothing new from this letter, since I did not conceal my design when I spoke with her. Mama Schläger[20] does not need to be informed of anything, I think.

As for you, my friends, I am confident of the continuation of your affec-

---

18. August von Kotzebue (born in 1761, assassinated in 1819), was a prolific writer and diplomat, who, after he moved to Berlin in 1803, attacked the Romantics in his journal *Der Freimüthige*.

19. *Chanoinesse* (Fr.)=Canoness. Refers to a common acquaintance of Caroline's and Luise Gotter's in Gotha. It seems Caroline did not entirely approve of her friend entering a religious order so that her consistent use of the title "la Chanoinesse" is probably sarcastic.

20. Madame Schläger, owner of the boarding school in Gotha where Caroline and Luise stayed for two years.

tion for me. Let people talk, you are not required to defend me and I can depend on myself. In addition, I do not need to assert that a hundred lies do not make one truth, that amongst other things there is not one word of truth in the story about Unzelmann,[21] nor in the rumor that there is dissension between Schlegel and myself, nor is it true that I did not wish the divorce. Rather, I wished it very much even though I did not reach the decision easily and was even foolishly hesitant.

I am trying to think how I could still speak with all of you before we part for such a long time—a meeting in a third place would be best of all.

Apart from the serious news, I would have a hundred amusing things to tell you. In society here everything is in such disarray that there are new alliances and infractions every day, everything is upside down—for example, Niethammer, Asverus, Vermehren, and Hufeland take part in a *witty* little gathering. Möller has gone completely mad, whereas he was only half mad before. Hegel plays the *galant*, the Cicisbeo for everyone. Everything amuses me as in a comedy, especially since Podmanitzky, through whom I generally hear of it, can narrate it so well. He . . .

[rest of letter not extant]

Translated from Erich Schmidt, ed., *Caroline. Briefe aus der Frühromantik* (Leipzig: Insel, 1913), vol.1, 175–78, 197–99, 306–8; vol.2, 352–58.

21. Friederike Unzelmann, a well-known actress of this time, who was a target for gossip claiming that she was the cause of the estrangement between Caroline and August Wilhelm Schlegel.

Introduction and bibliography by
MARJANNE E. GOOZÉ

Translation by
MARJANNE E. GOOZÉ
with
JEANNINE BLACKWELL

Henriette Herz

(1764–1847)

Henriette Herz (1764–1847)
steel engraving after A. Graff, owned and reproduced by
Schiller-Nationalmuseum/Deutsches Literaturarchiv
Marbach am Neckar
courtesy of Schiller-Nationalmuseum

The daughter of a Portuguese Jewish family, Henriette de Lemos was born on September 5, 1764, in Berlin. Her father was a physician, and her family socialized with other enlightened Jews in Berlin, particularly with the family of the philosopher Moses Mendelssohn. His daughter, Dorothea, was Henriette's closest friend. Known for her extraordinary beauty and talents, Henriette, even as a young girl, played a prominent role in the Jewish community. At the age of twelve and a half, she was engaged to Marcus Herz, a physician and student of Kant, whom she had never met and who was fifteen years her elder. On December 1, 1779, she was married, barely fifteen years old.

She received little formal schooling but picked up a host of languages—Hebrew, French, Italian, Spanish, English, eventually Latin, Greek, some Sanskrit, Swedish, Turkish, and Malayan—and was an avid reader of popular fiction. After her betrothal, Marcus broadened her intellectual exposure, as Henriette explains in the following chapters of her memoirs. Beginning in 1777, he gave lectures in Kantian philosophy and experimental physics at his home. Guests at these lectures included the young Alexander and Wilhelm von Humboldt, who soon befriended Henriette and joined her *Tugendbund* (Society of Virtue), a group of young people who, like freemasons or Pietists, wanted to "foment their spiritual-moral development and practice active charity," as they wrote in their "statutes."

Whereas Marcus Herz was utterly devoted to the ideals of the Enlightenment, Henriette was drawn to the new literature, and her talents as a conversationalist and facilitator were developed in the reading societies. During her engagement to Herz, she was introduced to the reading group which met weekly at Moses Mendelssohn's. While only Jews participated in this gathering, a second reading circle, organized by Marcus in the mid-1780s, included most of the prominent men and women of Berlin.

These groups, Marcus's lectures, and Henriette's beauty attracted many Jewish and aristocratic intellectuals to Herz's house which became one of the centers of cultural life in Berlin in the 1790s. Visitors of Herz's salon included Jean Paul Richter, Friedrich Schiller, Mirabeau, and Madame de Genlis, to name just a few. Many young Jewish women, among them Dorothea Mendelssohn-Veit, met their future Gentile husbands there. In 1802 the young Ludwig Börne came to live with the Herzes, but was sent away after Marcus's death in 1803, because he had fallen passionately in love with Henriette. After her husband's death, Henriette lived in financially tight circumstances, which were aggravated by the wars against France and which forced her to assume a position as governess. She never remarried, entertaining only platonic relationships with men, in spite of gossip to the contrary.

Particularly close was her friendship with the theologian Schleiermacher, which eventually led to her conversion to Christianity. Unlike many of her friends, who converted in order to marry or to be able to occupy positions in the Prussian civil service, Herz's conversion was one of conscience. She waited until after her mother's death out of respect for her feelings, and was baptized in a quiet ceremony outside of Berlin in 1817.

Until her marriage Henriette had never been outside of Berlin. When her financial situation improved slightly at the end of the Wars of Liberation, she traveled more frequently, and even spent two years (1817–19) in Rome with Caroline von Humboldt. Little is known about Herz's last years. Since many of her friends had died, she lived a withdrawn life, engaged in works of charity by teaching languages to children of poor families, and died shortly after completing her eighty-third year on October 22, 1847.

Herz's greatest talents, or at least the ones she was encouraged to develop, were conversation and languages. She ventured to write two novels which—after one of them was criticized—she subsequently destroyed.

Two works published during her lifetime are translations of English travelogues, *Mungo Parks Reise in das Innere von Afrika in den Jahren 1795– 97* (Geschichte der See- und Landreisen vol.12, Berlin: Haude und Spener, 1799) and *Welds des Jüngeren Reise in die vereinigten Staaten von Nordamerika* (in *Magazin von merkwürdigen neuen Reisebeschreibungen*, edited by J. R. Forster, Berlin: Voss, 1800). Herz did not destroy the fragmentary memoirs she began in 1818 in Rome and took up again in 1823, 1824, and 1829. Terrified at the idea that her innermost feelings and her exchanges with others could be made public, Herz burned most of her correspondence in the 1830s, but was soon persuaded that this was an irresponsible act. To compensate for the loss, she agreed to narrate her experiences to the writer Joseph Fürst, who, using her own memoir fragments and her then extant diary as a basis, wrote them down. A first edition of her memoirs appeared in 1850, three years after her death. It is a most vivid depiction of Berlin society in the early 1800s, and a moving portrayal of the life of an extraordinarily gifted woman.

BIBLIOGRAPHY

Herz's Works

Berliner Salon. Erinnerungen und Portraits. Edited by Ulrich Jantzki. Berlin: Ullstein, 1985. A paperback edition of selections from her memoirs and letters.

Henriette Herz. Ihr Leben und ihre Erinnerungen. Edited by J. Fürst. Berlin, 1850.

Henriette Herz. Ihr Leben und ihre Zeit. Edited by Hans Landsberg. Weimar: Kiepenheuer, 1913. Includes Fürst's memoirs.

Henriette Herz in Erinnerungen, Briefen und Zeugnissen. Edited by Rainer Schmitz. Frankfurt a. M.: Insel, 1984. The most recent collection of her writings, incorporating previous collections.

Schleiermacher und seine Lieben, nach Originalbriefen. Magdeburg: Creutz, 1910.

Geiger, Ludwig, editor. *Briefwechsel des jungen Börne und der Henriette Herz.* Oldenburg und Leipzig: Schulzesche Hof-Buchhandlung, 1905.

Putzel, Max. *Letters to Immanuel Bekker from Henriette Herz, S. Pobeheim and Anna Horkel.* German Studies in America 6. Bern: Lang, 1972. German texts with English commentary.

Secondary Literature in English

Hargrave, Mary. *Some German Women and Their Salons.* New York: Brentanos, 1912.

"Henriette Herz." *The Jewish Encyclopedia* vol.6. New York: KATV Publishing House, 1901, pp.366–67. A good brief overview of her life.

Hertz, Deborah S. *Jewish High Society in Old Regime Berlin.* New Haven: Yale Univ. Press, 1988. The most exhaustive study to date on the German salon.

Hertz, Deborah S. "Salonières and Literary Women in Late 18th-Century Berlin." *New German Critique* 14 (Spring 1978): 97–108.

Meyer, Bertha. *Salon Sketches: Biographical Studies of Berliner Salons of the Emancipation.* New York: Bloch, 1938.

Memoirs
of a Jewish Girlhood

(begun in 1818; published in 1850)

My father was a Portuguese Jew whose grandfather, along with many of his brothers in faith, was forced to flee Portugal to avoid falling into the hands of the Inquisition.

The earliest moment in my life I can remember is when I had smallpox. At that time, doctors neither inoculated nor vaccinated against the pox, letting nature take its course. Vaccination was perhaps still unknown. I had many sores but they were harmless, and although I was but two years old, I still remember, at this very moment of my advanced old age, the place in the room where my bed stood, and how someone gave me a small pound-cake with raisins as a present. My father was a practicing physician of good reputation and treated my illness himself. I was the first child from his second marriage. The children from the first had died even before their mother, and he loved me very much. Not long after the smallpox—I was probably around three years old—I had a miserable day. I was wearing my new shoes and fell down several times that day because the soles were very slick, and when I fell the last time, it almost cost my young life, because I fell against a sharp corner of the door and hit my head; my mother came over, and without checking to see whether or not I was injured, laid me across her knee and spanked me for my carelessness; my screams did not disturb her in administering what she thought to be justice, and when she released me, she saw my face and her apron full of blood—only then did she realize that I had hurt myself. The surgeon was sent for, and it was discovered that the wound in my head went right down to the brain; if this had been damaged I would have died, without salvation.

When I reached the right age I was sent to a school, and I can remember, as if it were today, that quite often as I was escorted there, I made up my mind to escape my chaperone somehow; but I was always held back by the thought of what would happen to me afterwards, and yet, I still wanted to do it again, almost every day. I was entrusted to very good people and I had a few girlfriends—one of them I still know; she was the governess for the youngest daughter of one of the most prominent princes in Germany and still lives with the young princess; at that time she already played the piano well (she was several years my elder); and that gave me the desire to study music as well, and, at my request, my parents found a teacher for me. The lessons were given in the so-called parlor; when I wasn't in school, I spent the rest of the time in the nursery, which was then the sole quarters for the children, who were not allowed to enjoy the presence of their parents, as they are now; only on rare occasions were they permitted to visit their mother during the course of the day, and she would come to see them even less often. I made rapid progress with my music, and when I was eight years old, I played at a public concert and received a lot of applause, although I now realize that this does not prove that I played even tolerably well, since the listeners were hardly capable of judging, and a pretty child easily pleases, even if she gives only a halfway decent performance. The audience was made up of people from the middle class, perhaps also some who could not even be counted in this group. However, I remember that besides many Jews there were also several officers—one of these played the cello and accompanied me; he was an acquaintance of my schoolmaster's, and two years ago, as a very old man, he was killed by horses run wild.[1] After the concert there was a dance, and my dancing pleased people as my playing had; the audience urged me to the dance floor and stood on their chairs in order to see me dance a minuet with my dancing master, a small elderly Frenchman. The middle class, to which I belonged, was at that time less opulent and had fewer pretentions to elegance than nowadays; there-

1. 1821. For information on the text I relied on the notes provided by Hans Landsberg and by Rainer Schmitz in *Henriette Herz in Erinnerungen, Briefen und Zeugnissen*, edited by R. Schmitz (Frankfurt am Main: Insel, 1984).

fore, my appearance with my parents at this public place—which no one of the middle class would now condone—and that gathering, where the society was very mixed, may well have laid in me the foundation of vanity which I have had to fight ever since.

I did not continue in music, for which I did not have any real talent; the teacher who had instructed me for a small fee had died, and the growing family did not allow my parents to provide me with another teacher. My parents were good friends with a wealthy Israelite family, outstanding people who gave their numerous family members the best education; these friends offered to have me educated with their children; I was taken to their house but disliked everything there so much that I always cried or screamed so that they eventually did not want me around any more. I am still friends with several members of this family, but several years lapsed between our first meeting and our becoming friends. Then I was sent to another school where I only learned how pleasant it is to be pretty, both through what was said to me and through what I heard young officers, who frequented the house, say to the other young girls who were either pupils or visitors. Among the latter there were two sisters, daughters of a wealthy Jewish family who had received an elegant but not quite solid and respectable education; their father was old and belonged to the completely unrefined class of Israelites; their mother was insane. The youngest daughter was very beautiful. Both were considerably older than I, received guests in their rooms, and it made me very happy when they invited me, too—for they also considered me very beautiful, and although I was still such a child that my teacher had to tie me to the bedpost to punish me for little misdeeds, a place from which I was soon to be freed by one or the other of the young gentlemen, I quite liked to be told that I was beautiful—why else would I recall several of those occasions still today? I had the reputation of being a beautiful child, and once when Princess Amalie, the sister of Frederick the Great, visited the branch-covered booth[2] at the home of one of the wealthiest Jews, I was brought there to be seen by her, and I may have

2. The sukkah, a branch-covered booth erected close to the synagogue during Sukkoth, a thanksgiving festival commemorating the escape of the Israelites from captivity. As an acculturated German Jew, Herz uses the High German equivalent *Laubhütte*, rather than a Hebrew or Yiddish reference. Similarly, she uses the German *Gesetz* for the Jewish Law, Torah.

looked quite pretty in my blue dress with colored flowers—I recall that the princess patted my cheeks and that I was terrified by her cross-eyed gaze.

I continued to enjoy visiting the two sisters mentioned above, and in my innocence I spoke about them at home, as well as about the officers' visits to the school, and my mother thought it best not to send me there any more, but instead to provide me with a few teachers for basic instruction in Hebrew, French composition, arithmetic, and geography. In the first language I began to translate the Bible, and I even tackled some of its commentators. My teacher in this as well as in other subjects was one of the most immoral men that my mother could have selected—my good mother believed she had chosen well, and only later did I come to realize how bad her choice had been. My parents themselves could not do anything for my education, even with the best intentions. My father's activities kept him away from home all day and often until late at night, and my mother had neither the talent nor the patience to teach me anything; also the number of my brothers and sisters increased,[3] and thus the household, and my mother worked diligently for the children and the house. Although I was the eldest child, who usually, as the first, is especially loved, my mother did not appear to love me all that much because as far back as I can recall, I was never treated affectionately by her as long as I lived in my father's house. That went so far that I even experienced her hostility when I was sick. I often had bouts of asthma, particularly when I had walked quickly, so that my bodice had to be loosened right away, and I remember that once, when the attack was very bad, I was laid across chairs in the parlor; my father was not at home, my mother was playing cards in the adjacent bedroom, and when my father came home she did not even tell him that I was ill. My father, on the other hand, was always very kind to me, even though he was very touchy and was often roused in anger against me by my mother. And while the constant scolding of my mother left me indifferent, an unfriendly word from my father would pain me profoundly. And when his indignation with me rose so high that he denied me his blessing (which observant

3. Henriette had four brothers: Abraham, Aron Beer, Isaak (Itzig), and Daniel Leib. Her sister Sara married a Mr. Nathan in Berlin; their son, the scholar Natorff, fell in a duel in 1833. Henriette's sister Johanna was married to a doctor in Prenzlau also named Herz. Her youngest sister Brenna de Lemos, a painter in pastels, died unmarried in 1815.

Israelites, according to law, still bestow upon their children on Saturday, laying a hand on their heads), then I was very unhappy and would not desist from begging and pleading until he was reconciled—on such occasions I was always angrier with my mother, because she was almost always the reason for my father's wrath at me; she became so odious to me because of her eternal bickering, which I found so unfair, that I often made faces behind her back whenever she left the room.

What I say here about my mother is what I felt toward her as a child; if it was a sin, then I committed it unknowingly and I consider the struggle that it is now costing me to write this down as a kind of penance. What might have allowed me to endure the oppression then was not given to me: it ought to have been the principles of religion. How much worse was the religious education of Jewish children then than now! The children, particularly the girls, were not really instructed in the *beliefs* of their parents, but were admonished to observe the *forms* of the religion; that is: they had to observe innumerable customs which it or, more likely, which the rabbis prescribed. A girl had to pray in Hebrew without understanding what she was praying, and I remember well how I thus prayed sometimes with devotion and fervor, but especially when there was a thunderstorm that I dreaded so: then I rapidly said random prayers one after another. Now the Jewish children do not do this any more, because the prayers have been translated into German, but—they are not the more pious for it: their parents, who were raised in the old way, threw off the bothersome observances of Jewish customs, which alone constituted the religion, as soon as they came of age. Nothing replaced these customs and thus they continued living without thinking of God, except, at the very most, in times of need. The children were then raised in the same way; parents did not want to teach them what they did not believe in themselves, and so they were raised—and are being raised still—with no faith—no devotion fills their souls, and they cannot pray to God when their hearts are oppressed and anguished with unending torment. Reason, which the more educated resort to as a support and help, does not sustain them in their deep sufferings. Happy is he whose innermost soul is ignited by the pure light of faith, at least later in life, so that he does not die without being filled with that uplifting blessed feeling of devotion. Thanks be to God's grace that I was given this good fortune.

I continue to write down the memories from my childhood. I already mentioned that I was called a beautiful child; now I was also called a smart child, and whenever the Jewish colony planned to engage in some festivities, I was chosen to present a song or to give a speech. Queen Ulrike of Sweden, the sister of Frederick the Great, once came to Berlin and wanted to attend the ceremonies of a Jewish wedding; she was supposed to be received in style—grand entrances, girls dressed in white, and all that—and I, a child of eight or nine years, was chosen to present a song with a little speech—all enchanted I waited for the day, when an infected eye made it impossible for me to enjoy that bliss; I then watched the festivities from a window and cried my sick eye sicker.

Once, several young people had decided to put on a play together, and my parents were asked to let me participate, and gave their permission. I had never been in a theater but had seen a performance of *Richard III* in the house of the above-mentioned wealthy sisters; I was therefore overjoyed to be permitted to stand on a stage, too—I was supposed to act the role of a country girl in an operetta; merry times were to start for me; the many rehearsals gave me an opportunity to go out; and to be with older people was particularly enjoyable. A young man who was very musical took on the task of teaching us the songs, and so he would come to my house often—I was about eight or nine years old; and this young man left such a deep impression on me, that I could think of nothing else but the time when he would return with his violin; I would go to the door and wait for him impatiently outside. Finally everything was put together and rehearsed, the little theater had been erected in the house of a wealthy Israelite woman, and the whole company of actors consisted of Israelites. The day of the performance had been announced, when, to the great horror of the group, the elders of the congregation issued a prohibition against putting on a comedy. To ignore the prohibition or to fight it was not done in those times. We were greatly distressed; we met and discussed and decided to go to one or the other respected man or to the elders of the congregation and to ask for permission—we went, we asked, in vain—we did not get it. Without telling anybody in the group or my parents, I made up my mind to go to the elders the following Sunday, the day on which they usually assembled, and ask them to permit our innocent amusement. I did what I had planned: I went all by myself to the assembly hall, stepped to the grilled window behind which sat the venerable men who were not a little astonished to see the bold little girl. First I uttered a few pleading words, then I told them that it did not become such dignified men to concern themselves with children's play—in short, I attained my goal.

Beside myself with joy, I ran from one group to the other. It was winter and the roads were slippery; I slipped and fell several times, without harm; I ran and ran without thinking how my parents would respond to my long absence from home. The well-merited reproaches that they gave me passed me by, because I was so elated with joy. The one comedy became three until the enterprise was eventually stopped by more prudent minds; the loss of time and the numerous disadvantages arising from such hustle and bustle, particularly for the children and young women, cannot be denied. Here, too, my vanity found ample sustenance; people admired my acting, my singing, but more so my figure and my face—although I cannot remember the latter, I only retain a very blurred image of my appearance—and I particularly pleased myself and others in my theatrical costume. A white silk skirt trimmed with rose-colored ribbons, a bodice of the same color, all covered with silver spangles, and a white silken hat with many porcelain flowers completed my finery. I was usually lifted from the stage after the play ended; I was kissed and embraced and received many flatteries. Now a more quiet life was to start for me, but before I continue, I want to speak about my parents and some of the people in our building with whom I lived almost exclusively.

My father was, as I had said before, a Portuguese Jew and had lived in Hamburg before he attended university; he had studied medicine in Halle and was the first doctor of the Jewish nation.[4] In Berlin he soon had a practice with his brothers in faith as patients; but at the beginning he was paid so poorly that he had to make do with potatoes or coffee at many a dinner, since he had to spend everything he earned on clothes, which were important to him—furthermore, there were not so many wealthy Israelites in Berlin then as there are now; some of those whom my father helped by lending them a couple of *Groschen* became very rich, but they would then not remember past times. My father married, his practice increased, and he could live without major worries—his wife died soon after having lost two

4. Herz is incorrect here. Her father was not the first Jewish physician.

daughters, and several years after her death he married my mother. I did not know my father as a young man, but he was supposedly very good-looking, which is evident from a picture of him as a young man which I own, and one could see traces of past handsomeness in his face until his death. His nose and his mouth—which, by the time I became aware of his appearance, lacked almost all teeth—were exceptionally beautiful; a gentle, extremely delicate expression in his face, the most shapely hands and feet, a noble posture and agility made him handsome even in old age: his language was pure, since all Portuguese Jews lack the Jewish jargon[5] and intonation. My father lived strictly according to the law of his religion, but he carried the gentleness and love of Christianity in his heart and was therefore tolerant with all those who acted against his faith. The household was set up completely in accordance with Jewish laws and customs. The work of a practicing physician was much more difficult then, since most physicians did not own a coach and horses, and since my father did not earn enough to keep any. Moreover, he would carefully lay aside any extra *Thaler* he could save for the constantly growing family. Until late at night he would visit patients, accompanied by a servant, who had to light his way with a stick lantern on dark winter evenings—how often did I see him come home, soaked by the rain or covered with snow! He enjoyed a healthy constitution, however, and although he never wore a topcoat or a cloak, he would only catch a cold, if anything. He dressed elegantly for those times: he would wear clothes made from fine cloth, silk, or velvet, trimmed with gold or silver braids, always shoes and silk stockings, silk vests and so forth, the finest linen, a wig and an elegant three-cornered hat—and although this attire began to be somewhat old-fashioned then, it suited him very well, and all the older physicians were distinguished this way by their dress. His neat cotton nightgown and the white cap for week-days, the red satin one with a matching cap and slippers for holidays were even more becoming than anything else he wore.

My mother, whom I knew only as an ailing woman with eyes infected by her incessant crying over the death of a two-year-old son, was supposed to have been very pretty, although I must admit that no traces of that former

---

5. The veiled reference in nineteenth-century discourse for speaking Eastern European Yiddish, or High German with a Yiddish accent.

beauty were visible. She was very strong-tempered and almost always in a bad mood because of her eye ailment, against which none of the medicines the best doctors and eye specialists prescribed was effective. She was skillful in needlework, but rarely had time to do any. She was thrifty, orderly, clean, very helpful and pleasant toward everybody and loved my father to distraction, a love that he returned with the same passion. I don't recall that they ever called each other by their proper names; they always called or addressed each other with made-up tender names and we never heard an argument or bitter words between them. My mother was a counselor to many people and an active support in times of pain and pleasure; these qualities made her beloved by many people, and she merited this esteem. She had a straightforward, clear mind, and without having been formally educated, she appreciated everything connected to higher learning; she loved to have people read to her and she had an excellent memory: whenever she had been to a theater, she would not only recount the plot of a play precisely, but also the sequence of acts and scenes. She loved her children, but perhaps believed that a lot of scolding was necessary to educate and to lead a household, and often her wrath was provoked by the most inconsequential incident, probably due to her poor health and the eye ailment—to think that just a little medication would have sufficed to cure it, if only the doctors had diagnosed it earlier! The illness was namely the following: The continuous wiping of her eyes after the death of the above-mentioned child caused the eyelashes to be bent inward, so that they finally grew inward from the lids—none of the doctors had noticed that for many years, and they always tried to cure the ensuing infections, until, after many years, a famous old eye doctor discovered the true root of the evil; too late to cure it, because her eyes were already bloodshot and blurred, but he was able to alleviate the burning pain by pulling out the eyelashes with a minute pair of tweezers. After that she had no more infections, but her eyes were almost destroyed and she could never again see clearly; yet she did not turn blind either, and almost every day the small, quick-growing eyelashes had to be pulled out to prevent further infection.

In my most immediate environment were an old aunt and her husband, both quite common people, who established their household in some rear rooms of our house and frequently fought and were not particularly liked by my mother. An old relative of my mother's, a highly unclean man, who often gave me sweets, lived in a small dark chamber inside the house. The other tenants in the house, all of them Israelites, were merchants who would often visit us in the evenings. The oldest son of these people, a completely deformed, dissipated youth, could have caused my downfall, because of my innocence, if God had not protected me.

I had to work a lot and was allowed to go out but once a week with the above-mentioned old great-aunt. I visited with her an old couple and their no-longer-youthful daughter, and I was very happy there, but my mother's constant scolding when I came home spoilt my pleasure. However, I may have deserved the scolding, because I was very unruly and messy, particularly the former. I never actually walked but ran and jumped: thus I recall that I once stopped short in my tracks asking myself whether I was able to walk at all! Real strangers were never invited for dinner by my parents, but my mother often received visits from women who were usually led to the sewing room, to which I was admitted for a few minutes to receive a small cake or an apple; such coffee visits would usually end with a game of cards. Once every year I would go with my parents to the great Italian opera—it was the heyday of the singer Mara. The sweets which were taken along and Mara were of equal importance to me —yet still I remember her wonderful voice when she sang the *mi paventi,* an aria she made famous, and the effect she had on the full opera house. During Frederick II's time, the parterre was full of soldiers, who were taken to the opera upon royal order; and nobody else could have a seat there. We had our seats in a box above the parterre, and we were often bothered by the noise made by the packed-in soldiers or by their whispering; they were not allowed to speak loudly; but whenever Mara sang one of her arias, not the most minute sound or movement, not even breathing, was to be heard—there was the deepest silence—and when she had finished, it was as if the whole assembly took a deep breath. My pleasure at the opera was spoilt by the scolding and bickering of my mother when we arrived home. Often the old aunt, who loved and spoilt me, would protect me from her wrath—I slept in her rooms and was always with her, and if she was in the kitchen, I rarely left her alone there, although my parents objected, and since I preferred cooking and cleaning to sewing, I often helped her and the cook as diligently and assiduously as I could. I stopped playing at a very early age, and earlier than might have been good for me, I turned to reading; I read proficiently and had to read to my mother many a winter's evening, before my father came home and when she had no visitors. On summer evenings, I was sometimes allowed to go for a walk in the streets with the old aunt or to go to a garden in which my parents lived one summer,[6] after my father had overcome a severe illness. I had only two playmates, girls of the same age, one of whom died early; the other one is still my friend; with those two and my younger sister I would walk back and forth in front of the house. This sister was much more loved by my mother, and therefore I did not like her; we often quarreled, once we even beat each other up, which made my mother very mad at me, so that I was not allowed to see her for a whole day—this pained me greatly, I sat down on the floor in a corner and cried the whole day—my aunt, in order to show my mother that I was deeply touched by her hardness, told her that I had wanted to kill myself with a knife (which was untrue); that did appease her, and I was allowed to sit at the table in the evening.

I cannot clearly say whether I am deceiving myself or whether it is the truth, but it seems to me that I felt and thought then as I would now if I, the old woman, were suddenly placed into that world again. I cannot recall any truly childish behavior or thought, except for my overwhelming mirth, which could not be dampened even by my mother's scolding. From early on, I had a tendency toward charitable acts, and in order to satisfy it, I borrowed five *Thalers* from a friend of the family; he notified my father, who, in turn, paid him back. I was severely questioned about why I had borrowed the money, and I admitted the truth and was forgiven.

We were seldom alone at home, because although we did not see strangers, the people in our house visited us very often—my mother usually played cards with one or another of them, and so did my father occasionally, whenever he did not come home too late from his calls. Usually, he would browse in sacred books instead; I could then do what I wished. I ran around with my younger brothers and sisters in the nursery, where I often heard stupid or bad things from people who frequently told ghost stories. From these tales I still get a slight feeling of horror at midnight. Or, I read bad novels and comedies or slept until mealtime in a corner of the

6. Garden property in the Tiergarten. It was the family's summer residence.

room. Our tenants were harmless people, except for the man previously mentioned, who was one of the worst sort, because without any shame and without any consideration for my innocence and youth he made the basest and most obscene remarks to me. Whenever he kissed me, and this he did very often, there was great passion in his kiss; I did not understand this, since I was only about ten years old; he had the free run of our house, and no one paid attention to him, and without being aware of it myself, I acquired from him the knowledge that there are two sexes. But this unpleasantness fortunately passed; it did not harm me, because a higher hand protected me. My daily routine was now set: during the day I worked with my aunt who taught me to sew, and in the evenings after supper, whenever my father alone remained awake, I sat with him while he read, preparing my lessons for the French teacher or reading myself.

Weddings provided my real entertainment; there was always dancing, and usually I could not fall asleep the night before in anticipation of these pleasures. However, I was often distressed that, although I could dance very prettily, older girls would be preferred to me, and then, in a corner of the ballroom, I would quietly shed tears that the next dance would dry at once—how I enjoyed myself! I was almost always cheerful and was often quite unruly! Still with all that, I sometimes had a dark, yearning feeling, then I sat on a balcony wrapped in a small fur jacket, gazing at the moon, and weeping without knowing why. *The Life of Siegwart*[7] and other such sentimental novels probably contributed to this mood, and I often thought that those abductions and wondrous things I had read so much about could also happen to me—I also had such a mania for reading those kinds of books that I often did not work at all, and since my aunt, who was supposed to teach me to sew, let me have my own way, my mother was forced to send me to sewing school. Now I could read very little on weekdays but made up for it on Saturdays and Sundays, and did it with such speed and assiduity that in one day I could read through several parts of a novel and would constantly run to the lending library not far from our house to pick up more books.[8] On Friday evenings I read aloud to my parents; my father

7. *Siegwart, eine Klostergeschichte* (1776) by Johann Martin Müller (1750–1814).

8. The lending library of the bookdealer and publisher Hans Friedrich Vieweg in the Spandauer Strasse.

preferred to hear plays; I also liked to read these aloud, preferring to read novels alone to myself since they always moved me to bitter tears, and I was ashamed to cry. Horror stories had an especially strong effect on me and everything I read in ghost stories was confirmed for me in the nursery. The sentimental inclination, however, came completely from within me, because no one I saw aroused it in any way, and though it stemmed from my vanity, it really emerged only now and then—as, for example, one summer when I would go with my aunt every evening to a garden where my father resided: I know that I would stand before the mirror every time and pinch my cheeks red, and sometimes the mirror would be covered because I was always looking in it. However, I paid little attention to my clothes, preferring most an outfit that I could scrub and cook in. Of my aforementioned playmates my favorite ones were a quiet, profound, thoughtful, cool, and very reasonable girl who had a good mind, but was without education or culture since her parents did not belong to the so-called enlightened class of Jews—she died of consumption after a short marriage—and another very lively girl, profound like the first, but warm, who would often enthusiastically glow for some hero or heroine in a novel—she had a keen mind and was unusually clever; her father belonged to the upper bourgeoisie and was a very respected scholar and loved my friend above all others and educated her himself.[9] We three girls, still practically children, lived fairly close to one another, and as soon as one of us was able to get out of the house, she would go visit the others. I was always making plans for the future with the second girl.

I was now twelve years old and was looked upon with favor as a beautiful child, unusually large for her age. An older man, a Portuguese Jew who happened to be in Berlin, asked for my hand; he was willing to wait three more years but wanted the assurance from my parents that he would then be able to take me home as his wife—he spoke of Moors and parrots that were supposedly on their way to Berlin and would bring his treasures along with them later—the story ended with him stealing a silver snuffbox from my father and disappearing.

My mother found it necessary to send me to a formal sewing school, be-

9. Dorothea Mendelssohn, who married and divorced Veit and married Friedrich Schlegel. Her father was the philosopher Moses Mendelssohn.

cause I could indeed speak French, dance, and read, but could neither knit nor sew, and the aunt who ought to have taught me was too lenient with me. I had probably gone to the sewing school for about six months when my mother told me that I should again learn sewing from my aunt, and how great was my surprise when my aunt told me in confidence that I was to be betrothed—to whom, I asked her, and she named the man: he was an up-and-coming physician—I had seen him a few times with my father and also at his window; he lived in our neighborhood, and I had to pass by his house whenever I picked up books from the library—then it so happened one winter day that I slipped in front of his house and fell with a horror novel in my hand: I was immensely embarrassed, for he was at the window. I was happy in a childish way about becoming engaged, and I pictured quite vividly how I would be taken on walks by my fiancé, how I would be provided with better clothes and a hairdresser, because up to now my hair had been done by my aunt who rubbed it with tallow and arranged it to her liking. Furthermore, I hoped to increase my pocket money which at that time amounted to two *Groschen* a month, and to partake of the small, somewhat finer culinary delicacies that were sometimes prepared for my father. Impatiently I awaited the day of the engagement which my aunt had secretly announced, telling me that my father would ask me whether I approved of his choice for me. The longed-for day came, the morning passed, and nothing was said to me—at the noon meal my father asked me if I would rather marry a doctor or a rabbi? My heart pounded, and I answered that I would be content with whomever he should choose for me. After the meal, my mother told me that that evening I would become engaged to Doctor Marcus Herz—she then gave a long speech, which at that moment was boring and unpleasant; but much later I remembered many good pieces of advice from it. She told me how I should behave toward my fiancé and how I should take her marriage as a model for my own future one—and it is true that there has never been a happier one.

The party assembled. I was in another room. At that time it was not the custom for the girl to be in the same room with her parents and the notaries, and only after she had formally been asked for her consent and had signed the marriage contract could she join the guests. In timid expectation I sat there all dressed up—glowing with anxiety—I wanted to sew but my hands trembled. I paced up and down the room, by chance passing the mirror and, for the first time, I considered myself more than pretty—the apple-green and white striped silk dress and the black hat with feathers suited me very well, my dark eyes sparkled from the blush of my cheeks, and my small mouth was gentle. Many years have passed since then, but the youthful face of that moment stands so vividly before me that I could paint it. I wanted to appear calm when the door opened and the notary and two witnesses entered—they asked me if I gave my consent to the union, and I stammered "yes." Shortly thereafter Marcus came, kissed my hand, and led me to the others. My parents were very content, tender and loving toward one another, as always; a neighbor pointed this out to Marcus saying that it was a joy to see such a marriage. Give me a few years, he responded, and you will see a second.

I knew little of my fiancé; he was fifteen years my elder, small and homely, but he had an intelligent face and a reputation as a scholar—he was one of Kant's favorite students—and had studied medicine as well as philosophy in Königsberg; he had also already published a few brief, discerning, philosophical papers. His early youth was spent in very ordinary circumstances, and his later solely in scientific circles, so that he did not get to know either people or the world, and thus his intellect was formed whereas his character was not. My life in my father's house remained the same, as well as my mother's attitude toward me. I was given neither more to eat nor better food than before, and it was always less than what I wanted to eat. However, I did receive six *Groschen* instead of two *Groschen* weekly[10] and had my hair done twice a week by a hairdresser. I was hardly ever allowed to go out, only seldom with my fiancé, and if I once in a while went out alone, I was always picked up early, because Marcus would come every evening to play cards, which bored me terribly, since I hardly knew one card from the other and always had to sit next to him at the card table, and often I had been called away from very enjoyable company to this boredom. I was almost never alone with Marcus, because I did not have a room of my own—whenever he left I accompanied him out, and if all was quiet in the house we stayed in the entry hall; his caresses

10. This is clearly an inconsistency, because before, Henriette had spoken of two *Groschen* as her monthly allowance.

were pleasing to me, though in my innocence I did not understand much, because in spite of everything that I had heard and seen, my mind had stayed absolutely pure. Once I asked a young woman in our house how babies were conceived—and she told me: when one thinks a lot about the same man. I would think a great deal about Marcus and I feared that this way, I would bring shame upon my parents. I was happy with the prospect of soon becoming a wife, so that I could go out and eat what and as much as I pleased. Marcus treated me mostly like a child, which of course I was, but it still vexed me when I was called one.

Marcus soon introduced me to many families he was friendly with. I did not like them very much; they belonged to the more distinguished kind and seemed unbearably stiff to me—I had to call on one family especially often, and Marcus soon came to regret having introduced me there—since one of the sons, with whom I accidentally found myself alone in a room, became so forward that only my loud screams rescued me.

The time approached which had been set for my wedding—my sister Hanne and I diligently sewed for my trousseau. Our household had also grown larger, for my mother had borne twins. My mother continually quarreled with me, and shortly before the wedding only the evenings were pleasant, because many young people, Marcus's friends, came and we joked and laughed a lot. Unpleasantness was not, however, totally absent from this scene—Marcus and my father often had strong disagreements concerning some of the articles of the marriage contract, and this was very painful to me—however, this was a very fleeting emotion, because all of the beautiful new clothes and the millinery which were laid out before me and the close prospect of freedom filled me with youthful delight.

The wedding day finally came, and although many, many years have elapsed since, I can remember practically every moment of that morning and of the whole day. With indescribable sadness I awoke, the thought of leaving my father hurt me deeply, and amidst a thousand tears I let myself be dressed in my wedding dress, which was of white satin, trimmed with red roses. The bridegroom came, and the guests arrived—shortly before the ceremony I tried to speak to my father alone—with hot tears I bade him to forgive everything I had done which had ever offended and angered him, and to give me his blessing; he did this, embraced me in tears, and said: "Child, don't break my heart." Until my last breath I will never forget these words. His blessing was heard by God—because I entered a rich, beautiful life. It was the first of October of the year 1779, I believe.[11] Much snow lay high in the courtyard where the baldachin stood, the canopy under which I was married, according to Jewish custom. Many distinguished people who knew Herz were present. A banquet which lasted until late that night closed the festivities. Herz's friend Friedländer and his wife accompanied the newlyweds home.

The First Three Years of My Marriage

Herz's barber was the first person to see the fifteen-year-old wife the morning after her wedding. Although many years have passed since then, I still know exactly where I sat and how I was dressed in a charming, very fashionable morning gown, and how proud I was of my new dignity as housewife, when the old barber entered the room. A cook, who would come early in the morning for my orders for dinner, and a somewhat drunken old woman, whom Herz had had in his service before, made up my household. That evening there was a ball at my parents' home. I dressed—was not pleased with myself—fussed with my finery many times, but still was not any more pleased with myself—the reason was that, according to Jewish custom, as a married woman I had to cover my hair completely, and the headdress, decorated with pearls and flowers, did not suit me at all; I arrived somewhat later than some of the guests, and my mother received me with indignation and rebuked me since here and there a little of my hair was visible from under the headdress—but how soon was all that forgotten, when my beloved father invited me to dance a minuet with him and thereby opened the ball with me! Herz did not dance. My father was already in his sixties and still danced with grace and agility, so that he drew the admiration of the numerous guests. I remember little more of the evening, except that I was bored and that I was happy when I saw the festivities ending. The next days were spent with visits and receiving guests; my new life actually began a few weeks later. All the young people who visited my father's house, most of whom were students, also came to my house

11. Henriette was married to Marcus Herz on December 1, 1779.

now, and not one among them was especially interested in me; nor did I find anyone more interesting than the other. Freely and cheerfully I associated with them, and my husband liked to have them in his home. My mother would visit me and was most of the time unhappy with everything she saw me do—alas, I guess she was right. My father came less often—it was, however, always an occasion when he came. A few of those young people and my mother usually ate Friday lunch with us. We were often at my parents' house where Herz played cards and I was bored.

I was happy, loving a thirty-year-old man with the love of a fifteen-year-old. I had read many novels and absorbed them. Herz laughed at me and when I reveled in my love, dancing around him, embracing him, he called me to reason. Dorothea[12] and I saw each other almost daily, and when we could not see one another, then we would write. Herz was the doctor in her father's house, our husbands were good friends, and if we did not see each other more often than we did, this was because we moved in different social circles.

Even when he was in Königsberg, Herz had heard about how widespread education was in Berlin, extending to all classes, and for that reason—even as knowledgeable as he was—he began his trip here with a certain trepidation.

A retort from a cobbler's apprentice soon reinforced his worst fears. He had lost one of his shoes underway and just after he arrived ordered another made exactly like the remaining shoe. When the shoe arrived, however, it was clear that this directive had not been followed, and furious, he asked the cobbler's boy whether he actually thought this shoe was an exact copy. As apparent as the difference was, it didn't even faze the boy a moment. He looked Herz scornfully up and down and then said: "Don't you know, little man, that no two things in the world are exactly identical?" Herz arose, disconcerted, paid for the shoe without a word, and let some time pass before he braved Berlin society again.

However, he soon realized that he did not have to avoid even the most sophisticated circles. He was at ease in any company by virtue of his knowledge, and of his ready wit as well; this inspired him with retorts most

12. Dorothea Mendelssohn-Veit.

incisive, though at times not very kind, which soon were making the rounds of the entire city.

Herz was already a respected physician even around the time of our wedding. Soon he was renowned, and this brought him into contact with many admirable families whom he treated for medical problems. In a short time, he began to hold philosophical lectures in our home and a very select audience found their way to them. These talks brought about an even greater extension of our social connections, since he sometimes would invite the more rigorous and interesting of his listeners to dine with us. Later he added well-received lectures on physics, which were illustrated by experiments using precise instruments and apparatuses. These talks were attended by people of the highest station, the inquiring mind as well as the merely curious, and added to our circle many of the most prominent celebrities. Even the younger brother of the King attended these lectures; the royal tutor Delbrück brought along his charge, the five-year-old Crown Prince, to show him some interesting experiments. I remember having executed some phosphorus experiments for the little Prince myself.

It is to these lectures that I owe, among other things, my acquaintance with the brothers Wilhelm and Alexander von Humboldt, who would become friends for life—a friendship that embellished my days of happiness and brightened my days of gloom. They had urged their tutor (the later Privy Councillor Kunth) to ask Herz's advice on the construction of a lightning rod, a rather unusual apparatus in the countryside in those days (around 1785), to be installed on Tegel Castle, which belonged to the Humboldt family. And soon Kunth introduced to us his two pupils, who joined our social circle in short order.

Under such auspicious circumstances, our house grew, and I can say without exaggerating that it became one of the most pleasant and sought-after houses in Berlin. If Herz was attractive because of his brilliant mind and his fame as a physician, I attracted—much time has passed since—because of my beauty. But I don't want to be unjust toward myself. At least I had an appreciation of the sciences. There was hardly a field of investigation in which I had not some kind of knowledge, and in some I became seriously engaged, such as physics and, later, several languages.

Even as young and ignorant as I was, our guests still conversed a lot with me because they were convinced that I was clever, since I was pretty; these conversations were not without their usefulness to me, for those who participated in them were primarily insightful people, and if they couldn't speak *with* me, they could nevertheless speak *to* me.

Herz was a keen critic. It didn't take much for him to condemn whole works for lack of clarity. He often liked to quote a saying from Malebranche that there was a whole class of prolific authors in whose works hardly one passage could be found that they themselves would have understood.

The appearance of Goethe's *Götz* [*von Berlichingen*] and [*The Sorrows of Young*] *Werther* marked a turning point in literature. It is understandable that such an event must bring in its wake a general literary schism. This happened within our marriage as well. I, the young woman with a lively imagination, was drawn to this rising star, Goethe. My husband, older, a personal friend of Lessing, regarded the latter not only as one of the greatest German critics, but also—contrary to Lessing's own view—as a great author; he disregarded everything in belles lettres that had not been written with Lessing's clarity and lucidity. He shared this opinion with several of his friends, including David Friedländer. When Friedländer came to him one day asking him to explain an obscure passage in a Goethe poem, hoping deep in his heart that he could not do it, Herz directed him to me with the words: "Go to my wife; she understands the art of explaining nonsense!"

Once, when Karl Philipp Moritz was with me, Herz came in with Goethe's poem "The Fisherman" in hand. "'Kühl bis ans Herz hinan! [Cool into deep in the heart!]" he cried. "Will one of you explain to me what that is supposed to mean?" "But who would want to understand this poem?" replied Moritz, pointing his finger to his head. Herz just stared at him. There are simply many things in poetry which are comprehensible only to those who have sensed the same thing or something similar, and I can definitely say that Herz had never felt anything like that.

With the advent of the Romantic School, my aesthetic sufferings rose to new heights; here everything was either untrue or incomprehensible to Herz. But those sufferings reached their pinnacle with Novalis. The uncluttered scientific mind has no sense for mysticism. And added to that was the problem that some of the passages in that poet's work were also unclear to me, even if I understood his spiritual strivings on the whole. Herz, who had only glanced through some of Novalis's works in order to joke about them, knew all too well how to find such passages. One day he read one to me and wanted me to explain it. After several vain attempts, I had to admit that I didn't understand it either. "But you think," said Herz with a sarcastic smile, "that the young oaf understood it himself?"

As much as Herz loved social life, he sought in it only a break from his real vocation. And this was indeed unremitting work, and he hated nothing more than whatever kept him from it: above all, the migraines which he frequently suffered. He resisted them as long as possible. If they became severe enough to keep him from his professional duties, his impatience and irritation at not being able to overcome them would reach the melting point. "But what happens," he shouted during one such attack of the malady, "when a general is struck by such a migraine on the day of the battle that decides the fate of a nation?"

My propensity for reading grew, and I could now satisfy it undisturbed. The first book which I read completely under the direction of my husband was Euler's *Letters to a German Princess*.[13] Even if Herz was too busy to instruct me thoroughly, he would still explain many things to me that I did not understand. In addition to his practice, he was occupied at that time with the translation of a short English brochure. I often glanced at the book wishing that I could understand it; this wish was soon satisfied in that my husband found an old Scotsman as a teacher for me. I made rapid progress but was interrupted since I had to dismiss the teacher because— he fell in love with me. Another was supposed to be found soon, but this was not to be because Herz fell dangerously ill. From the very beginning, he must have had a feeling it was coming, because when the Councillor of State Rose wanted to give him the honorarium for the lectures he was holding that winter, Herz did not want to accept it, saying that he might die. This was my first experience of real suffering. I had not been married a full year and loved my husband with the total devotion of a girl not yet sixteen years old. Even though this love was more planted in me than innate, I knew and expected nothing different or more beautiful. For seventeen days

13. Leonhard Euler's *Briefe an eine deutsche Prinzessin über verschiedene Gegenstände der Physik und Philosophie* (original in French: 1768–72). Herz no doubt read the German version, which started appearing in 1769.

and nights I did not even get to change my clothes. In the first days of his illness I alone cared for and sat with the beloved patient; on the eighth day I sat on his bed and he said to me that he wanted to entrust to me something that tormented him greatly. He told me about a horrible incident that had happened to a family we knew on the very day before he fell ill, asking me to call a relative of this family, because he needed to speak to him. I did what he wanted, and the man came. Herz spoke to him but did not mention the incident, and that evening it became clear that this story, told in great detail, was the fantasy of his sick mind, which was increasingly deranged by the rising fever and which involved me so sadly that, upon orders of the excellent Selle, Herz's doctor and friend, I had to avoid the patient's room altogether. Herz had never exhibited the slightest bit of jealousy, although many younger and older men came to our house, but suddenly it was aroused to such a degree that he did not want to see me any more, because, as he said, I was involved in immoral affairs with all the young people who attended or cared for him. I remained completely calm in the face of this accusation, since I was fully aware of my innocence and was convinced that such a thought could only be the product of Herz's sick imagination. The only possible cause I could think of was that the young people and I, who was practically still a child, laughed about the bizarre, often funny ideas Herz had. The removal from the sick bed, however, pained me greatly, and I sat quietly behind a screen, listening for the patient's slightest movement.

On the twelfth day of the illness which had turned into a severely high fever, Herz suddenly lost his speech, and the doctors believed his death to be imminent. I cannot say what I felt when I thought I heard one of them saying: "He is dying." I only know that I ran into the adjacent room where, almost unconscious, I paced in a circle, continuously repeating the words: "But I'm so young." Then I asked to be given an instrument with which I could kill myself. Later I found out that I had thrown open the window in order to jump out. The momentary danger passed, and with joy in my heart, forgetting that I was forbidden, I went to his bed, hovered over the patient, caressing him, and asked: "Are you better?" "Better?" was his answer, "I was almost dead, but go now, go!" I spent several days more in such a painful state—on the fourteenth day of the illness, the doctors' hopes were finally gone, that night would be decisive, and truly enough, that night the illness reached its peak. A thoughtless man among the attendants ran to my old father to inform him of his son-in-law's extremely precarious situation, and the shock immediately paralyzed my father's tongue. My good mother, who only left my house at night, now had to tremble for the life of her own beloved husband. After several hours and after administering many medicines, the danger abated and Herz recovered a little. My pain subsided as the good news of his improvement was brought to me, and my first thought was that my father should be informed immediately. The messenger found the dear pious man praying to God with devotion and fervor; he could only speak with his creator in thought, because his tongue was still bound—but when he received the joyous news, at that moment his tongue was freed and "God be praised" came from his lips. Surely never before has a more pious invocation been uttered by blessed lips. The doctors meanwhile still held little hope for Herz from this momentary improvement, and said that only a restful sleep, which he had not had in sixteen whole days, could possibly save him. For several days he had said in this constant delirium that he wished to sleep, but that it was impossible in this strange room and house; if only one would allow him to leave this hospital and bring him home to the room where the pictures of Leibniz, Euler, Lessing, and others were hanging (he was referring to our dressing room; his bed stood in his study because the bedchamber was too small), then he could sleep. The cold was very severe, and the doctors did not want to allow a transfer to a room which had not been thoroughly heated: my mother insisted that he be moved, and on the seventeenth day of his illness the doctors permitted the move, since they had completely given up on the patient—there was nothing more to lose. The day before, my mother had ordered the room heated; it was thoroughly warmed, and the patient was installed in his room at about noon, and almost immediately fell into a quiet, restful sleep which lasted six hours, while we tensely and anxiously waited, because Selle had said that it was uncertain whether the sleep, which now seemed beneficial, would not become the sleep of death. He awoke and the fever had broken. The crisis was caused by a fungus infection that went from his lips deep down into his throat. When he regained full consciousness, he was so weak that he could not even move a finger; he compared his strength with that of a fly. I will not mention my joy, as well as my parents' and the neighbors', over the sudden certainty of his recovery. The convalescence proceeded very slowly at first because of the fungus infection that was treated by the excellent Voitus, one of the doctors; once the infection passed, Herz's strength increased quickly. He was very happy, because he was very soon convinced that everything that had tormented him in his delirium—jealousy, removal from his own home, accidents which had befallen his friends, etc., were the products of his feverish mind. The great concern which friends and acquaintances had shown him, the loyalty of the young men, who were practically all aspiring physicians—among them one of my mother's brothers, a dear man who now (1824), seventy years old, is a country doctor—some are now dead, some are scattered worldwide—made Herz's cheerfulness return and I recovered my good spirits, even exuberance, as well; the recollections of all of Herz's fantasies were recorded by him for psychological reasons, and he described his whole illness in a letter written to a friend—who has since departed this world—and published an interesting abstract in Moritz's *Journal of Empirical Psychology*.[14]

Our earlier life now resumed. Herz was preoccupied with his increasing responsibilities; I sewed, washed clothes, scrubbed the floors, and went out; the latter only seldom. My new acquaintances were still somewhat limited, and of the old ones very few remained. I grew and blossomed more and more, neglected my toilette and hygiene outrageously, and my small household as well. I brought with me into marriage the disorder and slovenliness that had brought down on me my mother's justified wrath before I was married. My husband reprimanded me severely about this, especially when his undergarments were torn—clothing I had pulled out of some corner of the house. He summoned me and reproached me for it, with good reason. Since it did not do any good, he became seriously angry; even though I was frightened when he had me called to his room while he was dressing, it still did not accomplish anything, and it is remarkable that in later years when I went over to the other extreme, I still got scared, even terrified, when he had me called while dressing.

My vanity was fully indulged after Herz's illness. A Russian general came to Berlin, a man married to a lovely woman from the Black Sea re-

14. *Magazin der Erfahrungsseelenkunde.* Edited by Moritz, Pockels, and Maimon. Vol.1, Sect.2 (1783): 44–73.

gion. He lived in one of the best inns, where several elegant Polish ladies also lived; Herz was their doctor. These ladies had seen me and thought I was prettier than that Southern European woman; they wanted to convince her husband that they were right, and without my knowledge they organized a breakfast at which I was to be viewed. I don't remember any more which one of us won, but I can affirm that had I been the Phrygian shepherd, the lovely Southern European would have gotten the golden apple. I still see her before me in all her loveliness in a delicate white morning gown of gauzy, gracefully draping material and her long, floating black hair; the most graceful figure, the most delicate movements, and everything she said was childlike and naive; she might have been a few years older than I. My clothes were better, but couldn't have looked good on me since I had on a large headdress because I was required to keep my head covered. Even if disorderly attire and bodily neglect can be neither defended nor condoned, still the main reason for my attitude may have been my disgruntlement with myself because of that legally required headdress.

I saw Dorothea often, but even more often I was with a young girl from the neighborhood whom I had come to like, Marianne Schadow, and Mr. Reil, who was a student in Berlin at the time and who had been introduced to us by Goldhagen, Herz's friend in Halle. He took his meals with us, and his intellect, knowledge, and hard work won the hearts of Herz and my uncle. The girl and I were the same age and we both thought that great things would have to happen to us, since life simply could not go on in the calm, uneventful way it had until then. Sadly enough, her own life was all too short; she entered a liaison with a young man that took her life and her honor; she secretly eloped and soon died in childbirth. Yet that happened only at the end of the summer; during the previous winter I saw her almost every day, particularly when I came down with the measles and had to stay in bed and could see almost no one.

Shortly before my illness I had met a gracious young woman. She was from Prague, where she had escaped from an unhappy marriage into a convent. Her father, a pious Jew who followed the Jewish law, had her abducted from there, even though she had become a devout Catholic under the exhortations of the nuns. Her father left her in Berlin; we became close friends and saw each other often; later she became the wife of a gifted artist. Her sons became respectable artists as well, although her oldest died too young. I saw this woman often, and she and the previously mentioned friends livened up my sickroom. I soon recovered and became lovelier and healthier. My vanity also had reason to rejoice, for around that time Jewish women received permission to wear hairpieces, even though not their real hair, in public. Since my parents had nothing against this, a wig that suited me was made, and soon it too was put aside and was replaced with my own shiny, coal-black hair.

I lived happily and worked hard; our little house had many visitors and we in turn visited many homes, among others that of the friends whom Herz had described in that terrifying tale during his feverish hallucinations. This house was very elegant and terribly pretentious. We were invited there frequently. The men gambled and the wife and I took walks in the garden in the summertime. One evening it happened that we went into the garden and found there two men whom I did not know. Madame Cohen introduced us; the older was the English consul, a handsome man; the younger, an officer attached to the consulate. Both lived in this house; the latter offered me his arm and we were strolling in the rather small garden when Mme. Cohen heard a bell ringing and said she had to leave; her companion went along. They disappeared so quickly that I was alone with my companion before I could disengage my arm. I was disconcerted and did not grant the young man's request to stay longer in the garden, but rather hurried back into the house. Since we visited these so-called friends often, Ewart (the name of the young man) could see me frequently, and the English maid, probably at the instigation of her mistress, provided ample opportunities—which I probably would have recognized and not participated in had I been older than sixteen. But as it was, I let this happen, and let Ewart say flattering things to me when I met him by chance. It was not long before he came to visit us at home; he was very clever and knew how to win Herz over. They spoke French together since he did not know German, and very often he came at nine in the morning and stayed until two in the afternoon. We read, and he explained his love for me in the tenderest words which I did not exactly return, but which did not leave me unmoved, and I can say with complete honesty that I did not show him the slightest degree of favor, for I hardly even allowed him to kiss my hand. Yet I did not feel totally indifferent to him when he begged me on his knees for a kiss, with tears in his eyes. When I thought about Herz I wept about my offense against him which consisted of fleeting thoughts and feelings. How often did I ask Herz not to admit Ewart when he came early in the morning, so that he would not be with me so many hours. But Herz thought it shouldn't matter to me; I could just let him sit there and keep working. Where then was safety? Ewart appeared at all times of the day, neglected his customary circle of friends, which included the court, and was always where I was. When he could do it, he had himself invited to Moses Mendelssohn's home, which we frequented a lot. Since he found that he could not reach his real purpose, which I finally understood, through delicacy, he became aggressive and that saved my soul. I closed my heart to him, and turned him away from my door whenever I was alone. On a Saturday noon, I was returning home from my parents' and found him at my door just as I was entering; I had to let him come in, if only because the maid was present. We had hardly entered the room when he implored me to arrange a time when he could be alone and undisturbed with me; he knelt before me and swore that he would not rise until I had given him a time. I heard a doorbell ring, heard steps—I pleaded with him to stand up—to no avail— someone was approaching the door—he said it did not matter to him who was coming, whether my husband or a stranger—they were at the door, and I told him nine the next morning, while planning not to be there at that time. I was calm, and even if Ewart was the first man to make my breast heave with a different feeling than ever before, it was still only to an imperceptible degree, and it was more the English officer than the man in him that caused it.

Later that same evening, which I spent away from home, my maid told me while I was undressing that Ewart had been there several times and that he had given her a letter for me; I took it from her, didn't open it, slept peacefully and hurried the next morning before nine o'clock with the letter to a woman friend, Marianne [Schadow], whom I got to know better because her future husband, with whom she was living at the time, made a bust of me, and I asked her for her advice. I did not want to open the letter, but to send it back unopened or give it to my husband; she definitely advised against the latter, and her curiosity, perhaps also my own, led us to open the letter. Its contents are easy to guess; it was written in English, partly in verse, partly in prose, full of glowing passion. I was more and more convinced I should show it to my husband and then do what he told me. My relationship with Ewart had improved my English reading ability; we read a lot together, and so it is not surprising that I knew more English than Herz. So I had to translate the letter for him almost word for word; he stayed calm and said that I should send back all the books he had lent me and write him the following words: "Sachez la comédie est finie et que vous ne trouverez jamais plus ni moi ni mon mari à la maison."[15] It was no struggle to do this; I was relieved to do it, and my cheerfulness was not in jeopardy. Herz knew that I had begun this acquaintance at the Cohens' home. I kept silent about the opportunities that had been arranged for him to meet me there, and that was of course not right; but—so young, so beautiful—I could be forgiven for it. Several weeks passed without my seeing Ewart; it happened once—probably arranged—and he told me that he had been outrageously duped on account of me, that certain people (and he let me know that it had been these previously mentioned friends) had told him that it would be easy for him to get me to let him visit me once more; he realized now that this was impossible. I believed what he said, since I had never really trusted the Cohen woman; I spoke with Herz about it, told him everything, and since he had reason to maintain the favor of the Cohens, he allowed Ewart to visit us again. His behavior after that was totally different; but I am not so naive as to believe that this change occurred for the proper reasons, but rather think he became colder to me because of a liaison with one of the Queen's ladies-in-waiting who later became his wife. His visits became less and less frequent and finally stopped altogether; I remained calm, and when I saw him again years later, I was upset for a moment, but stayed calm. Several years later he became the consul at the court in Berlin, and I saw him very seldom, yet I remember that when I saw him for the first time after a long period, I was startled and my heart was beating fast. Thus ended my first encounter of this sort and I still thank God today that it did not drive me into ruin. His hand alone was able to protect me against that, and He held it gently over me. Dorothea knew part of this story, and she was just as naive and innocent as I; Marianne, whom I saw more often, knew more about everything because her friend and later husband was making a bust of me in his house, where she also lived, and

---

15. "Know that the comedy is over and that you will never again encounter me or my husband at home."

she was usually present for the sittings. Even though I saw Dorothea less frequently, she was closer to my heart, and she understood me, or better, understood my innocence much more, because she was herself innocent. Before knowing Ewart, I had never thought it possible for a married woman to be loved by a man other than her husband, or to be able to love someone other than him. As if by gradual magic, the curtain opened up behind which I saw and sensed a great new world! I often said this to Dorothea, whom I saw once a week during the reading circle she had organized in her home. . . .

Translated from *Mittheilungen aus dem Litteraturarchive in Berlin*, vol.1 (Berlin: Die Litteraturarchiv-Gesellschaft Berlin, 1896), 142–78. Amended with passages from J. Fürst, ed., *Henriette Herz. Ihr Leben und ihre Erinnerungen*, 2nd ed., (Berlin: Hertz, 1858), 96–100.

Introduction, bibliography, and translation by
LORELY FRENCH

Dorothea Schlegel

(1764–1839)

Dorothea Veit-Schlegel (1764–1839)
portrait by Philipp Veit
courtesy of Sächsische Landesbibliothek,
Dresden

Dorothea Schlegel was born Brendel Mendelssohn on October 24, 1764, in Berlin. She was the oldest daughter of Fromet Guggenheim and Moses Mendelssohn (an emancipated Jew and one of the most famous philosophers of the German Enlightenment). As was customary in Jewish families in Berlin, Brendel did not attend school but was educated by her father in religion, philosophy, literature, and practical humanitarianism. When she was nineteen, she entered into a prearranged marriage with the banker Simon Veit, a man she did not even know. She gave birth to four children, two of whom, Jonas and Philipp, survived infancy and became well-known painters. Dorothea, the name by which she called herself, confided to several friends that she was not happy in her marriage. One of her closest friends, the Jewish *salonnière* Henriette Herz, tried to convince her to divorce Veit, but Dorothea did not want to cause her father any worries. It was in Herz's salon, during the summer of 1797, that the thirty-three year old Dorothea first met the writer, critic, and philosopher Friedrich Schlegel, who was almost nine years younger than she. The ensuing love affair brought about Dorothea's divorce from Veit after more than fifteen years of marriage.

In 1799, upon invitation from Friedrich's brother August Wilhelm and his wife Caroline, Dorothea, Friedrich, and Philipp moved to live in the small community of writers and artists in Jena. Although Dorothea and

Caroline displayed mutual respect, there were considerable tensions because of the tight financial situation and personal/artistic rivalries. In Jena, Dorothea began work on her novel *Florentin* to provide support for Friedrich, herself, and her family. In 1801 the first and only volume of *Florentin* appeared anonymously, published by Friedrich Schlegel, whom readers believed to be the author.

In 1802 Friedrich and Dorothea resided briefly in Dresden and Leipzig before moving to Paris. Although Dorothea continued to write, she received little credit for her work. She helped with, and in many cases, completed several translations, essays, and critical reviews that appeared under Friedrich's name. She contributed to Friedrich's journal *Europa* from 1803 to 1805. With the help of her friend, the woman poet Helmine von Chézy, she translated and rewrote the story of the Arthurian magician Merlin (Leipzig, 1804).

In 1804 in Paris, Dorothea was baptized a Protestant, receiving the name of Friederike. She then married Friedrich Schlegel and moved with him to Cologne, where both converted to Catholicism in 1808. In Cologne, Dorothea translated Madame de Staël's novel *Corinne,* which appeared in four volumes in 1807–8 under Friedrich's name, and composed the story *Lother und Maller* from an unpublished medieval manuscript. Friedrich published it in 1805 and later included it, along with the Merlin story, in his own collected works (1823). From 1808 to 1816 Dorothea lived in Vienna where Friedrich, as secretary at the court chancery, became involved in Metternich's conservative politics; from 1816 to 1818, they resided in Frankfurt, where he held the post of *Legationsrat* at the *Bundestag;* and from 1818 to 1820, Dorothea stayed with her sons in Rome. After Friedrich's death in 1829, she was instrumental in the publication of his essays and lectures, including the editing of his *Philosophy of Language,* and the cataloging of some 180 notebooks of his unpublished manuscripts. Dorothea died on August 3, 1839, at the home of her son Philipp in Frankfurt am Main, where she had been living since 1829.

Throughout her life, she had considered her role to be the practical and spiritual supporter of her husband, his muse and helpmate. Her own literary production served to support the family, not to acquire literary fame. Her only original work, the novel fragment *Florentin,* was published under Friedrich's name and did not include the "dedication to the editor,"

Dorothea's somewhat bolder artistic justification (included here). Throughout her life, Dorothea was an enthusiastic, witty, observant correspondent. Her letters are not only important documents of the cultural life of the time and the private lives of the Romantic poets—they are also milestones in the development of a new language that vividly presents interior and exterior realities.

BIBLIOGRAPHY

Schlegel's Works

Briefe von Dorothea Schlegel an Friedrich Schleiermacher. Edited by Heinrich Meisner and Erich Schmidt. Mitteilungen aus dem Literaturarchiv in Berlin, N.S.7. Berlin, n.p., 1913.

Briefe von Dorothea und Friedrich Schlegel an die Familie Paulus. Edited by R. Unger. Deutsche Literaturdenkmäler 146. Berlin: B. Behr–F. Feddersen, 1913.

Briefe von und an Friedrich und Dorothea Schlegel. Collected and annotated by Josef Körner. Berlin: Askanischer Verlag C. A. Kindle, 1926.

Briefe deutscher Frauen. Edited by Fedor von Zobeltitz. Berlin: Ullstein, 1910, pp.275–304.

Das Volk braucht Licht: Frauen zur Zeit des Aufbruchs 1790–1848 in ihren Briefen. Edited by Günter Jäckel. Darmstadt: Agora, 1970, pp.245–76; 687–93.

Dorothea v. Schlegel geb. Mendelssohn und deren Söhne Johannes und Philipp Veit. Briefwechsel im Auftrage der Familie Veit herausgegeben. 2 vols. Edited by Johann M. Raich. Mainz: Kirchheim, 1881.

Eichner, Hans. "Camilla. Eine unbekannte Fortsetzung von Dorothea Schlegels *Florentin.*" *Jahrbuch des Freien Deutschen Hochstifts* (1965): 314–68.

Finke, Heinrich, editor. *Der Briefwechsel Friedrich und Dorothea Schlegels 1818–1820 während Dorotheas Aufenthaltes in Rom.* München: Kösel und Pustet, 1923.

Florentin. Ein Roman. Herausgegeben von Friedrich Schlegel. Vol.1. Lübeck: Friedrich Bohn, 1801.

Florentin (1801). *Frühromantische Erzählungen II.* Vol.7 of *Deutsche Literatursammlung literarischer Kunst- und Kulturdenkmäler in Entwicklungsreihen.* Edited by Paul Kluckhohn. Leipzig: Philipp Reclam, Jr., 1933.

Frauenbriefe aller Zeiten. Edited by Bernhard Ihringer. Stuttgart: Steinkopf, 1910, pp.207–10; 214–15; 233–34.

Frauenbriefe der Romantik. Edited by Katja Behrens. Frankfurt am Main: Insel, 1981, pp.329–69.

Schlegel, Dorothea. *Florentin: Roman-Fragmente-Varianten*. Edited with an afterword by Liliane Weissberg. Berlin: Ullstein, 1987.

Schlegel, Friedrich. *Geschichte des Zauberers Merlin*. In his *Sammlung romantischer Dichtungen des Mittelalters, aus gedruckten und handschriftlichen Quellen*. Leipzig: Junius'sche Buchhandlung, 1804. Reprinted as *Sammlung romantischer Dichtungen des Mittelalters. Erster Teil: Geschichte des Zauberers Merlin*. Vol.33 of *Kritische Friedrich Schlegel-Ausgabe*. Edited by Liselotte Dieckmann. Paderborn: Schöningh, 1980.

Schlegel, Friedrich. *Lothar und Maller. Eine Rittergeschichte. Aus einer ungedruckten Handschrift bearbeitet und herausgegeben von Friedrich Schlegel*. Frankfurt am Main: Friedrich Wilmans, 1809. Reprinted in *Kritische Friedrich Schlegel-Ausgabe* 33:377–452.

Schlegel, Dorothea and Friedrich. *Geschichte des Zauberers Merlin*. Afterword by Klaus Günzel. Köln: Eugen Diederichs Verlag, 1984.

Wienecke, Ernst, editor. *Caroline und Dorothea Schlegel in Briefen*. Weimar: Gustav Kiepenheuer, 1914.

In English Translation

Schlegel, Dorothea Mendelssohn Veit. *Florentin. A Novel*. Translated with an introduction and essay by Edwina Lawler and Ruth Richardson. Vol.1 of *Dorothea Mendelssohn Veit Schlegel (1764–1839): Life, Thought, and Works*. 1 vol. to date. Lewiston, N.Y.: Edwin Mellen, 1988–.

———. *Correspondence: The Berlin and Jena Years (1764–1802)* Translated by Edwina Lawler and Ruth Richardson. Vol.2 of *Dorothea Mendelssohn Veit Schlegel (1764–1839): Life, Thought, and Works*. Forthcoming.

———. *Camilla. A Novella*. Vol.3 of *Dorothea Mendelssohn Veit Schlegel (1764–1839): Life, Thought, and Works*. Forthcoming.

Selected Letters

To Carl Gustav von Brinckmann,[1] Berlin, 2 February 1799

Three weeks ago I was finally divorced from Veit, after many contestations, scenes, after much vacillation and doubting. Now I live alone, and from this shipwreck, which frees me from a long slavery, I have salvaged nothing but a very small income—on which I can live only if I am extremely thrifty—my high and cheerful spirits, my Philipp, some human beings, my piano, and the beautiful desk that you gave me and at which I am now writing to you. This is in a few words all I *own*—but how shall I enumerate everything that I *am rid* of?—Now, now I wish you were once again in our midst! You would do me a cruel injustice, dear friend, if you were not completely convinced that I think of you often, very often, with the friendliest interest; I at least firmly believe that if you were here now, I would count you among the small number of chosen people I have found on this occasion to be reliable and worthy to be called my friends. Oh my dear Brinckmann! I have come to know many people during this incident, which has demanded my total alert concentration—my long inactivity had prevented it until now: nothing had been important enough for me to draw my attention, not even the people who called themselves my friends—if I derived only this one advantage from it, it would still be worth the effort!—As if by a stroke of magic your letter arrived just when I have been

1. Carl Gustav von Brinckmann (1764–1847), Swedish diplomat and secretary to the legation in Berlin, was a close friend of Dorothea Schlegel, Rahel Varnhagen, and theologian Friedrich Schleiermacher.

feeling once more in my heart the need to gather close around me every-thing that is dear and valuable to me, and to enjoy my precious acquired possessions like a freed slave who may now for the first time call something her own after she has become her own master, and who now guards it with jealous care. Imagine how I feel—in all my life, this is the first time that I am free from the fear of having to bear an unpleasant conversation, an onerous presence, or even humiliating rudeness. I hardly feel it yet—I still feel like someone who has carried a heavy burden for a long time and be-lieves he feels it still, long after it has been thrown off. Now I am what I should have been a long time ago, dear friend! Now I am happy, and in good spirits—no more *horror,* no shame, you might not even find me so harsh any more, I live in peace with everything around me!—It was just in time—if I had not held onto that last happy moment and made use of it, it would have been too late, and—believe me—I would not have endured it—what the world calls an honorable old age would have been, for me, a disgraceful old age, I'm convinced, and I did not want to live through that—*my death* was certain, if I had had to live without dignity. Inner ne-cessity convinced me to take a step that, as you already know, has public opinion against it—the rumors may even reach Paris—of all the motives people will try to attribute to me, believe only what I have written you here—I have acted according to my conviction; that I had not done so ear-lier is inexcusable of me; I can state only one thing in my defense: until now I did not really know my rights, and the friends to whom I revealed myself did not share my opinion, so that I feared I would have to stand all alone. Schlegel, Schleiermacher, and [Henriette] Herz lent me their support—and now of course there is a lot of gossip—If only you were here, dear friend? . . . it is possible that I will leave Berlin soon; certainly not for-ever!!!—My income is very small, and Berlin terribly expensive, if one wants to live reasonably comfortably here. I would especially like to go someplace where the winter is not so long; I need a more beautiful environ-ment—and winters here are long and deadening.—. . . Schlegel is writing excellent things now; in the *Athenäum*—a novel—those are the real things—his plans are infinite, and aim at infinity. What a splendid soul this Schlegel is! To write about him to you would be a futile endeavor. You knew him briefly, you foresaw a lot in that short acquaintance—if only you were around him as I am, and could closely observe the unfolding of this rich, flourishing wealth of mind, soul, and life. You may envy me always for this pleasure, or better still, you may come and share it. . . .

To Rahel Levin-Varnhagen, 18 November 1799[2]

I wish you had received the letters I so sincerely and earnestly wrote to you in my mind; then I would have a good conscience. But I do not want to have a bad conscience any longer—I am doing well here, my friend. As you have rightly observed, I desire nothing more than to be merry! If I were not merry here now, then there would be no helping me. How could I not be happy? And were it only for the reason that now I am surrounded by people who don't just value what tradition has declared valuable. Here everyone thinks for himself!—And what kind of people do I live with? During the six weeks that I have been here, I have not heard a single word that caused me an unpleasant feeling. I am very content with Caroline, I am on the best of terms with her, and that is not an easy thing to achieve; for she does not even flatter once and never just to please; thus I had to pass a pretty harsh test by her before she accepted me, although she was friendly to me from the very beginning. What I really esteem in her, however, is her somewhat unrelenting, but always fair, straightforwardness and sincerity. Thus she very boldly passes judgment on every work of art and on everything in general; but what would be arrogant in others stems from her ingenuous candor and the spontaneously inconsiderate bent of her character. She is in truth really quite a good person, and every good trait she discovers in another she notes in its place. She has a rather high opinion of herself, yet in fact every upright person should have this high opinion, particularly when it is combined with a just appreciation for the merits of others, as it is with Caroline, who reveals herself naively at every opportunity, and never conceals the high esteem of herself in her heart while feigning it for another. One eats very well in her house; she plays the host-

2. Written after Dorothea and Friedrich Schlegel moved in with Caroline and August Wilhelm Schlegel. Their "ménage à quatre" turned out to be highly problematic because Dorothea and Friedrich were too poor to support themselves, and Caroline too critical of her as-yet-unmarried "sister-in-law." Dorothea's ambiguity toward the arrangement becomes apparent in her venomous little asides.

ess very well, with ease and grace. How well she would manage in someone else's house with her bold confidence and her carefree being is hard to say: she would certainly make life difficult for her hostess! But I have come to like her and to place boundless confidence in her. It is quite charming that this woman keeps so young, both physically and intellectually. What you told me about her coquettishness toward [August] Wilhelm Schlegel made me suspect from the beginning that she does not love him, of which I am now fully convinced.

I have seen Hardenberg,[3] he was here for a few days, and a look at his demeanor explained to me why he once escaped your attention; his friends claim that he has changed to his disadvantage; I claim, however, that one does not *become common*: one is born so.

And now finally: a bright spot in my life. I have seen Goethe! and not merely seen; he went on a walk with me and the two Schlegels for a good half hour, distinguished me with a glance as he was told my name, and conversed amiably and naturally with me. He made a great and indelible impression on me; to have this god so visible, in human form right next to me, and directly engaging me in conversation, was for me a great, everlasting moment!—I observed little of the awe-inspiring demeanor that everyone attributes to him; on the contrary, although my shyness and fear were great, they soon vanished and I developed a certain sisterly trust in him. It is certainly too bad that he is growing so corpulent; that spoils one's imagining a little! As he walked along with me and talked so amiably, I compared his personality with all his works that came quickly to mind, and I found that he looks most like the *Meister* and *Hermann*.[4] Least of all he resembled *Faust*, but I found in him very distinct traces of the *Miscellaneous Poems, Tasso, Egmont, Werther, Götz,* the *Elegies,* in fact everything, everything!—Even the fatherly tone in his last things became clear to me. He visits nobody except Schiller, whose wife is very sick; but Caroline gives me hope that he will accept an invitation to supper some time. When it

3. The Romantic poet Friedrich Leopold Freiherr von Hardenberg, or Novalis (1772–1801), friend of Friedrich Schlegel.

4. Dorothea is referring to Goethe's novel *Wilhelm Meisters Lehrjahre* (*Wilhelm Meister's Years of Apprenticeship,* 1795–96), his epic *Hermann und Dorothea* (1797), his plays *Faust* (1790), *Torquato Tasso* (1790), *Egmont* (1788), and *Götz von Berlichingen mit der eisernen Hand* (*Götz von Berlichingen with the Iron Fist,* 1773).

happens you shall hear about it. For you, my dear, actually deserve to be present!—Now here you have the joys I would like to share with you in greater detail, but I can spend only a little time on correspondence with my friends; I must work as much as my still precarious health allows.

To Friedrich Schlegel in Jena (1800)[5]

With deep joy I still remember the dear, cheerful morning when I first recalled the little stories in this book. They lay slumbering in my soul as violets during the winter; a new spring, the returning sun had awakened them all. Glowing and joyfully impatient, I wrote down the first pages and then placed them so contentedly and naively on my writing desk, as if I had completed a whole oeuvre; for what I secretly dreamed and imagined adding to the couple of pages was as good as written on paper, as far as I, the ingenue, was concerned. I did not have the courage to tell you about my playful fantasies, nor the time; you were so rich, you had so much to communicate to her who had waited for you so long; I forgot it myself, which will not surprise you. Finally, as you once expressed delight that I had begun to find the language to express my feelings, I summoned up my courage, and showed you those pages. And since moderation in my utterances has never been my forte, and since I easily go too far in this as in my reticence, now everything had to come out at once, because I had been silent for so long. And before you could think twice, I poured out everything pell-

5. This letter is in fact Dorothea Schlegel's unpublished "Dedication to the editor of *Florentin*," Friedrich Schlegel, who had published the novel in 1801 under his name. *Florentin* is narrated as a framed autobiography: Florentin, a young Italian nobleman, saves the life of Count Schwarzenberg in a hunting accident, becomes friends with him and is introduced to his family. He meets and falls in love with the Count's daughter, Juliane, who is, however, already betrothed to Eduard. During his stay at the Schwarzenberg castle, Florentin tells the story of his youth: his frightful novitiate as a Benedictine monk, his escape from the monastery, his adventures and open marriage with a woman who is then seduced by a cardinal. Afraid to destroy Juliane's and Eduard's relationship, Florentin leaves the castle before their wedding and travels to the Count's sister, Clementina, a saintly, charitable woman who, it is suggested, is Florentin's real mother. *Florentin* remained a fragment. Dorothea never wrote a second volume, although a novella and scattered notes were found among her papers, which suggest that at some point she was planning to write a sequel.

mell. You were the one who did not let me have peace until I had completed the work just as the world would have it, and I obeyed in humility; for it was not at all my will. To me, in my own way, it was more complete when I was carrying it secretly within myself and quietly shaping and reshaping it. My fantasy, hemmed in by nothing real, bothered by none of the obstacles the world puts in one's way, had mixed together the most delightful, marvelously colorful snippets (you yourself have often compared me to little Philipp, whose poetry begins rather sentimentally with a description of a rushing waterfall and then ends quite naively with a biscuit that a wanderer dips into the waterfall). I liked it better then than now, since I have been able to express so little of what I actually meant and I myself can't even recognize my own little images any more. Nothing in there is as gleeful and melancholic, as deeply moved and pleased as I myself was when it still lay inside me. I always believed that I wrote down exactly what was on my mind, but that was a delusion; out ahead of my pen floated the correct word; behind it were written totally different words that I did not recognize, just as one who tries to grasp a mercury ball with his fingers—when he believes he has caught it, he has only just separated off little pellets, while the actual large ball continues to escape him until it has become only pieces and he cannot find the whole again.

"But who would have such a mercurial fantasy?" I hear you ask—I am sorry to say I do, and the notion that I might be responsible for it now surprises and shames me not a little. Yes, you are to blame for it all, and for that reason it is only fitting that you allow me to dedicate to you alone what surely would not exist without you.

"And this is how it shall end?" *You* would certainly not ask this question, but you anticipate that many others who like an orderly, satisfying ending will.[6] *Satisfying ending*! Look, my friend, I had to stop at this word and could not go on writing for a long time. I felt as if I had to ponder what a *satisfying ending* really might be. What most people consider satisfying is not so to me. Ah, out there in reality, in certainty, that's where my melancholy and my dissatisfaction really start! My reality and my satisfaction lie in longing and vague intuition—I had raised my eyes, and behold! the sun

---

6. Dorothea alludes here to the fact that *Florentin* is a novel without closure: at the end, the hero simply disappears, never to be heard from again.

had gone down; across from me lay the beautiful mountains in autumnal, bluish haze; the highest peak shimmered and flamed in the glow of the departing rays, while the rest was swallowed up by deep shadows; and as I stood watching, delighted and moved, and saw the white stripes across the sky forming wondrous, light, transparent shapes and then destroying them again, and as I tried in childlike wonder to see in them here a familiar, life-like shape, or there a celestial being or the capricious product of a playful imagination, then suddenly the silver shimmer of the moon would glance across from beyond the mountains, as if she had been sent by the departing sun to console us for his departure. Imagine the whole picture! there was peace, movement and great tidings—the promise of an eternal present, of a new being in view of the apparent end.

How you smile at these dithyrambs and don't understand that this enthusiasm can overpower me in the midst of serene peace! I beg you, do not find it improper, and please accept that I mix everything together, and that I am always and everywhere *completely* myself; this has become clear to me now and I do not know any other way to let you know what has become clear to me: namely, that a poem need have no more final an ending than a beautiful day.

Usually, though, one finds no ending of a novel satisfying unless the person in whom one is most interested gets married or is buried, and people will complain that here neither of the two options brings us completely to rest. I am eager to learn your opinion on this matter; as far as I am concerned, though, I must admit to you that I am never totally satisfied unless the poet leaves something for me to think or to dream about. Thus I can occupy myself for a long time with one single story and enjoy giving it sometimes this, sometimes that ending. I am like those little girls who prefer to play with a naked doll which they can dress differently every hour and to which they can give a totally different appearance, than with the most splendidly and most perfectly dressed doll that has her clothes—and, with them, her final destiny—sewn permanently into place.

I ask once again: What should have become of this man you call the hero?—"Certainly, the hero of a novel must either get married or buried."—Married! Can we be at peace with that? Don't we see in Eduard and Juliane that marriage often starts all trouble and confusion?—Death! Yes, that would really be an ending to a novel with which we would have to make our peace. But here I must repeat my complaint and my regret that this book has been called a novel and not, as it really is, a true story.

For me the book thus ends here, for Florentin's influence did not extend any further. By the way, we do know that in reality he no longer trifled with serious matters, but did indeed carry out his decision, which for him was his destiny, and scorning the advantages, the niceties of culture, he returned to his beloved savages. He was leader and prince of an entire nation, which revered him as a god. Once more the family saw him in their plantations as a delegate of his people, to whom he proudly returned when they tried to convince him to stay. Since then we know nothing of him. Maybe he is still alive and tells his grandchildren of the doom-laden miracles and the glittering misery of the Europeans.[7]

To Rahel Varnhagen in Baden, Hitzing, 26 June 1815[8]

Dearest Varnhagen! Warmest greetings from our green surroundings, which are beautiful in spite of clouds and rain. We are in the midst of beautiful trees, which send you their greetings; at any rate I cannot understand anything in their incessant rustling and whispering and bending except greetings to all our dear friends.—Yesterday's good tidings are driving me to distraction; I cannot make myself sit down for sheer antsiness. The only thing I can manage is a letter to you, and that is the only reason I am writing to you today in particular; if you lived on the *Judenplatz* and I on the *Grüne Angergasse,* then we would already have got together long ago, laughing and crying with each other. The victory has cost us a lot. The death of the Duke of Brunswick is a great loss; they say the English suffered horribly, the general of their cavalry is supposedly dead and the heir to the

7. Dorothea is probably referring to her planned continuation of *Florentin*. According to a manuscript sketch that was found among her belongings but that was lost again during World War II, Florentin goes to America, where he is eventually joined by Juliane and Eduard, with whom he founds a utopian community.

8. Dorothea Schlegel writes of the defeat of Napoleon at Waterloo by the combined forces of Britain, Prussia, and Belgium from June 15–18, 1815. Her ardent German patriotism is colored by an archconservative monarchist stance toward the masses, one very different from that expressed by her contemporary Bettina von Arnim.

throne of Orange wounded. We will get the official details in today's newspapers, which have not arrived out here yet. Exactly as in [the battle of] Leipzig: on the sixteenth we were beaten or at least at a disadvantage; on the seventeenth a truce, missed opportunity on the enemy's part, strategically used peace on ours; on the eighteenth, victory! What I find most edifying is the fright, the disorder, the army deserting. Thus, with God's help, we will finally be freed from the specter of this so-called *Nation* and we will learn to realize that *masses* with no respect for birth, for innate, God-given law and order, with no restraint, with no obedience, with no sense of submission and with no faith in the divine order of the world, that such an untrammeled people, living only by its whims, never able to make uniform progress, only driven hither and yon always, and without cease, in tumultuous clutching at what is beyond them—we will finally realize that such a people is *not a nation*. Long live truth and order!

I have heard from Baroness Pereira that you are doing well in Baden. I wish I had confirmation of that from you! Friedrich sends you his regards. He is now undergoing a very thorough treatment by Koreff, which appears to have an excellent effect on him. I feel quite well and am pleased with the wonderful tranquility around me. Please give Baroness Arnstein, Frau von Ephraim, and Jettchen sincere and kind greetings *de ma part* and my congratulations. An affectionate embrace to Marianne. Adieu, I love you very much.

P.S. Schröder played Medea—I did not know this and thus did not see her perform. If we had not won the victory, I would have been inconsolable over this missed opportunity.

Translated from Ernst Wienecke, ed., *Caroline und Dorothea Schlegel in Briefen* (Weimar: Kiepenheuer, 1914), 287–289 [to Brinckmann]; and from J. M. Raich, ed., *Dorothea von Schlegel geb. Mendelssohn und deren Söhne Johannes und Philipp Veit. Briefwechsel* (Mainz: Kirchheim, 1881), vol.1, 21–23 [to Rahel Levin, 1799]; 58–62 [to Fr. Schlegel]; vol.2, 313–14 [to Rahel Varnhagen].

Introduction and bibliography by
SUSANNE ZANTOP

Translation by
JEANNINE BLACKWELL

Caroline Auguste Fischer

(1764–1842)

Since Caroline Auguste Fischer was neither the wife, nor the mother, nor the lover of any of the literary "giants" and did not take part in any illustrious literary circles, we have little information about this radically innovative, complex writer. All we have are a few scattered remarks about her unusual, unbourgeois life-style, and her novels and tales which permit us to form some idea of the inner struggles and social conflicts faced by an unconventional, creative woman.

Caroline Auguste was born in 1764, the oldest daughter of Karl Heinrich Ernst Venturini (1734–1801), court violinist at the Duchy of Braunschweig, and Charlotte Juliane Wilhelmine Köchy (1742–1825), daughter of a Brunswick tailor. Although her family belonged to the lower middle class and constantly struggled for financial survival, Caroline Auguste received an education well beyond her station. In the early 1790s, she married the Lutheran theologian and pedagogue Christoph Johann Rudolph Christiani, court preacher and founder of a boys' school in Copenhagen. The marriage was unhappy. Fischer's passionate longings and her inability to live within the narrow confines of a bourgeois female existence led to the rupture. In 1799, after she had borne two children and before she was officially divorced, Caroline Auguste moved back to Germany, leaving her son behind in Denmark; her daughter had died at age three. Caroline turned up in Dresden, where she lived with writer and scholar Christian August

Fischer (1771–1829) and published her first novels and stories about the struggles between social convention and creative desires, possibly to counter the antifeminist tracts produced by her partner. In 1803, she accompanied Christian August to Heidelberg but stayed behind with their newborn son Albert when Fischer left to become a professor in Würzburg. In 1808, however, she followed Fischer and married him, possibly to secure financial support for her illegitimate child. When the marriage was desolved by divorce seven months later, Caroline Fischer returned with her child to Heidelberg. Little is known about her subsequent life: she tried to make a living by running a girls' school in Heidelberg, by opening a lending library back in Würzburg, by writing novels and contributions to journals. None of her ventures were successful in the long run. Shunned by society, struggling with depression, Caroline Auguste Fischer died impoverished and forgotten in a Frankfurt hospital in 1842.

In her years of wandering, between 1800 and 1820, Fischer wrote a series of unusual, provocative novels and tales. Whereas her first two works relate, in rapid, dramatic succession, the trials and moral downfall of male protagonists from a man's perspective (*Gustavs Verirrungen* and *Vierzehn Tage in Paris*), her subsequent novels probe into women's responses to oppressive gender definitions; they denounce the institution of marriage and inhuman divorce practices, and claim women's right to sexual passion. In *Die Honigmonathe, Margarethe,* and *Justine,* Fischer juxtaposes women characters who embody the traditional ideal of "Entsagung" [renunciation] with passionate, articulate heroines who strive for self-realization as artists and human beings. Although none of them succeed in reconciling their desire for independence with their desire to be loved, this confrontation acts out the inner conflicts, the profound alienation women experienced under the existing double standard.

The doubling into a conformist self and a rebellious other is depicted in racial and political terms in the short story "William the Negro," which appeared in *Zeitung für die elegante Welt* in 1817 (numbers 97–101). The conciliatory ending, which unites the two realms, "black" and "white," Latin America and Europe, and integrates Molly into a traditional patriarchal marriage, should not deceive us: after all, the utopian reconciliation is preceded by a situation in which only William, the revolutionary black man, can understand the songs of the "mute" dreamer Molly, while racism and scorn are heaped on both outsiders. Under the guise of sentimental liberalism, the black man's struggle for independence from colonial rule is thus tied to the white woman's finding her own voice.

BIBLIOGRAPHY

For a more extended biography, bibliography, and discussion of Fischer's works see Susanne Zantop. "Caroline Auguste Fischer." In *Dictionary of Literary Biography: The Age of Goethe.* Edited by James Hardin and Christoph E. Schweitzer. New York: Bruccoli, Clark and Gale, forthcoming. There is as yet no secondary literature in English on Caroline Auguste Fischer.

Fischer's Works

Gustavs Verirrungen. Leipzig: Heinrich Gräff, 1801. Reprinted Hildesheim: Georg Olms, forthcoming.

Vierzehn Tage in Paris. Leipzig: Heinrich Gräff, 1801. Reprinted Hildesheim: Georg Olms, forthcoming.

Die Honigmonathe. 2 vols. Posen and Leipzig: J. F. Kühn, 1802. Reprinted, with an afterword by Anita Runge. Hildesheim: Georg Olms, 1987.

Der Günstling. Posen and Leipzig: J. F. Kühn, 1809. Reprinted Hildesheim: Georg Olms, 1988.

Margarethe. Heidelberg: Mohr and Zimmer, 1812. Reprinted Hildesheim: Georg Olms, 1989.

Kleine Erzählungen und romantische Skizzen. Posen und Leipzig: J. F. Kühn, 1818. Reprinted Hildesheim: Georg Olms, 1988.

William the Negro

(1817)

Molly was the youngest of eleven children. Her parents, shop-
keepers of meager income, saw her birth as more of a burden
than a delight, and seemed to have little love left over for her.
Since health and beauty were inherited in their family, they thought, without realizing it, that their children would thrive no matter how indif-
ferently they were treated, and so Molly felt like an orphan even in the
midst of her rowdy brothers and sisters.

In the winter they would call her the mute one and in summer the
dreamer. It was indeed true that when the snow lay on the fields or ice over
the streams, hardly a word passed her lips. But instead she carried on full
conversations with the birds, the flowers, and the trees as soon as spring
approached, and then she was oblivious to the nasty names her brothers
and sisters shouted when they rushed and tumbled past her.

Especially ridiculous to the children were the conversational replies
which Molly invented for objects which they knew to be lifeless; those responses were never more noticeable than after a rainfall, strong winds, or a
thunderstorm. But Molly's foolishness seemed to reach a climax when she
mourned because the sky was overcast, and then suddenly brightened up
and rushed among the flowers when the sunlight broke through. But because all their scorn seemed to be lost on her, the children finally decided it
was not worth their effort to harass her anymore.

That fulfilled Molly's greatest wish, for even though she paid little attention to her brothers and sisters, she was still pained and distracted by all their racket. She felt herself surrounded by harmonies which were so real to her on lovely days that she unconsciously matched them in her words and movements. She derived unspeakable pleasure from just this precise measuring of beat, and she could imagine nothing more splendid than if all life's tasks were so harmoniously arranged.

The natural result of this harmonizing was that everything musical gripped her soul with longing, and soon she played all sorts of instruments to perfection. She was, to be sure, misunderstood by her first teachers; they, like many of their artistic colleagues, considered surpassing difficulties to be the highest measure of art, and soon gave up on Molly, after they had tried in vain to convert her to their faith. But one man, with a more profound mind and great wisdom, took her under his wing and led her on the path that she had always sensed, but, misguided as she was, never found.

Her life was now transformed and she sang everything she had uttered before—except for the few things everyday life forced her to speak. Yet her private music was very different from what she played for strangers, for whom she learned difficult pieces not very close to her heart; the rest, she kept for her own lonely hours in the garden.

Yet she had an invisible listener. During those hours when she would sing, William, a young black man from the neighborhood, stood hiding behind the lilac bushes and did not stir from the spot as long as she stayed in the garden. How often, how gladly he would have fallen at her feet, had he not seen his own black face almost every time in the brook that meandered through the meadow behind the garden.

Ah! her cheeks could be compared without exaggeration, he thought, to the dawn, her dark blue eyes to the deep, clear blue sky, and her lovely blond hair to brilliant sunbeams. When she left the garden, he hid his black face in his hands and, his heart pounding, hurried back to his books.

He came from the hottest climes of Africa. He and his sister Saphi were once looking for gold nuggets in a stream, when they were assaulted by six white men, separated, and dragged off to the coast. Soon thereafter William was sold first to a Spanish, then to an English master, who allowed him to study. He soon left his white classmates far behind in schoolwork, and Sir Robert, his master, a declared enemy of the despicable slave trade, relished in anticipation what he might prove by William's example.

In San Domingo the yoke had already been shaken off and hopes were high that William's brothers in the rest of America would not have to bear it much longer either. But educated leaders were lacking, and Sir Robert strove to prepare William for such a position. The Negro's impassioned spirit seized upon this thought, never to let it go, and not only his classmates, but also several of his teachers soon found themselves left in his wake.

But as he came close to his goal, his strength seemed suddenly to leave him. He lowered his eyes to the ground when Sir Robert mentioned America, and the fate of his brothers forced from him merely more hot tears. "Molly, Molly!" he sighed in his lonely room. "Molly!" he cried aloud, wandering through forests, along cliffs, "Alas, why am I black! Molly, you divine white girl!"

Thus he cried one day as he thought the garden deserted; but Molly sat in the arbor and heard everything. How deeply and passionately she was moved by the intimate music of this soul, she who was so familiar with the meaning of tones. Her violent trembling kept her from leaving her seat. As she tried a second time to withdraw, her lute fell from the bench, an involuntary gasp betrayed her, and William stood before her.

Kneeling, he handed her the lute, passionately beat his breast, and touched his brow to the earth. Molly, deeply shaken, begged him with a gesture to rise, unable to utter anything but a soft, "Oh!"

"In our country," William said, "only the priests on the mountaintops are allowed to say, 'oh!' to the great spirit. None of us would ever dare to. But Molly is permitted. The great spirit cannot be angry with Molly. What is Molly asking for?"

"I only ask," she answered shyly, "that you rise."

"If William could ask for something," he said stepping in front of her with glowing eyes, "he would ask Molly for one of her divine songs."

In place of an answer Molly tuned her lute and sang first softly and trembling, then with a stronger voice, and finally with greatest fervor one of her loveliest and most secret songs. She had been silent for a long time, while William still listened, his ardent gaze fixed on her lowered eyes, when finally he grasped the hem of her dress and pressed it to his mouth, then to his heart.

But Molly saw her brothers and sisters in the distance, and for the first time she feared their scorn. "I must go!" she said, but when she saw William's pain, she added quickly and softly: "Tomorrow we will see each other again!" Only when she had left the garden did these words fall heavy on her heart; night fell, and it was morning before she could grasp how it had been possible to utter them.

William had in the meantime asked all his teachers to excuse him for the day—a request they granted all the more readily, since it was so untypical of him and since they had already worried about the boy's overworking. William was thus already behind the garden house at daybreak, his eyes trained on the garden gate. Yet he would have hardly caught a glance at her, had she known that he was not in his usual classes. Since he had to pass her house every day to attend them, she had carefully kept inside at the appointed hour.

She had barely stepped into the garden when William sprang over the thorn hedgerow, knelt next to the arbor, putting on his head a basket of flowers he had lowered over the wall with a ribbon. Agitated and frightened, she stepped back, but simultaneously saw the basket fall from his head and heard him sigh, "Molly!" A few moments later she found herself inside the arbor, amidst the flowers, and William at her side.

He told her how the whites had captured him, how horribly they treated him, how happy he was now under Sir Robert's protection; what deep pleasure the sciences afforded him, what a burning need he felt to provide the same joy to his brothers, and to free them from their interminable and despicable yoke.

The painting was sketched with tropic ardor, each word an image, each image pressing on her soul with gripping vitality. Molly saw the brutal whites, the blacks imploring heaven, the magnanimous Englishman coming to their rescue. Her lovely lips parted in astonishment, her eyes, no longer downcast, fixed on the flaming eyes and stirring speech of the noble young man.

"Wherever I turned," William continued, "I heard the haunting call of only one word: America! Now I only hear: Molly! Molly! Now I only sigh:

Molly. Why am I black? When you, Molly, are so heavenly white!" With these words William fell at her feet again and hid his face in his hands. Yet he abruptly rose, and seemed even taller than before.

"Must I despair?" he continued, "Will I never be allowed to raise my eyes to Molly? Yes, I am black! But am I not a man? Don't I have a heart? Does a white man sense Molly's worth as I do? Can he feel it? If I liberate my brothers, teach them to love and to follow the sciences, the arts, and human law, am I worth nothing? Molly! Am I worth nothing?"

His heart had already answered the question and given him the courage to take Molly's hand and press it to his heart. "Molly!" he repeated, "Am I not worth a glance from those lovely eyes?" And Molly leaned over toward him, but as she did a large tear held back too long dropped on his hand. "Oh no," he cried, turning away and dropping her hand. "I am only worth your tears. Molly can only give me her tears. Oh flee, you unhappy man! You belong in the burning deserts, where you can perish far from Molly."

With these words he stormed out of the arbor. But behind him he heard the mourning flutelike sound of her voice: "Oh stay here, William, stay!" and she fell into his arms.

When a noble black man loves a beautiful white woman, his love can hardly be compared to the love of a European man. For William it was a holy, consuming fire which put Molly into a trembling, continuous ecstasy. How far removed was his speech from that trifling and mawkish twaddle of the usual lover. What magnificent images he revealed to Molly's soul; and the heart and mind he unfolded before her in conversations made it impossible for her to separate her fate from that of this noble and spirited young man.

Sir Robert was informed of Molly's decision. His heart was proud, but his common sense told him that this could have a tragic outcome. The young man was to be sole inheritor of Sir Robert's large estate, and as such was not to be scorned by Molly's father, a poor merchant; he had won the respect and love of everybody around; and he left no doubt as to what he would one day accomplish for his people and for knowledge in general. But Molly was only fifteen years old, and one might easily conclude that her impressionable heart had led her astray.

Who, however, could muster the courage to open William's eyes? Ever since Molly had said to him, "William, I will never leave you," superhuman strength was at work in him, and if he had astonished his teachers before, they now had to admit that they would soon have nothing more to teach him. Sir Robert began to consider whether the confusion of a young girl, even if it were to the disadvantage of the poor little creature herself, might not be used toward the happiness, toward the liberation of a people.

Yet he could not answer this question to his total satisfaction, and he hoped that Molly's parents would decide the issue in a way that would please him, too. But convinced by their outrageous indifference that Molly would enjoy a better life under William's care or anywhere else but at home with these unnatural parents, he resolved not to meddle with fate. If the girl's sacrifice were needed for the great task, he could at least do everything in his power to assure its success.

A torturing disquiet—should he even call it a premonition—drove him to postpone the official betrothal. William had already asked him: "My generous benefactor, may William bring Molly to you today so that she might kneel with him before you?" Sir Robert answered, pressing his hand: "My good William, any day but today! You know what pressing affairs I must still settle. Let me enjoy your good fortune when my heart is unencumbered." Usually the same words were repeated afterward, sometimes with an almost imperceptible nod, yet always with a warm handshake and echoed with "my good William! my dear William!"

Three months had passed, however, and Sir Robert had not yet seen Molly. William no longer asked, but his countenance grew darker and his manner no longer had its former endearing candor. Finally Sir Robert said on a particularly pleasant day: "My dear William, I think it would be proper to go to Molly's home, but I am greatly repelled by her parents. If you are sure of her heart," he added gravely, "then give her my apologies and bring her to me."

On hearing these words William knelt at his benefactor's feet, embraced him, and refused to let him go. Only when Sir Robert mentioned the name Molly did he spring up, disappear in a flash, and appear a few moments later before Sir Robert, with the trembling girl in his arms. "She is afraid, my dear benefactor," he shouted, "she is timid! Oh, quickly, say something to her, so that you can see her eyes!"

"My dear William," answered Sir Robert in an uncertain tone, "you are holding Molly too tightly. Let her free, then she will hear me and answer me. I am after all your friend."

But Molly still stood before Sir Robert with downcast eyes and seemed barely able to stand. After William's abrupt, disjointed words of joy, she had assumed their betrothal to be imminent. She had tried to excuse herself on account of her clean yet inappropriately simple clothing, but William had not listened. He had understood only what he had already feared: that she would refuse him. In which case he had already decided to use the force of his love and his superior strength. She was in the garden at the time, the meadow gate was open, and thus she found herself in front of Sir Robert before she had time to think of further protest.

Her enchantingly innocent face, her long, silken, downcast lashes, her lovely blond hair falling far below her shoulders—Sir Robert gazed on all her charms with such visible sentiment that William could barely control his ecstasy. He bolted away to get Molly's lute, the harp, all her musical instruments, and, as he assured them, would have even brought the grand piano if Molly's parents had not stopped him.

Meanwhile Sir Robert had had time to compose himself and to ask Molly to sit beside him. His many questions, long since answered, which he knew had no rhyme or reason, came so fast and so chaotically that Molly, uncertain about which to answer first, finally raised her large, dark blue eyes to him. Both were struck as if by lightning. Molly saw to her surprise that the handsome young man with a noble gait whom she had thought to be Sir Robert's secretary due to his elegant yet extremely simple costume, was the man himself. Since she had imagined everything in his entourage to be covered in silver and gold, she had imagined the master of all those splendid people to be even more splendid than they, but also very old, she didn't know why. Now she saw a man of around thirty with a regal manner and with high nobility of mind written on his pensive brow.

Sir Robert was no less moved. Molly's face with her eyes wide open was totally different than when they were downcast. In place of the trembling girl frightened into reticence, he saw the triumphant eyes of intellect which almost forced him to lower his own. He had nothing more to ask, and was happy when William pressed Molly to play the lute.

Molly's voice was yet more triumphant than her eyes. William saw it with delight, and Sir Robert felt it with a kind of shudder. Yet he sought to compose himself and to draw Molly into the conversation to discover exactly how she was treated by her parents. Although she employed great kindness by merely hinting at, rather than describing, their behavior, he was convinced that she was not happy at all, and decided in spite of his recurring doubts to make at least William happy. The betrothal then took place; and when Sir Robert entered his lonely room, he sighed, as if finishing a day of heavy labor, "At least one of them is happy!"

Sir Robert was, however, mistaken. On the day of the betrothal, as he placed Molly's hand in William's, the Negro's gaze strayed from Molly, whom he wanted to see double, to a large mirror that reflected the group all too precisely back to his intoxicated eyes. Alas, he saw his own figure like that of an animal on its hind legs, standing next to that of the magnificent white man and the divine young girl. His arm sank and Molly's hand fell from his own. But neither she nor Sir Robert noticed this event, and soon thereafter he had time enough to cast himself to the ground in the garden and pressing his face and his heart to mother earth, weep out that feeling for which he yet had no name.

Only desire, often confused with love, is blind; but love, true, ecstatic love that permeates the innermost being—how could it be blind? It is rather to be known by its supreme and unerring divination; it spreads its wings with supernatural power where mere knowledge causes them to sink. And thus one could counter the claim, "What is blinder than love?" with the more truthful one, "What is more all-seeing than love?"

Alas, it was not just the brook nor the mirror, even less was it selfish jealousy that taught William to know himself; it was love, the innermost desire to make Molly happy, that opened his eyes. Could she be happy with him? That was the frightening question that tore his poor heart callously to pieces; the question he dared not pose to anyone but himself. For just that reason, however, his condition worsened, and could no longer be hidden from Sir Robert, as much as the master was preoccupied with his own.

Sir Robert felt like he had been startled out of a gloomy dream and held himself culpable for turning his whole attention to himself to the detriment of both his protégé and the great task he hoped to accomplish through William. All the more he forgot about himself now to seek with growing anxiety for the cause of William's dangerous melancholy.

Yet after many unanswered queries, William fell to his feet, his face bent to the ground, and pleaded: "My dear benefactor, let William go to America to his brothers! Then he will get better." Speechless with shock and foreboding, Sir Robert saw William rush out the door before he could even think of holding him back, and as he decided to follow, Molly entered the room.

She thought Sir Robert had business to attend to and she tried to withdraw, but he asked her to help him find William, who was probably in the garden. He was in fact there, but in a condition that caused them both great alarm. In spite of William's resistance, a call to the doctor proved necessary; and the diagnosis made them fear a consuming fever.

The secret that the unhappy youth had carefully kept was now revealed in his unconscious state, and Sir Robert as well as Molly saw with unspeakable confusion that he had long been aware of feelings which they had barely begun to admit to themselves. Molly no longer lifted her eyes, and Sir Robert drew back with a start whenever he happened to touch her garment in caring for the patient.

The day of medical crisis predicted by the doctor arrived; the unhappy youth might have to go alone to that dark, unknown land from which none ever return. In such a time petty passions disappear, and even great ones are softened. Sir Robert and Molly no longer took notice of themselves; William's survival was their only thought and wish; and as the crisis resolved itself positively, they embraced as brother and sister with lively cries of joy, and their former reticence was forgotten.

But soon William's glances reminded them of it, and it even increased, when William repeated his request to go to America. "I shall go with you!" cried Sir Robert, "And I," added Molly with a trembling voice, "will perhaps obtain permission from my parents to await William's return in Malaga, where I have an aunt." William did not reply to her response, and the journey was begun at his insistence several weeks before the most favorable season, against the advice of the ship's captain.

It was soon clear that the man had been right. For they were barely out of the Channel, when they had to batten down for a storm which pressed down on them. Since the ship was sturdy and the crew experienced, the captain was as determined to carry on now as he had been reluctant to go before the trip. But all human effort and expertise could not withstand the raging elements, and after they had swayed between life and death for three terrible days and nights, the ship was stranded near the island of Madeira. The crew was rescued and the cargo salvaged; there was hope that the vessel could be saved, too; but William had disappeared without a trace.

When Sir Robert expressed disquiet about his disappearance, when he repeatedly and untiringly searched for him, and when he was distraught as the search seemed futile, the uninformed crew members concluded that he must have lost a son or a brother. How great was their astonishment when they learned that the man in question was a Negro. They thought he must surely have cost quite a sum of money to justify Sir Robert's expenditure during the search; yet they considered the sum extravagant and the whole matter reprehensible since it was a bad speculation.

Three months had passed and all hope was gone, when news from San Domingo spread on the island. The blacks had won battles repeatedly, and one particular Negro, who had recently arrived from Europe, had distinguished himself by miraculous bravery.

"What is his name?" cried Sir Robert as he vehemently grabbed the hand of the newsgiver.

"William!" he responded, "did you know him?"

"He was my son."

"Impossible! I told you he was a Negro."

"All the same. When will you sail back?"

"Where?"

"To San Domingo."

"Heaven preserve me from that! The life of every European there has been forfeited. I escaped only by a miracle."

"It cannot be that bad!"

"Much worse than you think. And you will find that confirmed, if you can get any written news from there."

But the news was sought in vain, although Sir Robert took great pains to get it. Finally it seemed clear to him that he could find it out only in England; but the question whether Molly would accompany him there fell heavy on his heart. His feeling for her now could not be compared with the previous one. His whole life centered on Molly now. If she left him, he would return to the desert like the spirit of the dead.

Molly was no less affected. She now could compare her feelings for William to others, and had to call the former ones compassion. The most perfect of men revealed to her every day qualities and convictions that had enchanted her already when they were only described to her, and this man loved her—that was not to be denied. Molly trembled before the word Malaga.

Vacillating between seeking and fleeing each other, they met one morning on the shore as a ship was discovered on the southwestern horizon. "Molly! Molly!" cried Sir Robert, pointing there and holding her hand to his heart. But Molly did not respond, and Sir Robert would have discovered more consternation than joy in her face, if his gaze had not been set directly on the ship.

It approached, the Portuguese flag became visible, and preparations were made to receive it when it reached the harbor driven on by a brisk breeze. It came from Rio de Janeiro and, wherever it landed, had heard the news confirmed of the successful revolution in San Domingo; but had not been able to ascertain any details.

Thus Sir Robert's desire was again more provoked than satisfied, and his decision to take the Portuguese ship to return to Europe seemed to be most appropriate. Since Molly—if she did not want to go to England—could be delivered to her aunt along the way, the dreaded separation was postponed, at least until Lisbon.

But after their very pleasant journey they stayed in that city for several weeks without mentioning that aunt. Nor was she mentioned when a ship arrived from England. Sir Robert and Miss Molly, Miss Molly and Sir Robert—the names were heard together so often, people mentioned them with such tender respect, with such warm significance, that the sound of it became as common and the idea of separation as strange to them as the idea of death is to a healthy person. They were already booked on board, when it suddenly occurred to Molly that she ought to have paid at least one visit to her aunt.

This trip was as pleasant as the previous one, but they arrived in England convinced that they could no longer live without each other, no matter what the circumstances. However, they were prepared for any sacrifice, as soon as William asserted his previous claims to her, and Sir Robert redoubled his efforts and expense to gain certainty in the matter.

364

Two weeks after his arrival he observed, in Molly's presence, his banker entering with a letter. Trembling, he snatched it hastily. He tried to greet the man, but his voice failed him, and the latter, assuming it was important news, was courteous enough to withdraw. Sir Robert was now alone with Molly, but the letter lay unopened in his hands. Molly recognized William's hand, a shudder passed over her limbs and she had to brace herself to keep from falling.

Sir Robert noticed it, led her quickly to a chair, and said softly: "Yes, it is from William." Suddenly he cried aloud, lifting up the letter: "Molly! Before I open it, I will repeat here once more my secret vow: I will do nothing that is unworthy of that friendship, of the great goal for which I educated William. Molly! Have you heard my vow?"

A torrent of tears from Molly's eyes served as his answer. He sat down, opened the letter, and read:

"My dearest, unforgettable benefactor,

"William has caused you pain, but he has himself felt the deepest pain of all. One consolation remains to him: he can repay something he never hoped he could. To you he owes his better life; in return, he gives you his own life, he gives you Molly. Do not reject William's sacrifice! For it would not be a blessing to him. Although he does not live a happy life, at least he lives a dignified one. A great task stands before him, and he will achieve it. In three victorious battles he has won the name of savior. My benefactor! The sound of dropping chains is beautiful, and thus William, although abandoned by Molly, is not without beautiful music.

"What is it in that name? Will William become weak now? Will he forget that nature did not make him for that heavenly white girl? Molly! I renounce my claim on you! But give me recompense! Assure me that you will make the most noble mortal man happy. But also from him who has already given so much, I still demand something else, demand a vow that he will charge all his progeny to fight the battle for the rights of my people. Farewell! William is going into battle."

"My William!" cried Sir Robert, "I will never see you again! Oh, that vow has long been sworn, and it will be kept! You noble youth! Only now do I really feel what you were to me!"

At the sound of William's name called aloud, several servants came in and pressed Sir Robert for news. William had won their love and respect, and now people wished that Sir Robert demand his return as a sign of his gratitude after the successful fight for the freedom of his people. But in place of William, a few months later the news of his death arrived; the whole house mourned as if for a son.

Sir Robert and Molly dressed in mourning and their grief did not allow them to think of closer ties for some time. Yet they were suddenly brought about by Molly's father. He decided to marry her to a rich profiteer, and could only be pacified by Sir Robert's definitive proposal.

Soon thereafter the marriage took place, and rarely has been seen a more handsome and mutually deserving couple. Their happiness was increased by two lovely children, a boy and a girl, and it would have been complete, had it not been clouded sometimes with thoughts of William.

One day, as the first rays of the spring sunshine came to their estate and their children played around them in the garden room, little Betty let out a piercing scream, and hid her face in her mother's lap. When asked what was wrong, she pointed with her little hand backwards toward the door, and they saw a totally black, curly head peeking in.

Sir Robert rose to open the door, but before he could reach it, little George had pulled in a small Negro boy just his size, who ran all around the magnificent room with his eyes sparkling. Molly began to tremble violently, and Sir Robert bent down to the boy with a tenderness he could not suppress.

"Where did you come from, son?" he finally asked.

"From the meadow over there," answered the black boy. "There are flowers there and my father is there, too."

"What is your father's name?"

"William the Savior."

"My William, my William!" cried Sir Robert, bolting out of the room dragging the child along with him. There stood the noble Negro, his brow pressed to the trunk of a tree; but as he heard his name cried aloud he turned his tearful eyes and felt Sir Robert's arms embrace him.

Neither could say a word; but when Molly appeared, William shouted, pulling himself away with vehemence: "Go back, Molly! I have taken a black wife. The news of my death was a ruse; only that way could I force you! But you shall not forget me. I am leaving my son with you. He is named William. Farewell! I may not stay. Go back! Don't stop me! When the task is complete, we shall see each other again!"

Translation of "William der Neger," in *Zeitung für die elegante Welt,* 5 installments, vols.97–101 (19–24 May 1817): 785–823.

Introduction, bibliography, and translation of prose by
JACQUELINE VANSANT

Translation of poetry by
WALTER ARNDT

Sophie Mereau

(1770–1806)

Sophie Mereau (1770–1806)
drawing by unknown artist
courtesy of Bildarchiv preussischer
Kulturbesitz, Berlin

L iterary history has traditionally seen Sophie Mereau—like most other German Romantic women—as a functional adjunct: as a muse, as erotic impulse, as tragic victim who inspires the male poetic genius to greater flights of fancy. Sophie Mereau was that to her husband Clemens Brentano, but more important, she was a creative poet in her own right. By creating as characters iconoclastic, pleasure-loving women who chafe under society's bit, and by parodying the Sentimental literary topos of "virtue in distress," Mereau created literary models that both countered and affirmed the Romantic ideal. As a self-supporting divorced writer, she countered and affirmed it in her own life as well.

Sophie Friederike Schubart was born on March 28, 1770, in Altenburg in Thüringen, as the second daughter of Gotthelf Schubart, the ducal secretary, and his wife Johanna Sophie Friederike. As was typical among the upper bourgeoisie of the time, Sophie and her sister Henriette were educated at home in modern languages, music, and drawing. Her mother died when Sophie was sixteen years old, her father when she was twenty-one.

In 1793 Sophie married Friedrich Ernst Carl Mereau, a law professor at Jena with whom she had corresponded for five years. They had two children, a boy who died and a daughter, Hulda, Mereau's only child to reach maturity. The marriage was very unhappy; Sophie and Friedrich Mereau were granted a divorce in 1801 after an extended separation. While Mereau was living in Jena, she regularly met with the writers Friedrich Schiller, Johann Gottfried Herder, Friedrich and August Wilhelm Schlegel, Friedrich Schelling, and Caroline Schlegel and Dorothea Veit.

It was in 1798, at the home of Caroline Schlegel, that she was probably introduced to the then-nineteen-year-old Clemens Brentano, who became one of her most ardent admirers. They kept up a lively correspondence, which continued after Mereau moved from Jena to nearby Camburg. After the divorce from her husband, Mereau supported herself and her daughter with her writing and editing, thereby establishing herself as one of Germany's first professional woman writers. Conflict dominated her relationship with Brentano. Repeatedly, he tried to convince Mereau to marry him, and repeatedly, she refused, afraid to lose her freedom and, with it, her creativity. Her pregnancy finally brought about the marriage. After the wedding (in 1804) they moved to Heidelberg, where they maintained close contact with intellectuals and writers such as Friedrich Creuzer, Ludwig Tieck, and Caroline Rudolphi. In her three years of marriage to Brentano, Mereau had three children, all of whom died in infancy. She translated but did little original work during this time. Sophie Mereau died in childbed on October 30, 1806.

Mereau experimented with a wide variety of forms, short and long prose works, poetry, essays, and translations. Her earliest literary efforts were encouraged by Schiller who published some of her poems in his journal *Thalia* in 1791. Her first novel, *Das Blüthenalter der Empfindung*, appeared anonymously in 1794. Although in this novel a male narrator relates the adventures of two protagonists who struggle to be together, the main focus is the limitations women face in society. In 1797, eight letters from Mereau's next novel, *Amanda und Eduard*, were published in Schiller's journal *Die Horen*, and the completed version followed in 1803. In this epistolary novel, which can be viewed as a counterpart to Friedrich Schlegel's *Lucinde*, Mereau finds fault with marriages of convenience and criticizes her male contemporaries' concept of femininity. Two volumes of Mereau's poetry were published in 1800 and 1801. Her poem "Feuerfarb," printed in 1792 in the *Journal des Luxus und der Moden*, was set to music by Ludwig van Beethoven (Opus 52, 1805). Numerous short stories by Mereau appeared in journals from 1797 to 1805. In addition, Mereau translated extensively from French, Italian, Spanish, and English. She devoted much time to the works of Boccaccio and the letters and biography of the French courtesan Ninon de Lenclos. She also edited several journals for women, the best known of which is the journal *Kalathiskos*. Particularly noteworthy is her essay on the life of Ninon de Lenclos in which the courtesan demands the same rights in love relationships as are granted men.

Flight to the City, selected for this anthology, appeared in the *Taschenbuch für das Jahr 1806, der Liebe und Freundschaft gewidmet*. Like her other works, this playful, frivolous story of elopement, free love, and a *bohème* existence on the margins of good society contains a passionate plea for free choice, for love and pleasure without guilt and without society's interference. The advice with which Sophie concluded a letter to Clemens might serve as a motto for this story as well: "love to live, and live to love."

BIBLIOGRAPHY

Mereau's Works

Amanda und Eduard. Frankfurt am Main: Friedrich Wilmans, 1803.

Das Blüthenalter der Empfindung. Gotha: Justus Perthes, 1794. Reprinted with an afterword and selected bibliography by Herman Moens, Stuttgart: Akademischer Verlag, 1982.

Der Sophie Mereau Gedichte. Vienna & Prague: Franz Haas, 1805. The volume is a new edition of two earlier volumes of poetry which appeared in 1800 and 1802.

Kalathiskos, edited by Sophie Mereau. Berlin: Fröhlich, Vol.1 (1801) and Vol.2 (1802). Facsimile with afterword by Peter Schmidt, Heidelberg: Lambert Schneider, 1968.

Briefwechsel zwischen Clemens Brentano und Sophie Mereau. Edited by Heinz Amelung. Leipzig: Insel Verlag, 1908.

Lebe der Liebe und liebe das Leben. Edited with an introduction by Dagmar von Gersdorff. Frankfurt am Main: Insel, 1981. Correspondence between Clemens Brentano and Sophie Mereau; introduction emphasizes the effect of the Brentano-Mereau relationship on Mereau's work.

Frühling

(1800)

Düfte wallen—tausend frohe Stimmen
jauchzen in den Lüften um mich her;
die verjüngten trunknen Wesen schwimmen
aufgelöst in einem Wonnemeer.

Welche Klarheit, welches Licht entfliesset
lebensvoll der glühenden Natur!
Festlich glänzt der Äther, und umschliesset,
wie die Braut der Bräutigam, die Flur.

Leben rauscht von allen Blüthenzweigen,
regt sich einsam unter Sumpf und Moor,
quillt, so hoch die öden Gipfel steigen,
emsig zwischen Fels und Sand hervor.

Welch ein zarter wunderbarer Schimmer
überstrahlt den jungen Blüthenhain!
Und auf Bergen, um verfallne Trümmer,
buhlt und lächelt milder Sonnenschein.

Dort auf schlanken, silberweissen Füssen
weht und wogt der Birken zartes Grün,
und die leichten hellen Zweige fliessen
freudig durch den lauen Luftstrom hin.

Spring

(1800)

Fragrancies abound, a myriad voices
Carol in the air to left and right,
Newly young, all creaturedom rejoices,
Floating in an ocean of delight.

What resplendency, what light effuses
From vivacious Nature's glow of pride!
Festive shines the ether and encloses
All the land, as groom embraces bride.

Life flows out from all emblossomed branches,
Stirs in hiding under swamp and heath,
Burgeons forth where barren highland blanches,
Making do with rock and sand beneath.

What a lovely sparkle is outdoing
That fresh grove abloom in rosy haze!
And on mountains, ancient walls in ruin,
Falls alike its blithe and playful gaze.

There, on slender feet of silver gleaming,
Bows and waves the birches' tender green,
And their light and lissom twigs are streaming
Gaily down the zephyr's warming stream.

In ein Meer von süsser Lust versenket,
wallt die Seele staunend auf und ab,
stürzt, von frohen Ahndungen getränket,
sich im Taumel des Gefühls hinab.

Liebe hat die Wesen neu gestaltet;
ihre Gottheit überstrahlt auch mich,
und ein neuer üpp'ger Lenz entfaltet
ahndungsvoll in meiner Seele sich.

Lass an deine Mutterbrust mich sinken,
heil'ge Erde, meine Schöpferin!
Deines Lebens Fülle lass mich trinken,
jauchzen, dass ich dein Erzeugter bin!

Was sich regt auf diesem grossen Balle,
diese Bäume, dieser Schmuck der Flur:
Einer Mutter Kinder sind wir alle,
Kinder einer ewigen Natur.

Sind wir nicht aus Einem Stoff gewoben?
Hat der Geist, der mächtig sie durchdrang,
nicht auch mir das Herz empor gehoben?
Tönt er nicht in meiner Leier Klang?

Was mich so an ihre Freuden bindet,
dass mit wundervoller Harmonie
meine Brust ihr Leben mitempfindet,
ist, ich fühl' es, heil'ge Sympathie!

Schweige, schweige, eh' ein kalt Besinnen
diesen schönen Einklang unterbricht,
ganz in Lust und Liebe zu zerrinnen,
trunknes Herz, und widerstrebe nicht.

From *Der Sophie Mereau Gedichte* (Vienna: Haas, 1805), 44.

Dropped into a sea of sweet sensation,
Roves the soul in wondering content,
And sustained by joyous divination,
Plunges in a whirl of sentiment.

Love is who refashioned all these creatures,
His divineness shines upon me too,
And a bounteous springtime newly reaches
For my soul—foreboding told it true.

Let me sink to your maternal bosom,
Holy earth, oh my creatrix, do!
Let me feast upon your living fulness
And rejoice that I am sprung from you!

All that lives and stirs on this great ball,
All these trees, all that adorns this earth:
One dear mother's children are we all,
Children of eternal Nature's birth.

Do we not salute a single sire?
And the spirit that perfused their round,
Did it not raise up my own heart higher,
Not reverberate in my lyre's sound?

What allies me to their joys, so nearly
That by some miraculous decree
My own bosom shares in them sincerely,
Is, I feel it, sacred sympathy!

Silent! Silent! Lest the mind dismiss,
Coldly reasoning, this fair alliance!
Dare dissolve entire in love and bliss,
Rapturous heart, and offer no defiance.

An einen Baum am Spalier
(1800)

Armer Baum!—an deiner kalten Mauer
fest gebunden, stehst du traurig da,
fühlest kaum den Zephyr, der mit süssem Schauer
in den Blättern freier Bäume weilt
und bey deinen leicht vorübereilt.
O! dein Anblick geht mir nah!
und die bilderreiche Phantasie
stellt mit ihrer flüchtigen Magie
eine menschliche Gestalt schnell vor mich hin,
die, auf ewig von dem freien Sinn
der Natur entfernt, ein fremder Drang
auch wie dich in steife Formen zwang.

From *Gedichte*, vol.1 (Berlin: Unger, 1800), p.15.

To a Trellised Tree
(1800)

Wretched trellised tree! For, tethered tightly
To your chilly wall, you languish there,
Scarcely conscious of the zephyr's resting lightly
In the foliage of untrammeled trees,
But bypassing yours with careless ease.
Oh! The sight of you is hard to bear!
And imagination, image-bright,
By its airy magic brings the plight
Of a human shape before my gaze,
Who, forever severed from the liberal ways
Of nature, is coerced by alien norms,
Just as you are, into rigid forms.

Flight to the City

(1806)

I was born in a medium-sized town in Germany. My father was the first in his family tree to spurn the vine that had produced such rich harvest; for, since Noah's times they had all been vintners and winesellers, whereas he traded living vineyards for the dead parchment of a nobility patent.

Yet while my father lived more for future reknown, my mother sought the approbation of her contemporaries, and she went to such great lengths to earn the reputation of a learned woman that she gladly let everything else go to ruin. Her room was filled with nothing but large and heavy volumes, because she was embarrassed to be found reading a light, entertaining book. She read flowers as if they were a Latin dictionary; on paintings she studied nothing but the date, and she denied herself the vivid impression of a beautiful countryside, because she had made it a point of honor that she had become virtually blind by so much reading. She assembled around her all those who eternally strive for spirit and wit and never attain more than the ridiculous; here political tracts were read and astronomical calculations corrected, here the worth of great minds, of the nation, and the fate of states were decided.

My father had a good eye for art and was himself talented in several areas. Above all he revered and practiced dramatic art, and for this reason had a pretty theater built in one of his vineyards. He reserved for himself the noble roles and very often appeared as tyrant or hero. He had his own wardrobe made, which every visitor had to see who wanted to be seen by him. I was barely fifteen years old when I first performed all the lead roles to great acclaim in this temple consecrated to the arts. A young man from the neighborhood, whom I will call Albino, played the First Lover, and as such he told me so often that he loved me that he himself finally felt it and I believed it. Our imagination was kindled ever higher, and soon we were only playing ourselves in the most fervent roles. With what fire did we now portray the most difficult scenes!

The audience's most ardent applause gave our talents the praise which was actually due our hearts: they thought that deception had been heightened to truth, while we were actually giving them truth as deception. Only our lack of misfortune prevented us from being just like our dramatic models. But misfortune did not fail to come. My father, who with his delight for scenes thought continuously about sequels of future greatness and who indulged in imagined honors and honorary posts of his descendants, used his powers to stage my fate as well. Soon he found his opportunity. Not far from the town lived a country squire, who, just the opposite of my father, had always made it a point of honor never to change the custom which all his ancestors had followed without deviation, since the founding of the empire, just as a flock of sheep faithfully follow the footsteps of their shepherd. His son Vincent was the distinguished husband whom my father had selected for me. Nature had overendowed his body with flesh and bones just as it had underendowed his mind. Shooting swallows in flight, catching crayfish, playing dice, drinking, cursing, and fighting with the farmers—these no man understood better than he. He often honored our theater with his presence; several times we had tried to have him learn the part of the captain of the guard, or some other similar role—in vain. He had never been able to progress beyond the role of the stony commandant in the Don Juan banquet.[1] Once when I had reaped particular praise for my acting, he sought me backstage in order to pay me his tribute, too. He believed he could give me no more flattering proof of his admiration than his

---

1. The "stony commandant" refers to Molière's play *Dom Juan ou le festin de Pierre* (1665) or other adaptations of Tirso de Molina's *El burlador de Sevilla*, or Zamora's *Convidado de piedra*: Don Juan, who has dishonored and abandoned Doña Elvira and killed her father, the *commandatore*, in a duel, challenges the "devil" by inviting the Compture's stone statue to dinner. The statue arrives and takes the horrified Don Juan with him to hell. The reference here is, of course, ironic: the stony commandant does not utter a word.

inability to resist any longer the marriage proposal which my father had presented to his relatives, although he would be the first in his family to offer his hand to a commoner. To give this unbelievable honor credibility, he then forced upon me such coarse caresses that I had to resist him with all my might. My screams attracted others, who freed me this time from his loathsome presence. He, however, unaccustomed to restraining his desires, made the usual proposals to my father the very next day. The latter, overjoyed by the fulfillment of his greatest wishes, accepted the high honor with the basest of joys and set the wedding date for a few weeks later. My mother, herself above the paltry tasks of housekeeping, was content with everything just as long as she was not disturbed with such trifles. And thus even the usual solace was denied me, that an argument between my parents might ensue because of this match and that their war would guarantee my peace.

Meanwhile, time passed and our despair grew. We were now in actual, not dramatic misery and believed that we surpassed all our dramatic models. Long acquainted with the notion of elopement, we never hesitated a moment in reaching a decision; however, its execution appeared all the more difficult to us. We had no money; for fourteen days we discussed how we could remedy this deficiency, but we got no further on the last day than on the first.

The theater was the place of our secret rendezvous; here, where we had hatched our love, we hoped to see it fly. But we soon forgot to take the necessary precautions for keeping our secret. Lovers are like thieves who are initially unnecessarily careful, gradually become more negligent, then forget to take even the most rudimentary precautions, and are finally caught in the act.

One night when we showed up on stage at the usual hour—with pleasure do I now recall all the little circumstances surrounding that fateful event—Albino told me that his father, who was a notary, was holding a substantial sum of money to which his son could easily gain access. And since he was supposed to fetch his father from their dairy farm the following Sunday, he could have his carriage hitched as early as possible without creating any suspicion. Then I would turn up, he added, in our garden on the outskirts of town, and from there we would depart without further ado. Before another soul suspected our flight, we would already be far away, since we could take post horses at the next station. "Hey! Merry coachman, drive on," he added, and fired by his own description, began to canter around the stage. Soon, however, his gallop was broken in that he unexpectedly fell from his imaginary high horse and came to sit on something alive. Not knowing what had happened to him, he spurred his unknown steed with all his strength; the latter soon made a bold leap and threw his rider roughly to the floor. Albino let out a scream of horror assuring me that he had fallen over a human being, whereupon I ran like a flash to the kitchen to shed light, if possible, on the obscure mystery of this incident. When I returned, I saw him in the prompter's box and asked him, laughing, what had become of his horse? He, however, earnestly assured me that he had felt a human body under him, so that I finally began to fear our discovery. I supposed it could perhaps have been a servant eager to enter upon a nightly love affair with my father's wine. It was essential, of course, to find the culprit, in order to save our secret through our complicity in his own. But we searched long in vain until Albino eventually found a nightcap, which I recognized with horror as my father's. And sure enough, unable to sleep, he had come to the theater before our arrival in order to rehearse the role he was to perform in the play chosen for the wedding festivities. When he had heard us coming he suspected, as we had, an assault on his wine, quickly extinguished his light, and hid in the prompter's box. Since he had recognized our voices, he had stuck out his neck as far as possible to overhear our conversation, until all of a sudden he had felt the unwelcome rider on his shoulders, and, with a bold leap out of the box, he roughly threw off his burden.

Although Albino considered everything lost now and broke out in useless lamentation, I strained my imagination—which has always served me in moments of great distress—to find some means of escaping the impending danger and carrying out our plan, upon which such beautiful hopes were founded. I knew the value of the moment and therefore quickly decided on an idea which I immediately shared with my friend.

I told him: "We can now no longer doubt that my father overheard our plans; that father left without saying a word indicates he is afraid of damaging the wedding plans by creating a stir. Since he knows all the details surrounding our flight, he will doubtless want to wait for the moment of its execution and then try to stop it. Maybe he'll generously forgive me so that

I will be forced by gratitude to accept a marriage, which, as he very well knows by now, I abhor. Let us, therefore, my friend, use our involuntary trust in him to our own advantage and carry out immediately what we had arranged to do in a few days. Instead of taking the detour as planned, let us travel directly to B— where we will arrive in peace, while they will be in hot pursuit of us on the road which my father knows from our conversation."

"How ingenious and resolute you are," cried Albino, embracing me, "and how lucky I am to possess such an inventive and clever beloved. Here is my hand!—I entrust myself to you forever!—The only difficulty that remains is how to take out the carriage and horse without making noise, yet we will find a way to arrange that as well. While I strew the path from the stall to the street with straw, you can sneak up to your room and pack the essentials." I hurried there; my room was over my father's bedroom, and I opened the door half loudly, half softly, as people do whose clumsiness betrays what they want to conceal most. But I used the utmost caution when I left again, and I succeeded in slipping out unnoticed half an hour later with a small bundle of personal belongings. With easy step and heavy heart I reached my beloved, whose door I found open. By that time he had liberated his father's golden prisoners and enslaved his horse. We reached for the shovel and pitchfork and the courtyard was soon covered with straw, the horse was led out, and we were ready for departure without the sound of trumpets and drums.

We soon found ourselves on the main road. Fear made us cruel; our cruelty gave the horse wings; and we traveled so fast that we were in **, almost half the way, by daybreak; there we took post horses, and, without the slightest incident, arrived in B— at nightfall.

How boundless was our joy! We believed we had escaped the greatest danger of our lives; pain and unhappiness were no longer foreign to us, and we felt very innocent because we did not think at all about guilt! Months passed without our noticing it; youth, love, and pleasure bore us so lightly on their colorful wings that we did not feel the flight of hours. Life seemed eternal because we did not perceive its passing.

Soon we were suitably settled; all we lacked was a friend who could lead our inexperience down the primrose path of pleasure through his greater knowledge. That friend was also quickly found. Every day at the table in the inn where we normally dined, we would see a young man whose name was Felix and whom we found interesting because of his attractive countenance and his attentiveness toward us. Once, another man, who had seated himself across from me, had aroused Albino's anger because of some coarse jokes directed at me which had led him to utter some angry replies. The stranger, little impressed by Albino's youth and inexperience, said to him contemptuously: "Your speeches, my friend, are so impertinent that I would give you a slap in the face were I seated next to you; consider yourself slapped." Albino wanted to jump up when Felix, who sat next to us, held him back and answered the stranger jestingly: "And I, were I seated next to you, and if I had a sword, would drive it through your body; therefore, consider yourself as good as dead and be silent." The group laughed; the argument was forgotten. However, Felix's attentiveness and quickness remained unforgettable to us.

From this moment on we were inseparable. He combined the greatest finesse of living with the most graceful figure, the most animated conversation, and a score of talents, and we soon could not be without him. His advice, his desire determined everything we did. Then one morning he had gone out with Albino, and soon after that a young boy brought me the following note in his handwriting:

> Flee from your apartment if there is still time. I will expect you in the royal gardens. Do not lose a minute if you do not want to destroy your happiness.

Frightfully shaken, I immediately hurried to the appointed spot and found Felix alone and apparently greatly disturbed. My first word was a question about Albino. His silence made me all the more insistent, and he finally told me that when they had crossed the Lindenplatz, a tall brown-haired man in a gray frockcoat, black vest, and with roundly cut hair had confronted them. —"That was his father!" I cried out, "from your description I recognize him and see my entire misfortune at one glance!—Was he alone?" "No," continued Felix. "Two others were with him; the one, tall and strong, wore an iron-gray topcoat and a scarlet-red vest. The third appeared to be a lance-corporal." "The big man was my father," I cried again. Felix told me that he guessed it right away, for this man had grabbed Albino's arm and asked where his daughter was. "At that moment," he added, "I saw Albino turn pale with embarrassment searching for a reply. During the confusion I slipped away in order to report this incident to you immediately and, above all, to save you."

This was a dreadful moment for me! Without a home, without friends, with little money in this big city, I saw nothing before me but the most horrible ruin or a life of disgrace! I told Felix my story, entrusted him with my entire situation, and felt somewhat relieved when I saw him very moved and filled with vivid concern.

However, I could not reach any decision. My most pressing concern was to find a lodging; to live alone was a frightful prospect, and Felix suggested taking me to the wife of one of his friends. I gladly consented: he took me to her and introduced me to her as a relative of his. She appeared to be more delighted than surprised at my arrival. In a short time I was provided with every comfort, and Felix requested that I let him know if he could do anything else for me. All I wanted was to have news of Albino, and he promised to do his best to satisfy my wish. Alas! The uncertainty of his fate and my separation from him was the deepest pain I had ever felt, and my misfortune appeared so unique to me that I believed it would never end! My landlady tried in vain to cheer me up; I melted into tears and was deaf to all her attempts to console me. My sole activity was to look out of the window for Felix, who did not return until the next day.

His tale filled me with new afflictions. For a long time, he said with the utmost sympathy, he had fought with himself as to whether or not he should report the news he had learned; but to sustain my hopes would just mean to perpetuate my suffering, and the more cruel the truth the sooner I must learn to bear it. "You had hardly left your residence yesterday," he continued, "when the three strangers in whose hands I had left our poor Albino arrived at your door. They remained there through the night in order to wait for you, until, disappointed in their expectations, they disclosed themselves to the innkeeper, paid the bill, and left again taking along everything that belonged to you. I investigated as best I could to find out what might have become of Albino and finally found out that last night, a young man, who according to the description could be none other than he, had been taken prisoner and, the day after, had been taken away in a carriage, securely bound, to the fortress **."

This last piece of news was too horrible for words. I only saw and heard the misfortune of my friend and spent several days in the deepest despair. My courage had left me and my pain was so great that I wanted to deliver myself voluntarily into the hands of my father and thus share my beloved's fate! Felix held me back. He did not console me as long as I was inconsolable, but he mustered all his ingenuity as soon as he saw me calmer. The hope of ever seeing my darling again died a gentle death upon hearing his words, but the fear of my father and of prison came terrifyingly to life. To counter love Felix armed me with love of self, and he let the lure of enjoyment overcome my weakening pain. He reminded me of the first beautiful days in B—, which could easily return in even more beautiful shape. He described the attractions of a free life, the power which youth, intellect, and talents can exercise over feelings, the triumph of charm, and his victory over my imagination had already been decided long before my heart even thought of resisting.

Thus each moment had brought my pain imperceptibly closer to its end, and distraction completed what common sense had begun. The quick change of ever-new pleasures made me forget the permanence of love and of my vows.

Felix seldom left me alone, and I forgot all too soon how to be without him. Once he went out very early without returning to me at the usual hour. I waited for him the entire day in great distress until I finally saw him return in the evening, exuberantly cheerful.

"You are free now!" he called to me—because up until now the fear that my father might still be lying in wait for me secretly had held me back. "All danger is past, your pursuers are faraway—now you need not think about anything else than enjoying life and forgetting a passion that fate itself has forbidden." After that he told me in a roundabout way how yesterday, he had once again caught a glimpse of the tall, skinny man and the short, round one in the iron-gray coat; they had been on the road in an old-fashioned carriage. Immediately, he had climbed into a hackney coach and hurried after the two men. At the next station he had started a conversation with their servant and drunk heartily to his health. The trusting fool had disclosed to him all the secrets of his masters, who were indeed none other than Albino's father and my own. The servant had told him that the two old men had searched for their children in B—, where one of them had caught his son and brought him into safe custody, while the other had found the nest empty and finally, weary of searching, decided to return home without his daughter.

I must admit—since I have never wanted to adorn myself with noble sentiments I did not own—that when I heard of the danger I had luckily escaped and thought of the free, independent, happy life which smiled down on me now, I could not refrain from feeling the liveliest joy. Felix gladly joined in my transports of happiness. We danced and sang the merriest songs, and our hearts seemed now suddenly delivered from all worries, and our relationship freed from all constraints. But quickly I was stricken by my former pain. The thought of Albino's misfortune, for which I held myself alone responsible, stood before me like a ghost, and put all my exuberance, all my happiness to flight. I disengaged myself from Felix, and while he finished the song, I sat down in a corner of the room to bemoan my fate with bitter tears. He followed me and looked at me full of astonishment, but instead of giving way to my mood and showing me sympathy and comfort, as he had done before, he only looked at me attentively with a half-serious, half-roguish face, and finally cried out: "Truly, my dear, nature destined you to be an actress!"

This outcry took me so much by surprise that it calmed me down. However, we did not speak about it any more at present; our relationship remained as it had been; and with every day Felix seemed to become more obliging. His inventiveness in providing me with ever new forms of entertainment was inexhaustible. I saw in him the creator of my new existence and thought I should set no limits to my gratefulness. Once he took me to a theater where I had never been before. My landlady accompanied us, and as soon as we had taken our seats, Felix left us, for, as he said, he had to speak with someone.

As the theater filled with more and more people, my unease at Felix's failure to return increased, no matter what my companion said to explain it. The play began, but it did not entertain me. The actors appeared boring and conventional to me until the moment the buffoon entered. His first words made my heart beat faster; the tone of his voice entranced me. Everything seemed to take on life because of him; his impromptus moved the audience to transports of merriment. I, too, forgot myself and everything else around me and saw with delight the remaining part of the play, after which our servant told us that Felix had already gone home and we should not wait any longer for him.

When I entered my room, the man who had enchanted me so much on the stage jumped toward me with a mask over his face, gesturing to me playfully. His mood enraptured me irresistibly and without asking, without thinking, I felt myself caught up in the same giddy glee. Automatically, I assumed the role of his beloved, we surrendered to the whims of the moment and improvised a number of amusing scenes, which had probably never been performed in such a lively manner on stage. Finally, he took off his mask and I saw Felix, who confessed to his unconquerable penchant for the theater and encouraged me to join him. "Is there a more splendid life!" he cried out merrily, "than to devote oneself forever only to jest, to transform everything ponderous into joy! To produce this intoxication in others as often as one wants! To put false modesty to shame, to drive out complacency and to force pain to become enjoyment, against its will!— For us alone is the road strewn with flowers; foolish life, which for most people mixes a dose of vexation and boredom with every drop of joy, remains perpetually rich and new for us. We live in all times, run about in all walks of life, from beggar to king, and that is why we stay forever young. Lightly, like migratory birds, we wander through foreign lands, the strangest incidents seek us out, but we enjoy the sweetest freedom. So do not hesitate to follow me and swear allegiance to Thalia's flag, just as I swear allegiance to yours forever."

I had listened to Felix attentively and in thoughts added some of my own encouragements. To be looked upon with delight by all, I thought, to see oneself worshiped from all sides, loved and cheered—who could resist the temptation? "All right!" I cried aloud, "I shall follow your call! One day queen, the next shepherdess, the next a heroine, and in all forms beautiful, beloved, and exalted—who would not gladly choose this way of life? And even if profits are unsure, our calling speaks so loudly in us that it will secure for us not catcalls but curtain calls."

Once we had made our decision, the preparations for its execution were soon made as well. We wanted to leave B— and first perform at some other places in order to train ourselves some more. D— was the city we chose.

Everything was ready for departure when my landlady, pricked by her conscience, tried to dissuade me from my design. "You do not know," she said, "the path which you are treading. The prospect is attractive and seductive to a young heart who loves distractions. But the seed of the fruit does not match its peel. Consider the contempt which the crowds will hold for you and which will wear you down. The aristocrats will appear to love you, they will draw you toward them and take you from time to time into their circles. But in what manner is this done: 'Be our jester! Entertain us!' That is your ticket of entry; you have to pay for each praise with hard work. And just observe these proud children of Thalia in their mutual relationships. Almost all are completely without morals, without the slightest consideration for one another. Ruthlessly they tear each other to pieces with their love of slander at every possible opportunity. They are united without harmony, they are a whole without connection, they belong to each other without love and leave each other without pain. All these things, my child," she continued, "consider them well."

> Enough of wisdom's talk;
> Wild thoughts begin to rage.
> I'm off, to give my heart
> Completely to the stage!

I answered her laughing and with that our conversation ended. However, she had a different reason for moving my happy, conceited heart. She followed me to my room. "There is something else I want to tell you, dear child," she said there, "it may be more convincing, I hope, than all reasons of wisdom and eloquence. Listen carefully!"

"A young, very wealthy nobleman, who arrived here only a short time ago, saw you and immediately fell into the most vehement passion for you. If you are willing to accept the tribute he wants to pay your charms, you will soon be living better than a queen. The most exquisite table, a perfectly furnished house, the most beautiful equipage, obedient servants are awaiting you. Rather than wasting your time with the tedious learning of an arduous craft, you could indulge in sweetest leisure. Instead of a meager income, you could enjoy the most splendid luxury, and instead of being dependent on the moods of a despotic, ignorant public, you would acknowledge no one as your master but your lover. What am I saying: Master! since he will always be your most humble slave, attentive to all your desires and happy to oblige you whenever he can. A very considerable monthly allowance will provide for your finery, not to speak of the gifts—the expedient acquisition of which I will teach you. Would you be so blind as to let such good fortune slip through your fingers, since you are about as likely to get another such offer as you are to remain young and beautiful forever?"

What noble convictions! I thought to myself, while I could not hinder her words from having an effect on my fantasy. My vanity had already driven off, sitting on the silk cushions of the splendid carriage, to quench my thirst for pleasure by engaging in all the diversions I still hoped to enjoy. At the same time my selfishness had inspected with great pleasure the interior of a generously furnished house. Only my heart was not in it, and only out of curiosity did I ask my landlady whether she really had instruction to make all these offers? She left me immediately saying that she wanted to delight the young nobleman with the flattering prospects implied in my question and let him eliminate all my doubts himself.

Confused, with an empty heart but a head full of a thousand tempting images, and undecided about the choice I should make, I remained alone for some minutes until Felix entered and immediately settled all doubts. I told him what had happened. He laughed at the lady's "wisdom," but thought her foolishness so serious that he had my few personal belongings cleared out of her home immediately and did not leave my side until our departure, which followed in a few days.

We traveled to D—. Our trip was as merry as possible. Felix was always in the best of moods and delighted me with the cheerful exuberance of his wit. In order to travel more cheaply, we had joined with two other persons, whose company, however, soon became tiresome to us in every respect. Quickly, Felix thought of a ruse to rid himself of them. He pretended that he was stricken by recurrent violent convulsions; these became so apparent to our fellow travelers that they nervously asked about their cause. The rascal replied after some hesitation that he had had the misfortune of having been bitten by a rabid dog, and, since he had never fully recovered from this wound, he was now traveling to a famous surgeon who would help him regain his health. Quickly, as if they were already prey to the disease, they jumped off the carriage and completed the journey on foot, while we drove on leisurely and laughingly. By the time they finally arrived, worn out from heat and exhaustion, we had already exposed their gullibility, to the great pleasure of the company we had encountered.

With very high hopes we arrived in D—. I first performed the role of the maiden from Marienburg. My heart pounded fiercely when I threw a glance at the assembled crowd. But my fearful timidity itself brought me an advantage because it gave my acting a girllike shyness and my expression an uncommon warmth. The audience, which is always sympathetic to a tolerable figure, encouraged me so much with its lively applause that after the play was over, I found myself surrounded by a crowd whose sweet incense of flattery aroused in me the most pleasant bewilderment in the world. I was unaccustomed to such fragrant offerings and unpracticed in the divine art of pleasing everyone, but innate tact soon let me find the way. Meaningful glances, flattering replies, polite nonsense absentmindedly spoken, a loud laugh honoring an inanity—were sufficient to make everyone perfectly satisfied with me.

How many invitations did I receive after this day! How many splendid festivities were planned with me as their queen! Yet I never responded because I was honest enough to want to speak with Felix first and to arrange with him how I should behave. But I was astonished when he responded to all my remarks in the meanest fashion of the world; instead of the easy life he had depicted for me, he demanded the seriousness and circumspection of a matron and at once locked out all those sweet prospects! Astonishment made me speechless at first, but as soon as I regained my voice, I reproached him with bitter words in the most emphatic manner, about how little his present conduct corresponded with the free and happy life he had so often portrayed and how wrong and unnecessary it was to make life difficult for us and arbitrarily banish our every pleasure! Instead of calming me down, however, he laughed scornfully, saying he had only been testing his dramatic skills then and nothing could have been further from the truth. He removed his good mood like a mask, and hung all his worldly wisdom into the wardrobe with his costumes. Nothing remained of his wit but a few scraps, with which he miserably strove to patch over holes in his character.

How very betrayed I found myself! I had expected a jovial, easygoing companion and found a tyrant, who, like all other tyrants, showed himself to be as strict toward others as he was lenient toward himself, with the sad consequence that he stubbornly distanced from himself the pleasures he incessantly sought. I, on the other hand, held pleasure and freedom to be the sole requisites of life. They had led me into the arms of love and consoled me when love was gone. In order to be their worthy priestess I had chosen my present station, and it was natural that now I had to sacrifice everything else to them. For some time, I concealed my aversion for Felix, but since he did not change his conduct, I decided to take revenge. On the occasion of a new argument which arose because of some gifts I had received, I broke with him forever.

I was barely free when I became the object of the attentions of a young artist, who, like me, was just starting out in life. He was gentle, modest, and loving, and in him I found the complete opposite of the impetuous, despotic Felix. If Felix's love was a wild chant, which, unresolved, lost itself in harsh, discordant tones, the artist's love resembled the song of a shepherd's pipe, whose last tone arouses in us a wistful sadness over the transitoriness of beauty. A minor incident soon drew us even closer to one another. Felix, who since our separation had let me feel his hatred in every way, forgot himself to such an extent that he tried to insult me incessantly even during performances. Once, when we had to fence as part of our roles, he attacked me so crudely and fiercely that I was wounded. Without the quick assistance of my new friend I would have sunk to the floor.

I fell sick and had just recovered from the consequences of my fright when the company broke up, and I gladly seized the opportunity to travel with the larger part of the troupe to a small city, in order to leave D— and avoid the sight of Felix. Our trip was very unpleasant. The director, whose till was already ailing, had arranged the entire trip, including the cost of provisions, with a carriage lender, using his gold watch as payment, the one thing of value he still possessed. We were all packed into the big carriage; due to our imposed state of rest—we couldn't stir a limb—we longed for sweet repose. The more slowly we advanced the faster came our sighs. Whenever we finally reached an inn, we would find that instead of yielding the anticipated relaxation, all our previous trials had only been a preparation for greater hardships. The forced constraint of all limbs, some of which had fallen asleep on their own, would give way to equally forced activity. Wherever we arrived, innkeeper and wife, maids and servants alike, would look first at us, then at one another, in dumb bewilderment, and then break out in unabashed laughter, while one of us would scream for tea, the other demand food, and most call for wine. The men would curse, the women scold, and our leader, the man who had rented us the carriage, would look calmly at his watch to see what time it was.

I found it impossible to continue with these wild migrants and therefore hired a carriage of my own. I climbed with my friend into the carriage and happily pulled ahead, to the great vexation of the rest, who freely vented their envy. We arrived a day earlier than the others and introduced ourselves as a married couple to the company, whose jaws dropped as far down when they heard this news as their hopes over the chance of a new engagement sank. It was very hard just to find a place which could be transformed into a worthy scene for so many talents; finally, however, we succeeded in consecrating a big barn as a temple for the arts. As if a magic wand had been waved, there were now muses walking where Ceres had ruled before.[2] Out of the barn floor rose an amphitheater: where threshers had marked an uneven beat before, there were now the delicate whispers of violins and flutes. The mystical curtain covered the stage set, and those standing behind it wished for nothing more ardently than to encounter always full sheaves and never empty chaff. "Mohammed" opened the performance, but by the end of the piece, art had lost as much honor as the audience, and perhaps also the actors, had gained in pleasure.[3] Mohammed had artfully composed his turban from a nightcap of red wool and a muslin scarf, lent to him by one of his recent acquaintances. He had decorated it with a pair of shiny buckles, which he did not use today because he wore yellow slippers. His unlucky star, however, would have it that during one of the most moving scenes a curious spark came so close to this work of art that it was set aflame. Palmire rushed forth to put out the fire as quickly as possible but since her breath only appeared to feed the flame, the owner of the scarf eagerly dashed onto the stage to save her property and, to the de-

2. Ceres, Roman goddess of agriculture, had her temple in the plebeian quarters. The allusion to the goddess here ironically highlights the transformation of the barn into a temple of the arts.

3. Goethe's translation, in 1800, of Voltaire's drama *Le Fanatisme ou Mahomet le Prophète* (1742), his *Mohammed Fragments*, and his preoccupation with Islam in the *West-östlicher Divan* set the stage for the Mohammed dramas of the nineteenth century. Most of these plays were set during the siege of Mecca and revolved around the tension between religious fanaticism and sensuality.

light of the audience, quickly transformed Mohammed's turban into the headdress of a Jacobin. This unexpectedly hilarious catastrophe of the tragedy was so very much to the liking of the locals and put them into such a good mood, that they competed in their exertions to entertain the actors, inundating them just as much with compliments as with champagne. The happy spirits lasted for awhile; the actors believed they had found an earthly paradise here and lived in a perpetual state of intoxication. But the angel of necessity soon stepped before this paradise with his fiery sword. For with all this paradisiac splendor, everyone, even the director, had forgotten their earthly cares. Out of this forgetfulness, however, arose the awakening of all the debtors, and out of the awakening soon came the total dissolution of the entire troupe.

At this calamity I remembered the golden days I had once spent in B—, and I decided to travel there with my beloved in order to share with him all the advantages which I hoped to find there. Our way of thinking was so harmonious that no matter what I did, I could always count on his approval. He was the kindest, most pleasant man in the world, and never let any ugly mood of his darken a happy hour of mine. Since it is only natural to love those who give us but joy and no displeasure, I was also devoted to him with all my heart, and gladly gave up all the little pleasures which would have otherwise made me happy. Only my inclination for diversions and for everything new I could not and would not abandon but hoped to satisfy fully. I sketched a thousand ambitious plans for myself and my friend. With jokes, plans, and hopes, our journey passed both pleasantly and quickly.—We arrived in B—, where I immediately sought out my former landlady and found to my delight that she appeared to have forgotten all that had happened between us. We went to the theater and had not been there very long, when she pointed out to me a tall adventurously dressed man, who was sitting not far from us in a box. "Look, my child," she said, "that is the nobleman who would have gladly made your happiness and perhaps still wants to if your stubbornness permits." I looked at him more closely and my astonishment was just as great as my horror, when I recognized in him the Vincent whose love had once frightened me so. Sometime after my flight, he had set out from his father's house for B—, where he had seen me only in the evenings and, because of the distance and my different dress and manner, he did not recognize the old love in the new one. I hid my dismay as well as I could from my hostess and tried as much as possible to avoid his glance, for at his appearance, the old fear of imprisonment and paternal punishment was stirred up in me with new intensity. I trembled at the thought that his treachery could easily cost me my freedom, which I now less than ever thought of relinquishing. I therefore decided to leave B— as soon as possible and we traveled to H—, where I was engaged under very favorable conditions. The acclaim I now received to an ever-greater degree seemed to indicate very nicely the progress I had made along the way. I lived for some time very happily until death suddenly snatched my companion away from me. This loss made me serious for the very first time in my life. Yes, I would have abandoned myself completely to melancholy if the distraction of my situation, my youth, and my innate lightheartedness had not made it impossible and soon reconciled me to life.

One day, when I had returned to my apartment after a performance, intoxicated by unusually enthusiastic applause and tired from the exertion, a young man was announced who claimed to be an old friend. I was curious to know who it could be and awaited his visit with great impatience. He entered—seeing, recognizing, and flying into each other's arms was the work of a moment. "It is you!" we both called. "Yes, it is me and I am just as in love with you as I was then"—for it was none other than—Albino himself. We wanted to ask each other questions, but kissed instead. We were moved, but a smile held back our tears. It took a long time before a sober explanation could grow out of the intoxication of surprise and joy. Finally, Albino asked me how I had succeeded in escaping from the convent. "From a convent?" I cried in astonishment. "Did you lose your mind in that prison? All I want to know is how you were able to escape from your prison." "What do you mean?" he said in similar astonishment. "Surely, the whole world seemed a dungeon since I had to live without you, but I swear that I know of no other prison." "Is is not true then that you were arrested by our fathers in B— and taken into custody before Felix's eyes?" "Before Felix's eyes, you say?" replied Albino, "but it was he who told me that they dragged you out of our apartment and locked you forever away in a convent." "Oh! that vile man!" I cried out, "our trusting inexperience made us an easy prey to a cunning swindler who played cruel games with our trust."

Albino now decribed to me all the circumstances of the deception. "I loved the scoundrel so much," said he, "that he won my complete trust and I told him the circumstances of our story, to which I often added humorous descriptions of our families. He questioned me about the most insignificant details. At the time his questions appeared to me just as innocuous as they are now proof of his treacherous plans. On the unhappy day when I saw you last, I had asked Felix to go with me because I very much wanted to surprise you with a present or two. I found a ring in which two hearts had been very delicately joined. This ring, I determined, was to be yours. To ensure that it would fit, I asked Felix to return and take one of your rings away in secret. He promised to return right away, but I waited for him with great impatience, in vain. Instead I received a letter in which he implored me to flee without delay if I did not want to be robbed of your sight forever. He indicated a place where I should hide and which I should not leave for anything in the world before he himself would come to fetch me. He did not return until the evening, and oh, how skillfully did the hypocrite manage to etch on his face the lines of deepest distress and how skillfully did he feign sad confusion! He told me that your father had sought out your apartment, descended upon you there, and had taken you away on the spot. He himself had arrived at your place just at this moment and followed you to the outskirts of B—, where he learned from one of the servants that you were to be locked up in a convent for the rest of your life. As far as I was concerned, he added, an even more severe fate was in store, because I had been charged with robbery and the case against me demanded the greatest penalty. With feigned anguish Felix advised me to flee the country. The hope of being able to see you in better days made me heed his advice and take care of life and limb. I chose this place because I knew that similar circumstances had already assembled several of my countrymen here. Fate then seemed to replace by luck what it had robbed from me in love. I gambled, and time after time, I won significant sums, parts of which I invested in shipping ventures. I waited only until my ships returned safely before writing my father to learn from him whether it would be possible to buy my way out of the suit which your father is supposed to have filed against me."

How happy did Albino's words make me! His love gave my entire life a new, brilliant meaning. And how very much must he love me if he was totally content with the present, forgetting completely about the past! His plan to reconcile himself with our parents was very dear to me and its execution seemed all the easier since we were now united and outside the reach of their power.

We therefore wrote immediately to my brother who had once been Albino's trusted friend and had loved me very much. In a short time we received his answer which eliminated all remaining doubt. The favorable news arrived the same day as the expected ships, which returned with generous profit and placed us in possession of a fortune capable of dazzling the eyes and turning the heads of everyone at home.

Well endowed with letters of credit and in good spirits, we now started our journey home which at present had for us all the fascination distant places had once possessed and now lost. We lingered awhile in S— in order to see the local sights, including the theater. But how gladly I would have left this unseen, for the first thing that I saw was that buffoon whose voice had so often impressed me deeply. I was burning all over, whereas Albino, who stood next to me, appeared as cold as ice and seemed not even to notice my confusion. We returned to our inn where he suggested taking advantage of the cool of the night by departing immediately. I agreed with great joy. He left me, so he said, to settle the bill and hire the post horses. However, while I awaited his return with as much impatience as unease, he hurried back to the theater to look for the swindler whom he had immediately recognized. With much restraint, he first demanded an explanation for his treachery, because he probably felt that the theater was not a suitable place for revenge. Since Felix, however, took as cowardice what was only the result of intelligence, Albino went on to accuse him in no uncertain terms of vile and malicious behavior. Both drew their swords, but Albino was even more valiant than clever, and Felix more passionate than valiant. So the fight soon ended to Felix's disadvantage, who fell wounded to the floor. Albino, believing him dead, hurried back to me. Since the post horses stood ready, we departed immediately.

Only when we were alone did I dare question Albino about his long absence, because I had deliberately kept my curiosity in check in front of witnesses. His answers were so indefinite and his entire manner appeared so deliberately cold that my heart began to pound terribly; for I began to fear very unpleasant explanations concerning Felix. Hardly had we crossed the border, however, when my fears came to an end: Albino told me how he had recognized Felix immediately, then demanded an explanation and punished him. But in order to cause me no disquiet he did not want to tell any of this before we were completely out of danger.

We finally reached home. All our so-called adventures, which had appeared so strange and desirable before, now seemed ordinary and distasteful. The most exotic, unusual, and desirable thing of all seemed to us to be the happy peace of a secluded life. Our parents felt as much honored by us as they were pleased. What they would have otherwise condemned as a reprehensible prank was transformed into the product of a daring and genial spirit—due to our success, which in the eyes of the world justifies any action. Our miraculous fortune drew the attention of the entire little country and flattered and astounded them. It pleased us, however, to be able to use part of it to bring my father's affairs in order. His love of pleasure and his concern for the pleasure of others, combined with the total unconcern of my mother, had severely shaken his financial circumstances.

Our wedding was celebrated by the entire community. No pomp nor artificial solemnity glorified it, but everybody was seized by the madness of enjoyment; everywhere charming confusion held sway. Everyone believed to have found in our luck a guarantee of their own, and their simple, heartfelt joy was the greatest ornament of the festival.

Thus ended unexpectedly in comedy what had started out as sure tragedy. Nothing seemed funnier to us than to remember how we had once left our country as heroes, full of pathos, and now returned, imperceptibly transformed into married bourgeois. Yet, we gladly traded the flighty stage for the secure walls of domesticity. Cheerfulness and love remained with us; we lived with more happiness than merit, more tenderness than reason, and more lightheartedness than intelligence. If we had anything to wish for, it was to live ten lives so that we could love each other ten times over.

Translation of "Die Flucht nach der Hauptstadt," in *Taschenbuch für das Jahr 1806; der Liebe und Freundschaft gewidmet,* ed. U. Spazier (Frankfurt/Main: Wilmans, 1806), 137–84.

Introduction, bibliography, and translation by
KATHERINE R. GOODMAN

Rahel Varnhagen

(1771–1833)

Rahel Varnhagen (1771–1833)
pencil drawing by Wilhelm Hensel, 1822
courtesy of Bildarchiv preussischer
Kulturbesitz, Berlin

Rahel Varnhagen was renowned in her day for her performance at the center of her Berlin salon. A few nobility mingled there with political radicals and conservatives, leading minds of German Romanticism, German Jewish intellectuals, and actresses: a scandalous venture void of arrogance and prejudice save that of the proud heart. Of this ephemeral art form, the salon, we possess, of course, only accounts by its visitors. We are far more fortunate when it comes to Varnhagen's letters, a literary form in which she invested considerable creative energy and which bears witness to her unrelenting efforts to engage her correspondent and to the liveliness of her mind. Varnhagen also demanded involvement from her correspondents and the letters do not permit passive reading. They are grammatically imperfect (not infrequently to the point of opacity) and display eccentric punctuation; they are also strewn both with foreign loan words and her own peculiar but suggestive neologisms. She claimed never to have learned German properly (she was raised speaking Yiddish), but one suspects she prided herself somewhat on her unconventional usage, which she perceived as breaking rational constraints on personal expression. She complains that she cannot write a beautifully balanced, classical German sentence, but she strove for spontaneity; she might have viewed grammar as another convention to be broken.

From the time of their first publication in 1834 Rahel Varnhagen's letters have attracted attention; women in particular have been drawn to them. Varnhagen could not bear to have women "identify" with her, and yet that is precisely what they did. She disdained the women of her day whom she perceived to be bound by convention, but she admired many (indeed almost any) who broke consciously with it. She consistently encouraged her friends, men and women alike, to have the courage to follow their own inner voices. Despite, or perhaps precisely because of, Varnhagen's unending complaints, women have found her a source of consolation. Moreover, no nineteenth-century women readers report finishing her letters without a sense of her strength, pride, and energy.

Varnhagen was acutely aware of the prejudices of her day: sexism as well as anti-Semitism. Convention, and that included prejudice of any kind, restricted the full growth of human beings. She named prejudices and minutely described their painful effect on her, always upholding the vision of a world without artificial restrictions, a world of generosity. That does not mean she identified herself with the "causes" of women or Jews. Rather, she rejected being forced into categories by convention and not being seen for herself.

If anything, Varnhagen identified with the leading intellects of the day, making a cult of her intellect, her soul, and her unique personality. She prized especially what she saw as her talent for friendship. For her a generous friendship was a microcosm for a utopian social system. By practicing her talent she believed she was helping create better conditions for others. She adamantly affirmed the importance of her role in the salon and as friend and correspondent. She published only a few excerpts from her letters during her lifetime, but she planned an epistolary autobiography as an example of fortitude under desperate social conditions. She was an admirer of the French Girondist Count Mirabeau. Toward the end of her life she became interested in the Saint-Simonists.

The facts of her life can be summarized briefly. Rahel Levin was born on May 19, 1771, in Berlin, the daughter of the wealthy Jewish merchant Markus Levin and his wife Chaiche. Without formal education she soon learned nevertheless to astound family guests with her intelligence and candor. After the death of her stern father in 1789, the young Rahel began serving weak tea to her friends in the garret of her parents' house. This first salon was the more famous. Its unconventional gatherings ended, however, after Napoleon's conquest of Prussia in 1806 and with the growing anti-Semitism which accompanied Prussia's burgeoning nationalism. From 1819, several years after Napoleon's defeat, until her death in 1833, Rahel maintained a second salon in Berlin. However, the times and the people had changed, and this salon was no longer able to generate the same hopeful dynamism. By this time Rahel Levin had married Karl August Varnhagen von Ense, fourteen years her junior; they remained childless. Her long and close friendship with David Veit, a Jewish doctor, stemmed from the very earliest years of her first salon, as did her friendship with Rebecca Friedländer, who composed romantic novels under the pen name of Regina Frohberg. No doubt Rahel Varnhagen's closest, most intimate female friendship was with the controversial Pauline Wiesel. Wiesel, who had married a plodding businessman, became the mistress of Prince Louis Ferdinand of Prussia. After his death on the battlefield in 1806, Wiesel lived alternately with men or women, but always maintained a close correspondence with Rahel Varnhagen. Varnhagen had an affectionate, if not especially close relationship with her younger sister Rose, who married Karl Asser, a jurist from the Netherlands.

ANNOTATED BIBLIOGRAPHY

Varnhagen's Works

The following letters to friends and relatives constitute but a minuscule portion of those remaining to us. Various editions of her correspondence with different people have recently been collected in a ten-volume edition: Rahel Varnhagen. *Gesammelte Werke*. Edited by Konrad Feilchenfeldt, Uwe Schweikert, and Rahel E. Steiner (Munich: Matthes & Seitz, 1983). Marlis Gerhardt's handier, one-volume selection *Rahel Varnhagen. Jeder Wunsch wird Frivolität genannt. Briefe und Tagebücher* (Darmstadt: Luchterhand, 1983) is also a sign of the reawakened interest in Varnhagen's letters. Since the publication of both these editions, Deborah Hertz has found previously unpublished letters from Varnhagen to Rebecca Friedländer (*Rebecca Friedländer: Briefe an eine Freundin. Rahel Varnhagen an Rebecca Friedländer*. Edited by Deborah Hertz. Köln: Kiepenheuer & Witsch, 1988).

Hannah Arendt's biography remains the best from a psychological perspective.

Fortunately this is available in English: *Rahel Varnhagen. The Life of a Jewish Woman* (revised edition, New York: Harcourt Brace Jovanovich, 1974). Those readers more interested in historical background and detail (and who read German well) will find Herbert Scurla's *Rahel Varnhagen. Die grosse Frauengestalt der deutschen Romantik* (Berlin: Verlag der Nation, 1962) invaluable. A comprehensive bibliography of publications regarding her person or her letters can be found on pp. 451–62 of volume 10 of the Feilchenfeldt, Schweikert, and Steiner edition of her letters.

Secondary Literature in English

Bird, Alan. "Rahel Varnhagen von Ense and Some English Assessments of Her Character." *German Life and Letters* 26 (1972–73): 183–92.

Goodman, Katharine R. "The Cases of Varnhagen and Arnim." In Goodman. *Dis/Closures. Women's Autobiography in Germany between 1790–1914.* New York: Peter Lang, 1986, pp.73–120.

Goodman, Kay. "The Impact of Rahel Varnhagen on Women in the Nineteenth Century." In *Gestaltet und gestaltend: Frauen in der deutschen Literatur.* Edited by Marianne Burkhard. Amsterdam: Rodopi, 1981, pp.125–53.

Goodman, Kay. "Poesis and Praxis in Rahel Varnhagen's Letters." *New German Critique* 27 (Fall 1982): 123–39.

Guilloton, Doris Starr. "Toward a New Freedom: Rahel Varnhagen and the German Women Writers before 1848." In *Woman as Mediatrix: Essays on Nineteenth-Century European Women Writers.* Edited by Avriel H. Goldberger. New York: Greenwood, 1987, pp.133–49.

Hertz, Deborah. "Inside Assimilation. Rebecca Friedländer's Rahel Varnhagen." In *German Women in the Eighteenth and Nineteenth Centuries. A Social and Literary History.* Edited by Ruth-Ellen B. Joeres and Mary Jo Maynes. Bloomington: Indiana Univ. Press, 1986, pp.271–88.

Hertz, Deborah. *Jewish High Society in Old Regime Berlin.* New Haven: Yale Univ. Press, 1988.

Kahn, Lothar. "Ludwig Robert: Rahel's Brother." *Publications of the Leo Baeck Institute Year Book* 18 (1973): 185–99.

Litvinoff, Barnet. "Rahel Levin: The Apex of a Triangle." *German Life and Letters* 1 (1947–48): 211–27.

Matenko, Percy. "New Light on Rahel Varnhagen's Biography: Some Hitherto Unpublished Letters." In *Studies in German Literature of the Nineteenth and*

Twentieth Centuries. Festschrift for Frederic E. Coenon. Chapel Hill: Univ. of North Carolina Press, 1970, pp.35–46.

Weissberg, Liliane. "Writing on the Wall: The Letters of Rahel Varnhagen." *New German Critique* 36 (Fall 1985): 157–73.

Selected Letters

You can't write the person you want to spend your life with! Which thought, which breath wouldn't one want to tell him, show him? He could be our witness, confirm our existence!? And in terrifyingly dreary, almost unrecognized fear we waste our days well-behaved, cheerfully let ourselves be called reasonable, and are insane from cowardice. Public life—*life* is too all-inclusive—is arranged so that that's all right too; you get your results, but in sheer deprivation, shut out of the paradise where you may seek your own air, sustenance, and companions yourself: the fresh, healthy, never deceiving heart is called greed, banished to a kind of nursery, prison, or madhouse: and so we go grayly through the cities to the cemetery. God, where did I get that? I'll tell you. I feel a whole flood of tears in my breast over my heart; and everything reminds me of everything. Nothing seems detached to me anymore: I feel myself *totally* confined and my spirit is more alert than ever. I *don't* comfort myself with a life beyond! A beautiful life on *earth* wouldn't preclude that. Every moment heightens and sharpens for me the ever-more intimate profound feeling of the incomprehensible loss! Our organs are too mortal to comprehend it; and higher creatures surely grieve for us—we who are incapable of it and which I sort of *calculate*! Everything like me! The coldest, the least that we mortals can do—the enormous pain, the enormous loss, the impossibility of leaving the existing confusion other than by *dying,* disengaging, severing, isolating, only makes death *possible.* Understand this as all-inclusively as you can: in regard to human interaction, to the most profound tendencies and needs of the heart, to nature, which we temporarily call dead, to every constellation. You see, I know well why you don't write me! You have one great good fortune. According to its history in which the last ununderstood arrival of phenomena is called *chance,* and according to its inner eternal value! What a friend you have chosen, found, and sensed! I understand one person—you—totally. Can lend you, as though doubly organized, my soul, and have the immense power of doubling myself, without confusing myself. I am as unique as the greatest phenomenon on this earth. The greatest artist, philosopher, or poet is not above me. We are of the same element. Of the same order, and belong together. And whoever wants to expel the other, only expels himself. But *Life* was assigned to me; and I remained an embryo until my century, and am *totally* buried in rubble from the outside; that's why I say it myself. So that one image concludes this existence. And even pain, as I know it, is a life; and I *think* I'm one of those creatures which humanity should design and then doesn't need any longer, and can't do anymore. No one can comfort me: no such wise man exists: I am my own comfort; now that's still good fortune! But that's like insulting it: and I feel like I'm insulting it too. I'll define good fortune for you some other time. That's how things stand with me more or less. If you lived in the same city with me you would have infinite pleasure! You can't imagine how my life blooms eternally. But you would have to submit to the rule of only seeing me when I wanted. Just don't die! That depends totally on you. I certainly won't forget myself that way. People like us can only die *inadvertance*; I feel most acutely. And there is another way of holding onto your life; there are drops on other stars, which are sufficient by themselves to sustain a life spun on earth. The reversal, the nourishment of a more comprehended, coarser life, etc. !!! Have no fear! I am usually more serene. But when I wrote to people, it's as if the heavy, full horizon of my soul thundered forth. Heavenly people love thunder.[. . .]

To Rebecca Friedländer in Berlin (Frau von F.) Berlin, December 14, 1807

Read this letter as if it arrived next week. I wrote it yesterday. It's a good one.

Even though speaking and writing don't help anything, one should not stop speaking and writing! This dismal sentence, of which each half is true only in itself, is only a joke! This morning I wasn't being clear; and you didn't understand me either. What we talked about is too important to me and it reached a point where it must be made clear—all the more since our current half-understanding would have to lead to a wrong-understanding—that I not pursue it with you with all my strength and best insight [sic].

What we really understand by the word *human* is that creature which engages in rational association with its peers, in a relationship with a consciousness that we ourselves are able to shape, and are even compelled to shape continually. Whatever we may be, whatever we may do, we all have the need to be lovable. All of us follow this beautiful, pure, most human, lovable instinct. In the highest sense—but also right down to the most disparate—the whole life-web of humans as humans is nothing but this, modified into infinity. In you—as in any delicate, lively soul—this need is also very keen. But what in the world is more lovable—and happier—than a soul open to everything that can happen to human beings! And what else yields a purer frame of mind than this very condition, which through its permanence, through its sheer existence elevates and propagates itself! The entire world gains you and you gain the entire world! Give up the idea—still the mistaken opinion of so many good people—that you can comprehend but *one* object with your whole soul. Impress upon yourself the thought that for *one* moment the conviction takes root in you of what it is like to be lovable, and you are it! It is not, as you wrote me today, "work" which I demand—something you are incapable of today, something of which one is always incapable—rather I demand one moment of conviction, one moment of healthy attitude.

More humiliated than I one cannot be, more sorrow one cannot enjoy; a greater misfortune in *everything* one values most or least one does not experience, any greater loss one does not see; a more painful youth up to the age of eighteen one does not experience, more ill one cannot be, or nearer insanity; and I have loved. But when did the world not speak to me, when didn't everything human affect me, every human interest: suffering and art and jest! The moment pain and a searing longing tear the soul apart can't one, shouldn't one want to unearth the treasures of one's mind? *That* is when one must feed on one's supply, the supply of treasures, the supply of highest human interests, of *human* interest. Don't tell me that only natural gifts enable one to do this, and that I, for example, shouldn't compare myself with you. Anyone who can reason as you can about various matters *has* the power: only your interest lies in the wrong direction.

An educated human being is not the one whom nature has treated extravagantly; an educated human being is one who uses his talents benevolently, wisely, and appropriately in the highest manner: who wants to do this in earnest; who can gaze steadily where he is lacking and realize what he lacks. To my mind this is a duty and not a gift; and this alone constitutes for me an educated human. That's why I want you to see what you have failed to do. This raises one more to a general level—*à généraliser*—so that the general does not lead one to the specific, but the other way around. This is very lovable; this would make you *entirely* lovable. This you can *achieve*; for it comes suddenly through a thought; just as the opposite came to you also through a thought. And I repeat what I have already said: people like us will only get well when they conceive the greatest loathing for being sick; when they are permeated with the idea that to be healthy is highly lovable. You can't imagine how convinced I am: I'd like to give you that conviction in a potion. But it will work, I'm sure! Just be very coquettish!

To Pauline Wiesel   Berlin, March 12, 1810
                                                8:30 in the evening. Tuesday

It's a shame that I have not written you: a misfortune; a misfortune like every shameful act! Dear beloved friend[1] [Freundin und Freund]! Woe! —my injured heart weeps this woe! —Woe! That our life runs by without us liv-

---

1. Varnhagen addresses Pauline Wiesel as both a "Freundin," female friend, and a "Freund," the male counterpart. We can only imagine what she meant, but throughout the entire letter she uses the formal form of the pronoun "you" [*Sie*].

ing together. You are alone, separated from me, and I am alone, distant from you. Only once could nature let two such creatures live at the same time. In this age. Every day I see you, and nature, and me more. Away from you I do nothing but repeat every word, every little deed of yours, every expression, and believe me, I can name the principles of your entire being, your existence, better than you yourself: there is only *one* difference between us: you *live* everything, because you have courage and had good fortune; I *think* most things, because I had no good fortune and wasn't given any courage, not the courage to fly in the face of fortune and wrestle good fortune from its hands, I have only learned the courage to endure; but nature dealt grandly with us both. And we are made to live the truth in this world. And by different routes we arrived at one and the same point. We exist at the margins of human society. For us there is no place, no office, no vain title! *All* lies have one: the eternal truth—true living and feeling which can be traced uninterrupted to simple, profound natures, to a nature which we must comprehend—has *none*! And so we are shut out of society, you because you insulted it (I congratulate you on it! At least you had something—many days of pleasure!), I, because I can't sin and *tell lies* with it. I know fully your inner history. Every insult you heaped on society, even if it was justified for *you,* really wounded you yourself: I know step by step how it happened. You would gladly have been "a homey little wife, caressing and kissing your husband," as Goethe says in his distich; but it didn't work. And where is one to go with the terrible supply, with the whole apparatus of one's heart and life! Most people are not hyper-sensitive, self-destructive, self-sacrificing nuns. One would like to go to *war,* I would like to go myself, to seek nourishment for the promise with which nature sent us into life. By the just and almighty Lord, on the high seat of judgment, one goes to war for less than that! and is honored for it! If you had found a heart in Wiesel's breast, you would never have sought one elsewhere. But by his own deficiency, and his unfortunate superfluity of words, he reasoned your underdeveloped, all-too-cautious intellect astray. Your better awareness always existed at the margins. I know everything. Your strong *heart* is not made for suffering. It needs some *other occupation:* just so your eyes, your senses. I know you totally, far better than you yourself, Pauline, better than any person thinks he can know another. You were also right about Prince Louis Ferdinand. You know how I loved him: I still

412

study him intuitively; "there is nothing generous about him," you often said. You meant, giving in on the spur of the moment, and other things. But I know the fundamental part of him that really offended you. I understand everything *intuitively*. Even he couldn't envision the deep-seated will, the deep-seated desires of his own nature powerfully enough to bring about one unified action. He was often enmeshed in short-lived goals; what had been pounded into his head ten, fifteen, twenty years ago, and what his present soul no longer accepted, still seemed to direct his actions, or rather, he lacked the courage to show that his soul had changed, that he had different longings, different goals. So he made a mess out of nearly every hour of his life despite the finest, truest, most diligent disposition; and naturally had to wound his clear-sighted beloved every minute. This only made you flare up again, and—since the truth about all this can never be expressed—made you say a lot of false things. Now I perceive everything. Now that I dig untiringly inside myself and behold my spirit more and more by the blazing flames of my emotions. So it stands with us; and I can't come to you! But, Pauline, I have *not* given up! Everything I do is based on that. Until now I could do nothing. Now I hope that some of our inheritance will be forthcoming, and just think! Moritz will probably marry.[2] Then I will be all alone again on earth. From now on I won't see [Rebecca] Friedlaender anymore (she's taken the name Frohberg), she's too insufferable, unnaturally *pauvre* by nature, but pretentious. Now and then I go into society; I have no set group, none which pleases me, as much as before. Not *one* person, man or woman, with whom I can go for walks, never mind to the theater. Every day I become less and less able to make the effort to seek out such a person. And too proud. I would rather bitterly sacrifice forever whatever I got *that* way, even if it was my due, than take just one step toward it.— Except for the six weeks he was in Königsberg, Moritz has lived with me the whole winter, and he is still here. I gain little pleasure and quite a bit of trouble from him. I exist for him only in passing, even though he takes care of me financially, and is, *en gros,* generous to me. Another burden for my

2. Refers to the Levin family's financial problems which began in 1806–7, and lasted until 1812. Her oldest brother, Markus, managed the family fortune, but it was invested jointly so that Varnhagen did not actually have access to her share. As a result she often mentions financial difficulties. Her brother Moritz married Ernestine Victor in 1811.

heart! Now I have a young man,[3]—I wrote you last spring that I went walking in the meadow with him and that I cried out for you: my whole soul loves him, must love him, because his qualities demand it. He loves me too, like one loves the sea, the configuration of the clouds, a gorge. That is *not* enough for me. *Not any more.* Whomever I love must want to live with me; stay with me. (Campan[4] still writes frequently, but only recently love letters saying that I should come.) So I'll *definitely* tear *this* arrow out of my heart, too, and let one more wound hurt, and heal, and scar. And now, if two hundred *Louis d'or* lay next to me like one miserable visiting card, I would leave tomorrow without saying good-bye. Except for you, *my* friends all think I can love on air, and live. They like to see games of the heart like mine, and I am supposed to live without love! It's over, it's too much!—One more thing, Pauline! Every day I become more like you. Here and there I meet pleasant people, but in eight days I know them totally, and then that's it. . .

To Rose in The Hague   Karlsruhe, Friday, January 22, 1819
                                        12 o'clock noon. Warm, rainy weather
Dearest Rose of my Heart!

It grieved me that your eagerly anticipated stay in Brussels was so unhappily and miserably upset! *Poor* Karl![5] That is the very illness that I had when you gave birth to Louis and which kept me in bed for thirteen weeks and convalescing for a year. God preserve us! What can I say! And those are the blows of fate, whose bruises do not go away. I'm speaking of you as well. I would tell you to spare yourself, to cheer yourself up, if I did not know that it was totally useless. One doesn't do it anyway. On the con-

---

3. This could refer to Karl August, whom she met in the spring of 1808. But it sounds more like Alexander von Marwitz, whom she met on May 19, 1809. Marwitz (1787–1814) was a university friend of Karl August's and became a close frined of Rahel's. He died in the Wars of Liberation.

4. Henri de Campan (1784–1820), son of French author Madame de Campan, lady-in-waiting to Marie Antoinette. Varnhagen met him when he came to Berlin as part of the French occupation after 1806.

5. Varnhagen's sister married Karl Asser (1780–1836), who was a lawyer in Amsterdam, later in Brussels.

trary, people want to save up after they've spent a lot, and feel guilty if they so much as gasp for breath! So pass the lives of slaves to reason and guilt! I, on the other hand, eat half a chicken now every day, because nothing provides such light nourishment, and delicate, damaged organisms need this especially. Distract yourself, with your donkeys' milk, i.e., visit places where new objects, words, and people move you, refresh your blood, life, nerves, and thoughts. We women need this doubly; for men's preoccupations, in their own minds at least, are also business which they have to consider important, which flatter their ambitions; in which they see themselves making progress, in which they are already spurred on by their interaction with people: while we have only degrading piecework before us—petty expenses and arrangements which have to depend on the position of men. It's ignorance of human nature when people imagine our intellect to be different, constituted for other needs, and that we could live, for example, totally off the lives of our husbands or sons. This demand arises solely from the supposition that a woman's soul knows nothing higher than the demands and expectations of her husband, or the talents and desires of her children: then *every* marriage, in and of itself, would be the highest human condition: but this is *not* so: one loves, protects, cares for the desires of one's loved ones; accommodates oneself to them; makes them one's greatest concern and most urgent occupation: but they cannot fulfill us, restore us, refresh us for further activity and effort; or strengthen and empower us for our entire lives. This is the reason for the many frivolities which you see in women and believe to see in women: according to applauded convention they have no room for their own feet, they must put them wherever the husband just stood or wants to stand; and see with their own eyes the whole lively world, like one who has been magically turned into a tree with roots in the earth: every attempt, every desire to dissolve this unnatural condition is called frivolity, or considered punishable behavior. That's why you and I must get ourselves reinvigorated! Right after he had read me your letter, Varnhagen forgot all arrangements with various friends for the coming summer and immediately proposed visiting you—health and the weather permitting. I laid the matter before him, and he immediately agreed. But, dear Rose, I don't want to talk of a trip yet: especially since it is January and there's time until June.—

—Nor will I do anything foolish or extravagant: even with the greatest freedom: and I am a foundering slave to Reason. That's what people justifiably call what's most advantageous: except that too often people judge this from too low a perspective, and too subordinate: that's my mistake, too: and therefore I do harm to health and a better, higher life; because health only flourishes in a higher life. I have been out twice since mid-November: I had to avoid the weather: and I am only passably well: as you know: even so I have avoided really bad spells. Varnhagen has been in bed with the flu since the day before New Year's Eve: quite ill.—I also suffered: his little room was warm and small, and I had to go through the cold to get there. That took its toll on me. I, too, am ill and *imbécile* from lack of ideas and distractions. I cannot stand that; and never could!!!—But it's all right now: *par ci par là* one gets through. Because of rising blood pressure and my eyes I cannot read continually. Still, I read a lot. You see my handwriting, after a while I get pithy.—Write soon, beloved! That you heard Catalani[6] is a comfort to me! Your Schiller and Goethe also please me. Study the latter especially! Do you have his life and everything by him included?—

Adieu. Dear child! Write soon! I too get few letters from home, and so little in them as possible: my heart is badly burned on that score. Adieu, Your R.

Dore[7] sends her regards! To Mr. Asser, too, and I do too again! Greetings! He should take care of himself and spare himself for quite awhile, and drink champagne and use iron drops. That helped me.

Translated from Karl August von Varnhagen, ed., *Rahel. Ein Buch des Andenkens für ihre Freunde* (Berlin: Duncker and Humblot, 1834), vol.1, 264–67 [to Veit]; 323–26 [to Friedländer]; vol.2, 563–66 [to Rose]; and from Ludmilla Assing, ed., *Aus dem Nachlass Varnhagens von Ense. Briefe von Chamisso, Gneisenau, Haugwitz . . . et al.*, vol.1 (Leipzig: Brockhaus, 1867), 290–94 [to P. Wiesel].

6. Angelica Catalani (1780–1848), Italian soprano.
7. Dorothea Neuendorf, Varnhagen's servant.

Introduction, bibliography, and translation of letters by
MARJANNE E. GOOZÉ

Translation of poetry by
WALTER ARNDT

Karoline
von Günderrode

(1780–1806)

Karoline von Günderrode (1780–1806)
woodcut, 1880
courtesy of Bildarchiv preussischer Kulturbesitz, Berlin

Karoline von Günderrode's life and work are defined by irreconcilable conflicts: her desire to be loved and accepted conflicted with her passion for writing; her financial situation undermined her social standing; her longing for action was thwarted, as she saw it, by her femaleness. "I have no mind for feminine virtues, for feminine happiness. The wild, the great, the brilliant things are what I love. There is an ill-fated incongruity in my soul; and it will and must remain that way, for I am a woman and have desires like a man, without the strength of a man," is how she described her situation in 1801 in a letter to a friend. These conflicts were translated into her writings and account for the rebellious, explosive, even tortuous nature of her literary production.

She was born in Karlsruhe on February 11, 1780, the eldest of six children. Her father, a court adviser and writer, died in 1786. Karoline was educated at home by her mother, Louise, a learned woman who had studied Fichte's philosophy and had anonymously published short essays and poems. In May 1797, Karoline entered the *Cronstetten-Hynspergisches Damenstift* in Frankfurt am Main, a Lutheran cloister for unmarried and widowed women from certain upper-class families. In Frankfurt she pursued her private studies in history and philosophy and spent long hours reading, despite her frequent severe headaches and vision problems. She corresponded regularly with her friends, Lisette von Nees and Susanne

Heyden, two exceptionally educated women, and befriended the Brentanos—Bettina, Clemens, and Gunda—with whom her life and literary production remained intertwined until her death. Karoline met Bettina in 1801 at the home of Sophie von La Roche, the Brentanos' grandmother, who later published one of Günderrode's earliest works in her journal *Herbsttage* (1805). In 1799 Günderrode fell in love with law historian Karl von Savigny, who, afraid of the intensity and absoluteness of her feelings, limited their interaction to an intellectual friendship and married Gunda Brentano. This same scenario repeated itself with Clemens Brentano, whom she met in 1801 as well: although Clemens wrote her passionate letters and recognized her talent, he married the writer Sophie Mereau in 1803. And yet again, in August of 1804, Karoline became unhappily involved with Friedrich Creuzer, a classics professor in Heidelberg. When Creuzer finally rejected her love and returned to his wife, Karoline committed suicide (1806).[1] For years, she had carried a dagger around with her. She had always maintained that it was best to live fully and to die young. Death, it seems, provided an escape, if not a refuge, from an uncompromising life.

Life and art are intimately tied in Karoline von Günderrode's short oeuvre. The clash between desire and convention and the need to hide the true nature of her feelings in order to be accepted made her resort to gender reversals and "masks." In her letters she sometimes refers to herself as a male friend or in the third person masculine; some of her love poems are written from a "male" perspective, although they were originally addressed to a man. Her dramas, which are considered her least successful works, include scenes of violence, suicide, and exile. The exotic settings and themes emphasize the power of men to shape their fate and women's lack of power to do so. Both her poems and her dramas have one pervading theme—death. It is not seen as a negative force, but as a place of hope and union. Her early "Apocalyptic Fragment," included here, embodies this longing for death and the dark mysticism she shares with the German Romantics; it advocates unity of spirit with nature and a belief in the drive for

---

1. For a very personal account of Günderrode's friendship with Bettina von Arnim and her suicide see Bettina von Arnim's *Report on Günderode's Suicide*, reproduced on p.455 of this volume.

fulfillment, oneness, and truth inherent in all elements of the world.

Christoph von Nees published two volumes of her writings under the pseudonym "Tian" in 1804 and 1805; a third was prepared for publication, but not published during her lifetime. Although her work and exceptional promise were widely commented on at the time, Karoline von Günderrode did not enter the literary canon, not even after the publication of Bettina von Arnim's *Die Günderode* in 1840, which contained many of Günderrode's letters and poems. Until Günderrode's recent "rediscovery" by Christa Wolf, German literary historians had been more concerned with her suicide than with her literary production. A kindred spirit, the American philosopher/writer Margaret Fuller, who translated Bettina's book in 1842, was the first to recognize and praise the "wild graces of style" both of Bettina von Arnim and her friend Karoline von Günderrode.

BIBLIOGRAPHY

Günderrode's Works

Günderrode, Karoline von. *Gesammelte Werke*, 3 vols. 1920–22. Reprinted Bern: Lang, 1970.

———. *Der Schatten eines Traumes. Gedichte, Prosa, Briefe, Zeugnisse von Zeitgenossen*. Edited by Christa Wolf. Darmstadt and Neuwied: Luchterhand, 1979.

Geiger, Ludwig. *Karoline von Günderode und ihre Freunde*. Stuttgart, Leipzig: Deutsche Verlags-Anstalt, 1895. Includes works by Günderrode.

Preisendanz, Karl. *Die Liebe der Günderode. Friedrich Creuzers Briefe an Caroline von Günderode*. 1912. Reprinted by Bern: Lang, 1975.

Preitz, Max. "Karoline von Günderrode in ihrer Umwelt." *Jahrbuch des Freien Deutschen Hochstifts*, 1962, 1964, and 1975 (with Doris Hopp). Correspondences with Günderrode, excellent documentation.

Schwartz, Karl. "Karoline von Günderrode." *Allgemeine Enzyklopädie der Wissenschaften und Künste*. Edited by J. S. Ersch and J. G. Gruber. Vol.97. 1878. Reprinted Graz: Akademische Druck- und Verlagsanstalt, 1977, pp.167–231. The most complete biography of Günderrode. Contains source material and works not found elsewhere.

Secondary Literature in English

Arnim, Bettina von. *Goethe's Correspondence with a Child.* 3 vols. London/Berlin, 1839. 1:81–122. Bettina's account of her friendship with Günderrode and Günderrode's death reproduced in this volume.

Arnim, Bettine von. *Günderode.* Translated by Margaret Fuller. Boston: Peabody, 1842. Selections from Bettina's book. Includes some works by Günderrode.

Fuller, Margaret. "Bettine Brentano and Her Friend Günderode." *The Dial* 2 (January 1842): 313–57.

Wolf, Christa. *No Place on Earth.* Translated by Jan van Heurck. New York: Farrar, Straus, & Giroux, 1982. A novel presenting a fictitious encounter between Günderrode and Heinrich von Kleist.

Selected Letters

Karoline to Clemens Brentano [1803?]:

I don't know if I indeed talked the way you make my letter sound in yours, but I find it bizarre to listen to how I speak, and my own words seem almost stranger to me than a stranger's. Even the truest letters are only corpses, in my view; they depict a life that once inhabited them, and even though they look at first as if they were alive, the moment of their living is already past. That is why it seems to me (when I read something I wrote some time ago) as if I were seeing myself lying in a coffin, and my two selves were staring at each other in amazement.

My trust was certainly not a lovable child. She did not know any nice stories to tell, yet those around her were always whispering, "Be sensible, child! Don't go any farther!" Then the child grew confused and awkward. She did not quite know how to be sensible and wavered this way and that. Can you blame the poor thing? But the child is not obstinate; if she is welcomed into the house in a kind and friendly way, she will turn around and come in, rather than staying outside in the street.

Don't talk to me any more about doing "good turns." I always have to laugh at that part of your letter. I won't be able to use those words any more; besides, it always makes me think of turning somersaults. I have never really understood what you meant by it; it only seemed silly to me although I did not know why.

I know few people and maybe none very well, for I am very unskilled in observing others. So, if I understand you at one particular moment, I cannot generalize from that to all the other moments. There are probably very few people who can do so, and I am certainly not one of them. Right now I think of you—that it would be good to look at you—and pleasurable; but that one should only want to *look* at you. Is this notion true or false? Karoline

Karoline to Clemens Brentano (June 10, 1804):

Before I can answer your serious questions[2] seriously, I must beg you most urgently to remove this dreadful wig you have forced upon my head and that I really can't wear, because it would inhibit me too much. So, right at the beginning of my letter, begone with it, so that I can move freely.

How I got the idea to have my poems printed, you want to know? I have always had a secret inclination to do so—why? and what for? I rarely ask myself. I was very happy when someone was willing to represent me at the publishers. Easily, and not knowing what I did, I have destroyed the barrier that separated my innermost heart from the world; and I have not regretted it as yet, for always new and alive is my desire to express my life in a permanent form, in a shape worthy of joining the most excellent minds, greeting them and sharing their society. Yes, I have always been drawn to that community; it is the church toward which my spirit is continuously making its earthly pilgrimage.

2. Karoline is responding to Clemens Brentano's letter of June 2, 1804, in which he comments on the fact that her authorship of the poetry collection was disclosed in an article in Kotzebue's journal *Der Freimüthige*. Clemens writes that the author of that article must be a mere scribbler because he praises Karoline. "You can only be praised by someone who loves you personally and who knows your history," Clemens tells her. Furthermore, he criticizes her for "hovering between the male and the female" and for being "too learned." "It is," he writes, "as if a modern sage had found some fortunetelling doves from antiquity, had poked their eyes out and had put them in his wig, for your songs are all such profound, fortunetelling turtle-doves."

Since I want to be very honest with you today, I must tell you something more: I don't feel a genuine relationship with you yet; if there can be one— and that would please me—it must be at your initiative; however, if it can't be, it would hardly distress me. My connection to you is not friendship, not love; my feelings thus require no relationship; they resemble far more the interest one might have in a work of art; but confused, misunderstood relationships might dull this interest for me.

Don't go on to tell me that it is my nature to be reflective, or worse, that I am mistrustful; mistrust is a harpy who greedily throws herself upon the gods' feast of enthusiasm and sullies it with impure experience and vulgar cleverness, which I have always scorned to do when dealing with any person of quality.

Give my best greetings to your wife; I also look forward to seeing her and your child, who I imagine is very sweet.

You have given me much pleasure with your *Ponce de Leon.*

Karoline to Friedrich Creuzer (April 23, 1805):

Last night I had a wondrous dream that I cannot forget. I seemed to be lying in bed, a lion lay to my right, a she-wolf to my left, and a bear at my feet! All of them halfway across me and sound asleep. Then I thought, if these animals were to wake up, they would get angry at one another and tear themselves and me apart. I became terribly afraid and I drew myself quietly out from under them and escaped. The dream seems allegorical; what do you think of it? Since I realized what Susanne Heyden[3] will probably write you, my good spirit has left me; I am walking around in unfamiliar territory. Inside I am restless and everything is strange to me. Even you are strange to me, not because of my feelings, but because of the gulf I know there is between you and me and that I perceived *more clearly.* I seem to be banished from my sweet home and I am as much out of place in my own thoughts as I was last night with those wild animals that my weird dream gave me for companions.

3. Susanne Heyden, half-sister of Karoline's friend Lisette Nees von Esenbeck, served as Günderrode and Creuzer's go-between.

Karoline to Friedrich Creuzer (Nov. 18, 1805):

My whole life remains dedicated to you, beloved, sweet friend. In such surrender and in such unconditional love, I will always belong to you, live for you, and die for you. Love me always, too, beloved. Let no time, no circumstance come between us. I could not bear the loss of your love. Promise me never to leave me. Oh you, life of my life, do not forsake my soul. See, everything has become freer and purer for me since I renounced all earthly hope. The fierce pain has dissolved into sacred melancholy. Fate has been conquered. You are mine beyond all fate. It cannot tear you away from me any more, now that I have won you in this way.

Translated from L. Hirschberg, ed., *Gesammelte Werke der Karoline von Günderode,* vol.2 (Berlin-Wilmersdorf: Goldschmidt-Gabrielli, 1920–22), 257–59 [to Clemens Brentano, 1804, and Creuzer, Nov. 1805]; "Unbekannte Briefe der Karoline von Günderode an Friedrich Creuzer, mitgeteilt von Paul Pattloch," In *Hochland. Monatsschrift für alle Gebiete des Wissens, der Literatur und Kunst,* vol.53 (Oct. 1937–38): 53–54 [to Creuzer, 23 April 1805]; and Ludwig von Pigenot, ed., *Karoline von Günderode: Dichtungen* (Munich: Bruckmann, 1922), 209–10 [to Clemens Brentano, 1803].

"Two Poems"

Einstens lebt
ich süsses leben
(1804–5)

Einstens lebt ich süsses Leben,
denn mir war, als sey ich plötzlich
nur ein duftiges Gewölke.
Über mir war nichts zu schauen
als ein tiefes blaues Meer
und ich schiffte auf den Woogen
dieses Meeres leicht umher.
Lustig in des Himmels Lüften
gaukelt ich den ganzen Tag,
lagerte dann froh und gaukelnd
hin mich um den Rand der Erde,
als sie sich der Sonne Armen
dampfend und voll Gluth entriss,
sich zu baden in nächtlicher Kühle,
sich zu erlaben im Abendwind.
Da umarmte mich die Sonne,
von des Scheidens Weh ergriffen,
und die schönen hellen Strahlen
liebten all und küssten mich.
Farbige Lichter
stiegen hernieder,

Once a Dulcet Life
Was Mine
(1804–5)

Once a dulcet life was mine,
For I seemed all of a sudden
But a fragrant wisp of cloud;
Nothing to be seen above me
But a deep-blue ocean sea,
And I sailed now here, now yonder
Lightly cradled by the waves.
Gladly in the heavens' ether
Did I flit the livelong day,
Then would settle, gaily tumbling,
By the rim of Earth, recumbent,
As she, steaming, incandescent,
Having loosed the Sun's embrace,
Hies to bathe in vesper cool,
Be refreshed by evening breezes.
Then the Sun, by parting's sorrow
Seized, embraced myself instead,
And her lovely lambent rays
Laved and loved and kissed me all.
Colorful lusters
Toward me descended,

hüpfend und spielend,
wiegend auf Lüften
duftige Glieder.
Ihre Gewande
Purpur und Golden
und wie des Feuers
tiefere Gluthen.
Aber sie wurden blässer und blässer,
bleicher die Wangen,
sterbend die Augen.
Plötzlich verschwanden
mir die Gespielen,
und als ich traurend
nach ihnen blickte,
sah ich den grossen
eilenden Schatten,
der sie verfolgte,
sie zu erhaschen.
Tief noch im Westen
sah ich den goldnen
Saum der Gewänder.
Da erhub ich kleine Schwingen,
flatterte bald hie bald dort hin,
freute mich des leichten Lebens,
ruhend in dem klaren Aether.
Sah jetzt in dem heilig tiefen
unnennbaren Raum der Himmel
wunderseltsame Gebilde
und Gestalten sich bewegen.
Ewige Götter
sassen auf Thronen
glänzender Sterne,
schauten einander
seelig und lächelnd.
Tönende Schilde,
klingende Speere

Skipping and sporting,
Cradling on zephyrs
Balmy bodies;
Purple and gold
All their attire,
Like the profounder
Riches of Fire.
But they grew wan,
Paler and paler,
Sunken their cheeks,
Breaking their eyes.
And of a sudden
Vanished my playmates,
And when my eyes sought
Sadly to hold them,
I saw the hulking, hurrying shadow
Eager to snatch them,
Bent on pursuit.
Deep in the west
I still saw the flash of
Gold on their garments.
Then, lo, I spread out
Small wings of my own;
Fluttering to and fro,
I rejoiced in the aerial life,
At rest in the lucence of ether.
I saw rare and wondrous objects,
Figures also, move in space,
In the sacred, deep, unfathomed
Ranges of the firmament.
Gods immortal
Seated on thrones
Of brilliant stars
Eyeing each other,
Blissfully smiling.
Clanging shields,

huben gewaltige,
streitende Helden;
Vor ihnen flohen
gewaltige Thiere,
andre umwanden
in breiten Ringen
Erde und Himmel,
selbst sich verfolgend
ewig im Kreise.
Blühend voll Anmuth
unter den Rohen
stand eine Jungfrau,
Alle beherrschend.
Liebliche Kinder
spielten in mitten
giftiger Schlangen.—
Hin zu den Kindern
wollt ich nun flattern,
mit ihnen spielen
und auch der Jungfrau
Sohle dann küssen.
Und es hielt ein tiefes Sehnen
in mir selber mich gefangen.
Und mir war, als hab ich einstens
mich von einem süssen Leibe
los gerissen, und nun blute
erst die Wunde alter Schmerzen.
Und ich wandte mich zur Erde,
wie sie süss im trunknen Schlafe
sich im Arm des Himmels wiegte.
Leis erklungen nun die Sterne,
nicht die schöne Braut zu weken,
und des Himmels Lüfte spielten
leise um die zarte Brust.
Da ward mir, als sey ich entsprungen
dem innersten Leben der Mutter,

Ringing spears
Wielded by towering
Heroes in combat;
Powerful wild-beasts
Fleeing before them;
Others were wreathing
Earth and Heaven
With wide-flung rings,
Pursuing themselves
In eternal orbits.
Blossoming grace
Amongst those crude ones,
A maiden was poised,
All overmastering.
Lovely children
Played in the midst of
Poisonous snakes.—
Thither I meant to
Flutter my way next,
Play with the children,
Also to kiss
The maiden's feet;
But a deep-down longing held me
Prisoner within myself;
And I felt as if I had been
Wrenched from such sweet flesh at one time,
And were feeling only now
The bleeding wound of pain gone by.
And I turned my flight to where
Lay sweet Earth in blissful slumber
Cradled in the arms of Heaven;
Softly now the star-song sounded,
Lest it rouse the lovely bride,
And the ether's breezes wafted
Softly by the tender breast.
Then I felt that I was sprung

und habe getaumelt
in den Räumen des Aethers,
ein irrendes Kind.
Ich musste weinen,
rinnend in Thränen
sank ich hinab zu dem
Schoosse der Mutter.
Farbige Kelche
duftender Blumen
fassten die Thränen
und ich durchdrang sie,
alle die Kelche,
rieselte Abwärts
hin durch die Blumen,
tiefer und tiefer,
bis zu dem Schoosse
hin, der verhüllten
Quelle des Lebens.

From L. Hirschberg, ed., *Gesammelte Werke der Karoline von Günderode,* vol.3 (Berlin-Wilmersdorf: Goldschmidt-Grabrielli, 1920–22), 11–15.

From the Mother's inmost life,
And I staggered about
The spaces of ether,
An erring child.
I had to weep;
Streaming with tears I sank
Down to the Mother's lap.
Colorful cups
Of fragrant flowers
Caught up the tears,
And I passed through them,
All those calyxes,
Trickled downward
On through the flowers,
Deeper and deeper
Down to the womb,
To the shrouded
Wellspring of life.

Die eine Klage
(1804–5)

Wer die tiefste aller Wunden
Hat in Geist und Sinn empfunden
Bittrer Trennung Schmerz;
Wer geliebt was er verlohren,
Lassen muss was er erkohren,
Das geliebte Herz,

Der versteht in Lust die Thränen
Und der Liebe ewig Sehnen
Eins in Zwei zu sein,
Eins im Andern sich zu finden,
Dass der Zweiheit Gränzen schwinden
Und des Daseins Pein.

Wer so ganz in Herz und Sinnen
Konnt' ein Wesen liebgewinnen
O! den tröstet's nicht
Dass für Freuden, die verlohren,
Neue werden neu gebohren:
Jene sind's doch nicht.

The Prime Lament
(1804–5)

Whom in soul and mind oppresses
The profoundest of distresses,
Parting's bitter smart,
Who had cherished what was taken,
By his dearest was forsaken:
The beloved heart,

Tastes within delight the burning
Tears, and love's perennial yearning
To be one in twain,
Find in one the other ever,
Thus the bounds of self to sever
And all being's pain.

Who with all her heart and nature
Came to love a human creature
Ah! is not consoled
By the thought that joys departed
Usher in some newly started—
They can't match the old.

Das geliebte, süsse Leben,
dieses Nehmen und dies Geben,
Wort und Sinn und Blick,
Dieses Suchen und dies Finden,
Dieses Denken und Empfinden
Giebt kein Gott zurück.

From *Gesammelte Werke,* vol.2:14.

That sweet state of living, learning
Both accepting and returning
Words and looks and airs,
Eager search and joyous ending,
Sentiment and apprehending,
Not a god repairs.

Apocalyptical
Fragment
(1806?)

1. I stood on a high rock in the Mediterranean Sea; before me, the East; behind me, the West; and the wind lay still upon the sea.

2. The Sun sank; scarcely was it hid from sight, [then] the dawn of morning began to rise. Morning, noon, evening, and night chased one another in giddy haste across the dome of heaven.

3. Astonished, I saw them circle round; my blood, my thoughts, moved not more swiftly. Time, while it without me conformed to new laws, went on within me at its wonted pace.

4. I would have rushed into the morning-red, or have bathed myself in the shadows of night, hastily, with her, flowing on, away from this slow life; but sunk in contemplation, I grew weary and fell asleep.

5. Then I saw before me a sea, girt in by no shore, neither to the East, the South, the West, nor to the North. No breeze swelled the waves, but from its depths was moved, as if excited by inward fermentation, the immeasurable sea.

6. And many forms rose from the depths of the sea, and mists arose and were lost in the clouds, and again, in sudden lightnings, saluted the parent waves.[4]

---

4. I would like to suggest another reading of the German here which would do more justice to the erotic-maternal overtones of the original (Fuller translates the *Schoss des tiefen*

7. And always more manifold arose these forms from the deep. I was seized with giddiness and dread; my thoughts were driven hither and thither, like a torch by the stormwind, till my memory was extinguished.

8. As I again awoke, and began to know of myself, then I could not tell whether I had slept ages or minutes; for, in the dull, confused dream, there had been nothing to remind me of time.

9. It was dark within me, as if I had rested in the bosom of the sea,[5] and risen from it like the other forms; to myself I seemed a drop of dew; I moved merrily to and fro in the air, and rejoiced, and my life was that the sun mirrored himself in me, and the stars looked upon me.

10. I let myself be borne upon the breezes, I joined myself with the evening-red, to the ocean-colored drops; I ranged myself with my playfellows round the moon, when she would hide herself, and accompanied her path.

11. My past was entirely past; I belonged to the present solely; a longing was in me, which knew not its aim. I sought ever, and what I found was not what I sought; and with still more ardent longing was I drawn forth into the Infinite.

12. Once was I aware that all the forms, which had ascended from the sea, returned to it and were again produced[6] in changing forms. This apparition surprised me, for I had known of no end. But now, I thought, my desire is also to return to the source of life.

13. And, as I thought of this, and felt more life than in all my past conscious being, was suddenly my mind embraced as by overwhelming mists; but they vanished soon. I seemed no more myself; my limits I could no longer find; my consciousness I had transcended; it was greater, different, and yet I felt myself in it.

14. I was released from the narrow limits of being, and no single drop more; I was restored to the all, and the all belonged to me. I thought and felt, flowed as waves in the sea, shone in the sun, circled with the stars; I felt myself in all, and enjoyed all in myself.

Meeres—Schoss meaning both lap and womb—either with "depths" or with "bosom"): "And myriad forms rose up from the sea's deep womb, and mists rose up and sank into clouds in pulsating bolts that touched the birthing waves."

5. Alternative reading: "womb of the sea."

6. Alternative reading: "again conceived."

15. Therefore, who has ears to hear, let him hear. It is not two, nor three, nor a thousand, but one and all; it is not body and spirit separately, one belonging to time, the other to eternity, but one, belongs to itself, and is, at once, time and eternity, visible and invisible, constant in change, an infinite life.

From *Günderode. Correspondence of Fräulein Günderode and Bettine von Arnim,* trans. Margaret Fuller (Boston: Burnham, 1861), 12–13.

Introduction, translation of *The Queen's Son,*
and corrections and amendments to Bettina von Arnim's(?)
Translation of *The Report on Günderode's Suicide* by
JEANNINE BLACKWELL

Bibliography by
EDITH WALDSTEIN

Bettina von Arnim

(1785–1859)

Bettina von Arnim (1785–1859)
medallion picture by Achim Bärwald, courtesy of
Bildarchiv preussischer Kulturbesitz, Berlin

Elisabeth Catharina "Bettina" von Arnim née Brentano assumed an array of public and private masks that attest to the versatility of her character and literary production: the *enfant terrible,* the *Wunderkind,* the *salonnière,* the social activist, and the subordinate admirer of Goethe and the Prussian King. Although none of these masks represent the "true" Bettina, literary and cultural historians have always attempted to characterize her by one or the other exclusively.

The seventh child of Maximiliane (von La Roche) Brentano (who died in 1793) and the Frankfurt merchant Peter Anton Brentano (who died in 1797), Arnim began writing early, tutored by her grandmother, the author Sophie von La Roche. As a young woman, Arnim developed close friendships with members of her older brother Clemens's Romantic circle, particularly with Achim von Arnim, who was to be her husband; with Karl von Savigny, her future brother-in-law and later Prussian Minister of Justice; with the poet Karoline von Günderrode, and with Johann Wolfgang von Goethe, the grand old man of German letters. Arnim recreated three of these friendships by casting their correspondence and private writings posthumously into the form of epistolary and lyric memoirs.

Bettina and Achim were secretly married in 1811 and had seven children. Her literary career did not start until the death of her husband in 1831. In short order she produced the works for which she has become famous in German literary history: *Goethe's Correspondence with a Child* (1835), a compilation of erotic letters by the seventeen-year-old Bettina to the admired poet; *Günderode* (1840), a recreation, in letters and poems, of Bettina's effusive friendship with Karoline von Günderrode until Karoline's suicide in 1806;[1] and *Clemens Brentano's Wreath of Spring* (1844), a collection of her deceased brother's early poetry. Recent reappraisal of Bettina's works has brought to light her political writings, which reflect and accompany her activism in the 1840s and '50s: *This Book Belongs to the King* (1843), a plea for social reform; *The Book of the Poor* (1844), her unfinished collection of case studies of the impoverished lower classes in the Prussian province of Silesia; *Ilius Pamphilius and Ambrosia* (1848), a political pamphlet in epistolary form; and her *Letter to the Dissolved Prussian National Assembly, Voices from Paris* (1848). Bettina took an active part in relief work during the cholera epidemic of 1831; she wrote publicly for the emancipation of the Jews, and in support of Polish freedom fighters and Silesian weavers. After the revolt of the Silesian weavers, for which she was held partially responsible, publication of her work was temporarily stopped and she was arrested. Yet Bettina would not be silenced. Even after the failure of the German Revolution in 1848, she continued to lobby for reform in a second book addressed to the Prussian king, *Conversations with Daemons* (1852). As a sympathizer with the Revolution, she worked toward the release of imprisoned radicals and dropped the aristocratic "von" from her own name.

In the midst of this political-literary activity, she also held a renowned salon, as did her erstwhile friends Rahel Varnhagen and Henriette Herz, to mediate between various factions of politically involved Romantics. She befriended the brothers Grimm, who dedicated their fairy-tale collection to her; Heinrich Heine; and Karl and Jenny Marx.

Although her children followed the more nationalist conservative bent of their father, Bettina herself remained a recognized liberal and political activist until her death in 1859.

Only a few of Bettina's fairy tales were published during her lifetime, and these were largely ignored by the critics. "The Queen's Son," meant to

---

1. Although Bettina entitled her work *Günderode*, with one "r," the official spelling of Karoline's name is Günderrode.

be included in Achim von Arnim's journal *Der Einsiedler* [The Hermit] in 1808, was not published until 1913 under the misleading title "Der Königssohn." This *Kunstmärchen* [literary fairy tale], written before the brothers Grimm published their collection of *Kinder- und Hausmärchen* in 1812–15, constitutes Bettina's attempt to recapture, through repetition of key words and shifts in rhythm and tense, the oral quality of the folktale. If read symbolically, it provides both a commentary on the divisions within contemporary society and a model for the reconciliation between "man" and nature, male and female, the powerful and the powerless.

Bettina's poignant and painful personal account of the suicide of her friend Karoline von Günderrode (probably written in 1808 and incorporated into her 1840 work) was almost simultaneous with her fairy tale. It is doubly touching because of the leitmotiv of Günderrode's tale—which had become "too sad to finish." It is as if Bettina's work of grief demanded telling the tale to its end.

BIBLIOGRAPHY

Von Arnim's Works

Arnim, Bettina von. *Werke und Briefe*. Edited by Gustav Konrad. Vols.i-iv. Frechen: Bartmann Verlag, 1958–63. *Briefe*, edited by Johannes Müller, Vol.v. Frechen: Bartmann Verlag, 1961.

———. *Sämtliche Werke*. Edited by Waldemar Oehlke. 7 vols. Berlin: Propyläen-Verlag, 1920–22.

———. *Werke*. Edited by Heinz Härtl. Vol.i: *Goethes Briefwechsel mit einem Kinde*. Berlin and Weimar: Aufbau Verlag, 1986. Vol.ii: *Die Günderode. Clemens Brentanos Frühlingskranz*, 1989. Three further volumes are forthcoming.

———. *Werke und Briefe*. Vol.i: *Clemens Brentanos Frühlingskranz. Die Günderode*. Edited by Walter Schmitz and Sibylle von Steinsdorf. Frankfurt: Deutscher Klassiker Verlag, 1986. Vol.ii: *Goethes Briefwechsel mit einem Kinde*. Edited by Sibylle von Steinsdorff, 1988. Two further volumes are forthcoming.

———. *Bettina von Arnims Armenbuch*. Edited by Werner Vordtriede. Frankfurt am Main: Insel, 1969.

———. *Die Günderode: Briefroman*. With an afterword by Christa Wolf. Frankfurt am Main: Insel, 1981.

————. *Achim und Bettina in ihren Briefen: Briefwechsel Achim von Arnim und Bettina Brentano.* Edited by Werner Vordtriede. With an introduction by Rudolf Alexander Schröder. 2 vols. Frankfurt am Main: Suhrkamp, 1961.

————. "Bettina von Arnim und ihr Briefwechsel mit Pauline Steinhäuser." Edited by Karl Obser. *Neue Heidelberger Jahrbücher* 12 (1903): 85–137.

————. *Bettina von Arnim und Rudolf Baier: Unveröffentlichte Briefe und Tagebuchaufzeichnungen.* Edited by K. Gassen. Greifswald: Universitätsverlag Ratsbuchhandlung L. Bamberg, 1937.

————. "Bettina von Arnims Briefe an Julius Döring." Edited by Werner Vordtriede. *Jahrbuch des Freien Deutschen Hochstifts* (1963): 341–488.

————. *Bettine von Arnim und Friedrich Wilhelm IV.: Ungedruckte Briefe und Aktenstücke.* Edited by Ludwig Geiger. Frankfurt am Main: Rütten und Loening, 1902.

————. *Bettinas Leben und Briefwechsel mit Goethe.* Edited by Fritz Bergemann. Leipzig: Insel Verlag, 1927.

————. *Bettina von Arnim. Die Sehnsucht hat allemal Recht: Gedichte, Prosa, Briefe.* Edited by Gerhard Wolf. Berlin: Buchverlag Der Morgen, 1984.

————. *Der Briefwechsel Bettine von Arnims mit den Brüdern Grimm.* Edited by Hartwig Schulz. Frankfurt am Main: Insel, 1985.

Arnim, Bettina, and Gisela von Arnim. *Das Leben der Hochgräfin Gritta von Rattenzuhausbeiuns: Ein Märchenroman.* Edited by Shawn Jarvis, Frankfurt: Fischer, 1986.

Betz, Otto, and Veronika Straub, editors. *Bettine und Arnim: Briefe der Freundschaft und Liebe.* 2 vols. Frankfurt: Verlag Josef Knecht, 1986, 1987.

Conrad, Heinrich, editor. *Frauenbriefe von und an Hermann Fürsten Pückler-Muskau.* München: Georg Müller, 1912.

Varnhagen von Ense, K. A. *Aus dem Nachlass Varnhagen's von Ense: Briefe von Stägemann, Metternich, Heine und Bettina von Arnim nebst Briefen, Anmerkungen und Notizen von Varnhagen von Ense.* Leipzig: F. A. Brockhaus, 1865. Conrad and Varnhagen contain important pieces by Bettina von Arnim not found in the Collected Works edited by Konrad Müller.

Herzhaft in die Dornen greifen. Bettina von Arnim: 1785–1859. Frankfurt: Freies Deutsches Hochstift, 1985. Catalog of an exhibit commemorating Bettina's two-hundredth birthday.

In English Translation

Arnim, Bettina von. *Günderode. A Translation from the German by Margaret Fuller.* Boston: Elizabeth Palmer Peabody, 1842.

Arnim, Bettina von. *Goethe's Correspondence with a Child.* 3 vols. London: Longman, Orme, Brown, Green, and Longmans, 1839. Anonymous translation, presumably by Bettina von Arnim herself.

Arnim, Bettina von. *Goethe's Correspondence with a Child.* Translation, Anonymous, part of the translation by Bettina von Arnim. Lowell: D. Bixby, 1841.

Secondary Literature in English

Blackwell, Jeannine. "Fractured Fairy Tales: German Women Authors and the Grimm Tradition." *Germanic Review* 62 (Fall 1987): 162–74.

Collins, Hildegard Platzer, and Philip Allison Shelley. "The Reception in England and America of Bettina von Arnim's 'Goethe's Correspondence with a Child.'" *Anglo-German and American-German Crosscurrents.* Edited by Philip Allison Shelley with Arthur O. Lewis, Jr. Vol.II. Chapel Hill: Univ. of North Carolina Press, 1962, pp.97–174.

Drewitz, Ingeborg. "Bettina von Arnim: A Portrait." *New German Critique* 27 (Fall 1982): 115–22.

Fuller, Margaret. "Bettine Brentano and Her Friend Günderode." *Dial* 2 (1842): 313–57.

Helps, Arthur, and Elizabeth Jane Howard. *Bettina: A Portrait.* London: Chatto and Windus, 1957.

Hertz, Deborah. *Jewish High Society in Old Regime Berlin.* New Haven and London: Yale Univ. Press, 1988.

Jarvis, Shawn. "Spare the Rod and Spoil the Child? Bettine's 'Das Leben der Hochgräfin Gritta.'" *Women in German Yearbook* 3 (1986): 77–89.

Pross, Helge. "A Romantic Socialist in Prussia." *German Quarterly* 27 (1954): 91–103.

Waldstein, Edith. "Romantic Revolution and Female Collectivity: Bettine and Gisela von Arnim's 'Gritta.'" *Women in German Yearbook* 3 (1986): 91–99.

Waldstein, Edith. *Bettine von Arnim and the Politics of Romantic Conversation.* Studies in German Literature, Linguistics, and Culture. Vol.33. Columbia, S.C.: Camden House, 1988.

The Queen's Son

(1808)

Once upon a time there was a King who had a magnificent land, and from his castle on a high mountain he could see far into the distance. Behind the castle, beautiful gardens had been laid out for his pleasure; they were surrounded by splendid rivers and dense forests full of game. Lions, tigers had their dwelling there, wild cats crouched in the trees, foxes and wolves roamed in the thicket, white bears and also ones with golden fur often swam across the rivers in pairs and came into the king's garden. In the treetops nested the eagle, vulture, and falcon. The forests were a true kingdom of animals which put borders around that of the King, and it was seen as theirs alone.

But then the King took a wife for her beauty and to have children. When she was with child, the common folk rejoiced that they would have an heir to the throne and held the woman in high esteem for it. But the time for the birth passed without her bearing a child. This made the King very sad for he believed that his consort was ill and would soon die, yet she kept on taking food and drink like a healthy woman. But she stayed with child for seven years. The King grew angry at her deformity, and thought that she had sinned against God, since He was punishing her so. He had her rooms separated from his own, and she was forced to live in the rear part of the castle. There she carried her heavy burden slowly and sadly through the lonely gardens and saw the wild animals coming out of the forest to drink on the far bank of the river. When springtime came and the old lions and tigers came with their young and nursed them, she often would wish in deep despair that she, too, was a beast of prey in the forest, wresting her food from life in a raging fight, just to feed her young. "But like this," she said, "I must wander here through the garden with heavy pace and heavy care. Every year I see you bearing your fruit, and I see how you raise your young ones in your wild, rough way. But I, the Prince's daughter, the Queen, shall never raise my own noble progeny, and will be unhappy and hated by the King, my husband."

Then, one day, as she sat in a lonely spot under a palm tree, she felt pains, and she bore a son. He seemed to have the strength of a seven-year-old boy, for as he came into the world, a wild she-bear had ventured across the river, and he was barely out of the womb before he chased after her, catching her by the pelt; the bear swam back across and carried him off with her into the forest. Then the Queen cried out in a powerful mother's voice: "My son, my only born, is in the forest and will be devoured by the wild animals!" The King's guards came running and charged into the river toward the forests with bludgeons, bows, and arrows, to recapture the son of their lord. But when the animals saw these violent people invading their kingdom, they rushed from the forests onto the shore to defend themselves. The bears sat up erect and stretched out their claws, the lions bared their teeth and twitched their tails, the tigers roamed back and forth on the shore with fiery eyes, the wolves howled, the elephants stirred up dirt and pushed boulders into the water, the birds flew from their nests and made the air heavy with horrible shrieks so that none of the brave knights dared to climb up the bank. Thus they swam back to the deserted Queen, for they believed that the King's son was indeed lost. But when they came to her, they found that she was again in labor bringing six more children into the world, each of them happier and stronger than the last. So there was little grief for the lost son. She was brought before the King with the six babes as a glorious mother, and he received her with honors and jubilation.

The children grew, the Queen cared for them with great patience and gave them nourishment, but when evening came and she had put them to sleep, she would go behind the castle to the spot where she had sat and the she-bear had taken her child. She would go down to the water to try to lure her son out of the undergrowth. Deep in her heart she worried very little about her other children, only about this one, and she could not convince herself that he was dead; she was like a shepherd who cares more about the one lost lamb than about the whole flock and believes this lamb to be the best and only one. She is no longer afraid of the wild animals whenever she hears them howling in the night, and whenever one animal wanders into the garden, she runs up to it and asks about her child, but they don't understand her. Then she becomes impatient and desperate, she threatens and pleads and grabs the bears by the fur and says, "You have stolen my son from me!" They seem to care nothing about it, though, and act like animals do; they recognize the woman and do her no harm.

When she returns to the castle, she wipes away her tears and bends her face over the restless children, thus hiding her tears, and says, "My poor children are restless and cold, I must warm them and feed them so they will quiet down." Thus she hides her sadness from people the whole day long and never turns her face to the sunlight, for she is ashamed that she feels more love for her lost son than for the others. She raises them, to be sure, with great patience and wisdom during the day. But in the evening, when the children are asleep, she searches after her son. She tells the great hawks that glide high up in the sky, flying back and forth, to take her boy some food. She says, again and again, "Oh, you winged creatures, if only I could float in the air and look down into the thickets to seek my son. Oh tell me please if he is still alive or if you have seen him dead?" When the birds scream incomprehensibly in the air, she thinks she can understand them, and pushes back her hair, the better to hear. She would think the birds were calling to her that he was alive and would come to her soon. She tries hard to interpret their cries; she even speaks to the bees and the buzzing insects that hover over the water, they swarm around her, humming and buzzing, each in its own way, and then they fly away again—Oh, poor Queen, not even one wild, ignorant animal will give you counsel, they know nothing of human lament! For humans persecute them and have no communion with them at all, humans stalk after them to get their skins or to eat their flesh, but never did a human turn to them in sorrow, asking for consolation. Many a noble beast has grieved for the freedom which cunning humans have robbed from it; they grieved that they must serve as slaves, which was not their task, and which went against their very nature, and they have gotten only dry hay to eat for their pains, when they could have eaten fresh, tender leaves in the forest. And they grieved that they had to be bridled and be ruled by the whip. So animals do not trust humans, and avoid their path. And when they are cornered and helpless, they attack people and tear their bodies horribly, just to protect their freedom or their young.

Meanwhile, the children were growing up and were raised in wisdom; they were peaceable in spirit and noble in every respect. The King could not decide on which to bestow the crown, for it could not be said which was the firstborn or which would be better at ruling. When they competed in a game for a prize, it often happened that they all won the same prize or that they all excelled in their own special way. The King could not love one of them more than the others, for each was handsome and their demeanor was like the iridescent feathers of an alluring bird in the sunshine; if it turns this way, then the red or green shimmers most splendidly; if it turns that way, then another color shines forth or yet another, or if it struts and moves its wings, the colors change as fast as lightning, one as beautiful as the next; one cannot decide which is the most breathtaking of all. Or they were like a rainbow, where all the colors are beautifully combined, spanning over the distant sky, so that each seems to grow out of the other. But the King did not have the right to divide his land or to give it more than one ruler. So he had a large crown made from pure gold which would encompass the heads of his six children and he said to them: "As long as your hearts stay as pure as this gold and you hold together as one, so that all your heads are encompassed in this ring, and you embrace each other in love, I will be able to say: my land has only one lord and although it has many bodies, it has only one spirit."

Then he had a great feast prepared, at which the people could see the new kings. All the nobles gathered at court; out in the open air there was a great throne of gold where the King's sons sat, and the King placed the crown on their heads. The quiet, lonely mother was dressed in jeweled splendor, with golden veils and cloaks, and there was jubilation at her appearance. People call her the glorious mother and play splendid music on all the instruments to honor her. But she hides her face behind the veil and weeps bitter tears for her lost child. Then her sons step down from their

453

seats, fall to their knees, and ask for their mother's blessing. She stands up and, with her right hand, blesses her children, but she holds her left over her heart in memory of her son.

The wild animals had heard the celebrating throughout the land and had grown restless; they swam across the rivers in great hordes. When the guards brought this horrible news, all the people fled to their homes, but the mother would not leave, for she had no fear. Her sons did not want to desert their mother when she did not heed their pleas, and stayed to protect her. The horde of animals came onward and among them appeared a beautiful face that looked upward toward the sky, and seemed to be a human, only more beautiful and noble. He rides on the backs of the lions and tigers, jumping gracefully from one to the other. When his mother sees him, she says, "This is my son," and goes bravely to meet him; she embraces him and feels a stone move from her heart. The animals recognize the woman and do her no harm. But the boy had no human language, he could only express his will through signs. Therefore he takes the crown and turns it seven times around his head; and with a strong hand, he tore an olive tree out of the earth, and gave each of his six brothers a branch, while keeping the stem for himself, to mean, "I am the master! But you shall all live with me in peace." And he became King of the animals and of humankind in spirit, without language.

Translated from "Der Königssohn," in *Westermanns Monatshefte,* vol.113 (1913): 554–58.

Report on Günderode's Suicide[2]

(1808/1839)

"[...]It is quite impossible for me to write of Günderode on the Rhine: it is not that I am so sensitive, but I am on a spot not far enough removed from the occurrence for me perfectly to review it. Yesterday I went down yonder where she had lain; the willows are so grown that the spot is quite covered; and when I thought how she had run here, full of despair, and so quickly plunged the violent knife into her breast, and how long this idea had burned in her mind, and that I, so near a friend, now wandered in the same place, along the same shore, in sweet meditation on my happiness—all, even the slightest circumstance seeming to me to belong to the riches of my bliss—I do not feel equal at such a time to arrange it all, and pursue the simple thread of our friendship's life from which I might yet spin the

2. Bettina von Arnim's *Report on Günderode's Suicide* (as it is entitled, for example, in Elizabeth Bronfen's edition of *Die Günderode*. Munich: Matthes & Seitz, 1982, p. 372) is in fact an excerpt from a letter to Goethe's mother, supposedly written sometime in October 1808, which Bettina von Arnim included in volume 1 of her letter-collage *Goethe's Correspondence with a Child*. The following translation (London, 1839), printed by the Berlin publisher Trowitzsch & Sons, was presumably made by Bettina von Arnim herself. It is reproduced here unchanged; we adjusted the spelling to American usage and corrected only typographical errors or obvious mistakes that may have been due to Bettina's faulty English or editorial oversight. The punctuation was left basically intact, except in places where it made no sense.

whole—No! It distresses me and I reproach her, as I used to do in my dreams, that she has left this beautiful earth: she had yet to learn that Nature is possessed of spirit and soul, holds communion with man and cares for him and his destiny—that "promises of life" float around us in the air—yes! she used me ill! she fled from me in the moment when I would have imparted to her every enjoyment.—She was so timid; a young Canoness who feared to say grace aloud: she often told me that she trembled when her turn came to pronounce the *benedicite* in front of the other canonesses. Our communion was sweet—it was the epoch in which I first became conscious of myself.

She first sought me out in Offenbach; she took me by the hand and begged me to visit her in the town; afterwards we visited every day; with her I learned to read my first books with understanding; she wanted to teach me history, but soon saw that I was too busy with the *present,* to be held long by the *past.* How delighted I was to visit her! I could not miss her for a single day, but ran to her every afternoon: when I came to the cloister-gate, I peeped through the keyhole toward her door till I was let in.—Her little apartment was on the ground floor, looking into the garden: before the window grew a silver poplar, which I climbed to read aloud. At each chapter, I clambered one bough higher and thus read down to her—she stood at the window and listened, speaking to me above; every now and then she would say: "Bettine, don't fall." Only now do I realize how happy I then was; for all—even the most trifling thing—is impressed on my mind as the remembrance of enjoyment.

She was as soft and delicate in all her features as a blond. She had brown hair but blue eyes that were shaded by long lashes: when she laughed it was not loud, it was rather a soft, subdued *cooing,* in which joy and cheerfulness distinctly spoke: she did not walk, she *moved,* if one can understand what I mean by that; her dress was a robe which encompassed her with caressing folds; this was owing to the gentleness of her movements. She was tall of stature—her figure was too flowing for the word slender to express; she was timid-friendly and much too yielding to make herself prominent in society. She once dined with all the canonesses at the Archbishop's table; she wore the black dress of the order, with long train, white collar, and cross; someone remarked that she looked amidst the others like a phantom—a spirit about to melt into the air.

She read her poems to me and was as well pleased with my applause as if I had been the great Public; and indeed I was full of lively eagerness to hear them: not that I seized upon the meaning of what I heard; on the contrary, it was to me an "element unknown" and the smooth verses affected me like the harmony of a strange language which flatters the ear although one cannot translate it. We read *Werther*[3] together and conversed much upon suicide. She said, "To learn much, to comprehend much, and then die young! I would not like to live, after youth had left me." We read what the Greeks said of Phidias's Jupiter Olympus, namely that a mortal who left the earth without seeing him had been cheated of what was most splendid. Günderode said: "We must see the Olympian; we will not belong to the unblessed who thus leave the earth." We laid the plan of a journey, devised our route and adventures, wrote everything down, pictured all before us—our Fancy was so busy that Reality could hardly have afforded us a better experience. We often read in this fictitious journal and delighted in the sweetest adventures, which we had there met with: invention thus became as it were a *remembrance,* whose relations still continued their connections with the *present.* Of that which happened in the real world we communicated to each other—nothing: the kingdom in which we met, sunk down like a cloud, parting to receive us to a secret Paradise—there all was new—surprising; but congenial to spirit and heart; and thus the days went by. She wished to teach me Philosophy; what she imparted to me, she expected me to comprehend and reproduce in my own words in writing. The essays which I wrote on these subjects she read with wonder: they did not contain the most distant idea of what she had communicated; but I maintained that I had understood it so. She called these themes revelations, enhanced by the sweetest colorings of an ecstatic imagination; she collected them carefully and once wrote to me: "Thou dost not yet understand how deep these openings lead into the mine of the mind; but the time will come when it will be important to thee; for man often goes through desert paths—the greater his inclination to penetrate, the more dreadful is the loneliness of his way, the more endless the wilderness. But when thou becomest aware how deep thou hast descended into the spring of thought

3. Johann Wolfgang von Goethe's popular novel about unrequited love which ends in the suicide of the protagonist, *The Sorrows of Young Werther* (1774).

and how there below, thou findest a new dawn, risest with joy again to the surface, and speakest of thy deep-hid world—then will it be thy consolation; for thou and the world can never be united; thou wilt have no other outlet, except back through this spring, into the magic garden of thy fancy—but it is no fancy, it is Truth which is merely reflected from it. Genius makes use of Fancy to impart or instill the Divine, which the mind of man could not embrace under its ideal form; yes! Thou wilt have no other way of enjoyment in thy life than that which children promise themselves from magic caverns and deep fountains, through which one comes to blooming gardens, wonderful fruits, and crystal palaces, where yet-unimagined music sounds, and the sun builds bridges with his rays, upon which one may walk with a firm foot straight into its heart. All this in these pages of thine will form a key, with which thou mayst perhaps unlock deep-hid kingdoms; therefore, lose nothing nor contend against that desire which prompts thee to write, but learn to labor in thought, without which Genius can never be born in the spirit: when it becomes incarnate in thee, then wilt thou rejoice in inspiration, as the dancer rejoices in music."

With such wonderful lessons did Günderode nourish the infancy of my mind. I was then on a month's visit to my grandmother at Offenbach, to enjoy the country air on account of the fragile state of my health: how then must such letters have affected me? Did I understand their contents? Had I an idea of what I myself had written? No! I knew as little how to interpret the text of my written inspirations as the composer knows how to trace the text of his improvisations to its source: he throws himself into a finer element than himself; it bears him, it nourishes him, his food becomes Inspiration; this incites and charms without empowering him to give it a palpable construction, although it raises the faculties, purifies the mind and touches the soul. Thus was it between me and my friend: melodies streamed upon my heightened fancy; she listened and felt an endless pleasure in them, perceiving all that which would have only disturbed me, had I retained them. She often called me a Sybil who dare not preserve her own predictions; her summons charmed me, although I felt a sort of fear; my spirit was bold and my heart timid; yes, there was indeed a struggle within me—I wanted to write, I looked into unfathomable darkness; I was obliged to exclude the external light; I liked best when I had shaded the window, and yet saw through the curtain that the sun was shining outside:

a nosegay whose colors stole through the half-light could fix me and set me free from inward anxiety, so that I forgot myself while I gazed on the shadowy gleaming of the flowers, and scent, color, and form made a beautiful whole; here I learned truths, from which I went forth into dreaming, and which suddenly set my spirit free, so that with quiet composure, I could comprehend and impart my forebodings—while I saw the flowers illumined only through a crevice in the shutter, I discerned the beauty of color, and the excellence of beauty; color itself became a spirit, which addressed me like the scent and form of the flowers.—The first thing which I thus learned was that everything in Nature's images is of divine origin—that the divine spirit is beauty, nursed in the lap of Nature—that beauty is greater than man, but that knowledge alone is the beauty of man's free mind, which is above all corporeal beauty.—Oh! I only need "to dive into the fountain," and I could perhaps again tell all which I learned by my communion with the color, form, and scent of that nosegay. I could relate still more, which would sound wonderful and peculiar enough; but I should fear it would not be believed, or be considered as raving and folly—but why should I conceal it here? Whoever reads this will realize that he has often noticed the wonderful phenomena of light; as they form new images through color and accidental or special media. Thus was it then with my soul, and thus it is even now. The great and piercing eye of the spirit was arrested by an internal ray of light; it must perforce drink it in without being able to free itself by self-willed reflection: my friend knows well what enchantment is caused by this spellbound gaze on a ray of light—the spirit of color—and he knows as well that the semblance is not semblance, but *truth itself.*

As soon as I came forth from this internal contemplation, I was dazzled; I saw dreams, I pursued their forms; this made no difference in the common intercourse of life, for herein I fitted without impediment, because I never really moved in it; but I say, without fear, to my Lord, whose blessing I now beg upon his child: I had an inward world and secret powers, and senses by which I lived in it; my eye saw clearly great visions, as soon as it was shut; I saw the heavenly globe; it revolved before me in immeasurable greatness, so that I could not see the great whole, although I had an idea of its rotundity; the starry host passed on a dark ground before me; the stars were dancing in pure spiritual figures, which I grasped as spirit; monuments formed themselves of columns and shapes, behind which stars passed away, others dipping into a sea of colors; blooming flowers came forth and grew up on high; distant golden shadows covered them from a still higher white light, and thus vision followed vision in this inward world. At the same time my ears perceived a fine silver ringing; by degrees it became a sound, which grew louder and more powerful the longer I listened; I rejoiced, for it strengthened me and gave strength to my spirit, to harbor this mighty sound within my ear. If I opened my eyes, all was gone! all was still! and I perceived no interruption, only I could no longer distinguish this so-called real world (in which other men maintain that they exist) from this world of dream or fancy; I knew not which was sleeping and which waking; nay, I at last believed that I only dreamed the common life, and I must to this day leave it undecided, and shall be in doubt for years to come. I was so certain of being able to float and fly, I was inwardly proud of it and rejoiced in the consciousness; a single elastic pressure on the tip of the foot—and I was in the air; I floated slowly and gracefully two or three feet along the earth, but soon touched it again, and again flew off—and floated to the side, and thence back again; thus, to my unspeakable pleasure, I danced to and fro in the garden by moonlight; I floated over the stairs up and down; sometimes I raised myself to the height of the lower boughs, and chirped among the branches: in the morning I awoke with the full persuasion that I could fly, but during the day forgot it.—I wrote to Günderode, I know not what—she came out to me at Offenbach, looked at me anxiously, and made perplexing inquiries after my health; I looked in the glass: my eyes were become darker than before; my features were incomparably finer, the nose so small and thin, the mouth so full and the complexion quite pale: I rejoiced, and saw my figure with delight; Günderode said I should no longer remain so alone, and took me with her to town. A few days passed and I was attacked by fever; I laid myself to bed and slept, and know nothing more but that I slept. At length I woke; it was the fourteenth day since I had first slept: when I opened my eyes, I saw her faltering figure, moving to and fro, wringing her hands. "But Günderode," said I, "why are you crying?" "Be God forever praised!" cried she, coming to my bedside, "Art thou at length awake? Art thou again restored to consciousness?" From this time forth, she would not let me read any Philosophy, nor write any more essays; she firmly believed these to be the source of my illness. I was well pleased with my figure; the paleness which remained after the fever delighted me beyond measure; my features appeared to me very expressive; the eyes which were become larger prevailed, while the other parts of the face retained an ethereal pallor: I asked Günderode whether she did not see therein the first traces of transfiguration.

Here I have broken off, and have not written for many days; anguish rose before me with such earnestness and weight that it would not give way to thought; I am still young, I cannot accomplish the monstrous task.

Meantime they have here been making harvest-home; vinedressers crowned with leaves brought the grape must down from the hills amidst shout and song, preceded by pipes to which they danced. Oh thou! who reads this, thou hast no robe so soft that it may enwrap the wounded soul! What dost thou not owe me, that I make the sacrifice of allowing thee to touch my wounds! How canst thou repay me?—Thou wilt never repay me! Thou wilt not call and invite me to thy side; and because I have no shelter in love, thou wilt not harbor me, and thou wilt grant no relief to my yearning! I see that I shall stand by myself, alone, even as I today stood alone on the bank with the gloomy willows, where the death-shiver still hovers over the spot: there no grass grows; there she pierced her beautiful body at the very point where she had been taught to find her heart most surely. O Jesus Maria!

Thou! my Lord!—thou! flaming Genius above me! I have wept, not for her I have lost, who like the spring-breeding gales encircled me, who protected, inspired me, who entrusted to me as my goal attaining the loftiness of my own nature; I have wept for myself, with myself; I must become hard as adamant against myself, against my own heart; I dare not complain that I am not loved, I must severely chastise this passionate heart; it has no right to demand, no! it has no right—thou art mild and smilest upon me, and thy cool hand assuages the glowing of my cheeks; this shall content me.

Yesterday we sailed up the Rhine in vine-decked boats to view the hundredfold celebration of the vintage on both vineyard shores. Ours was a merry crew; they wrote wine-inspired songs and sayings, and set them afloat in empty bottles, swimming down the Rhine; on each heap of ruins great firs were placed, which were set on fire at twilight; from the

Mäuseturm[4] in the midst of the proud Rhine rose two mighty pines, their flaming charred boughs fell into the hissing flood: from every side it thundered with fireworks and rockets, and beautiful bouquets of fireballs rose virgin-pure into the air, and on board the boats songs were sung, and in sailing by, people threw garlands and grapes at each other. When we came home it was late, but the moon shone bright: I looked out of the window and still heard from the other side the roar and revelry of the homecoming, while on this side, where she had lain dead upon the bank, all was still. — There is no one now, thought I, who asks after her; and I went toward the spot, not without a shudder, no, I was afraid when I saw from afar the mist hovering over the willow-trees, and I almost turned back, for it was as if it were she herself who undulated, hovered, and expanded there; I went toward the spot, but prayed on the way that God would protect me. —Protect?—from what? From a spirit whose heart during her life was full of willing love toward me; and now that it is freed from its earthly shell, should I flee from it in fear?—

Ah! perhaps she has passed onto me the better part of her spiritual wealth, since her death. Fathers pass on an inheritance to their children; why not friend to friend?—I cannot explain how oppressed I feel!—Perhaps she, the friendly bright one, may have thus enriched my mind! As I returned from her grave, I found some people who were looking for their cow which had strayed—I accompanied them: they guessed immediately that I had come from thence; they had much to relate about Günderode, who had often entered into friendly chats with them and given them alms; they said that as often as they passed by yonder place, they said a pater noster; I have also prayed there, both to and for her soul, and have bathed myself in the moon's light, and have cried aloud to her that I yearned after her and those hours in which we harmlessly exchanged with one another thought and feeling.

She told me little of her other concerns; I do not know in what connections she stood except with me; she had indeed spoken to me of Daub in Heidelberg and also of Creuzer, but I was ignorant whether the one was dearer to her than the other. I once heard of it from other people, but did not believe it. One day she met me with a joyful air and said: "Yesterday I

4. Medieval tower on an islet in the midst of the Rhine, near Bingen.

spoke with a surgeon, who told me it was very easy to make away with one's self"; she hastily opened her gown and pointed to the spot below her beautiful breasts; her eyes sparkled with delight. I stared at her; for the first time, I felt uneasy. "Well," I asked, "and what shall I do when thou art dead?" "O," said she, "ere then, thou wilt not care for me any more; we shall not remain so intimate till then, I will first quarrel with thee."—I turned to the window to hide my tears and my anger-throbbing heart—she had gone to the other window and was silent—I took a secret glance at her; her eye was raised to heaven, but its ray was broken, as though its whole fire were turned within. After I had observed her awhile, I could no longer control myself—I broke out into loud crying. I fell on her neck, tore her down to a seat, and sat upon her knee and wept many tears and *for the first time,* kissed her on her mouth, and tore open her dress and kissed her on the spot where she had learned to find the heart; and I implored her with tears of anguish to have mercy upon me, and fell again on her neck, and kissed her hands which were cold and trembling, and her lips were convulsed, and she was quite cold, stiff, and deadly pale, and could not raise her voice: she said slowly: "Bettine, don't break my heart." I wanted to come to myself and not give her pain; I smiled, cried, and sobbed aloud, but she seemed to grow more anxious: she laid herself on the sofa. Then I tried to jest and to make her believe I had taken all as a joke. We spoke of her will; she bequeathed something to each one—to me a little Apollo under a glass-bell, upon which she had placed a laurel-crown; I wrote down everything. As I went home, I reproached myself that I had been so upset; I felt that it was all a jest, or indeed *fantasy* which *"belongs to a realm that does not maintain its truth in reality."* I felt that I was wrong and not she, who had often spoken to me in this manner.

The next day I brought her a young French officer of Hussars, with his high bearskin cap; it was Wilhelm von Türkheim, the handsomest of all youths—a true child, full of fun and good-nature, who came unexpectedly. I said: "There, I have brought thee a lover who shall make life again pleasant to thee." He dispelled all melancholy; we joked and made verses; and since the handsome William maintained that he had made the best, Günderode wanted me to present him the laurel-crown; I would not hear of a diminution of my legacy. At last I was obliged to make over to him half the crown and so I now have only the other half.

When I once visited her, she showed me a dagger with a silver hilt which she had purchased at the fair; she was delighted with the beauty and sharpness of the steel. I took the blade and tried it on my finger, drew blood immediately, and she started. I said: "Oh, Günderode, thou art so timid and canst not look on blood and yet constantly cherishest an idea that implies the firmest courage!—But I am fully persuaded that I of us two am more capable of daring such a thing, although I would not kill myself; but I have courage to defend myself and thee in the hour of peril; and when I now press on thee with this dagger—see! how art thou terrified!"—She retreated in alarm; my old rage was again roused, under the mask of maddest willfulness; I pressed more and more earnestly upon her, she ran into her bedchamber and took refuge behind a leathern chair. I buried the dagger in it and tore it to pieces by repeated stabs; the horsehair flew about the room; she stood supplicating behind the chair and begged me not to hurt her. I said: "Rather than suffer thee to kill thyself, I myself will do it." "My poor chair," said she—"What! Your chair indeed! it shall serve to make the dagger blunt!" Therewith I gave it without mercy stab on stab, till the whole room was one cloud of dust; then I flung the weapon so far away that it flew clattering under the sofa. I took her by the hand and led her to the garden, into the vine-bower; I tore off the young grapes and threw them before her feet and trod on them and said: "Thus dost thou abuse our friendship." I showed her the birds in the branches and that till now we like them had lived sportively, but were constant to one another. I said: "Thou mayst depend upon me, there is no hour of the night which, if thou wert to utter a wish, would make me hesitate for a moment—come to my window at midnight and whistle, and I will without preparation go around the world with thee; and what I would not dare for myself, that I dare for thee. But thou—what right hast thou to cast me off? How canst thou betray such constancy? And now promise me that thou wilt no more intrench thy timid Nature behind such cruel, boastful notions." I looked at her—she was ashamed and hung her head and looked away and was pale—we were both a long time still. "Günderode," said I, "if thou art in earnest, give me a sign!" She nodded.

She made a journey to the Rheingau; from thence she wrote me a few lines, once or twice—I have lost them or else I would insert them here. Once she wrote as follows: "When one is alone upon the Rhine, one becomes quite melancholy; but in company, the most awful spots become just the most charming. I, however, like to greet alone the widespread, purple sky of evening; then I invent a fairy tale as I wander on, which I will read to thee. I am every evening curious to know how it will proceed; sometimes it becomes quite awful and then rises again to the surface."

When she returned and I wished to read the tale, she said: "It is become so mournful that I cannot read it; I dare not hear any more about it and cannot write any more on it—it makes me ill," and she took to her bed and stayed there several days; the dagger lay at her side; but I paid no attention to it, it lay right next to the night-lamp, when I came in. "Bettine, three weeks ago my sister died; she was younger than I—thou hast never seen her; she died in rapid decline." —"Why do you tell me this now for the first time?" said I, "Why, how could it interest thee? Thou hast not known her, such things I must endure alone," she replied with tearless eyes. This sounded odd to me; to my young nature, all brothers and sisters were so dear that I believed I should have been in despair, if one had died, and that I could have given my life for any one of them. —She continued: "Only think! three nights ago, this sister appeared to me; I lay in bed and the night-lamp was burning on that table; she entered slowly in white garments, and remained standing at the table; she turned her head toward me, inclined it, and gazed on me. At first I was frightened, but soon became quite tranquil; I sat up in bed to convince myself that I was not sleeping. I gazed at her also, and she seemed to nod her assent to something—took the dagger, and raised it toward heaven with her right hand, as if to show it to me, and laid it down again softly and soundlessly. And then she took the lamp, lifted it up as well, and showed it to me, and as if to signal to me that she wanted me to understand her, she nodded softly, carried the lamp to her lips and extinguished it—only think," said she with a shudder, "extinguished it!—and in the darkness my eye still felt her form; and then an anguish fell suddenly upon me, which must be worse than the death struggle; yes! for I would rather have died than have borne such anguish any longer."

I had come to take leave, because I intended going to Marburg with Savigny,[5] but now I wished to remain with her. "Go by all means," said she,

---

5. Friedrich Carl von Savigny (1779–1861), a distinguished jurist and law historian, was married to Bettina von Arnim's sister Gunda.

"for I go also the day after tomorrow to the Rheingau." So then I went away. —"Bettine," she called to me at the door, "remember this story; it is certainly noteworthy!" These were her last words.

From Marburg I often wrote to her at the Rheingau of my curious way of life. I lived the whole winter on the mountain, just below the old castle; the garden was enclosed by the fortress-wall; I had an extended view from the window, over the town and the richly cultivated Hessen countryside; Gothic towers rose in every direction from out the snow-layers; from my bedchamber I used to enter the garden; I clambered over the fortress-wall and climbed through the deserted gardens; where the gates could not be swung back, I broke through the hedges—there I sat on the stone-stairs; the sun melted the snow at my feet. I searched for mosses and carried them home in their frozen beds. I had thus collected from thirty to forty mosses, which in my cold chamber all blossomed round my bed, in little earthen dishes placed upon ice; I wrote to her about this, without saying how it really was; I wrote in verse: "my bed stands in the midst of a cold country, surrounded by groves which bloom in every color; and there are silver groves of primeval growth, like those on the island of Cyprus; the trees stand in close rows, weaving together their mighty boughs: the lawn from which they spring is rose-red and pale green; I, this day, carried the entire grove on my benumbed hand into my cold ice-bed land." To this she answered also in verse:

> This moss of a primeval age
> Which thus spreads forth its carpetage;
> I doubt if hunters scour its vales
> Or frisking lambs browse in its dales,
> If Winter cover it with flakes
> Or Spring, its blooming flowers awakes;
> But still the midge's humming song
> Echoes its green-clad groves among;
> From waving trees of silvery hue
> Hang tiny drops of glist'ning dew:
> And in each dew-drop, sparkling sheen
> At once reflected lies the scene.
> Thou must other riddles try
> If thy wit may mine defy.

We were now involved in the proposition and solution of riddles; every moment I met with some little adventure in my walks, which, concealed in a double sense, I sent her to solve: she generally gave a childlike merry solution. I once described to her a hare, which met me in a wild lonely woodpath, as an elegant knight; I called it *la petite perfection,* and said it had captivated my heart—she immediately anwered:

> To a plain which was pleasant and green
> There came a knight of a noble mien;
> Who bid the trumpet sound for repast,
> And all hares fled trembling at the blast;
> Thus I hope ere long will a knight to thee come,
> Thy heart by hares thus captive taken
> From all these wights to set at freedom
> And there fresh ardor to awaken.

These were allusions to little love-adventures. Thus passed a part of the winter. I was in a most happy frame of mind; others might call it overexcitement, but to me it was natural.

On the fortress which surrounded the large garden was a watchtower, and within stood a broken ladder; just by us, a house had been broken into; the thieves could not be traced, but were believed to have hidden themselves in the tower; I had taken a survey of it by day and knew that for a strong man it was impossible to ascend by this rotten, nearly stepless, and heaven-high ladder; I tried it, but slid down again as soon as I had made a short way. At night after I had lain a little while in bed and Meline was asleep, the thought would not let me rest; I threw a gown about my shoulders, stepped out of the window, and passed by the old Marburg Castle; there the Palatinate Philip with Elizabeth peeped laughing out of the window; I had already often enough by day viewed this stone group, leaning arm in arm out of the window, as if they would survey their possession; but now at night I was so afraid, that I hastened away with lofty jumps to the tower; there I laid hold on the ladder and helped myself up, God knows how; what was impossible for me by day, succeeded by night under the beating anxiety of my heart. When I was nearly up I halted; I considered that the thieves might really be above and there attack and throw me headlong from the tower; there I hung and knew not whether to go up or down, but the fresh air which I scented enticed me up—how I felt there, when suddenly by snow and moonlight I surveyed widespread Nature, alone, assured—the great host of stars above me! Thus it is after death; the freedom-striving soul, which most painfully feels the burden of the body in the moment, when it is about to cast it off, is at length victorious and becomes free from anxiety—there my only feeling was to be alone; nothing then charmed me like solitude; and before this blessing all else must yield. I wrote to Günderode that once again all my happiness depended on the humor of this caprice. I wrote to her every day, what I did and thought upon the open watchtower: I set myself on the parapet and let my legs hang down.—She continually desired to have more of my tower-inspiration; she said, "It is my cordial! Thou speakest like a prophet arisen from the dead." —But when I wrote to her that on the wall which was scarce two foot wide, I ran round about and looked merrily at the stars, and that though at first I felt dizzy, I was now quite bold, and that it was the same to me there above as if I were on the ground, she anwered me: "For God's sake! don't fall; I cannot yet make out whether thou art the sport of good or evil spirits."— "Don't fall!" she again wrote, "Although it were pleasant to me to hear thy voice from above, converse upon death, yet I fear nothing so much as that thou shouldst fall crushed into a miserable and unwilling grave!"—But her exhortations caused in me neither fear nor giddiness; on the contrary, I became foolhardy; I knew well, I had the triumphant conviction that I was guarded by Spirits. Strange it was that I often forgot it and that it often waked me in the midst of sleep, and I hastened forth at uncertain hours of night; that on my way and upon the ladder I always felt the same anxiety as on the first evening, and that always when above, I enjoyed the blessing of a breast freed from a heavy weight. When the snow lay there above, I wrote Günderode's name in it and: "Jesus nazarenus, rex Judaeorum" over it as a talisman of protection, and then I felt as if she must be shielded from all evil suggestions.

At this time Creuzer came to Marburg, to visit Savigny: as ugly as he was, it was at once inconceivable how he could interest a woman. I heard him use expressions in speaking of Günderode as if he had a right to her love; in my connection with her, separated as it was from all outward influence, I had never before suspected this, and was in a moment most violently jealous. In my presence he took a child on his lap and said: "What's your name?" "Sophia." "Well, as long as I am here, you shall be called Caroline; Caroline, give me a kiss." At this I became angry, tore the child from his lap and carried it out, away through the garden onto the tower; when above, I placed it in the snow, near her name, and laid myself also there with my burning cheeks, and cried aloud, and the child cried too; and as I came down, Creuzer met me. I said: "Out of my way! begone!" The philologist apparently fancied that Ganymede would hand him Jupiter's goblet!

It was New Year's Eve; I sat on my tower and looked into the depth below; all was so still—no sound even to the furthest distance; and I was sad about Günderode, who had sent me no answer; the town lay beneath me, as all at once it struck midnight: then arose a roar, the drums beat, the post-horns crashed, they fired guns, they hurrahed, the student-songs sounded from all sides, and the shouts of jubilee increased till they surrounded me almost like a foaming sea—forget it I never shall, but I cannot say how wondrous it seemed to me there above on that giddy height, and how by degrees it again became still, and I found myself quite alone. I returned home and wrote to Günderode; perhaps I may yet find the letter among my papers, and then I will insert it. I know that I begged her most ardently to answer me; I wrote to her about these student-songs, how they echoed to heaven and roused up the depths of my heart; yes! I laid as it were my head at her feet and prayed for an answer, and waited with a burning longing a whole week, but received no response. I was blind, deaf, without perception. Two months passed away and I was again in Frankfort: I ran to the cloister, opened the gate and lo!—there she stood and looked at me, coldly as it seemed. "Günderode!" I cried, "may I come in?" She was silent and turned away. "Günderode, say but one word, and my heart beats against thine." "No," said she, "come no nearer, turn back again, we must at any rate part." "What does that mean?" "This much! That we have been deceived in one another and do not belong together." Ah! I turned away. Alas, the first despair! the first cruel blow, so dreadful to a young heart! I, who knew nothing but entire submission, nay, abandonment to my love, had to be thus rejected!—I ran home to Meline, I begged her to go with me to Günderode, to see what was the matter with her, and to induce her to allow me one look at her face; I thought if I could only once catch her eye, I should have her in my power. I ran across the street and remained standing at her door; I let Meline enter alone; I waited, trembled and wrung my

469

hands in the little narrow passage, which had so often led me to her. Meline came out with tear-swelled eyes and drew me away in silence. For a moment grief overcame me, but I was soon again myself. Well, thought I, if Fate will not be kind, then we'll play at rackets with her. I was gay, I was merry, I was overexcited, but at night I wept in my sleep. On the second day, I took the route leading to her dwelling; and then I saw the house of Goethe's mother, whom I did not know well and had never visited. I entered: "Frau Rath," said I, "I have lost a friend in the Canoness Günderode, and you must supply my loss." "We will try," said she; and so I went to her every day and set myself on the "ottoman" and made her tell me all about her son, which I wrote down and sent to Günderode. When she departed for Rheingau, she sent me the papers back: the girl who brought them said the Canoness's heart had beat violently as she gave them to her, and that to the maid's question of "what message" she had answered: "Nothing."

A fortnight passed and then Fritz Schlosser[6] came; he asked me for a line to Günderode, as he was going to the Rheingau and wished to make her acquaintance. I said we had quarreled, but begged him to speak of me and mark what impression it made upon her. "When do you go?" said I, "tomorrow?" "No, in a week." "Oh, do go tomorrow, or you will find her no more—it is so melancholy on the Rhine," said I jestingly, "she may do herself some mischief." Schlosser looked at me anxiously. "Yes! Yes!" I said petulantly, "She will plunge into the water, or stab herself out of mere caprice." "Do not libel her," said he; and now I began to do so in right earnest. "Take heed, Schlosser—you find her no more if you delay according to your old custom; and I tell you go rather today than tomorrow and save her from the unreasonably melancholy humor"—and in jest I described how she would kill herself, in a red gown, with loosened bodice, and close beneath her breast the wound: this was called wanton wildness in me, but it was unconscious excitement in which I described the truth with perfect accuracy.

On the next day Franz [Bettina's brother] came to me and said: "Girl, we will go to the Rheingau; there thou canst visit Günderode."—"When?"

6. Friedrich Christoph Schlosser (1776–1861), then a history student and from 1817 onward Professor of History in Heidelberg.

I asked. "Tomorrow," he said. —Ah! I packed up with such precipitation; I could hardly wait for going. Everything that hindered me was pushed hastily out of the way; but several days passed and the journey was still put off; at last my desire for the journey was changed into deep mournfulness, and I had rather have stayed behind.

When we arrived at Geisenheim, where we put up for the night, I lay at the window and looked on the moonlit water; my sister-in-law Antonia sat by the window; the maid who laid the table said: "Yesterday a young and beautiful lady who had been residing here for six weeks made away with herself at Winkel; she walked a long time by the Rhine, then ran home and fetched a handkerchief: in the evening she was sought in vain. The next morning she was found on the bank among the willow-trees; she had filled the handkerchief with stones and tied it about her neck, probably because she intended to sink in the Rhine, but as she stabbed herself to the heart, she fell backwards, and a peasant found her thus lying under the willows by the Rhine, in a spot where it is deepest. He pulled the dagger from her breast and flung it full of horror far into the Rhine; the sailors saw it cast in the air, and so came up and carried her into town." —At first I had not attended, but at last, listened with the rest and cried: "That is Günderode!" They talked me out of my belief and said it must certainly be some other, since there were so many from Frankfort in the Rheingau. I allowed myself to be convinced and thought, "exactly that which one prophesies generally does not come true." That night I dreamt she came to me in a boat adorned with garlands to be reconciled with me; I sprang out of bed and into my brother's room and cried: "It is all false, I have just had so vivid a dream!" "Oh," said my brother, "do not build upon dreams!" I again dreamt that I rapidly crossed the Rhine in a boat to seek for her; the water was murky and weedy, and the air was dark and it was very cold—I landed on a swampy shore; there was a house with damp walls from which she floated forth and looked anxiously at me, signifying to me that she could not speak: I ran again to the room of my brother and sister and cried: "No! It is surely true! for I dreamed that I saw her and asked: 'Günderode, why hast thou done this to me?' " and she was silent and sank her head mournfully and could not answer. Then in bed I reflected on it all, and bethought me that she had formerly said she would break with me before she completed her purpose; now our separation was explained, and that she would give me a sign, when her resolution was fixed; this then was the story of her dead sister which she had imparted to me half a year ago; her determination was then already taken.—Oh! tell me, ye lofty souls, what mighty power moved this lamb in innocence, this timid heart, thus to act?

The next morning we sailed at an early hour further up the Rhine. Franz had ordered the boat to keep on the other side to avoid coming too near to the spot; but there stood Fritz Schlosser on the bank, and the peasant who had found her was showing him where the head had lain and where the feet, and that the grass was still laid—and the boatman steered involuntarily in that direction, and Franz unconsciously repeated after the peasant all that he could hear at that distance; and thus I was compelled to listen to the dreadful fragments of the story, about the red gown, unlaced—and the dagger, which I knew so well, and the handkerchief of stones about her neck, and the gaping wound—but I did not cry—I was silent. Then my brother approached me and said, "Take courage, girl!"—We landed at Rüdesheim; the story was in everyone's mouth. I ran past them all, with the speed of wind, and up Ostein mountain, half an hour without stopping. When I came to the top, my breath was gone and my head burned—I had far outstripped the rest. There lay the splendid Rhine with his emerald island gems; there I saw the streams descending to it from every side, and the rich peaceful towns on either bank, and the blessed lands on either side: then I asked myself if time could not assuage my loss, and then I resolved to raise myself above this grief, for it seemed to me unworthy to utter grief which the future would enable me to master.

From *Goethe's Correspondence with a Child* (London: Longman, Orme, Brown, Green, and Longmans, 1839), 83–122.

Introduction, bibliography, and translation by
DAVID WARD

Annette von Droste-Hülshoff

(1797–1848)

Annette von Droste-Hülshoff (1797–1848)
portrait by J. Sprick, 1838
courtesy of Bildarchiv preussischer Kulturbesitz, Berlin

Millions of German and American readers know Annette von Droste-Hülshoff as the author of a single novella, *Die Judenbuche* (The Jew's Beech Tree, 1842), yet that text has little in common with the bulk of her writing—intensely personal verse and a prose specifically grounded in her native Westphalia. Thus the only nineteenth-century woman represented in the German literary canon appears in a way that obscures more than it reveals of her particular contributions. A profound and deeply troubled spirituality characterizes much of Droste's lyric poetry, especially the breviary cycle *Das geistliche Jahr* (Spiritual Calendar, 1820/1839–40); a powerful bond with the landscape, people, and folk culture of her native Westphalia underlie one of her several epic poems, "Schlacht im Loener Bruch" (Battle at the Quarry of Loenen, 1838), her prose *Bilder aus Westfalen* (Pictures from Westphalia, 1842), and her two unfinished novels: *Bei uns zu Land auf dem Lande* (Out at Our Country Place, begun 1841) and the largely autobiographical *Ledwina*.

Anna Elisabeth (Annette) Freiin von Droste-Hülshoff was the second of four children born to the Catholic aristocratic family of Therese (née von Haxthausen) and Clemens August von Droste-Hülshoff. A premature baby whose health always remained fragile, Droste moved within narrowly defined limits, both physically and psychologically. She never married, continuing to live on a family estate with her mother after her father's death in 1826. Her travels consisted of extended visits with relatives or close friends in Westphalia, along the lower Rhine, and at Meersburg, where she lived and wrote during several yearlong sojourns in a tower overlooking Lake Constance. For most of her life, Droste shared her writing only with family members and a small circle of friends. Although many of her poems were finally published during the last decade of her lifetime, *Ledwina* and the second half of *Das geistliche Jahr* appeared in print only after her death.

Among her literary friends were Professor Anton Matthias Sprickmann of Münster, the popular writer Katharina Busch, Adele Schopenhauer, and, later, Levin Schücking, her closest collaborator, who made a career of publishing and promoting Droste's writing after her death in 1848.

The inward-looking intensity of her poetry and her relatively reclusive life have led several scholars to compare Droste with Emily Dickinson, whereas her marshes and moors inhabited by demonic nature spirits invite comparisons with Emily Brontë.

In *Ledwina*, Droste constructs a narrative from her own immediate environment. Although she reworks and refracts this material so thoroughly that no figure or situation corresponds exactly to fact, her family saw itself reflected and seen through so clearly that they urged her not to publish it. Hence the text she had worked on intermittently between 1819 and 1826 remained in manuscript until Droste's collected works were published by Levin Schücking in 1884.

Much has been made of an episode in 1820, when two students from Göttingen were each courting Droste. When she rejected the one, he returned to the university and persuaded the other to join him in denouncing her as arrogant and manipulative. This supposedly marked the end of Droste's constant efforts to secure affirmation from others, which had characterized her youth. She turned away from her younger brother's jovial and boorish student friends and their flirtations. She also stopped work on *Das geistliche Jahr,* which she had begun in order to please her resolute and businesslike mother who had always been cool toward her.

The depictions in *Ledwina* of such a dutiful but undemonstrative mother and of the immature self-importance of such a brother are part of the process by which Droste examines her own surroundings to locate a space of freedom for herself. She does not find one. The limitations on that freedom become a crucial subtext for the entire narrative. With her frailty and frequent crises of health, Droste was constantly aware of the nearness of death. Through Ledwina's severe chest pains, Hollberg's dangerous fevers, and Clemens's drowning, the urgent reminders of mortality form a backdrop against which the actions of the living and their responses to the day's events stand out in high relief.

The second limitation Droste explores here is the social status of her gender. The unfreedom of women in every phase of life and in every station is foregrounded: from the widowed mother who must hand over to an arrogant and unappreciative son the estate she has administered at great personal cost, to the sisters wondering about who will marry Therese and whether her future husband will permit them to retain their close ties to one another, to the woman in Warneck's anecdote who goes mad with shame when her husband's bankruptcy leaves her with the reproaches of his creditors, and another who renounces speech for fourteen years in order to live in harmony with a quarrelsome husband.

Droste also explores a wide range of individual responses to this unfreedom—from occultism, dreams, and visions to madness and death. Like many works of German Romanticism, *Ledwina* remains unfinished. The final scene, with the three figures at nightfall with their backs to the reader and to each other, is reminiscent of Caspar David Friedrich's paintings. The predominance of dreams and visions, too, echoes a proclivity of the Romantics. But the anchoring of this text in the concrete social realities of her class and region and the knowing humor—that is never patronizing—with which she includes bits of local folk life have more in common with the realism of the later nineteenth century. Finally, the corrosive visionary quality of Ledwina's sleeping and waking dreams is much closer to Trakl and the Expressionists of the twentieth century than to the Romanticism of a Novalis or an Eichendorff.

BIBLIOGRAPHY

Droste-Hülshoff's Works

Droste-Hülshoff, Annette Freiin von. *Sämtliche Werke.* Edited by Clemens Heselhaus. Munich: Hanser, 1966.

———. *Historisch-kritische Ausgabe, Werke—Briefwechsel.* 23 vols. Edited by Winfried Woesler. Tübingen: Niemeyer, 1978–.

———. *Spiegelbild und Doppellicht: Prosa, Briefe, Gedichte.* Edited by Helma Scheer. Darmstadt: Luchterhand, 1983.

Annette von Droste-Hülshoff. Edited by Sarah Kirsch. Cologne: Kiepenheuer & Witsch, 1986.

Note: Each of the latter two selections from Droste's works include a flawed version of *Ledwina* not based on the historical-critical edition, although the volume of that edition containing *Ledwina* appeared in 1978.

In English Translation (Recent Titles)

Browning, Robert M., editor. *German Poetry from 1750 to 1900.* Foreword by Michael Hamburger. German Library vol.39. New York: Continuum, 1984. Contains two Droste poems.

Cocalis, Susan, editor. *The Defiant Muse: German Feminist Poems from the Middle Ages to the Present, a Bilingual Anthology.* New York: Feminist Press, 1986. Contains two Droste poems with new English translations by Ruth Angress, Susan Cocalis, and G. M. Geiger.

Flores, Angel, editor. *An Anthology of German Poetry from Hölderlin to Rilke in English Translation, with German Originals.* Garden City, N.Y.: Anchor Books/Doubleday, 1960. Contains eight Droste poems with English translations.

"The Jew's Beech Tree." Translated by Michael Bullock. In *Three Eerie Tales from 19th-Century German.* New York: Frederick Ungar, 1975, pp.99–151.

Secondary Literature in English (Recent Titles)

Note: a systematic compilation of the secondary literature on Droste through 1983 comprises volume 14, part 2 of the historical-critical edition included in the list of Droste's works.

Brumm, Anna Marie. "The Poetry of Regionalism, Feminine Voices of the Nineteenth Century: Emily Dickinson and Annette von Droste-Hülshoff." *Comparative Literature Quarterly* 21. 2 (June 1985): 83–91.

———. "Religion and the Poet: Emily Dickinson and Annette von Droste-Hülshoff." *Dickinson Studies* 59 (1986): 21–38.

———. "Time, the Bride, and the Double in the Poetry of Emily Dickinson and Annette von Droste-Hülshoff." *Dickinson Studies* 61 (1987): 27–38.

Guthrie, John. "Tradition and Innovation in Droste's Ballads." *Forum for Modern Language Studies* 23 (1987): 325–40.

Lietina-Ray, Maruta. "Annette von Droste-Hülshoff and Critics of 'Die Judenbuche.'" In *Woman as Mediatrix: Essays on Nineteenth-Century Women Writers*. Edited by Avriel H. Goldberger. New York: Greenwood, 1987, pp.121–31.

Morgan, Mary E. *Annette von Droste-Hülshoff: A Biography*. New York: Peter Lang, 1984.

Pickar, Gertrud Bauer. "'Perdu' Reclaimed: A Reappraisal of Droste's Comedy." *Monatshefte* 76.4 (Winter 1984): 409–21.

Toegel, Edith Maria. *Emily Dickinson and Annette von Droste-Hülshoff: Poets as Women* (Diss., Univ. of Washington, 1980).

Ledwina

(1819–26)

T he river made its way quietly, unable to carry along any of the
blossoms and twigs on its mirror; just one figure, like that of a
young linden tree, drifted slowly upstream. It was the lovely, pale
image of Ledwina, who was returning home from a long stroll along its
banks. When from time to time she stood still, half tired, half lost in
thought, then the river was unable to steal any rays of light, any bright or
gentler play of color from her young figure, for she was as colorless as a
snow blossom, and even her lovely eyes were like a pair of faded forget-me-
nots whose true-blue devotion had remained but whose radiance had vanished.

"Tired, tired," she said softly, and slowly lowered herself into the tall,
fresh green grasses along the bank, which stood around her like the green
border surrounding a bed of lilies. A pleasant freshness wafted through her
limbs, so that she closed her eyes in rapture, but suddenly a painful cramp
jolted her upright. In an instant she was standing, one hand firmly pressed
to her ailing breast, and shaking her blond head in indignation at her
weakness, she turned away quickly as if to leave and then came back almost defiantly; she stepped close to the bank and looked, alertly at first and
then dreamily, into the river.

A large rock protruding from the river spattered bright droplets about,
and the little waves flowed and broke so delicately that the water here
seemed as if veiled by a fine net and the branches inclining along the bank

flitted away in its mirror like green butterflies. But Ledwina's eyes rested upon her own image, as the curls fell from her head and drifted away, her dress tore to shreds, and her white fingers disintegrated and floated apart, and as the cramp quietly began to yield, it was as if she were dead, and decay were dissolving, eating its way through her limbs, and each element were tearing away its own.

"Foolishness!" she said, coming quickly to her senses, and turned with a stern streak in her gentle features onto the highway along the river, while her eye combed the broad, empty landscape for cheerful objects. A repeated whistling from the direction of the river went unnoticed, so that when a moment later a big black dog with its head lowered came racing across the field directly toward her, she screamed and fled in terror to the river and, as the animal was at her heels, jumped in feet first. "Pst, Sultan!" came a voice beside her, and at that moment she felt herself caught by a pair of ungentle hands and set back onto the riverbank. She turned around, still quite stunned and frightened. Before her stood a big, foursquare man whom she recognized as a butcher by the sheep that hung around his neck like a fur collar. Each observed the other for a moment, while the man's face filled with the most obvious scorn mixed with irritation.

"What did ye jump like that for?" he finally blurted out.

"Oh, God," Ledwina said, ashamed of herself, "I thought the animal was rabid."

"Who? My dog?" the fellow said, offended. "He ain't even mean, and he never bit nobody."

Ledwina looked at the dog, who now sat listening beside his master as if he understood, like a sphinx.

"Are ye all wet now?" the butcher began.

"Not very," Ledwina replied, while with his staff the man measured the depth of the water beside the large rock Ledwina had reached in her watery excursion.

"But ye feel miserable, that much I do see," he said then. "I'll just see that I get ye into that house yonder."

Indeed, Ledwina did need his support badly, and it was only with great effort that she reached the farmhouse, which lay about a hundred paces from the river. Meanwhile her helper went on endlessly about how to recognize a rabid dog.

481

The old peasant woman quickly put aside her spinning wheel when Ledwina appeared at the door with the words "Make fire, Lisbeth, I have had a fright and caught a chill." The butcher began immediately to recount their adventure.

"Make fire!" Ledwina repeated. "I've got my feet wet at the sandpit."

The rescuer wanted to make the affair with the young damsel into something more perilous. "It's our mistress," said the old woman, now calmed. She put wood on the fire, set a chair beside it, adjusted a cushion on it, and went to the cellar to fetch a glass of fresh milk. The butcher, abandoned in the middle of his best speech, called after her irritably, "A schnapps, good hostess!"—"We don't give out schnapps," said the woman from the cellar doorway; "this once you can have a glass of milk free of charge."

"Young lady," the butcher started in again, "I tell ye, ye could have been drownded." Ledwina had to smile. "Only if I had lain in the water face down," she said to herself and reached into her basket for her purse. "Ye are not the sturdiest sort either," he replied, and a trace of bitterness crossed Ledwina's face as she offered him a coin.

"Heaven forbid," he cried out, "saving somebody's life—ye cannot put a price on that," while almost acting as though he would refuse the proffered money as something beneath his dignity. "Well, but you also brought me here," Ledwina said almost irritably. "Well, if that's what ye mean," said the rescuer and took it quickly, for since Ledwina had turned toward her basket he thought she was going to put the coin away again.

The peasant woman brought the milk. The butcher muttered: "Now if that were a good glass of beer." But he thought better of it, talked on about paying and being able to pay well, and finally went away.

"It is often like that all day long," said the peasant woman to Ledwina, who was beginning to feel quite cozy in front of the fire, "if we wanted to put up with having all kinds of people in the house, there would be customers enough for the best tavern. People think money rules the world. Our Klemens often has to get up in the night and guide travelers past the *Grafenloch*. He's not really happy about that, but it's not good to let people just tumble into the water."—"That's right," said Ledwina, already half asleep. "My mistress is sleepy," the old woman said, smiling, "I will fetch another pillow."—"No, please," Ledwina called quickly after her, rising from her chair, but Lisbeth had already returned with two pillows, one of which she laid on the ledge beside the stove and the other on the arm of Ledwina's chair. Ledwina, who, with a kind of sickbed defiance, seldom indulged herself, laughed aloud with pleasure at being so nice and comfortable. "Tell me something about the days back when you lived in the castle," she said amicably, and the woman began telling about dear, departed Grandpapa, and how the tower that burned down years ago was still standing then, and Ledwina's head slumped lower and lower, and the image produced by those of the woman's words that she heard emerged clearer and clearer, until she saw Grandfather as a little, gray man, quite friendly, he was dead of course, but still he kept shooting at the ravens in the old tower with his birdshot; there was no bang, but they fell very nicely—and softer and softer came the sounds of the old woman, who peered from time to time at her mistress from behind the spinning wheel, until finally those sounds, too, were quite asleep. Then she stood up gingerly, tiptoed over to Ledwina and slowly bent over her to make sure she was resting well. It was a moving sight, the earnest, old face of the peasant woman bending over the youthful, pale face of her mistress, one steeped in the silent melancholy of dream, the other in the imminent and inevitable demise of them both, the mature sheaf saturated with life above the delicate, sun-scorched blossom. Then she got up, took flax from a cupboard and began very quietly to comb it; but her expression was more earnest than before and yet very tender.

This had gone on for a while, when the door was opened rather ungently and with the words "Mother, here I've brought you a new chair," her son appeared, clattering and banging. He held a spinning chair he had fashioned for her in secret; "the other one really is too high for you," he continued. His mother gestured angrily with her hand indicating Ledwina's presence, but she was already awake and looking around, bright and refreshed. "Oh, I'd like to . . ." the old woman muttered. "I slept very well by your fire," the young woman said very amicably, "but it is good that I've been wakened, or I would have had to go sleepwalking tonight; I mean," she continued with a smile, as both gave her a questioning look, "if I nap during the day, I can scarcely sleep that night; then I get up from time to time and walk about my room; it's not good for me, but what is one to do with the long night? It will soon be five; now it's time for me to go," and as she passed through the door: "Was this chair made by your son? He is quite a craftsman."—"And sometimes quite a bungler," said the old woman, whose annoyance lingered on, but Ledwina was already gliding upstream like a gazelle, for she thought of her poor, sick breast only when sharp pains reminded her of it, and then she so loathed this sad and anxious sheltering, this pitiful, cautious life where the body governs the spirit until it, too, becomes as infirm and impoverished as the body itself, loathed it so much that she would gladly have let all her life's energy, which was glimmering out a spark at a time, flare up and expire in a single blazingly brilliant day. In this, too, her pious heart maintained the upper hand over her furiously flaming spirit, but never has a martyr offered up his life to God more purely and painfully than Ledwina sacrificed by renouncing a more beautiful death in the flame of her own spirit.

* * *

Things must have been rather different than usual as Ledwina entered the brightly lit living room, for she was not scolded at all, the usual bitter fruit of the aimless roaming she found so sweet but unsettling. Her sister, Therese, was surely busy enough fishing around for a knitting needle she had dropped, but Mother also said nothing, continued knitting in silence, and blinked her eyelashes emphatically; that was always a particular sign, that she was enraged or deeply moved or even embarrassed, for this clever woman, for whom a rather public and often complicated life had secured complete mastery over all untoward outbreaks of inward stirrings in deed and in word, herself did not know how thinly the veil of her features covered her soul, and healthy eyes, though they be inexperienced, required but very slight acquaintance before they often understood her better than she did herself, what with the manifold distractions of her house and children. Ledwina would gladly have spliced herself quietly into their company, but her work lay in the drawer of the table at which her mother was sitting. That was bad; meanwhile she sat down very softly on the sofa, which stood in the shadow side of the room, and said not a word. Little Marie entered the room and, with a loud, rather silly laugh, ran up to Ledwina: "Ledwina, have you heard the great big news?" Ledwina paled with alarm in unnaturally tense expectation, and Mother said hastily: "Marie, fetch me my handkerchief; I've left it in the garden among the pines." Marie turned around on the spot, but said before she left "By the time I get back you'll have heard it all; Therese's heart will burst if she doesn't say." She laughed out loud and raced off a little clumsily.

"You must both watch yourselves around the child," said mother earnestly. "Children's ears are known to be the keenest and we adults are often careless in that regard; in Marie's case it is merely impertinence, not the start of selfish impudence, which at best burns out the soul to a hollow shell—Karl" she turned to Ledwina, "received letters today, which among other things portend that one of his acquaintances from the university might pass this way and pay him a visit; you have surely heard his name mentioned, Römfeld, the so-called handsome count. From time to time Karl has told us all sorts of things about him, all sounding quite romantic, and you two were uncautious enough to tease him; I allow such things to occur, although in the end they mean little. I think that as long as real evil is not present, then in God's name one must occasionally tolerate some frivolity. I must admit that I was thinking of Marie as little as you were, but assuming that such things leave no further impression on her still very childish heart, how is one to teach her not to repeat such conversations without almost violently furthering those very impressions, for you know she would be childish and lively enough to regale the count with his own biography."

"She must be told," remarked Karl, who was pacing up and down the room, "that she is not helping anything at all; that gossiping itself is awful enough"—"Do you know a way to teach that to such a lively child without doing harm?" the mother replied sharply. "Well, *we* never gossiped when *we* were little," said Karl. The mother hesitated for a moment and then said, as if reluctantly: "Maybe she is also livelier than all of you." Karl flushed red and said half to himself: "And pretty ill-behaved sometimes, too."—"All children misbehave some at that age," the mother replied sternly, "and besides, she always obeys *me*; if that is not true with others, the fault must lie on both sides." Both were irritated, and a heavy silence fell. "Who has sent you letters?" Ledwina began softly and timidly. "It's just one," said Karl, "from Steinheim; he's got a good post at Dresden, and since he'll be traveling by way of Göttingen, he'll stop by here to bid a final, merry farewell to student life; and Römfeld is from Dresden and is just now returning, so they'll be traveling together. Steinheim already seems to be feeling pangs of guilt about the uninvited guest."

This last he said half turned toward his mother who, while generous and pleasant in her hospitality, always reserved the right of invitation entirely for herself.

"We know him already," she said, and then quickly, before Karl could answer that this concern applied not to Steinheim himself but to Römfeld, "Ledwina, where were you this afternoon?"

"Down along the river," Ledwina replied.

"You stayed a long time," her mother said.

"I spent a long time with old Lisbeth," Ledwina responded, "I enjoy being there very much."

"They are good people, too," said the mother; "rather proud, but that does no harm in their position; it keeps them honest in every regard."

"It was really painful for me," spoke Karl, "to find our old stock of domestics almost entirely depleted."

"For me, too," said the mother energetically. "I would gladly raise them back from the grave, even if I had to fill the coffins with gold in their place. So often we made harmless fun of them, calling them the family heirlooms, but truly, such people are not as much placed by God in our hands as we in theirs, and other than the guardian angel there is no more devout protector—and other than a parent's love no purer affection than the quiet and profound ardor of such trusted servants toward the house to which they are grafted, in which all other wishes and affections, even those for and toward their own kin, have had to melt away."

Toward the end of her words, Frau von Brenkfeld was deeply moved. Her voice was firm, but the gentle play of the most beautiful sentiments in the earnest features of her face gave them an indescribable grace. All the while, Ledwina had been watching her mother constantly and had grown pale as a sign that a thought had stirred her deeply.

"Yes," she said now very slowly, as if her senses came to life only gradually in the process of speaking, "that is true: we are brother and sisters, but I am sadly sure that we would not be able to sacrifice ourselves for each other with that quick, decisive certainty that knows no choice, of which the lives of faithful servants give us countless examples."

Karl looked at her rather obliquely, and dear Therese extended her hand to her reassuringly, and they exchanged a tearful glance. Ledwina said firmly: "Yes, Therese, that is true, but it doesn't make us worse; the old folks are just better."

"That is why it's called a servant's loyalty," Karl began, "and of a very particular kind, something like love for the royal house, for which everyone gladly sacrifices himself, even when sometimes the beautiful old trunk puts out branches that are quite withered and sickly; but I always find old people curious, and above all I like to talk with them. I find it strange to see an entire generation, insignificant as far as their actions are concerned, living on long past their already forgotten death in their often so significant personality within these few gray, decaying monuments, not to mention when one is fortunate enough to come across the living monument of some great mind of the past. I always prefer such little freely sketched portraits to the most beautiful galleries of famous biographies."

"It seems to me as well," said Therese, "that the pet flaws of old people are—almost like those of children—often bothersome, but in essence less serious or in fact more superficial than those of youth. Lack of consideration for the comfort of others is the first and most obtrusive trait the elderly take on, led to do so by general cares and the bitter comparison of their own weakness with the youthful strength of their surroundings, the root of all botheration, a small sin, but a great burden for others."

"The latter is true," said Karl, "without confirming the former. I for example have rediscovered many a youthful flaw enlarged and in truth quite grotesquely petrified among the elderly, which, so close to the grave, is for me one of the most ghastly of sights."

Frau von Brenkfeld, raised in the good old days when one honored not only one's elders but age itself, days now gone without a trace almost like the antediluvian era, shifted her chair.

Oblivious to her, Karl continued to declaim, while the stem of his pipe governed his diction: "Ambition among the nobility, which though not exactly good, one so easily excuses in the name of greatness, ambition becomes the ruthless and revolting thirst for fame. The half-scorned, half-lauded thrift of the middle class becomes ghastly miserliness, about which one does not know whether to laugh with Democritus or to weep with Heraclitus. The often pleasant tomfoolery of the lesser folk becomes the most shocking insensitivity and disregard toward those they otherwise hold closest and dearest. And often all these traits together can be found among all the classes; and just as their speech is seldom childlike and usually merely childish, so they are often childish and mean out of sheer malice."

Again he began to pace more and more furiously.

"Old people are good," said Marie, who was again sitting beside her mother and knitting away, and Frau von Brenkfeld nearly had to laugh out loud despite her irritated state, for according to the precocious scale by which children judge age, this defense was made on her behalf. "You can all be glad," she said, "that you weren't young thirty years ago; back then people never became adults in the eyes of their parents. As a rule, the one side never talked back and the other only seldom gave any reasons."

"It is bad enough," Karl said softly, "that it is different on average now. Obedience to one's parents is a law of nature and nearly as precious as one's conscience. I am convinced that the root of nearly all the prevalent moral ills lies in its neglect. Man is capable and willing of many excesses, once he has trod that law, however respectably, underfoot. There is something strange and moving about a law of nature."

"And besides," said Therese, "everyone needs someone—be it spiritual or secular—to obey besides God: that keeps him soft-hearted and Christian."—"I believe," added Ledwina, "that if there is some basis for what Karl said just now about old people, it can be found in the utter lack of an object of obedience; they show obedience to their regent, but without feeling it, for all business is usually taken out of their hands."—"True by and large," said Karl, "yet the thirst for fame is an exception."—and then quickly: "Nota bene, old Franz is dead now; and how did he come to die?"—"Of a fever in his chest," replied Therese, and Ledwina, whose face again colored with a pale hue, added in a quiet voice: "He caught a chill last winter going out to clear a path for me through the snow."

She stood up and moved to a chest of drawers standing in the shadows, as if she were looking for something, for she felt that this time the droplets that formed so readily in her eyes would become too heavy for them.

"You wanted to live to be a hundred," Marie laughed. "Just think, Karl, Ledwina thought she could live to be a hundred if she went for a walk every day; that's what old Mr. Nobst in the storybook did, too."

The mother said, as if she had overheard Ledwina's words: "He had been through the snow to Emdorf."

"He lived to be old enough," said Karl, "I believe he was past eighty; I won't live that long."

Ledwina, meanwhile, was bent over an open drawer, deeply hurt. It was as if they wanted to take this heartrending but precious gift of a sacrificed life away from her, and she pressed it and held it close. In fact the illness that killed their faithful servant, old Lisbeth's husband, could be ascribed to several causes, as is almost always the case when very old people pass away, and so out of that popular but misplaced considerateness that wounds the heart rather than healing, outrages rather than touching, Frau von Brenkfeld tried to rob that most probable reason of sacredness and to leave only the halo of that last sign of loyal attachment.

Meanwhile, Marie had run up to Ledwina and tormented her with the question she kept repeating between peals of laughter: "Ledwina, you're really scared of death, aren't you? How old do you want to get, Ledwina?"

Ledwina, thinking herself in her agitated state even more the center of attention than she was, would have liked to answer her, but she feared the trembling sound of her own voice; she bent over from one side to the other while the child, who had slipped under her arms and now squeezed in front of her by the drawer, endlessly repeated her question and her giggling and kept her eyes fixed on Ledwina's. Finally she replied rather steadily and—under the strain—louder than usual: "I am somewhat afraid of death, as I believe almost all people are; for not being afraid either goes against nature or rises above it. I would not wish the one, and the other can be achieved only by means of a very long or very pious life." The little one crawled back under Ledwina's arms and, laughing, hopped onto her chair.

Ledwina, too, had taken courage from her speech and returned rather calmly to her sofa. Karl, for whom further conversation was usually dead once he had the information he had demanded, while he went on spinning his own thoughts, now stood still and said: "The old chap was a genuine philosopher; he could have set our scholars' heads spinning. I've been a student for three years now, and our professors run around all day like Diogenes with his lantern pursuing useless questions, but I have seldom encountered such oversubtle ones as the old genius used to come up with. He had taught himself to play the clarinet, too."—"He used to play it back when he was young," Marie piped up. Karl spun his pipe around impatiently in his hands and then went on quickly: "But the curious thing was that he knew answers to every question, and for him they were always sufficient, even though the acuity of the answer was never in proportion to that of the question. Pride lays its eggs in every nest."

"Your father, may he rest in peace, was very fond of old Franz," said Frau von Brenkfeld gently, but earnestly. Without a thought, Karl answered: "Yes, except for the lessons, they were practically raised together, and that's what gave him his vitality." Then he came to realize by himself what she had implied, and went on with a rare, tender look in his eyes: "When he talked about how they used to sneak away and smoke out of hollowed-out chestnuts and how they stood by each other in guilt and punishment, I would always be quite spellbound; it's true, many's the precious hour that died for me with that man."

"For me, too," their mother said, struggling to keep back her tears, "and since then, old Lisbeth has grown quite feeble."

"Widows in general have something odd and usually unpleasant about them," said Karl, sidetracked once again, "especially when the children are still minors."—"Minors, what's that?" Marie interjected. —"Most of the time they lack strength, and in any case they are a mote in the eyes of the world, and then the world takes away their power and their glory; people see only their harshness toward debtors, which verges on the criminal, all out of duty. There's just no other way, but it usually leaves behind some scars. Governing never does a woman any good."

"Widows are good," said Marie in an offended tone, and Karl, who did not grasp the connection, shot back: "So are children, when they keep their traps shut," then looked at his mother and shrank back in double alarm. Frau von Brenkfeld was struggling mightily against a sensation more of melancholy than of anger, a feeling she considered wrong, since Karl had spoken on the whole rightly and certainly without ill intention, but to be reminded of the harshness of those circumstances, thanks to her deceased husband's bigheartedness and the resulting confused state of his ledgers, to which she, enduring the hardest of inward and outward struggles, had had to sacrifice for eight years of her life all her good health and often enough her most sacred feelings—to hear that harshness described so summarily and as if judgmentally by the very one for whom above all she had gladly made that sacrifice, this cast a cloud of sorrow and desolation into her soul that all the rays of obedience and filial love were incapable of dispersing. Her widow's veil had suddenly been transformed from a mourning crepe to a leaden cloak that would almost have stooped honor to the ground, since her husband's disproportionately large loans ruined people after his death whom he had tried to help during his life. He had taken their blessing with him and left his executors and his hard-pressed widow with their curse. Also, for a while now her otherwise strong heart had been attached with great weakness to Marie, the only one of her children for whom she was everything, while the others' hearts were beginning to turn to the foreign gods. In her relationship with her daughters these pangs had been less acute, since the mother's multifaceted and versatile knowledge of the world combined with the children's unconditional obedience to balance out Ledwina's greater depth of thought and delicacy as well as Therese's particularly clear and lucid frame of mind. But the homecoming of Karl, whom the university now returned to her completely educated, by the measure of his personal receptivity to education, but otherwise or perhaps for that reason a bit overmature and overfree, that homecoming had changed from a celebration of her widow's rule to its aggrieved burial rite, if only in her own mind, since now Karl was moved by duty and conscious decision to strive to be that which once timid reverence alone had made of him. But the very fact of this constantly visible effort, his frequent failure born of misunderstanding because he now lacked the intent, anxious respect of the child, the now-obvious cohesion and mutual support among brother and sisters told her distinctly how loosely the crown rested upon her head, held in place only by her perceptive but dutiful administration. She had sent Karl out into the open air like a luxuriant but delicate hothouse plant, with tears, worries, and her blessing, and she could not conceal from herself that, were she to release him now without any of these, he would only miss the last of them, and this only out of conscious thought and religiosity, not out of that timid, pious feeling that conceives of the world without the mother's blessing as a world full of rapacious animals. Marie he tolerated only out of consideration for his mother, and his irritable temper had to burst forth just as the girl had come to seem almost the only child she really had, and yet in just this matter she could say nothing without displaying the utmost tactlessness. Here, too, Karl understood her feelings only in rough outline as they arose, and he did not reflect on them at all; he paced back and forth, smoked, and was still a bit puzzled but entirely calm. Ledwina would have grasped all this with the greatest sensitivity, but a string painfully struck earlier continued to reverberate so sharply within her that it drowned out any other sound. Indeed, she could ruminate on a thought for a very long time and was often still taking her breakfast when the others had already consumed an important midday meal, an insignificant tea with a lot of amusing pastry wares, and were about to sit down to dinner. Only Therese, who always stood like the angel holding the flaming sword before her people and the olive branch above them, had to bear the entire burden of this moment and searched anxiously for unobtrusive, agreeable things to say.

"Why do you always choose that tiresome path along the river, Ledwina?" began Frau von Brenkfeld in a steady voice, to break the endless silence.

"I am very fond of that path," replied Ledwina. "I believe the water is a large part of it."

"You have the river below your window as well," her mother said, "but • it is such a convenient stroll for reflection; that is why one can easily go farther than one should."

"I must confess," declared Karl, "that now in particular this countryside strikes me as quite pitiful indeed. One walks as if on a tabletop, the countryside before us just like that behind us, or rather there is none at all: the sky above us and the sand below us."

"This countryside could be a lot less picturesque than it is," said Ledwina, "and I would still be fond of it; I will not even mention the memories that reside in every tree, for in that respect it would be incomparable, but just the way it presents itself here and everywhere, I would find it most appealing and valuable."

"*Chacun à son goût,*" replied Karl, "after the exceptions you just made, I don't know what attracts you: the prickly heather-bushes or the boring willow-trees or the golden mountains that a magic wind bestows upon us within an hour's time."

"The willows, for example," replied Ledwina, and a melancholy but animated energy poured across her features, "I find they have something moving about them, a curious reversal in nature: the twigs colored, the leaves gray, they remind me of beautiful but weakly children, their hair bleached by a single night of terror. And above all the profound calm in some areas of this landscape: no work, no shepherd, only all kinds of large birds and the solitary, grazing cattle, so that one never knows, is one in a wilderness or in a land without deceit, where property knows no guardian other than God and the general conscience."

"It is not hard," replied Karl, smiling, "to find some beauty in a thing so cherished, but I assure you, one cannot travel twenty miles without those pretty, romantic trappings falling away, and what remains behind, naked, is half desert."

"The desert," replied Ledwina, likewise smiling and as if dreaming, "the desert may hold grand and awesome delights."

"Child, you're cracked," said Karl and laughed aloud.

Ledwina spoke on slowly: "To be placed suddenly in its midst, without knowing surroundings that are similar and yet entirely different from these, and above all not having been made to suffer by them, and now for a long way nothing but the yellow, shimmering expanse of sand, no limit but the sky, which must descend in order to contain infinity and now stands over it, aflame; instead of the clouds the sky-high, shifting pillars of fire, instead of the flowers the colored, burning serpents, instead of the green trees the awful natural forces of lions and tigers that shoot through the rustling sandy billows like dolphins through foaming waves—it must be like the ocean."

Karl had stood still in astonishment; then he said with a foolish expression: "And what if the shifting pillars of fire paid us a visit or the flowers of the desert formed a wreath around us or the awful natural forces decided to have a go at us?"

Ledwina felt a nasty chill. She bent over without answering to pick up a ball of yarn from the floor.

"My God, child," cried out Frau Brenkfeld, whom this quick movement had given a glimpse of her not-yet-completely-dried shoes, "you are all wet!"—"I am a little wet," Ledwina replied, brought low by contrary feelings. "And you've been sitting here like that this whole time," her mother replied reproachfully. "Lie down this minute, you know in God's name well enough how little you can stand."—"Yes," said Ledwina curtly and stood up so that she in her sensitivity might escape all further admonition. "You lay yourself right down, and drink tea," her mother called after her. She turned around in the doorway and said with forced amiability: "Yes, surely." Therese followed her out.

* * *

"You still haven't drunk anything," declared Therese with a gentle reproach as she entered the bedroom once more a quarter of an hour later with a glass of water and saw the cup dutifully filled before her departure still untouched; "if mother were to come in now," she went on, "you know how she insists upon her instructions."

"Oh, God, I haven't drunk it yet? What if mother came!" Ledwina repeated, startled out of a deep reverie, and in an instant she handed Therese the emptied cup; "I feel so hot," she said, then restlessly thrust the bedcurtains far back and laid her burning hands in the sister's lap.

"You drink too swiftly," the latter said. —"I wish I could drink that glass of water," replied Ledwina. "You drink your tea, it is much better for you," Therese answered sympathetically, "you can make that sacrifice for your health, it is but a little wish."—"Oh, and it only comes from the top of my heart," smiled Ledwina, "and now sit down here with me and recite something to me. Lying in bed is so wretched; it won't be dark for a while yet, and then the long night!"

Therese sat down on the edge of the bed and unintentionally breathed a deep sigh. Ledwina smiled anew and very amicably, almost joyfully. "This day," said Therese profoundly, "has been so insignificant outwardly and yet inwardly so rich; so much has been thought through, and said aloud as well, that could not have come to such clarity in years, like the focal point of an age."—"Yes, indeed, so much," replied Ledwina expectantly, and at this moment only one thing stirred softly in her thoughts. "I wish," Therese continued, "that our Karl looked a little less imposing, so he would be respected a little less. Everything revolves around him, and Mother turns red every time he says with his officious air: 'report that to my mother!'"

As mentioned earlier, Ledwina had completely missed that portion of the preceding conversation to which Therese was referring, and now her mind held firm to another course as well. So she did not at all grasp it in its profound pain. "Yes," she said, still in her reverie, "so much was said that one forgot the first thing for the next. I wonder whether Steinheim has changed as well." Therese turned crimson. "I do not wish it so at all," she continued; "it always seems to me he could only lose in the process."

Therese poured her another cupful with some effort. "I can see him now," Ledwina began, "as he is asked a question and as that dear, honest face always answers so amicably; an utter calm befalls one, if one dwells on that face a while."—"That may be," said Therese anxiously. Ledwina glanced up at her. "Don't you think so?" she asked earnestly. "Oh, no," said Therese in greater confusion, and she broke off very abruptly. But Ledwina had sat upright and clutched her hand tightly. "Please, please," she said in urgent fear, "remain silent, but do not lie," and with a soft sound of the deepest melancholy Therese lay upon her breast and wept and trembled so that the bed-curtains shook. Ledwina held her firmly, and her face had risen like a moon that shone watchfully over her sister. The two drew apart after a long, full moment and sought their lost composure, the one on the silken bedcover, the other in the band around the teapot, which she unfastened, rather than tying it tighter, for it is a characteristic of the best and most wonderful of people that they are ashamed when an un-guarded moment has betrayed how tender they are, while those poor in spirit who are not promised the kingdom of heaven cannot forget in all eternity if they once come upon a touching thought, like the blind hen find-ing a pea.

"I have often looked quite ridiculous and vain in my own eyes," Therese finally began; "in yours, too?"—Ledwina had to laugh and looked at her inquiringly. Therese went on: "Obscure to the others and clear only to me; it is depressing, Ledwina, to be the only one to notice such a thing; it leaves one quite perplexed. Inwardly I've always burned with shame when I saw one or the other of our women friends making a show of her imagined con-quests. It is so ugly and so common. Modesty offers one no protection any-more, and I find it all so sad. Oh, Ledwina, am I imagining all this? I have nothing to build on but my most devout faith."

"You go ahead and build your house," said Ledwina, moved; "you have a good foundation, concealed but solid, that will not sink beneath you."— "He never said anything like that to me," Therese replied, her eyes burning holes into the floor. —Ledwina said reflectively and sweetly: "For all the others, nothing; for him, everything. Were it another man, you would not have such faith, either. Oh, Therese, you will be very happy; I say that freely and am not ashamed. All of us seek once, though most frequently in-cognito, but I have ceased seeking, for I know that I will not find."— Therese responded humbly: "I cannot demand as much as you."—"That doesn't mean a thing," Ledwina replied with a tone of gentle reproach;

"you can't believe that yourself; you are more pleasing to God and man, that much I know." Therese was quite alarmed and began to interrupt, but Ledwina gestured earnestly with her slender, white hand and continued: "It's true: my loose and foolish temperament has so many sharp points and dark corners, it would take a soul of curious proportions to fit into it completely."—Shaken, Therese took both her hands and said, turning her head as if looking for something in order to conceal the signs of her extreme emotion: "Oh, Ledwina, I won't even begin to tell you how much many people care for you, but in the end you, too, will find the one you will cherish most. God will not be deaf to such pure and quiet supplication."

Ledwina, for whom the conversation was becoming too taxing, said as if flippantly: "That's right. As they say, there's no pot so bad that a lid can't be found for it, but God only knows where my chosen one lives; perhaps at this moment he is hunting tigers; it's the right season, and then, you think Steinheim's love has remained unnoticed? Don't you believe that! Have I said a word to you before? And yet for half a year I have been absolutely certain of everything, and in my thoughts I can no longer separate the two of you. But how can you believe that our mother should express herself on such a delicate matter on the basis of mere appearance, no matter how reliable it seems? Or Karl, who holds honor and propriety almost too dear? Often, and secretly laughing, I have imagined the battle of those two, trying to appear neither intentionally disruptive nor negligent. Believe me, were Steinheim able to forget you or pass you over, the two of them would remain silent and compose themselves, but their faith in mankind would be gone, along with yours."

"But even today, where the decision is so very near at hand," Therese replied in anguish, "not the slightest sign in gesture or in words."

"Oh, Therese," said Ledwina, smiling, "I see now that love makes people stupid. This avoidance of his name, this delicate, obvious circumventing of his whole visit, which was after all the most central thing in the letter—does all this mean nothing to you? I'm telling you, Therese, I knew nothing when I entered the room today, but I drew back and sat waiting in the greatest suspense, believing that the next sound would bear the secret; especially in our mother's face, the whole open sea of emotions was billowing."

Therese had gradually raised her head and now she looked at Ledwina in awkward expectation, like a child looking at her father when she knows he is about to give her a present. "Well, I want to imagine it to be so, and I cannot well do otherwise," she said bashfully, "but please, please, no more talk about it!" After a few moments she continued sadly: "One shouldn't become so entrenched in one single hope; happiness is too round a ball for that." She fell silent and grasped cup and teapot as if she were about to pour. Then she said: "I'll be right back," and went out, for she was trembling so that she had been unable to lift the pot.

* * *

After a long while she returned with quiet footsteps, and leaning far forward she strained to look across at her sister, for she thought she might have dozed off and she did not dare approach her on account of the fresh evening air that wafted from her clothes, for she had been outdoors, deep, deep in the underbrush, and had wept and sighed her fill, and now she was once again silent and attentive, for this sweet, most cherished soul led a double life, one for herself, one for others, and the former always emerged to fight for the latter, except in place of a sword it bore the palm frond of the Passion. She stood thus for a while. No curtain rustled, but deeper, heavier breathing reached her and gave her, along with the certainty of her sister's slumber, a melancholy worry. She sat down very quietly by a window. The sun was setting, and its last rays rested upon a willow on the far riverbank. The evening breeze stirred its branches, and thus they emerged from the light and appeared in their natural color, then swayed back into the golden radiance. For in Ledwina's sickly, agitated state, this glistening play of natural forces could easily have become a sinister image of captivity within a scorching flame, which one strives to escape constantly but in vain, for one's foot is rooted in the tormented earth. But Therese had come to feel indescribable serenity in observing the heavens' pure swells of gold and all the lovely hues of the landscape; her thoughts had become a quiet and fervent prayer, and her eyes were fixed keenly on the twilight glow, as if here the partition between heaven and earth were thinner; and it seemed to her as if the rays drew her sighs aloft with them, and she lay her radiant face against the pane, but now that the sun was completely gone and the evening sky, too, was beginning to deny its color, her wings drooped as well, and again she grew sadder and did not know why. The cattle came slowly, lowing, into the yard, and just then the reddish twilight climbed higher, and a fresh wind drove the rose-colored herd across to the castle as well. "Now all will be well," she said rather loudly, meaning the weather, and started with alarm because she had forgotten her slumbering sister, but suddenly an indescribable confidence encompassed her, and these unintentional words spoken aloud seemed to her like divine inspiration. From now on she was completely calm and she remained so until the hour that was to decide her fate.

So it is that even the most lucid, secure souls have their moments when belief in a secret, spiritual mirroring of all things in one another, the much-denied oracle of nature, touches them powerfully; and whoever contradicts this, his hour has not yet come, but it will come, even if that hour be his last.

Therese rose up as if from a heavy dream and stole across to where Ledwina lay. In her sleep she lay motionless, almost rigid, and her face was pale as marble, but within her breast life was straining with heavy and restless movements. Therese watched anxiously and then gently laid her hand upon the area around the heart, which rose with furious pounding. Had she not known that sudden wakening of her sister always produced a terrifying panic, she would not have left her in this anxious, numbing repose, but now she cast a worried look at the sleeping figure, blessed her for the first time in her life, drew the bedcurtains wide open, closed those of the windows, and then went out gingerly, and looking back sadly, with the intention of looking in on her later.

* * *

It was deep in the night when Ledwina woke from her slumber. Outwardly, she had slept deeply, and Therese had been back, unnoticed, hours before, and left again, reassured, as her sister now seemed to be resting more easily. But within Ledwina, a horrific dream world had opened up, and it seemed to her as if she were walking with a large company, among them all her relatives and many acquaintances, to attend a theatrical performance. It was very gloomy, and the entire company carried torches, which cast a yellow flame-light everywhere: especially the faces seemed hideously altered. Ledwina's guide, an old but insignificant acquaintance, was very anxious and warned her of every stone in her path. "Now we are at the churchyard," he said, "take care, there are a few fresh graves." At that moment all the torches flared up, and Ledwina caught sight of a large churchyard with a numberless crowd of white gravestones and black mounds that alternated in regular succession, so that the whole looked to her like a chessboard and she laughed aloud when it suddenly occurred to her that the one she loved most in the whole world lay buried here. She knew no name and had no more exact image than the human form itself, but it was certainly her beloved, and with a shattered, fearful whimper she tore herself loose and began searching between the graves and digging up the earth here and there with a little spade. Now she was suddenly the spectator and saw her own figure, deathly pale, with hair flying wildly in the wind, burrowing among the graves with an expression in those distracted features that filled her with terror. Now she was again the seeker herself. She lay down across the gravestones to read the inscriptions and couldn't decipher any of them, but she did see that none was the right one; she began to be wary of the mounds of earth, for the thought of sinking into one had begun to take shape; nevertheless, the compelling force of the dream practically shoved her toward one gravestone, and no sooner had she trod on it than it collapsed. She actually felt the momentum of the fall and heard a crash splintering the boards over the coffin, in which she now lay beside a skeleton. Oh, and it was her beloved, she knew that right away; she embraced and held him more firmly than we are able to grasp thoughts, then she sat upright and looked at the grinning skull in search of features for which she herself had no norm. But there was nothing, and besides, she couldn't see right because there were snowflakes falling, even though the air was warm and humid. Incidentally, it was now day. She grasped one of the still-fresh, dead hands, which disengaged from the skeleton. That did not frighten her at all. She pressed the hand ardently to her lips, then set it back in its former place and pressed her face firmly into the moldering dust. After a while she looked up; it was night again, and her former guide stood very high atop the grave with a lantern and asked her to go with him. She answered that she would stay down here always until she was dead; he should go and leave her the lantern, which he immediately did, and for a while she saw nothing but the skeleton, which she caressed with heartrending tenderness. Suddenly, a child stood beside the grave with a basket full of flowers and fruit, and she recalled that it was one of those who circulate in the theater with refreshments. She bought all the flowers in order to adorn the corpse, while she carefully and calmly picked out the fruits and gave them back. And as she tipped the basket over, there were so many flowers that they filled the entire grave. This delighted her greatly, and once her blood was flowing more gently, the idea took shape that she might reconstruct the decayed body out of flowers so that it might live and go with her.

While selecting and arranging the flowers she awoke and, since with dreams only the very last impression is ever carried over into waking life, she felt rather calm, but unbearably hot. She sat up and looked about the room, still a bit distractedly. The moonlight shone on the curtains of one of the windows, and since the river flowed beneath, they seemed to swell and recede like the water. The shadow fell across her bed and lent the white bedcovers this same trait, so that she felt herself to be underwater.

She observed this for a while, and the longer she did so the more ghastly it seemed; the idea of a water sprite changed to that of a corpse submerged in the river, being slowly consumed by the water, while the inconsolable parents cast their nets futilely into the inaccessible realm of that element. She began to feel so ghastly that, after some scruples on account of the burning heat in her body, she decided to get up and draw back the curtains. The night was surpassingly beautiful, the moon stood clear in the deep blue, the clouds camped darkly on the horizon in a heavy mass stacked high, and the thunder rumbled softly and yet mightily, like the roar of a lion.

Ledwina gazed hungrily through the pane, the gray silvery light fell across the landscape like an elfin secret, and thin, dim luster welled across the grasses and weeds like fine threads, as if the pixies were bleaching their airy veils. At the river the air was quite still, for the willows were standing as if petrified and not a breath stirred their tousled hair, but in the distance the poplars were shaking and holding their white sides up to the moonlight, so that they shimmered like the silvery lanes in dreams and fairy tales. Ledwina looked and looked, and her foot took root ever more firmly at the enticing spot, and soon she was standing, half unwittingly, half reproaching herself, wrapped in a heavy cloth, at the open window. She shivered softly at the very fresh air and the haunting scene. Her gaze took in the clear light above her and the gentle light below her in the river, then the ominous, looming background, and it all seemed to her like the proud and dignified salute at sea of two brightly lit royal barges, while the general populace stands at a distance, crowded together and milling, and its muffled murmuring resounds across the water.

In the distance by the river a third light appeared, a dim, wavering little flame like a hazy meteor, and she did not know, was it really a will-o'-the-wisp or was it being carried by human hands, more for company than as a guide through the night's deceptive light. She fixed her gaze upon it as it slowly danced closer, and its uninterrupted approach spoke for the latter impression. She was so lost in alien realms that now she imagined the wanderer as a gray sorcerer looking for mysterious herbs in the damp heath marshes. There really were many conjurers, so-called spellmakers, in that region, as there are in all lowland regions where along with the heavy, misty air people breathe in despondency and a certain unhealthful gravity—the belief in ghosts; these sorcerers, usually respected old locals, are with few exceptions as guileless as their children, and they practice their ghostly work almost never for profit, but instead as a precious arcanum, acquired by chance, to be employed in performing neighborly favors. Thus even to themselves they adhered strictly to all the little circumstances that lend such matters a chilling effect, even for utter nonbelievers, like keeping strict silence, picking their herbs by the full moon or on a certain night of the year and so forth, and so it would have been nothing impossible to come upon such uncanny fellows during a nocturnal walk. But the little flame wavered closer, and soon Ledwina could recognize it as the burning wick of a lantern that a man was carrying, while a figure on horseback followed. She reasoned that it was probably a nocturnal traveler being led by someone who knew the way past the river's deceptive inlets. The fairy realm was destroyed, but a human sentiment of the most profound sadness took hold of her regarding the unknown man with whom she was experiencing a beautiful night and yet who rode past her as he rode past the rocks of his path and would know nothing of her if one day he read of her death in the newspapers. Now he was opposite the manor house, where the walkway was paved with stones; a slow clopping of hooves echoed her way, and she strained her vision to capture a hint of a figure from this fleeting image.

Suddenly a cloud sent out as a herald by the conspiracy on the horizon passed across the moon; it grew quite dark, and just then a heavy, splashing fall reached her ear, followed by violent thrashing and the loud, anxious cry of a man's voice. Ledwina leapt back from the window in terrible alarm and wanted to hurry to their aid, but her legs carried her only as far as the middle of the room, where she collapsed, but without losing consciousness. She screamed repeatedly as if in utter terror, her voice almost breaking, and within a minute her mother, her sister, and nearly all the female servants were gathered around her. They picked her up, carried her to bed, and thought she was delirious, since she kept crying out anxiously: "Open the window!—in the river—he's in the river," and trying to break loose. Marie, who was crying aloud in her fright, was nevertheless the first to distinguish the cry from the river amid all the loud confusion. They threw open the window, and soon the castle's servants, still quite numb with sleep, were hurrying to the riverbank with poles and hooks. His quick horse had borne the traveler back out of the waves into which he had followed the will-o'-the-wisp in the hand of his guide, since he had been trotting along very close behind him. He stood dripping wet beside his panting horse; in his fear he had been about to climb back into the water to save the life that was floating away, since this unfamiliar place offered him no other assistance.

Therese stood wringing her hands by the window and listened to the sounds of the searchers amid the storm that had broken out with frightful vehemence; the thunder rolled without pause, the water danced in ghoulish delight over its fallen prey and splashed foaming spray into the eyes of those who sought to snatch him back from it. The stranger stood on the bank, trembling with cold. Instead of going to the manor house, he wanted to take a boat out on the raging waves. "Do you want to take your own life as well?" said the old steward. "I think one is enough."—"Oh God!" cried the stranger in anguish, "I talked him into coming; he did not want to leave his old mother, who was afraid of the storm. For God's sake, a boat, a boat!"—"You can't have a boat; we have none," said the steward. The stranger held a lantern up to the latter's face and, since in the false light he seemed to be laughing, he grabbed him furiously by the collar and shouted: "A boat, or I'll throw you into the water, too!" The steward looked him steadily in the eye and said: "We don't have one." The stranger was skeptical and confused: "Then how did you get here?"—"Across that bridge there," replied the steward. "A bridge," the stranger said limply; he let the man go, and rushed in a panic to join the searchers. "I have something here," one called, and he threw a white object onto the bank, which was recognized as the lost man's cap. They searched here more diligently, but the hooks passed through the foaming water in vain. "We're not going to find him," called another, wearied by the fruitless and nearly pointless work; "the storm is too fierce."—"The water won't give him back, either," yet another shouted; "it hasn't had any human flesh yet this year."— "No?" replied another, and with horror the stranger saw that after this exchange all energy was visibly extinguished. He offered them money upon money, and to please him they went on looking, but so dejectedly that they were soon splashing their poles and hooks into the water just for appearance's sake.

Therese, meanwhile, had not left the window. "I don't hear anything," she whined, turning to Ledwina, whom she was horrrified to see half dressed and about to climb out of bed. She closed the window quickly and urged her trembling sister back into bed, to which the latter finally agreed, on the condition that all news be reported to her as quickly as possible. Therese promised everything and figured she would be able to live with her conscience afterwards. She had composed herself with great effort and now she said much to Ledwina that was consoling, both spiritual and worldly, until her sister finally grew quite still and, in utter exhaustion, fell asleep again. Then she went to prepare a warm room and a bed for the stranger, who after many hours finally came into the manor house, chilled through and through and shaking inwardly. Then she lay down herself— hoping that perhaps the dawn might grant her a little relief, since the day ahead would require all her energy—having first arranged for a chambermaid to sleep by the door to Ledwina's room.

* * *

It had struck seven when Minchen tiptoed into the bedroom and found her mistress already fully dressed. "What's the news, Minchen?" she said uneasily and fastened the last clasp. "The new gentleman is doing fine," the girl answered. "But the messenger?" asked Ledwina. "God only knows," replied Minchen, and they both fell silent. "It isn't much use hoping," Minchen said, and then began weeping bitterly. Ledwina stared ahead and asked: "Don't they know who it was?" "Yes, they do," replied the sobbing girl, "it's Klemens, old Lisbeth's son; oh, my God, what a scene the poor old woman has been making!" and she wept loudly. Ledwina sat down on the bed and buried her face in the white pillows, then she rose, white as snow, and said: "Yes, God must know," took her handkerchief from the table and slowly walked out of the room.

In the living room, all had gathered around the breakfast table when Ledwina entered. The almost too dazzlingly handsome stranger stood up and bowed. Karl said politely and with dignity: "That is my eldest sister," and to Ledwina: "Count Hollberg." They sat once again around the bountiful table and the conversation continued rather awkwardly about all sorts of events in Göttingen, the single known point the two had in common.

"Miss Marie, be careful," the stranger said, turning from the conversation toward Marie, who repeatedly held an open quill knife up to her mouth to test the steel. Marie turned red and laid the knife down.

"That's right, Marie is her name," said Frau von Brenkfeld with a polite smile.

"I believe I could tell you all by name," replied the count energetically and his radiant eyes passed around the circle, "Steinheim is a faithful composer of portraits; believe it or not, I recognized you all immediately."

"You have seen a lot of Steinheim," said Karl.

"Oh, quite a lot," Hollberg replied quickly; "in the past year each day, or rather nearly the whole day. As a favor to him I even audited a set of lectures I had no need to enroll in otherwise." Karl gave a very dry laugh.

"As long as you were there," the Count continued, "one couldn't really get close to him, for his heart may be open for several absent friends but always for just one who is present. I never had an excuse to visit him and he did not come to our *Commercen*[1] at all. But now," he continued, with a quick, sparkling glance, "now I believe I am deceiving neither myself nor others when I say we love each other very much."—"I conceived such an affection for him when we first met in the library. He was sitting by the window, reading *The Merchant of Venice* by Shakespeare, a play that for

---

1. Formal gatherings of the *Burschenschaften*, German student fraternities, complete with uniforms, toasts, special songs, and assorted rituals.

some perverse reason did not appeal to me back then as much as the other works of that giant; for," he went on with a childlike laugh, "unfortunately I always have to wear the fashion of the day for a while, and so I was just then resplendent in wildly romantic thundercloud gray embroidered with serpents and demons; I must have been a magnificent sight!"

Jovially he looked around the room and into the embarrassed face of Frau von Brenkfeld, who had no idea how to reply. Then he nodded amiably and said: "Yes, it's true, madam, in N. it was once fashionable for people to remove their heads and charge into the forests in droves, looking not for mushrooms but for revelations from the spirit world, and I was there with them, and therefore the *Merchant of Venice* did not suit me—there's not the least bit of a ghostly thrill in it. Well, I went up to the reader and intended to dazzle him with my opinion, but a Spanish proverb says: 'Many a man goes out to shear and comes home himself shorn.' Now tell me, my dear lady: how can someone of otherwise incorruptible reason now and again be so utterly mad?"

Karl tried to help himself by laughing and said: "Steinheim writes quite diligently about you."—"Then you know my name as well?" Frau von Brenkfeld spoke out of embarrassment, not noticing how out of place her question sounded. The stranger reddened and said: "I beg your pardon, Madam?" Then he looked down and said in a modest voice: "Do you not celebrate your name day on November nineteenth?"—"That's right," Frau von Brenkfeld replied; "my name is Elisabeth."—"The three young ladies," the count went on, "would be Miss Therese and Miss Marie. The name of the third is hard to remember and I fear guessing wrong; it must sound something like Lidwina or Ledwina."—"Exactly like the second," replied her mother and looked at Ledwina, and the count nodded, smiling amicably in her direction; she, however, did not notice this, since her mind was dwelling just then on the joy of Therese, whom she was so glad to see receive this soothing oil upon what she thought to be still heavy seas.

"Can't you tell me," said Karl, "when Steinheim is coming here?"—"Surely as soon as possible," the count replied with a long, telling look. Karl pursed his lips and said: "I plan to take a short trip, so we might miss each other, but I'll postpone or cancel it, depending on how things turn out. "A trip—to where?" asked Ledwina in surprise, and the annoyed Karl replied curtly: "To the Harz Mountains, maybe," and then to the count: "We had expected to see you here together." The count said amicably as he shook the black curls back from his broad forehead: "You see what good intentions Steinheim has toward me; but I must decide for myself what risks I dare take. If you had refused me your hospitality—" Frau von Brenkfeld started to break in politely, but the count went on: "A cherished source of joy is spoiled for me: I intended to surprise my sister on her birthday; thus the unhappy idea of enlisting the aid of a lovely night." Then he suddenly frowned, stood up, and left the room.

"How do you like him?" said Frau von Brenkfeld, looking up as if from deep anxiety, to Ledwina. She shook her head with a curious smile and said: "I don't know yet, but he's very unusual."—"There's something childish about him," Karl broke in, "but that's part of his illness."—"Is he ill?" Ledwina spoke tensely; "he looks quite fresh, almost too fresh."— "Oh, God, how he wanted to look fresh," Karl replied, "it really gave me a shock when I saw him. When I was in Göttingen he was always pale as the grave, so for a long time they called him Pallidus, until finally it was no longer a joking matter, but now—" Karl paused gravely and then continued: "I recall once we had a good *Commerce* in Ulrich's Biergarten and, since several of us were picking bunches of wildflowers as we walked, somebody finally tossed out the question of what the so-called flower of death actually was, since many call the dark red corn-poppy, others the bright red carnation, and still others only tall yellow flowers by that name; and he said with such melancholy: 'It seems to me the bright red one deserves this name most of all, bright red is the proper color of death after all. Dear God, how beautifully can those flowers of death blossom, and so short a time before they fall off!' Then he stayed behind and was silent the whole evening long, for along with his beautiful, intelligent mother—and against the will of all the relatives—his father had dragged consumption into the family."

"I find that truly bad; you use such harsh expressions, Karl," said Therese, who had been back with the others for a few minutes now, "there is truly enough evil in the world; one need not flaunt the word." Karl was offended and hence he spoke coldly: "Based on his personality, maybe I can also call it mad; I would then have to assume that, due to some *idée fixe,* he considered her healthy. I, for one, would not be moved even by the most ardent passion to knowingly poison my entire lineage."

Therese, who for understandable reasons was much inclined in Hollberg's favor, said this time quickly and without reflection: "But what if, in addition, he can now neither love nor marry?" Karl stopped short, gave her a mocking look, tipped his finger lightly against her forehead, and said with emphasis: "Oh blind world, how you stumble in the dark!" Therese drew her head back indignantly, but she said nothing, because it annoyed her no end to have said something silly now, of all times, and it bothered Ledwina even more, who essentially considered her sister not only richer in heart and mind but also smarter with her clearheaded prudence than their brother who was knowledgeable and strong, but limited in his often exaggerated self-importance. "Be that as it may," Karl continued earnestly, "suffice it to say, the whole family with all its intellect and infirmity has burned up like a meteor, all but him and a sister, in whose cheeks the flowers of death already bloom. The poor fellow could well make his fine speeches. Death has knocked hard upon his heart many a time already, and now it is lodged right inside."

There was a knock at the door, and a farm laborer entered in his stocking feet. "Your grace," he started in, "that new gentleman is asking for people in the village who will go in exchange for money and good words to look for Klemens. If that is as it should be, then the thing must be done, but they'll not find him, the water is too long, he's probably ten hours away by now."—"I will speak with the new gentleman," said Frau von Brenkfeld; "you go ahead," and once the laborer had left she looked at her children in silence; then she said: "That terrible restlessness! I'm afraid I couldn't keep company with him for long." Then she went out to have a word with the count.

Karl watched her go and then said with an embarrassed laugh: "I'm just glad that his stay here is not on my account; I was afraid all this would happen. Hollberg has been spoiled his whole life long. I suppose there were four of us who liked him. We had undertaken to make quite the dapper ladies' man out of him. He went along with it all, too, but in the middle of the best *Commerce,* something—usually something utterly insignificant—could suddenly take hold of him so profoundly and curiously that he ruined all our fun with his odd mood; it's interesting now and then, but always terribly disconcerting, especially since he never really understood student life, staying aloof at our gatherings as if he were among philistines; on points of honor he was as guileless and trusting as if he were among brothers, and he could have got into the nastiest of quarrels, but everyone knew and went easy on him."—"So he was probably well loved?" asked Therese. "Oh, yes," replied Karl, as he looked about the room for his mislaid tobacco pouch; "besides, being at once guileless and noble is the surest way to gain everyone's regard; there's something princely about it."

Therese turned to Ledwina: "There is a something special about innate gentility."—"Its possessor may risk much," replied Ledwina, "as long as it violates only outward forms that do not touch one's inward sense of honor, and even those only without ill intent."—"Oh yes," said Therese, "then I prefer it even to beauty—and not only in a man," she continued, absorbed in her pleasant thought, "it would be my choice for myself as well."—"Oh, I agree," replied Ledwina, and Karl, who now rejoined them, said: "I for one would not like to be treated with such consideration; it always smacks a little of the deference shown to women." Therese looked up in exasperation; then she began to laugh, first quietly and then more and more heartily. "It really is awful," she said, trying in vain to control herself, "to have to laugh so foolishly."

Their mother returned with the count. "Surely you agree," she was just saying.—"Yes, of course," he replied and looked glowingly around the room, "Madame's word is law, I was just thinking of his mother."—"His mother," said Frau von Brenkfeld, "might be better able to stand the sight of the corpse in a few days than now, at least I hope so."—"I don't believe so," the count responded in agitation; "she is inconsolable, the son was all she had." Frau von Brenkfeld spoke earnestly: "You are mistaken; we all cannot determine how much a truly Christian and sturdy soul from the lower classes, and above all a woman, is able to endure, no more than we are able to imagine the uninterrupted chain of cares and privation of which her life almost always consists; believe me, what one generally sees is nothing." The count raised his burning face and said: "I beg your pardon, Madame? Oh, excuse me!" He was silent a few seconds as if gone numb, then he spoke again: "Just think what the water will do to him. Surely the old woman will keep going to the river until it spits him back out, and then she won't recognize him." He rose hastily, said "Excuse me" once more, and left the room.

Frau von Brenkfeld watched in surprise as he left and then said: "Is it illness or obstinacy?"—"Both," replied Karl phlegmatically, and thus the conversation went on—in sharp strokes, often unjust, always missing the mark—between people one would have to consider to be good, a conversation concerning a soul that could not be handled delicately enough and that with all its transparent clarity still had to burn up because of these constantly misunderstood sentiments.

Frau von Brenkfeld was just saying: "Every day I see better how thankful I must be to God that I was born among seven sisters, and right in the middle, neither the eldest nor the youngest," when Marie hurried in and called out anxiously: "Oh Mother, the count is sitting on the balcony, and he's white as snow."—"My God," said Frau von Brenkfeld, "is he feeling ill?"—"Yes, he is," replied Marie, "he had put his head down on the stone table and didn't even see me."

They rushed out; the count tried to deny his obvious frailty with a few strained, confused words, but his senses seemed to desert him more and more, and while he labored with his last remaining consciousness to make light of his condition, he allowed them to more carry than walk him to his room. After half an hour he definitely had a violent fever, and the morning was spent anxiously waiting for the family doctor, whom they had summoned immediately.

* * *

"What do you say about our patient?" asked Frau von Brenkfeld as the man returned to the room. Doctor Toppmann slowly took his hat from the mirror table beside the flowerpots and deliberately brushed away a bit of pollen with his sleeve. Then he said: "Not much; I know too little about his constitution and one cannot speak with him, since he's completely incoherent."—"My God, since when?" cried Frau von Brenkfeld; "I knew nothing of that."—"It seems that he was not so before," responded the doctor, "only since he woke up just now."—"That is extremely sad," replied Frau von Brenkfeld heatedly; "for God's sake, he couldn't die, could he?" Doctor Toppmann made one of his oddest faces and said: "We could all die;

and besides, one mustn't think such a thing until the opposite is impossible."—"Certainly not," Therese spoke up; "I beg you, do not deceive us in this matter." Toppmann squinted with his left eye and asked: "Why?"— "One would be more careful," replied Therese; "one would know in any case what to do."—"Well, what does one do?" asked Toppmann. "Oh God," Therese replied, "we have a thousand other reasons, don't change the subject!" Toppmann was silent a while, then he said earnestly and to all present: "I know you will leave nothing undone that stands within your power and knowledge; therefore, keep the room cool but above all without the slightest draft, and see to it that the medication is taken properly; also, for the time being the patient must not be left alone. Tomorrow morning I'll be back, if nothing special happens before then." He bowed and started to go, then turned around, and said: "Nota bene, don't go near him any more than absolutely necessary; it could well be a matter of his nerves." He bowed again and left.

Karl said: "I think I can recall every word I've ever heard Toppmann say; that comes from the unforgettable facial expressions his words are molded into, or rather the other way around."—"He speaks very little anyway," their mother replied; "by his standards he spoke quite freely today."—"Therese really squeezed it out of him, too," Karl answered, looking after Therese, who had just left the room with a sign of extreme inner turmoil. Karl continued: "I once tried to make a collection of the different variations on his basic facial expression, long ago, before I went to Göttingen, and to that end I made a stroke upon a sheet of paper each time I thought I had discovered something new, but got so confused that I only got to about forty, and I must admit that this work of carefully noting all sorts of distortions, imagined and real, into which I thus eventually threw myself with a real passion, finally began to bring on a weakness and such a stupid distractedness, that I count this among the most dangerous occupations of all. I just can't understand how caricaturists manage to stay out of the madhouse."

"It has long been known," replied Frau von Brenkfeld, "that such artists, the satirists in literature and life and the most famous buffoons of the theater included, are at least usually severe hypochondriacs."

Amid these conversations, Ledwina had quietly slipped away and out of doors in order to conceal and perhaps to relieve a pressure, both physical and mental, that was overpowering her. She was drawn powerfully to the riverbank, as if there were something left to be rescued, and a thousand miraculous possibilities that could be called so only for her danced in frightful images about her burning head. First she saw the lost man with a thornbush holding his pale and trembling face above water by part of his hair, while the remainder of it, torn loose from his head, swayed from the waving twigs of the shrub; his bleeding limbs were hurled against the rocky bank by the waves in cruel rhythm. He was still alive, but his strength was gone and he could only wait in ghastly mortal fear until the pounding waves had torn out the last hair. Then another vision, equally ghastly and fearsome. She slipped silently along the wall beneath the window where her mother sat, who looked not ahead nor about her, rather talked quickly and intently with Karl about all sorts of things that were quite indifferent to her, in order to conceal the ill humor that had come over her irresistibly since the count's arrival and that had been heightened by the doctor's report to a level that she herself must have felt to be unjust. Poor Klemens was surely the reason for that part of her mood which was genuine sorrow; in addition, an exaggerated fear and almost childish caution against any contagion was part of the fixed household regimen, and thus a quiet dislike and unwavering unfairness toward the count lodged within Frau von Brenkfeld, who saw him threatening, on top of all her other worries and crises, to contaminate her clean and wholesome house, and upon whom his role—guiltless though it be—in the lad's death had already cast a slight shadow, which at the time she had not traced to its root, or perhaps not felt it enough at all, to wipe it away. Yet even now she was still fair enough to realize something unjust within herself, and with her profound, personal goodness she would not now want to judge him or even speak about him. The same was true of Karl, only for other reasons, and it must have been most entertaining for an observer to hear a conversation between the two so thoroughly boring to both parties yet carried out with such liveliness and often such engaging comments.

* * *

A coach clattered over the drawbridge and a team of six yellow duns trotted into the yard.

"Bendraets!" said Karl. "I'm deserting," replied his mother, flushing red

with bad temper, and she went out to receive these guests who were unwelcome at any time. The two little perfumed misses had already disappeared into the house by the side of their tall *Referendarius*—as the young,
ever amiable tutor, Herr von Türk, was known everywhere in the area—in
order, as they put it, to mobilize Ledwina-dear and Therese-dear a little, by
the time their mother, slowly emerging from the carriage, returned Frau
von Brenkfeld's greeting.

The women took possession of the sofa, and the lady of the house's eye
rested ever more congenially upon the wrinkled, melancholy features of
her neighbor who, in answer to a question, related, with a casual air born
of embarrassment, that her husband and their sons had gone out for some
hunting with young Warneck, but that they would be in this area toward
noon and would be looking in on them then. Sympathy with the constantly
burdened woman made Frau von Brenkfeld answer very graciously, and a
gentle, quiet conversation began between the two women who would so
gladly have confided in each other and yet were never able to, because the
multiple burdens of family relations compelled a good, guileless soul to
seek her salvation in intrigue. The conversation turned to Baron Warneck,
owner of the adjoining estates, who had returned from years of travel a few
months before.

"He is a man of much intelligence," said Frau von Brenkfeld. "Surely, of
quite excellent talents," replied Bendraet, "and a very virtuous man."—
"Do you mean in terms of courage or legally?"—"The latter, actually,"
smiled Bendraet, "although I believe it is true in both regards."—"We
know little about him," replied Brenkfeld, "yet I am happy to think the
best of him. My Karl rode over to his place recently because of some small
hunting violations, and he praises the baron's fairness and neighborly
spirit. The owners of Schnellenfort are always of interest to us; our proper-
ties and rights overlap with theirs in an unpleasant way. May God grant
him a peaceable wife," she added significantly. "What do you think,"
Bendraet asked with a hard stare, "there's talk it'll be Claudine Triest."—
"Really?" replied Frau von Brenkfeld smilingly. "I thought there was talk
of Julie Bendraet."—"Yet he has given us no reason to think that," replied
the blushing Bendraet; "on the contrary, he seems rather to betray a small
preference for Elise, but in any case"—she hesitated and grasped her
friend's hand—"it's really ridiculous in such matters to pass judgment

even before one's opinion is asked for, but anyway Elise would hardly choose Warneck. The baron has traveled too much and too merrily ever to settle down. He must have a lively and vivacious wife who will share the burdens and the enthusiasm of his diversions with him. That would be nothing for my little homebody. May God grant her," she added softly, "a quiet, homey fate, where she won't be reminded that she is less pretty and vivacious than Julie." Frau von Brenkfeld squeezed the speaker's hand gently, and the latter continued in a livelier tone: "But let me return the favor in kind, I seem to have made good Herr Türk quite happy with our little trip here. His full heart pours itself out daily into the most beautiful poems in honor of Ledwina."—"Oh, he writes poetry?" laughed Brenkfeld. "Oh, yes," replied Frau von Bendraet, "quite nicely, and I really do believe he's beginning to go a-courting."—"But for Ledwina he wouldn't do; she is too delicate for him. She's not healthy, either," said Frau von Brenkfeld defiantly. "Oh, yes, she is," replied Bendraet quickly and anxiously; "I think she is improving greatly and looks much better."

Both were silent for a little while; then Frau von Brenkfeld said: "You haven't seen her lately."—"But I have heard it," replied Bendraet, "from the black-haired music teacher in Erlenburg; he said recently that she looked more beautiful and well than ever."—"Wildmeister, you say?" said Frau von Brenkfeld, and she looked sadder still. Then she regained her composure and quickly went on. "As long as Türk doesn't have a better living, he won't do for any of his kind."—"He does have an estate," said Frau von Bendraet. "Ach, dear child, why not call it a farm. The little knightly privileges won't improve it much."—"He will have a good position," said her neighbor. "Let's hope so, but it will take some time until then; the post as *Referendarius* isn't very significant." Bendraet grew very red and said: "He is cheerful and well mannered; he could well please someone. Is a mother supposed to impede her children's happiness and success and then leave behind a house full of daughters she hasn't provided for?—Of course," she interrupted herself, "your daughters do have a prebend, but not every family has that advantage." "Even if the opposite were true," replied Brenkfeld, "the decision to support one's daughter for life is better than the likelihood that the family will later spend generations trying in vain to patch up the sad circumstances of her descendants."

The lanky *Referendarius* and Julie interrupted this conversation. The tall fellow told them that Miss Therese was so busy cooking and roasting for their furtunate, unfortunate guest that there was no talking to her, and Miss Elise had wanted to relieve her of some of those pleasant chores, and had thus remained behind with her.

Frau von Brenkfeld related the story of the previous night. Madame Bendraet was surprised that she had not mentioned it earlier.

"I don't like to present my guests with unpleasant things," the lady of the house replied. "Herr von Türk," Julie called out from Therese's embroidery frame, at which she had seated herself, "you must challenge Frau von Brenkfeld to a duel: she calls a handsome young man an unpleasant thing." Frau von Brenkfeld looked serious, and Türk did not know how to act. "Just don't spoil anything, dear," her mother called to her. "Heaven forbid," Julie replied, "I wouldn't dare touch it."

Now she stood up and began to pester poor Türk mercilessly with jokes that were now flat, now incisive, often including the two women in an irresponsible and disrespectful manner, and thus sorely troubling the tall man, who liked to be on good terms with all the world.

Therese, meanwhile, stood outside the sick man's door as if on burning coals. She had just sent in a glass of lemonade and was trying with her best words to coax Elise away quietly, while the latter stepped from one edge of the door to the other in order to steal a glimpse of the stranger.

"Elise," said Therese, "the servant will come out and bump your head with the door."—"I beg you," whispered Elise, "find some pretext to get me in there."—"My God, how can there be such a pretext?" Therese replied. She urged her to wait for Karl, who was inside and would tell her everything.

Now Elise wanted to watch for when Karl came out. Therese grew impatient and had a servant call Karl. He appeared, hurried and irritable, greeted Elise hastily, gave them a quick, short report, and returned into the sick man's room. Elise seemed offended or embarrassed; she left with Therese, and they rejoined the others.

Elise sat down immediately at Therese's embroidery frame and began working energetically. Türk paid her the obligatory compliments for her industry, for each of which he had to endure mocking words from Julie. Thus the morning passed. They suddenly noticed Ledwina's absence and comforted themselves with the knowledge that she had gone for a walk.

Frau von Bendraet had just said: "Our gentlemen are overdue," when Marie called out: "Look, Mother, a man on horseback!"—"That is my husband," said Bendraet. "And another one," Marie shouted, "and another one," she shouted with emphasis. "There will be one more, dear," Madame Bendraet said, and she turned apologetically to the lady of the house.

The new arrivals dismounted. Herr von Bendraet made many polite remarks and kissed Frau von Brenkfeld's hand. Baron von Warneck was still in the yard, taking care of something on his boots, while Junker Klemens Bendraet did not miss the chance to twist the other's spurs down underneath his boots.

"Don't play stupid pranks," his brother said, but Warneck laughed, put everything in order, and they went into the house. Hunting stories and politics were discussed, and noon arrived, long awaited and yet unexpected.

* * *

Therese had opened the door of the dining room, in which the guests were already inspecting the English etchings on the walls, when she looked behind her, because she heard Ledwina's footsteps on the stairs. She was about to turn around hurriedly, for her sister, flushed and exhausted, had just let herself down onto one of the steps, but Ledwina waved her away hastily, imploringly, and Therese walked on through the open door. Not long thereafter, Ledwina also appeared, and everyone sat down to eat. Elise wanted to sit next to Ledwina-dear, but Therese drew her over to her own side.

"You can help me serve," she said, and that was just fine with Elise as well.

Conversations around the table began and faltered again. Herr von Bendraet spoke of a trip he intended to take.

"If I ever win the lottery," Julie called out, "I'll do nothing but travel; I can imagine no greater happiness."—"I believe," Elise replied, "that too much traveling is not good for a young lady; it makes her restless and dissatisfied back home. I would rather stay home and let other people tell me about their travels. Oh, how delightfully Baron Warneck entertained us yesterday! You must also have many stories to tell, Herr von Brenkfeld."— "Has Warneck spoken to you often of his travels?" Karl asked. "I don't like to think of how often we—or actually just I—have already pestered Herr von Warneck. In truth, the less I expect and even desire to see for myself, the less I can do without the substitute: a lively description."—"Warneck is a man in torment," laughed Julie; "I'm always afraid he'll stay away entirely, for all the trials he must endure from Elise."

Elise gave her a sharp look, and Karl said: "If Warneck tells you much about his travels, then my small experiences will profit you little; for he has observed and explored the same regions that just flew past me like images in the *laterna magica*."[2]

He gave a nod toward Warneck, who turned away from a conversation with Louis Bendraet because he had heard his name mentioned. "I was saying that you have not only seen more than I; you have also seen all those places I could tell about."—"If you look at it that way," replied Warneck, "the many travelogues would surely have left nothing of those very regions behind for us. It is the different perspectives and sensations, the little accidents and incidents of the journey that make a travel tale from the hundredth teller as noteworthy as from the second, and especially in Switzerland, where the most gripping views of nature are as common as our daily bread; who could believe they had seen it all? Let's assume I've seen the waterfall at Schaffhausen glistening in the sun, but you saw it in a storm or a fog, what different and yet equally wonderful spectacles! And I have seen but little of the magnificent gorges and caves, as I tend to become dizzy easily."—"I have climbed around in quite a few of those caves," said Karl. "It must be a curiously pleasant feeling," interjected Louis Bendraet, "in the full possession of one's vital energies to walk beneath the earth, as if buried, within the damp and moldering rock. I would like to do that too."—"Some hero you are," his brother called out, "you want to go on breakneck climbing expeditions, and you get dizzy as quick as an owl. Listen, Louis, if you want to go traveling, you'll have to take Warneck along; he'd have to lead you by a rope like a cow and if need be sling you over his shoulder."—"What do you think, Louis," Warneck laughed; "that would look unpoetic, and besides, think of the cave women and mountain elves and the gnomes that conjure up a hump on people's backs. I'm afraid that wouldn't have a good effect on your figure."

2. Device for projecting silhouettes onto a wall by means of a lantern.

Everyone laughed, Türk and Louis included.

"Once," said Karl, "I almost did think I saw a cave ghost. Six of us had climbed into a ravine in * * *. The two Briehls, the two Herdings, Rolling and me. The others had got tired and were resting in a shabby mountain tavern. The entrance was low and narrow, and the very deep Black Forest made it even darker. We had scarcely gone a few steps when we were in utter darkness. Our guide was about to light the torches we had brought along. That took longer than usual."—"That was a blunder on the good man's part," interjected Klemens von Bendraet, "he should have done that outside the cave." His mother gestured to him indignantly, and Karl continued: "I forgot to say that it was raining some; so while the man is struggling with the flint, through the shouts of my companions, who were testing the echo, I hear something sliding across the cave floor, and suddenly something is wrapping itself around my knees and grunting and pulling at my clothes and trying to drag me to the ground. I admit that I gave a shudder. 'Good friend,' I called out, 'let's have some light! There's something here, but I'll try to hold onto it.' And I reached down into a bristly bunch of hair or fur, I knew not what. And then it began grunting and thrashing about and growling: 'I call upon the Apostle Peter.'—'What, you're here?' our guide cried; 'don't be afraid, gentlemen, that's just a poor soul; he won't harm you.'

"Just then the torch lit up, and I saw a ragged, emaciated fellow of about forty, lying before me on his knees and holding me fast. I held his head back by the hair, and the earth-colored, disfigured face stared at me and grunted. The guide said: 'Now be quiet, Seppi, these here are the blessed apostles'; then he pointed to the youngest of the Herdrings with his long curls and said: 'See her? That's Maria Magdalena.' The poor fellow let me loose right away and crawled into a corner of the cave, where, as we saw now, there lay some straw. The guide apologized later for not telling us about their madman. He thought he was the angel Gabriel and this cave the holy sepulcher, which he was guarding, allowing no one to enter but the apostles and sainted women; but anyone could claim to be these. He had been ill, and our innkeeper thought he had not yet returned to the cave."

"The poor fellow had a hellishly boring job," said Klemens.

"And besides," said Karl, "he thought that as an angel he was not allowed to eat anything but herbs and fruits—raw ones at first—and what he found in the mountains; afterwards, they got him to accept under this rubric all sorts of vegetables and fruit, with the exception of apples, which he took to be from the tree of knowledge, and peas; why he wouldn't eat these, I cannot say."

"Probably," called Klemens, "on account of the innocent pea aphids that are in them sometimes."

"And did you go farther into the cave?" said Julie.

"Yes, Miss," Karl replied, "we were ashamed to turn around, which actually each of us would probably have rather done, for we had all been shaken by the sight of nature's greatest horror. But as it happens—I don't know whether I should say 'thank God' or 'unfortunately'—, as it happens that such sad impressions, when they do not touch upon our own fate, fade away so easily, after a few days we thought about it only so far as to call Fritz Herdring 'Maria Magdalena,' and so all that remained of the whole ghastly story was a tired joke."

A brief silence ensued. Then Warneck began: "Madness is a matter that religious and secular laws should forbid one from examining and brooding over too severely. I believe that nothing leads more easily to Freethinking."—"To the madhouse, rather, I would think," Türk remarked. Warneck replied: "To the one or the other, and quite easily to both at once."

Again a silence, then Warneck said: "I have had some ghastly experiences of this sort as well, but none is more vivid in my mind than the impression of a woman in Westphalia, whom I found in the company of a gloomy, sullen, and no longer young maid standing beside the door of the inn at which I was lodging. The old woman's stunted physiognomy, mad, but without a trace of wildness, stirred my sympathy, and I stopped a moment by her side. She was slowly gnawing a hard, dry crust of bread; then she stopped, as if in alarm, put her finger into her mouth and held in her hand the ruins of a tooth that had just fallen out. Now she drew a filthy piece of paper from her bag, unfolded it, and placed the tooth in with several other old pieces of teeth. The maid replied to my inquiry that her aunt kept all her teeth as they fell out, so that—here the creature made a face to begin laughing; it made me feel quite ill—well, anyway—so that when she eventually got to the place where there was weeping and rattling of teeth, she wouldn't need to weep all the time, but would be able to rattle her teeth sometimes instead. The innkeeper told me later that she had always been a virtuous woman, but after her husband, a small shopkeeper, had gone bankrupt and far into debt besides, and several families who were ruined by his bad debts had heaped curses on her in their initial anger, she had gone mad and now thought herself damned because of the bankruptcy. Only in springtime, when the cowslips—also called 'keys of heaven'— blossom, was she content; she would carry large bouquets of them by day and by night because she thought if she died during this time she would be able to unlock the gates of heaven with them. When the flowers began to go by, she would become more and more anxious and searched finally with the greatest effort for the last flowers, even when the blossoming season was over; afterwards she had to stay in bed a long time, she had exerted herself so."

Warneck was silent, and a general conversation about madness, human spiritual powers, etc. evolved and soon was lost in other topics. —

* * *

The afternoon was spent taking strolls, hitting balls, swinging, and all sorts of the most restless activity. Herr von Bendraet played piquet[3] with Warneck, and Julie chased about with Türk, who seemed at times infatuated and at others wholly exhausted, and who made futile attempts in the brief interludes to strike up a conversation with Ledwina.

Elise sat at the frame and was showing her a new stitch, which Ledwina then tried for herself. "Miss Ledwina," said Türk, "can do anything she is shown."—"And Herr von Türk," replied Julie, "can find something to say about everything, but it isn't as becoming."

Karl and Louis came in and asked about Klemens.

"I thought he was with you," said Elise. "No no," Karl answered, "we were talking about Italian art. Then he said, if we were going to trot out the beaux arts he'd rather be hanged. Later he returned with a few stray goose feathers and some birchbark and asked us to commend our beautiful thoughts to eternity. In a moment a shepherdess would come walking by, endowed with all the attributes of the arts and of wisdom; we should just keep an eye out for her; meanwhile he was going off to idyllize with the

---

3. Card game for two players.

women harvesting grain in the field over there. And with that he ran off."

"And an old, dirty peasant woman came by, lugging her milk bucket," Louis laughed; "the hangman only knows how she looked. She had decorated her skirt with perhaps twenty rags of different colors. By attributes of the arts he probably meant an old, shriveled goose wing that she had picked up somewhere."

"So he is probably in the field now," said Therese.

"I've looked across the whole field from the wall there, and I can't see him."

The game of piquet was over; Bendraet had lost and stood up grumpily. Then Klemens came in, blond curls tangled about his flushed face.

"Maria Magdalena," cried Julie. "Where were you all this time?" Elise asked. "In my coat," he answered. "But, my God, are you about to laugh or cry?"—"I'm about to pull the rug out from under you," he answered, still half grumpily, and then broke more and more into irrepressible laughter. He escaped through the window to the other young people, speaking to them in low but animated tones. A cheerful mood got the upper hand there as well, and one could see that he was being teased. The manor clock struck five. Warneck was going to take his leave and return to Schnellenfort, but Frau von Bendraet asked him to have dinner first with them.

"If you can't stay the night," she said, "it's still just half an hour from Lünden to Schnellenfort, and the moon is bright."—"And you must tell us all about your travels," Elise interjected. —"Oh, you already know most of it," replied Warneck. "Still," he added with a laugh, "the most curious sight I've encountered in all my travels is one I have not yet mentioned. It was in the most southerly regions of France, where it struck me as even stranger than if it were to be found here."—"Well?" said Julie.

Warneck, smiling, paused a moment, then he said: "A woman who has never disagreed with her husband."—"Don't play tricks on us," Julie said with a confused laugh, and Türk called out: "Did you hear that, Warneck? Miss Julie thinks your strange experience is just made up."—"I don't believe it either," said Klemens, "or did her husband put a muzzle on her?"— "Not much better," said Warneck: "she was a deaf mute from birth."— "And yet married!" Therese spoke. "That, Miss," replied Warneck, "is actually what is so curious and at the same time repulsive about the whole affair. She was not much better than an animal, but she had a few hundred guilders."—"That's as it should be," shouted Klemens; "it's impossible to imagine a more agreeable wife."—"Klemens, Klemens," said Frau von Bendraet, "there you go again, talking off the top of your head!"—"That was just a slip of the lad's tongue, Madame," Warneck responded; "just look how red he is getting." And he put his hand against the young Bendraet's cheek. Klemens slapped at his fingers half in embarrassment, half in jest.

"By the way," Karl began, "in these parts there is in all seriousness a peasant woman who, resolving to live in peace with her husband, did not speak a single syllable in fourteen years."—"That's right," Frau von Brenkfeld said. "We know this woman very well. She had suffered long and much from her husband's quarrelsome ways. All at once she stops talking; at first people think she's angry, then mad, then mute. And so it continues for fourteen years. The husband dies. On the day of his burial she begins talking again and insists that it will comfort her even in her dying hour that she kept to her resolve. Now she could think of her departed husband without uneasiness and regret, for in fourteen years there had been no disagreement between them."—"That is a lot," said Warneck. "Is the woman still alive?" asked Louis. "Yes, indeed," replied Frau von Brenkfeld, "near Endorf in the little red house by the highway. "I do know that woman," said Klemens. "I don't," replied Louis, "but I'd like to know her." Klemens leaned toward him and said in a half whisper: "Don't strain yourself, sonny, she's an old witch, and there are no pretty daughters, either."— "Cut it out!" said Louis. Warneck laughed and shook his finger at him. "Well, what is it now?" said Klemens loudly; "I just said that the woman has no children, but a dozen squawking babies would have loosened the words from her tongue." Warneck replied teasingly: "It almost seemed to me that what you said had sounded different; but I won't make you even redder than you are; you're blooming like a rose already."—"Almost as red as he was when I caught him kneeling at Claudine's feet," called Julie. "Hmm," Klemens growled to himself, "soon I might like Fräulein Blankenau more than Fräulein Triest. All this word-chiseling and quibbling can get awfully tiresome."—"Excellent," replied Julie, "even if part of it is a little envy of the better artisan."—"I can tell," Klemens called, "you're working on getting me to tease you back, but I truly wouldn't know what with, unless I were to drag up your love for that well-patched gentleman."—

"You needn't say anything about that," Julie replied with a laugh; "if the poor scoundrel made a better living, he surely would not keep patching his old coats for so long."—"It is scandalous enough that art must go begging for bread," interjected Louis. "And actually," said Julie, "he's Louis's ideal and not mine."—"Ideal is a big word," Louis answered; "thank God I can raise my thoughts higher than that, but as for my taking Wengenberg's part, that seems to me very natural, and a wonder that I am the only one in our house who does; after all, music is a language that even children and savages supposedly understand."—"Which of the two do you take me to be?" asked Julie. Louis leaned over in her direction and said softly: "For a child, and a savage one at that."

Julie leapt up quickly and attacked him with great alacrity. Louis tried to defend himself, but the blows fell like snowflakes on his cheeks and shoulders and back, so that Louis, his head tucked between his shoulders, tried in vain to push now this, now another member of the company between himself and his attacker, and found peace at last only when he joined the ladies on the sofa. Meanwhile she went on shouting: "You ought to go to Erlenburg, that's where you belong, you troubadour, you moonbunny!"

The little war was over. Louis caught his breath. Julie looked down at her little reddened hands and stepped up to Baron Warneck: "Don't be angry; I pushed you around pretty good. Why do you stand there like a wall? The wall has to come down when the enemy is behind it."

Warneck looked into the tender, bright red face, and a gentle emotion flitted across his face. He lowered his sharp glance into her eyes and said: "Could it be that Miss Julie knows herself so little?" Then he quickly turned to the others.

The coach pulled up and the beautiful, richly bridled riding horses pawed the pavement. The riders put them through the most beautiful parade steps before the window, and the visit was over.

"Klemens can't even keep his own shame to himself," Karl began as he and his sisters watched the departing horses through the windowpanes. "Do you know what that teasing about his red face was about? Out in the field a pretty peasant girl gave him a good slap in the face and, once he thinks it over, the whole matter seems so ridiculous that he can't keep it to himself. He's always like that. He's not really any worse than other people, but he always tells all the wicked things he knows about himself, and a bit more and other things as well, without thinking about it."

"I find him very awkward company," replied Therese.

Meanwhile, their mother sat by the other window and thought about her poor, burdened, dejected neighbor—mother and wife and yet an orphan; in her mind's eye she saw her dragging herself, aged and haggard, through the spindly, rickety bower of her last and dearest hopes. She thought about her own children, their discipline, their obedience, their childlike attentiveness, and in comparing her heart grew soft through and through with melancholy and regret. She took a prayer book from a drawer of the table and went to her room. —

* * *

Meanwhile, Karl was informing Therese about the patient's condition, which seemed to him very comforting. The sick man was fully alert and had slept very soundly for several hours. "I beg of you," said Therese, "do take particularly good care of him; we cannot."

Karl responded with this and that and Therese became distracted, for she had just seen Ledwina walk across the yard and into the garden, and the sight of her slow, exhausted step, the delicate, gently curved figure, whose colorless, richly garlanded head, like the peony blossoms, seemed to grow too heavy, lay with melancholy anxiety upon her heart. Karl was just saying: "I'll go up to his room again."—"Do that," she replied; then pensively and restlessly she strode out into the expansive and beautifully laid out garden of the castle. She saw Ledwina from a distance, sitting at the edge of the park beneath the old linden tree, her arms crossed over the stone table and her face pressed against them. Then it occurred to her that she had seen Count Hollberg in a similar pose that morning, fainting and pale; she remembered everything that Karl had said about his illness, and she was taken aback by the similarity, for how could she have ever acknowledged to herself about Ledwina all that she had immediately accepted as undeniable in the count's case! Indeed, it is a beautiful sign of loving hearts to care thus for the object of their love as if there were no worries, and to cling to hope with fierce, heartrending blindness when it is long since gone for everyone else. A mood of anxiety overtook her, which she did not want Ledwina to see. She was about to turn around when her sister raised her head and looked in her direction. She tried now to get hold of herself, walked up to the linden tree, and sat down beside her.

Ledwina looked up and said faintly: "My God, if Lünden were as near as Erlenburg!"—"But thank God!" replied Therese, "it's more than that distance again from here; now we're sure to have a couple of months of peace."—"Klemens for example," said Ledwina, "and I really do believe that Adolfine Dobronn could take him."—"Oh, without a doubt," Therese countered. Ledwina replied: "And perhaps Linchen Blankenau as well—my God, if I had to become that person's wife, I couldn't stay alive for long." As if worn out by the thought, she rested her head on Therese's shoulder and spoke again: "No, I probably wouldn't die, but my mental powers would be crippled and I would lose all the thoughts that are dear to me; I would become half mad, or actually, dull-witted." She reflected awhile, then she said: "Anyway, Therese, I am so demanding and have so little sense for other people's views; that is one of my greatest faults. God knows what lessons may still await me. I admit that I have a great fear of a sister-in-law. Maybe she will have no heart for me." Then she said with a quick gleam in her tired eyes: "No, that's not it, but I do fear I'll have none for her. A wall will stand between us, that she is supposed to replace Mother and you for me and cannot, since by then you will be long since gone and happy."

Therese gently placed her arm around her strangely moved sister and grew sadder herself: "Dear Ledwina, don't waste away your life worrying about the future; it will come by itself, without our dragging it in with our fears and worries."—"And for that very reason," answered Ledwina spiritedly, "we must become familiar with the thought in advance so that it is not too hard for us later. Do you know that it is sinful to succumb through one's own fault to a fate that is so commonly borne? But," she said more slowly, "when I imagine another woman governing here in Mother's stead and sleeping in the bed before which we have so often stood and bid her good night."—She turned restlessly to every side. "But that will never happen," said Therese. "Mother will probably stay here. Karl is really so reasonable; his choice won't turn out to be so bad that Mother would have to move away."—"But what then if Mother is dead?" Ledwina replied. "Mother," Therese said sadly, "thank God, may well live longer than we."—"But that time will finally come," Ledwina interrupted. Then she gently put her arm around Therese's neck and spoke on, leaning close against her shoulder, softly and apprehensively. "You see, Therese, in our attic there are so many old family portraits, but in most cases we do not really know whom they represent, and yet these are all our ancestors and they lived here, God knows in which rooms, and they had brothers and sisters, had children, who looked at and preserved these pictures with joy and reverence, and perhaps later on with the most cherished, most touching memories, and now? How do they look? Remember the old woman—the one with the black cap—now her eyes and nose have been poked out, too. That was surely done on purpose because she actually looks so ugly." She took a deep breath and went on: "In the end, the past—the dearest, most cherished relics—are trod under foot. Think, if Mother's picture—" She began weeping violently and clutched tight to her sister. Therese had to hold herself together with force; every fiber of her heart was in pain, but she kept a firm rein, and said: "Ledwina, calm yourself, don't do yourself harm. Why do you force yourself to seek out objects that must shock you and make you ill? Now I ask you, if you love me, pull yourself together and speak and think of something else."

Both were silent. Ledwina stood up and walked up and down the garden a few times. Then she sat down again beside Therese, who began talking about all sorts of things. She answered in such a way that Therese had to be aware both of her goodwill and of its utter weakness. The sun began to set and its gentle rays danced through the branches of the linden tree across the girls' gowns and Ledwina's silently trembling face.

"What a beautiful evening it's becoming!" said Therese. "Yesterday at this hour poor Klemens was still alive," sighed Ledwina. "Are you seeking out sad things again?" Therese said gently. "Is one day's worth of remembrance," replied Ledwina, "too much for a lad who was his mother's only comfort? Listen to me!"

Now she told of how she had walked along the river, always upstream, struggling with the ghastly, senseless images, how she had almost got a grip on herself and intended to turn around, just this one more little inlet—and a faint, shimmering light peeked out of the water through the dense bramble bushes and over to her. Secretly shivering, she decided it was the sun's reflection. Then light clouds wafted past, the sun's gold vanished from the current, and the secret light flamed more brightly through the dark leaves.

"Can you comprehend, Therese," she said, "that I was thinking of the tales about lights that keep watch over the drowned? However, I did not give in; quickly I walked toward it; then it flamed up brilliantly and disappeared, and as I stepped into the thicket, it was poor Klemens's lantern, burned out, tangled in the vines, bobbing on the water. I knelt on the bank and released it from the brambles, but as I held it in my hand, so cold and wet and extinguished, it was as if it were a dead, stiff part of the lost man. I left it on the riverbank." With a shiver she pressed close to Therese. "But what is that?" she said, pointing to the ground. "What do you mean?" replied Therese. "It seems I see more than the shadows of the trees."—"And ours as well," said Therese. —"It's probably nothing; listen, as I was returning and came to the sand pit, I saw Lisbeth in the distance coming out of her house. Oh, Therese, she has gotten so small, I almost didn't recognize her. She walked ahead of me for a long while without seeing me, staring instead fixedly into the water. You know, she is always so tidy. Oh, God, she looked so distraught. Half of her gray hair hung out below her cap. I could stand it no longer and walked on past her. The bell struck noon in the village and the prayer bell began to peal. I said as I passed her: 'Praise be to Jesus Christ!' She did not look up, instead pressing her hands together and saying: 'In all eternity, in all eternity, Amen,' loudly, and over and over again. I could still hear it when I had gone quite a way further on."

"God will comfort her," said Therese, deeply moved, and she looked down. It seemed to her as well that between the shadows cast by the trees she saw another figure eavesdropping. She looked about quickly, but it was nothing.

"It's getting too cool for you, Ledwina," she said, standing up, and her sister, trembling with secret fever chills, followed willingly. In the yard they encountered Karl. Therese let her sister go on ahead and told him what she had observed, and he walked quickly into the garden; then she hurried after the mournfully pacing figure.

Translated from *Annette von Droste-Hülshoff, Historisch-kritische Ausgabe: Werke, Briefwechsel,* edited by Winfried Woesler, vol. 5 (Tübingen: Niemeyer, 1978–), 77–121.

Selected
Bibliography

I n the past ten years, several literary histories and encyclopedias of German women writers have appeared: the anthology *Gestaltet und Gestaltend. Frauen in der deutschen Literatur* (Amsterdamer Beiträge zur neueren Germanistik 10. Amsterdam: Rodopi, 1980) edited by Marianne Burkhard; Elisabeth Friedrich's encyclopedia *Die deutsch sprachigen Schriftstellerinnen des 18. und 19. Jahrhunderts* (Stuttgart: Klett, 1981); the anthology of essays *Frauen. Literatur. Geschichte. Schreibende Frauen vom Mittelalter bis zur Gegenwart* (Stuttgart: Metzler, 1985) edited by Hiltrud Gnüg and Renate Möhrmann; the *Lexikon deutschsprachiger Schriftstellerinnen 1800–1945* (Munich: Deutscher Taschenbuch Verlag, 1986) prepared by Gisela Brinker-Gabler, Karola Ludwig, and Angela Wöffen; and, most recently, the two-volume anthology of historical-critical essays *Deutsche Literatur von Frauen. Vom Mittelalter bis zur Gegenwart* (edited by Gisela Brinker-Gabler, Munich: Beck, 1988). Barbara Becker-Cantarino's *Der lange Weg zur Mündigkeit: Frau und Literatur (1500–1800)* (Stuttgart: J. B. Metzler, 1987) is the first modern narrative history of German women writers. It traces the "long road to emancipation" from the Middle Ages until the end of the eighteenth century, yet does not include women writers whose life and work transcended the eighteenth century. With the exception of witch hunt studies, which abound in this country, there are as yet few works in English that analyze

German women's culture of the early modern period. For a more extensive bibliography, which includes works in German, see the "Selected Bibliography on German Social History and Women Writers" in the *Women in German Yearbook 1989.*

General Overviews and Anthologies

Blackwell, Jeannine. "Women's Literary Culture and the Tradition of Life Narration." In *Bildungsroman mit Dame: The Heroine in the German Bildungsroman from 1770 to 1900* (Diss. Univ. of Indiana, 1983), pp.55–92.

Cocalis, Susan. Introduction to *The Defiant Muse. German Feminist Poems from the Middle Ages to the Present.* New York: Feminist Press, 1986.

Cocalis, Susan L., and Kay Goodman, editors. *Beyond the Eternal Feminine: Critical Essays on Women and German Literature.* Stuttgart: Akademischer Verlag H.-D. Heinz, 1982.

Evans, Richard J., and W. R. Lee, editors. *The German Family.* Totowa, N.J.: Barnes and Noble, 1981.

Fout, John C. "An English-Language Bibliography on European and American Women's History." In Joeres and Maynes, *German Women in the Eighteenth and Nineteenth Centuries,* pp.368–423.

Koonz, Claudia, and Renate Bridenthal, editors. *Becoming Visible: Women in European History.* Boston: Houghton Mifflin, 1975.

Mitterauer, Michael, and Reinhard Sieder. *The European Family: Patriarchy to Partnership from the Middle Ages to the Present.* Chicago: Univ. of Chicago Press, 1982. Translated from 1977 German edition.

Sagarra, Eda. *A Social History of Germany 1648–1914.* New York: Holmes and Meier, 1977. The last chapter is on women.

Waldstein, Edith. "German Literary Studies and Feminism: The Women's Studies Connection." *Women's Studies Quarterly* 12 (Fall 1984): 14–17.

Wilson, Katharina M., editor. *Continental Women Writers.* New York: Ungar, 1988.

Women in German Yearbook: Feminist Studies and German Culture. Vol.1–. 1985. Lanham, New York, London: University Press of America.

Middle Ages to 1700

Bainton, Roland. *Women of the Reformation in Germany and Italy*. Minneapolis: Augsburg Publication House, 1971.

Bolton, Brenda. "Mulieres sanctae." In Susan Mosher Stuard, editor. *Women in Medieval Society*. Philadelphia: Univ. of Pennsylvania Press, 1976, pp.141–58.

Davidson, Jane. "Great Black Goats and Evil Little Women: The Image of the Witch in Sixteenth Century German Art." *Journal of the Rocky Mountain Medieval and Renaissance Association* (1985): 141–57.

Dronke, Peter. *Women Writers of the Middle Ages. A Critical Study of Texts from Perpetua (+203) to Marguerite Porete (+1310)*. Cambridge: Cambridge Univ. Press, 1984.

Fox, Matthew, editor. *The Illuminations of Hildegard von Bingen*. Santa Fe, N.M.: Bear & Co., 1985.

Horsley, Richard A. "Who were the Witches? The Social Role of the Accused in the European Witch Trials." *Journal of Interdisciplinary History* 9 (1979): 689–715.

Horsley, Ritta Jo, and Richard A. "On the Trail of the 'Witches': Wise Women, Midwives, and the European Witch Hunts." *Women in German Yearbook* 3 (1986): 1–28.

Irwin, Joyce. "Society and the Sexes," In Steven Ozment, editor. *Reformation Europe: A Guide to Research*. St. Louis: Center for Reformation Research, 1982, pp.344–59.

Kieckhefer, Richard. *Repression of Heresy in Medieval Germany*. Philadelphia: Univ. of Pennsylvania Press, 1979. Detailed information on the Beguines and their persecution.

Kieckhefer, Richard. *European Witch Trials: Their Foundation in Popular and Learned Culture 1300–1500*. Berkeley: Univ. of California Press, 1976.

Kunze, Michael. *Highroad to the Stake. A Tale of Witchcraft*. Translated by William E. Yuill. Chicago: Univ. of Chicago Press, 1986.

Lehrman, Sara. "The Education of Women in the Middle Ages." In Douglas Radcliff-Umstead, editor. *Roles and Images of Women in the Middle Ages and the Renaissance*. Pittsburgh: Center for Medieval and Renaissance Studies, 1975, pp.133–59.

Levack, Brian P. *The Witch-Hunt in Early Modern Europe.* London and New York: Longman, 1987.

Lucas, Angela M. *Women in the Middle Ages. Religion, Marriage and Letters.* New York: St. Martin's Press, 1983. On Gandersheim, pp.143–47.

Midelfort, H. C. Erik. *Witch Hunting in Southwestern Germany, 1562–1684: The Social and Intellectual Foundations.* Stanford: Stanford Univ. Press, 1972.

Midelfort, H. C. Erik "Heartland of the Witchcraze: Central and Northern Europe." *History Today* 31 (Febuary 1981): 27–31.

Midelfort, H. C. Erik. "Witchcraft, Magic, and the Occult." In Steven Ozment, editor. *Reformation Europe: A Guide to Research.* St. Louis: Center for Reformation Research, 1982, pp.183–209.

Miles, Margaret R. *Image as Insight: Visual Understanding in Western Christianity and Secular Culture.* Boston: Beacon Press, 1985.

Monter, E. William. "The Pedestal and the Stake. Courtly Love and Witchcraft." In Claudia Koonz and Renate Bridenthal, editors. *Becoming Visible: Women in European History.* Boston: Houghton Mifflin, 1977, pp.119–36.

Monter, E. William. *Ritual, Myth, and Magic in Early Modern Europe.* Athens, Ohio: Ohio Univ. Press, 1984.

Monter, E. William. *Witchcraft in France and Switzerland: The Borderlands during the Reformation.* Ithaca, N.Y.: Cornell Univ. Press, 1976.

Moore, Cornelia Niekus. "Anna Hoyers' 'Posaunenschall,' Hymns of an Empire at War and a Kingdom Come." *Daphnis* 13 (1984): 343–62.

Moore, Cornelia Niekus. "Books, Spindles, and the Devil's Bench or What is the Point in Needlepoint?" *Festschrift Blake Lee Spahr, Chloe* 3 (1984): 319–28.

Moore, Cornelia Niekus. *The Maiden's Mirror: Reading Material for German Girls in the Sixteenth and Seventeenth Centuries.* Wolfenbütteler Forschungen 36. Wiesbaden: Otto Harrassowitz, 1987.

Ozment, Steven E. *When Fathers Ruled: Family Life in Reformation Europe.* Cambridge, Mass.: Harvard Univ. Press, 1983.

Petroff, Elizabeth, editor., *Medieval Women's Visionary Literature.* New York, Oxford: Oxford Univ. Press, 1986. Contains translations of writings by Hildegard von Bingen, Mechthild von Magdeburg, and St. Gertrude the Great.

Petroff, Elizabeth. "The Visionary Tradition in Women's Writings: Dialogue and Autobiography." Introduction to *Women's Visionary Literature*, pp.3–59.

Sticca, Sandro. "Sin and Salvation: The Dramatic Context of Hrotswitha's Women." In Douglas Radcliff-Umstead, editor. *The Roles and Images of Women in the Middle Ages and the Renaissance*. Pittsburgh: Center for Medieval and Renaissance Studies, 1975, pp. 3–22.

Strauss, Gerald. "Lutheranism and Literacy: A Reassessment." In *Religion and Society in Early Modern Europe 1500–1800*. Edited by Kaspar von Greyerz. London, Boston, Sydney: Allen and Unwin, 1984.

Symphonia. A Critical Edition of the 'Symphonia armonie celestium revelationum' [Symphony of the Harmony of Celestial Revelations]. Edited and translated by Barbara Newman. Ithaca: Cornell Univ. Press, 1989.

Wiesner, Merry E. *Working Women in Renaissance Germany*. New Brunswick, N.J.: Rutgers Univ. Press, 1986.

Enlightenment to Romanticism (1700–1848)

Although eighteenth- and early nineteenth-century literature by English and French women writers has received considerable attention, critical works in English on German women writers are comparatively scarce. Listed here are only general overviews or investigations relating to women's socioeconomic situation. Bibliographies of individual authors are attached to their respective biographies.

Becker-Cantarino, Barbara. "Outsiders: Women in German Literary Culture of Absolutism." *Jahrbuch für Internationale Germanistik* 16.2 (1984): 147–77.

Bell, Susan G., and Karen M. Offen. *Women, the Family, and Freedom. Vol.1: 1750–1880*. Stanford: Stanford Univ. Press, 1983.

Blackwell, Jeannine. "An Island of Her Own: Heroines in the German Robinsonades from 1720 to 1800." *German Quarterly* 58 (1985): 5–26.

Boettigheimer, Ruth B. "Tale Spinners: Submerged Voices in Grimm's Fairy Tales." *New German Critique* 27 (1982): 141–50.

Boettigheimer, Ruth B., editor. *Fairy Tales and Society: Illusion, Allusion, and Paradigm*. Philadelphia: Univ. of Pennsylvania Press, 1986.

Boettigheimer, Ruth B. *Grimm's Bad Girls and Bold Boys: The Moral and Social Vision of the Tales*. New Haven: Yale Univ. Press, 1987.

Bruford , W. H. *Germany in the 18th Century. The Social Background of the Literary Revival*. Cambridge: Cambridge Univ. Press, 1971; first edition 1935.

Cocalis, Susan, and Kay Goodman, editors. *Beyond the Eternal Feminine: Critical Essays on Women and German Literature*. Stuttgarter Arbeiten zur Germanistik vol.98. Stuttgart: Akademischer Verlag H-D. Heinz, 1982.

Dawson, Ruth. "Women Communicating: Eighteenth-Century German Journals Edited by Women." *Archives et Bibliothèques de Belgique* (1983): 95–111 (Actes du 6e Congrès International des Lumières, Bruxelles, 1983).

Dawson, Ruth. "'And this shield is called—self-reliance.' Emerging Feminist Consciousness in Late Eighteenth Century." In *German Women in the Eighteenth and Nineteenth Centuries. A Social and Literary History*. Edited by Ruth-Ellen B. Joeres and Mary Jo Maynes. Bloomington: Indiana Univ. Press, 1986, pp.157–74.

Frederiksen, Elke. "German Women Writers in the Nineteenth Century: Where Are They?" In Cocalis and Goodman, *Beyond the Eternal Feminine*, pp.177–201.

Goodman, Katherine R. *Dis/Closures: Women's Autobiography in Germany 1790–1914*. New York, Bern: Peter Lang, 1986.

Hausen, Karin. "Family and Role-Division: The Polarisation of Sexual Stereotypes in the Nineteenth Century: An Aspect of the Dissociation of Work and Family Life." In Richard J. Evans and W. R. Lee, *The German Family*. Totowa, N.J.: Barnes and Noble, 1981.

Hertz, Deborah. "Salonières and Literary Women in late 18th-Century Berlin," *New German Critique* 14 (Spring 1978): 97–108.

Hertz, Deborah. *Jewish High Society in Old Regime Berlin*. New Haven and London: Yale Univ. Press, 1988.

Joeres, Ruth-Ellen Boetcher. "German Women in Text and Context of the Eighteenth and Nineteenth Centuries." In *Internationales Archiv für Sozialgeschichte der deutschen Literatur* 11 (1986): 232–63.

Joeres, Ruth-Ellen Boetcher, and Mary Jo Maynes, editors. *German Women in the Eighteenth and Nineteenth Centuries. A Social and Literary History*. Bloomington: Indiana Univ. Press, 1986.

Madland, Helga. "Three Late Eighteenth-Century Women's Journals: Their Role in Shaping Women's Lives." *Women in German Yearbook* 4 (1988): 167–86.

Moebius, Helga. *Woman of the Baroque Age*. Translated by B. Chruscik-Beedham. Montclair, N.J.: Schram, 1984.

Paulsen, Friedrich. *German Education. Past and Present*. Translated by T. Lorenz. New York: Scribners, 1908. On women's education, see pp.232ff.

Petschauer, Peter. "Eighteenth-Century German Opinions about Education for Women." *Central European History* 19.3 (September 1986): 262–92.

Petschauer, Peter. "Improving Educational Opportunities for Girls in Eighteenth-Century Germany." *Eighteenth-Century Life* 3 (1976): 56–62.

Schreiber, Etta S. *The German Woman in the Age of Enlightenment. A Study in the Drama from Gottsched to Lessing*. Morningside Heights, N.Y.: Kings Crown, 1948.

Tatar, Maria. *The Hard Facts of the Grimms' Fairy Tales*. Princeton: Princeton Univ. Press, 1987.

Tilly, Louise, Joan Scott, and Miriam Cohen, "Women's Work and European Fertility Patterns," *Journal of Interdisciplinary History* 6.3 (Winter 1976): 447–76.

Ward, Albert. *Book Production, Fiction and the German Reading Public 1740–1800*. Oxford: Oxford Univ. Press, 1974.

The Contributors

WALTER ARNDT, Professor Emeritus of Russian and Sherman Fairchild Professor in the Humanities at Dartmouth College, has won awards from the American Philosophical Society, the National Endowment for the Humanities, the Guggenheim Foundation, and many others for his translations from Russian, German, and Polish. His verse translation of Pushkin's *Eugene Onegin* (1963) won the Bollingen Prize for Translation in poetry; his other translations include Goethe's *Faust,* an anthology of Anna Akhmatova's poetry, and Wilhelm Busch's satirical picture stories, among them the notorious *Max and Moritz*. His most recent work is a collection of seventy-five poems by Rainer Maria Rilke (*The Magic of Rilke,* Univ. Press of New England, 1989).

JEANNINE BLACKWELL, Associate Professor of German and Acting Chair of the German Department at the University of Kentucky, has written on women's literature in the genres of fairy tale, *Bildungsroman,* Robinson Crusoe stories, and religious confessions. She is writing a book on witch-trial testimony and women's visionary literature in Europe from 1450 to 1750.

RUTH P. DAWSON, Associate Professor in the Women's Studies Program at the University of Hawaii at Manoa, is especially interested in German women writers of the late eighteenth century. Two of her recent publications are "Frauen und Theater: Vom Stegreifspiel zum bürgerlichen Rührstück," in *Deutsche Literatur von Frauen,* edited by Gisela Brinker-Gabler (Munich: C. H. Beck, 1987) and "'And this Shield is Called—Self-Reliance.' Emerging Feminist Consciousness of the Late Eighteenth Century," in *German Women in the 18th and 19th Centuries: A Social and Literary History* (1986).

BRUCE DUNCAN, Professor of German at Dartmouth College and Associate Dean of the Humanities, has written on Achim von Arnim, Gerstenberg, Goethe, J.M.R. Lenz, Lessing, and Schiller, and is currently involved in a project that explores the pedagogical uses of the computer for studying German and German culture.

LORELY FRENCH, Assistant Professor of German at Pacific University, wrote her dissertation at University of California, Los Angeles, on *Bettine von Arnim: Toward a Women's Epistolary Aesthetics and Poetics* (1986). Her article "'Meine beiden Ichs': Confrontations with Language and Self in Letters by Early Nineteenth-Century Women," is appeared in the *Women in German Yearbook 5* (1989).

KATHERINE R. GOODMAN is Associate Professor of German at Brown University. She is the author of *Dis/Closures: Women's Autobiography in Germany 1790–1914* (New York/Bern: Peter Lang, 1986) and coeditor of *Beyond the Eternal Feminine: Essays on Women and German Literature* (Stuttgart: Stuttgarter Arbeiten zur Germanistik, 1982).

MARJANNE E. GOOZÉ, Assistant Professor of German at the University of Georgia, also works predominantly on Bettina von Arnim and the epistolary mode. She has written on questions of gender and textuality, the Berlin *salonnières,* and on Kafka and Hölderlin, and contributed to the forthcoming *Dictionary of Continental Women Writers* (Garland Press). She is currently preparing a book on Bettine von Arnim's epistolary autobiography.

CORNELIA NIEKUS MOORE, Professor of German and Dutch and Associate Dean of the College of Languages, Linguistics, and Literature at the University of Hawaii, Honolulu, received her Ph.D. at Indiana University. Her publications include *The Maiden's Mirror: Reading Materials for Girls in the Sixteenth and Seventeenth Centuries* (Wolfenbütteler Forschungen, Wiesbaden: Harrassowitz, 1987).

JANICE MURRAY received her M.A. in German Literature at the University of Heidelberg. She is a Ph.D. candidate in Germanic Languages at the University of California, Los Angeles, and is currently writing a dissertation on the correspondence and literary reviews of Caroline Schlegel-Schelling.

JULIE PRANDI has been the recipient of a Fulbright Graduate Fellowship and a study grant from Columbia University while teaching there. She earned her Ph.D. from the University of California, Berkeley, and is currently an Assistant Professor of German at Illinois Wesleyan University. Her publications include *Spirited Women Heroes: Major Female Characters in the Dramas of Goethe, Schiller, and Kleist* (New York: Peter Lang, 1983).

DENIS SWEET, Associate Professor of German at Bates College, has written on the art critic, historian, and essayist Winckelmann and on the literature of the German Democratic Republic. His translation of Hans Mayer's *Aussenseiter, Outsiders: A Study of Life and Letters,* was published by MIT Press in 1982. He is currently preparing a book on the Nietzsche reception in the GDR.

JACQUELINE VANSANT, Visiting Assistant Professor of German at Miami University, earned her Ph.D. from the University of Texas, Austin. Her research includes articles on modern Austrian literature, on Sophie Mereau, and Bertolt Brecht. She is author of *Against the Horizon: Feminism and Postwar Austrian Women Writers* (Connecticut: Greenwood Press, 1988) and general editor of the German textbook *Blickwechsel* (Boston: Houghton Mifflin, 1990) and of *Deutsch lernen im Kontext* (New York: Random, 1989, with Robert Didonato and Ronald Walker).

EDITH WALDSTEIN, Associate Professor of Humanities at Wartburg College, is the author of *Bettine von Arnim and the Politics of Romantic Conversation* (Columbia, S.C.: Camden House, 1988). She has written articles on other German Romantics and on Christa Wolf. Together with Marianne Burkhard, she edited the first three volumes of the *Women in German Yearbook: Feminist Studies and German Culture* and is currently editing an anthology of essays on German eighteenth-century women writers.

DAVID WARD, Assistant Professor of German at Dartmouth College, who works primarily with postwar German prose, has been translating since he served on the editorial staff of *Dimension: Contemporary German Arts and Letters* (1975–78). Among his translations are Bertolt Brecht's unfinished play *Fatzer* (with Andrzej Wirth and A. Leslie Willson), the novel *Tauben im Gras, Pigeons on the Grass* (New York: Holmes and Meier, 1988) by Wolfgang Koeppen, and Heinrich Heine's articles on the Salon of 1831, "French Painters," for *Paintings on the Move: Heinrich Heine and the Visual Arts,* edited by Susanne Zantop (Lincoln: Univ. of Nebraska Press, 1989).

SUSANNE ZANTOP, Associate Professor of German and Comparative Literature at Dartmouth College, holds degrees both in political science and literature. This interest in literary and extraliterary discourses is manifest in her book *Zeitbilder: Geschichte und Literatur bei Heinrich Heine und Mariano José de Larra* (Bonn: Bouvier, 1988), in her edition of essays on literature and painting, *Paintings on the Move: Heinrich Heine and the Visual Arts* (Lincoln: Univ. of Nebraska Press, 1989), and in her current project on Latin America in the literary imagination of the German Enlightenment.

Volumes in the EUROPEAN WOMEN WRITERS SERIES include:

Woman to Woman
By Marguerite Duras and
Xavière Gauthier
Translated by Katherine A.
Jensen

Nothing Grows by Moonlight
By Torborg Nedreaas
Translated by Bibbi Lee

Music from a Blue Well
By Torborg Nedreaas
Translated by Bibbi Lee

*Why Is There Salt in the
Sea?*
By Brigitte Schwaiger
Translated by Sieglinde Lug

*On Our Own Behalf:
Women's Tales from
Catalonia*
Edited by Kathleen McNerney

Mother Death
By Jeanne Hyvrard
Translated by Laurie Edson

Artemisia
By Anna Banti
Translated by Shirley
D'Ardia Caracciolo

Maria Zef
By Paola Drigo
Translated by Blossom
Steinberg Kirschenbaum

*The Panther Woman:
Five Tales from the Cassette
Recorder*
By Sarah Kirsch
Translated by Marion Faber

The Tongue Snatchers
By Claudine Herrmann
Translated by Nancy Kline